Platform Strategy for Global Markets

Hirofumi Tatsumoto

Platform Strategy for Global Markets

Strategic Use of Open Standards and Management of Business Ecosystems

Hirofumi Tatsumoto
Graduate School of Business Sciences
University of Tsukuba
Tokyo, Japan

ISBN 978-981-33-6788-3 ISBN 978-981-33-6789-0 (eBook)
https://doi.org/10.1007/978-981-33-6789-0

This Springer imprint is published by the registered company Springer Nature Singapore Pte Ltd.
The registered company address is: 152 Beach Road, #21-01/04 Gateway East, Singapore 189721, Singapore

Preface

This book attempts to uncover how platform firms have gained dominant competitive strength in the new industrial environment. It also explores how such an incredible competitive edge will impact the global industrial structure.

The new industrial environment is a phenomenon symbolized by the terms *openness* and *globalization.* In this analysis, the author defines openness as "the sharing of technical information by multiple companies through open standards" and globalization as "the creation of a single ecosystem (global ecosystem) by companies from advanced and emerging countries". In such an industrial environment, network effects are likely to occur. A platform strategy is a competitive strategy that maximizes the use of network effects.

A platform firm is a firm implementing a platform strategy that leverages network effects in the ecosystem. This definition simply shows that platform firms are very different from traditional product firms. Product firms are categorized by the products that they offer, like automotive companies and semiconductor companies. However, platform firms are categorized by how they deliver their products or services, rather than by the types of products or services that they offer. So, a firm selling smartphones can be a product firm or a platform firm.

Since a platform firm is defined as such based on the way in which it implements its strategy, platform firms can be observed in various business ecosystems. This volume covers multiple ecosystems including those of mobile phones, semiconductor manufacturing equipment, personal computers and automotive electronics. In these ecosystems, the presence of platform firms has a considerable influence on industrial evolution.

Platform firms are frequently studied due to their strong presence in business ecosystems. However, little is known about what strategic actions platform firms carry out or what conditions ought to exist for the strategic actions of platform firms to be successful.

This is partly because past platform research relied on case studies that focused only on highly successful platform firms, and thus had too much of a survival bias. Investigations of the sort are of little use to practitioners who are serious about developing their own platform strategies or to policy-makers who are considering fostering and regulating platform firms. There is also a danger to researchers, in that such work might be regarded as little more than "mere bragging about successful companies".

For this reason, the approach adopted here is orthodox in management research, as it entails: (1) firstly, identifying the business ecosystem as an industrial environment, (2) then, building a theoretical framework on platform strategy and ecosystem evolution from prior studies, and (3) finally, conducting case studies and empirical research on platform strategies and initiating discussions around the evidence gathered.

Many management researches follow a simplified method and explore only one of these three elements. However, the present book deals thoroughly with each of them, which requires an enormous amount of time.

Indeed, the author conducted more than 100 interviews with companies in Europe, the United States, Japan, China, India and other countries. All of these were backed up by facts and figures to provide rigorous evidence for the analysis. Besides the case studies, an empirical analysis was carried out on the performance of the platform strategy, which is rare in platform studies.

Every chapter tries to offer explanations and discussions based on such hard evidence and data, since the author believes that it is most important to look closely at the phenomenon in question when considering a new management strategy. On the other hand, theory building is also vital because a theoretical lens is necessary to measure the phenomenon. Therefore, the author's actual research activities moved back and forth between theory building and fact finding.

The strategies of platform firms are very different from the typical strategies of traditional product firms and include a wide range of strategic actions: two-sided market strategy, bundling strategy, strategic standardization, positioning at the hub, entry into peripheral markets and inter-firm relationship management. This exploration illuminates the above actions in detail. Furthermore, most surprisingly, based on the evidence from the chapters, the author concludes that the success of platform firms should trigger an international change in industrial structures.

Platform firms strategically use open standards, which quickly spread and turn into international standards. Currently, most of these international standards are created by industries in developed countries. Therefore, if platform firms emerge, the readers might guess that the global economy is likely to be dominated by companies from developed countries, since international standards benefit developed-country firms. Yet, the conclusion of this book is just the opposite. The rise of platform firms changes the existing industrial structures, as it helps companies from developing countries enter global ecosystems, and its pressure for structural change leads to an international transformation in the division of labor between developed and developing countries.

The intended audience for this book is primarily academic researchers in business strategy. It is also suitable for undergraduate and graduate students, who want to conduct case studies and empirical research in this area. The author would be glad if those who are involved in strategic planning for companies or engaged in policy-making for industrial development read this book.

Although this is a professional academic publication and therefore contains a lot of academic language, which may be intimidating for practitioners, the author believes that the concepts and theories covered are essential for strategic planning in the new industrial environment. In order to think about business strategy in such a new environment, a new common language for business strategy is needed—and the author hopes to have provided the foundations for it. It would be a great pleasure if the readers could learn something valuable from the findings of this book.

Tokyo, Japan Hirofumi Tatsumoto

Acknowledgements

I would like to thank the many people behind the writing of this book, which could not have been completed without their support.

At the University of Tokyo's Graduate School of Economics, Manufacturing Management Research Center (MMRC), I encountered corporate behavior analysis based on product architecture and was able to conduct the core research for this book. Professors Takahiro Fujimoto and Junjiro Shintaku gave me enthusiastic guidance and training as a researcher throughout my time in undergraduate and graduate school. I went on overseas surveys with Dr. Koichi Ogawa, a former MMRC researcher. He taught me the joys of field research and the significance of discussions among researchers between surveys. In that period, I often went to Taiwan with Dr. Momoko Kawakami of the Institute of Developing Economies (IDE-JETRO) and Dr. Hsu Ching-Ming, a former MMRC researcher, and we were able to obtain valuable research results. I would like to thank everyone who presented me with exceptional research opportunities.

For the research on IP and standardization management, I wish to thank Prof. Toshiya Watanabe (Center for Policy and Vision Studies, University of Tokyo), Prof. Kenichiro Seo (NPO Industry-Academia Collaboration Promotion Organization) and Prof. Toshifumi Futamata (Center for Policy and Vision Studies, University of Tokyo). They provided me with their latest findings and also taught me the importance of returning research results to business practitioners.

At the University of Hyogo, where I worked from 2009 to 2012, I had the chance to collaborate with excellent colleagues. Professors Takahide Yamaguchi, Naotoshi Umeno, Dr. Shingo Nishii and Prof. Masaru Harada offered me further research opportunities and I am greatly indebted to them.

In those years, I had the privilege to contribute to Prof. Gawer's book on platform strategies, published in 2009. In 2010, I was hosted by Prof. Cusumano and stayed at MIT as a visiting researcher. The experience at MIT had a great influence on the matters addressed here. Professors Gawer and Cusumano guided me in connecting the series of studies in this book with the theme of platform strategy.

Since 2012, I have been working at the Graduate School of Business Sciences, University of Tsukuba, and have completed this book with brilliant colleagues. I am grateful to Profs. Naoki Makimoto, Yasufumi Saruwatari, Tadahiko Sato and Koken Ozaki for their advice on statistic techniques. I would like to thank Profs. Hiromichi Yoshitake and Nobuyuki Inamizu for their support in both research and educational practices.

The material presented here was also enriched through active discussions with the participants in a seminar at the University of Tsukuba's Graduate School. Kazuki Aruga, Junko Taguchi, Hiroko Haga, Kazuko Nakanishi, Ken Shimamoto, Kenichi Shibata, Hirokazu Hara and Iichiro Yamaguchi carefully read the initial draft of this publication and offered thoughtful comments. I would like to thank all the graduate students in the seminar for their support.

The research network has provided me with great intellectual stimulation in my academic career. I would like to express my gratitude also to Prof. Fumihiko Ikuine of Chuo University, Profs. Akio Tokuda, Tetsuo Yoshimoto of Ritsumeikan University, Junichi Tomita and Chikako Takanashi of Toyo University, Yoshikazu Shusa, Masanori Yasumoto and Kodo Yokosawa of Yokohama National University, Wooseok Juhn of Chukyo University, Tamiko Kasahara of the University of Shizuoka, Masato Itohisa of Hosei University, as well as Prof. Mitsuhiro Fukuzawa of Seikei University.

Some of my collaborators and research supporters have already passed away. Mr. Kenichi Imai was a researcher at the Center for Asian Economic Research and I was allowed to accompany him on his survey trips to China. He taught me that regional economic research is only possible when you can understand the hearts and minds of the people of a region. Mr. Yoshinobu Tsuji was the Director of the Standards Division of the Ministry of Economy, Trade and Industry, and he helped in my early standardization research. He was a wonderful visionary and his support enabled me to achieve great success in standardization management research. I also accompanied Prof. Tomofumi Amano of the University of Tokyo on overseas research trips to China and Thailand. This reminds me of the good old days. Professor Amano's research was inspiring and it influenced not only myself but also many other researchers of my generation. I hope that the completion of this book will serve as a testament to their lives in some small way.

I would like to thank the companies interviewed for this book. Voices from the field have always been valuable teachers for me. Including informal conversations, the volume of the interviews that I completed would be several times larger than the list at the end of Chap. 9. Some of the companies no longer exist. I cannot reveal their names, as I do not want to inconvenience them, but this publication is the result of their living voices.

In addition, this research was supported by a number of financial grants. My activities were funded by JSPS JP22683007, JP25705011 and JP16K03850. I am grateful to Yuko Fujita of Yuhikaku for her support in publishing this book. I also received financial support from the late Ryoji Takenaka, my uncle.

I would like to thank my family, Naomi, Kyoko and Ryuichiro. This book would not have been completed without the support of my wife Naomi. I would like to express my deepest gratitude to her.

Finally, I would like to thank my father and mother, Hideki and Noriko Tatsumoto, for watching over me during years of research. My father worked for a long time as a professor at the Faculty of Engineering at Chiba University before he passed away suddenly in May 2016. I would like to dedicate this book to my father.

Hirofumi Tatsumoto

Contents

Chapter 1
Open Standards and Rise of New Competition: Why Do Open Standards Generate New Patterns of Competition?

Open standards are the basis for collaborations among firms that create open industrial clusters or business ecosystems. Since standards severely affect their behavior and performance, firms always pay attention to standardization and many studies have focused on open standards (David and Greenstein 1990; Jorde and Teece 1990; Farrell and Saloner 1988; Besen and Farrell 1991; Funk 2002; Kajiura 2007; Yamada 2007; Ogawa 2009; Harada 2008; Tatsumoto et al. 2010; Tatsumoto and Takanashi 2010).

Standardization consists of standard setting and diffusion. In the former stage firms create the specifications of a standard, while in the latter stage they share those specifications with other firms. Based on the characteristics of these processes, there are three approaches to standardization, resulting in different types of open standards. De facto standards are automatically defined through market share dominance, while de jure standards are established by public committees, such as ANSI and ISO/IEC. Consensus standards, which have grown in popularity since the 1990s, are set by consortia, forums or alliances of firms and have different features depending on the standardization process.

This chapter describes the three approaches to open standards and the growing influence of platform firms due to the frequent development of open standards.

1.1 Impact of Open Standards

1.1.1 What is an Open Standard? Three Types of Open Standards

Open standards are one of the common characteristics shared by rapidly growing industries in the 1990s, including the personal computer, cell phone and DVD sectors. These industries are all based on open standards that help firms collaborate to achieve cost reductions and utility enhancements, benefiting both consumers and the firms

H. Tatsumoto, *Platform Strategy for Global Markets*,
https://doi.org/10.1007/978-981-33-6789-0_1

themselves. Open standards also play a role in attracting large numbers of newcomers to the market, thus turning the industry into a gigantic business ecosystem with a variety of economic entities and achieving considerable economic growth. Firms cannot survive in such an open industry if they do not fully embrace this trend.

With the rapid growth of ecosystems, open standards are increasingly influencing firm behavior worldwide. They encourage global information sharing and serve as a common basis for innovation, also in collaboration with foreign firms. International open standards, conducive to cross-boundary activities, facilitate the development of a regional cluster into a global ecosystem featuring firms from different countries that collaborate for innovation. From the point of view of business strategy, firms cannot ignore open standards.

Three types of open standards exist today, each with specific characteristics, summarized in Table 1.1. The first type, de facto standards, have been used for many years in various industries. Assume that a certain component becomes very frequently traded in an industry, so that a growing number of manufacturers start designing their products based on that component. As more and more products adopt

Table 1.1 Comparison of three standardization processes

	De facto standards	De jure standards	Consensus standards
(i) Membership for standard setting	One or several firms. When multiple firms set a standard, their combined market share should be below a certain threshold that does not violate antitrust laws	Fixed membership of multiple firms. They set a standard based on the principle of unanimous agreement	Initial membership consists of firms that come together freely. Members cannot stop other firms from joining the consortium. Based on majority decision
(ii) Scope of standard setting	The design that has become dominant through market trading becomes the standard	The standard is determined prior to actual market trading, although the specifications most prevalent in the market are generally proposed as the initial draft	The scope of standardization can freely (flexibly) be determined. It may be a technology not yet introduced into the market
(iii) Degree of disclosure	Member firms arbitrarily decide to whom and to what extent the standard should be open	The standardized content is disclosed to third parties (openness)	The standardized content must be disclosed to third parties (information openness)
Examples	Mainframe (IBM), VTR (JVC)	ISO/IEC/ITU-T	PCI SIG, DVD Forum, AUTOSAR, ETSI, NIST and other (regional) standardization organizations recently established

the component, its interface works as a common basis for collaboration. Eventually, the interface becomes an actual open standard, approved by all the players in the industry. This open standard, formed through market trading and perceived as an industrywide standard because of its dominance, is called a de facto standard. De facto standards draw on the market model; that is, the interface or protocol that is used by most firms is perceived as the industrywide standard.

The second type, de jure standards, have been used for as many years as de facto standards. The development of de jure standards is essentially independent of the market process, since a de jure standard is formally set by a public committee of experts. The committee members exchange information and decide the specifications of the draft standard. If conflicts arise around the content, an integrated version of the draft standard is developed through discussion and then published.

After the standard is published, firms in the industry are required to adopt it and, in extreme cases, the de jure standard may be rendered mandatory by law. Such a standard may have a large impact on the industry and, at the same time, raise concerns about violating antitrust laws, as it is established away from the market process and can impede fair competition. Firms in the private sector, therefore, often hesitate to organize draft-writing groups for de jure standards. This is the reason why national governments or standard development organizations usually develop de jure standards and why the process of de jure standard setting is carefully conducted in a formal manner.

The third type, consensus standards, are standards defined by a consortium. To create a consensus standard, firms freely come together to form a consortium, develop a draft standard through knowledge sharing among members and then publish it for other firms in the market. The firm group that comes together to establish a consensus standard is typically a consortium, but it may sometimes be a forum or a set of alliances. All types of firm groups are essentially the same, in that they always act as draft-writing organizations.

Unlike the case of de jure standards, no formal arrangement, such as governmental guidance, is needed to form a consortium. Therefore, multiple consortia targeting the same system may emerge at around the same time and compete with one another. Firms in the market choose from among the various competing standards and one of them eventually becomes the industry standard, perceived as the dominant, industrywide common basis.

Compared with de facto and de jure standards, consensus standards are relatively new, which is mainly due to institutional reasons. Indeed, before the 1990s, firms somehow hesitated to create consortia, because of concerns about antitrust laws when they gathered to form groups of firms. To reduce their hesitations and encourage firm collaborations, a set of guidelines for antitrust laws was published in 1980. In addition, the National Cooperative Research Act (NCRA) and the National Cooperative Research and Production Act (NCRPA) were introduced in 1980 and 1993, respectively, to encourage joint research and production. These guidelines and laws succeeded in creating a relaxed atmosphere, resulting in an increasing number of consortia for the development of standards. Owing to this change, consensus standards have been gaining popularity since the 1990s.

The three types of open standards provide a critical tool for firms in the industries in which inter-firm collaborations are necessary for product development or in which connectivity across systems is important to ensure user benefits. For example, a large system consisting of many modules or a system connecting other systems need open protocols or interfaces for compatibility. A development project for such a large system necessarily relies on a group of firms and on a common basis using open standards. Open standards work well in industries where cross-firm collaborations are inevitable in order to achieve innovation. Technology industries, including electronics, telecommunications and computers, fall into this category, and the most recent example is the Internet industry, where companies customarily use other companies' web services through open application programming interfaces (APIs). As a consequence, the strategic capability to employ open standards matters in these industries. In Sect. 1.1.2, we discuss open standards from the strategic viewpoint.

1.1.2 Open Strategy Using Open Standards

Open standards essentially contribute to cost reductions and utility enhancements by providing a common basis for firm collaborations. However, in terms of business strategy, they are crucial for any firm not only in its collaborations with other firms but also in the strengthening of its own business over other firms. Such a strategy, based on inter-firm collaborations and on building the firm's own strength over its rivals, is referred to as an open strategy. Firms often pursue an open strategy using open standards. As explained in Sect. 1.1.1, we currently have three types of open standards, each with different strategic implications, shown in Table 1.2.

Table 1.2 Strategic implications of open standards

Type of open standard	Strategic implications	Pros	Cons
De facto standard	The standard is easy to monetize	Arbitrary changes to the standard to meet the firm's needs	The standard is very difficult to develop because this requires holding a dominant position in the market
De jure standard	A legal barrier against new entrants	Mandatory by law	Relatively slow pace of standardization due to its formality
Consensus standard	Wide range of objectives: – sharing knowledge for collaborations – compatibility and connectivity – drawing up an investment roadmap	Building a common base across firms in the industry	Little practice because of its newness as an approach for open standards

By adopting de facto standards for their open strategy, firms can easily monetize them, since they can flexibly change standards to fit their strategy without any arrangement with other firms. This ease of monetization is an advantage of de facto standards. On the other hand, it is very difficult to establish de facto standards as industrywide standards. The fact that a firm establishes a de facto standard virtually means that it occupies a dominant position in the market of the target system. This is the reason why pursuing an open strategy based on de facto standards is fundamentally difficult.

Differently from de facto standards, de jure standards have no connection with business strategy in terms of monetization. Yet, they have a distinct advantage that the other two standards do not have, as de jure standards can build a barrier against new entrants. Typically, the firms that exploit de jure standards introduce a conformity test that checks performance and does not allow any product to be launched until it meets the set performance standards. For example, air conditioners have a standard for energy efficiency, and no product appears on the market unless it passes a performance test confirming its compliance with the standard. The conformity test works as a barrier against new entrants that do not yet have the skills to achieve the set level of performance. This entry barrier becomes even harder to overcome when the conformity test is made mandatory by law. From the perspective of business strategy, the function served by de jure standards is important when firms want to avoid competition with new entrants in the market.

Despite this unique advantage, de jure standards have the major disadvantage that the firms tasked with drafting them often need a long time to develop and publish draft standards. This is because they all have to agree, even by making compromises, otherwise they have to continue their negotiations in order to eliminate disagreement. In the worst case, i.e., if they do not come to an agreement, they have to abandon the standard drafting activity altogether.

From a strategic point of view, consensus standards are a much more complex tool than the other two standards. As mentioned above, de facto standards are used for monetizing, while de jure standards are intended to build barriers against new entrants. On the other hand, consensus standards are used for a variety of strategic objectives, and their basic function is to establish a common basis in the industry. Specifically, three cases of consensus standard usage can be identified.

The first function is to share knowledge with other firms for collaboration purposes. The draft-writing firms include technological information and industrial context into the draft standard that they want to share with other firms in the industry. Since open standards turn this knowledge into an explicit form, any firms that are new to, or unfamiliar with, the industry can increase their skills to reasonable levels using the standard and begin collaborating with other firms.

The second function is to ensure compatibility and connectivity of interfaces or protocols. A system comprising many modules or connected to other systems has interfaces with protocols. In order to guarantee their compatibility or connectivity, some formal conformity testing is necessary, for which firms often employ consensus standards.

The third function is to share an investment roadmap among peers in the industry. Firms operating in industries characterized by rapid evolution of technology often need synchronization of individual investments in the same technological generation. Things become much more difficult when the necessary investments are distributed across many firms and, in this case, using a consensus standard helps streamline the process. For example, the semiconductor industry is currently going through a phase of rapid technological evolution and its production processes feature various manufacturing machines of the same technological generation. Equipment providers need cross-firm synchronization to develop and produce their equipment, otherwise their investments become worthless, as no other equipment of the same technological generation is available. They thus use consensus standards to draw up a roadmap and share it with other firms in the industry.

Consensus standards are flexible and useful to achieve strategic objectives related to building a shared cross-firm basis. As explained above, this type of standard is often employed to share knowledge, provide compatibility and draw up roadmaps. However, it also has drawbacks due to its newness, compared with the other two standards. Indeed, consensus standards began spreading in the 1990s, following the relaxation of antitrust laws. This encouraged joint research and production, which, in turn, led to an increase in the number of consortia, producing many consensus standards but having little practice in their usage. Hence, it is paramount for firms to learn how to use consensus standards for strategic objectives and accumulate sufficient practice through business experience.

1.1.3 Outcomes of Open Standards

Open standards are a very important strategic tool for implementing open strategies. They are also effective for establishing collaborations among firms and strengthening their business. This is the main reason why firms frequently use them to pursue open strategies.

Although open standards are mostly adopted by firms for the sake of their own business, they produce outcomes that are likely to transform industrial structures. One of their main outcomes is the creation of an open area in the target system, and this knowledge becomes common to all the firms in an industry through standardization. Before discussing why this open area is able to change industrial structures, let us explore the connections among the three types of open standards and their outcomes in terms of open area.

Table 1.3 Comparison of the three types of standards

Type of standard	Model of standard setting	Model of standard diffusion	Open area outcomes
De facto standard	Market model (unilateral information exchange)	Market model (competition among standards)	Smaller open area
De jure standard	Non-market model (bilateral information exchange)	Non-market model (no competition or mandatory)	Smaller open area
Consensus standard	Non-market model (bilateral information exchange)	Market process (competition among standards)	Larger open area

Table 1.3 compares the models and outcomes of the three types of standards.[1] As mentioned above, standardization consists of two phases, standard setting and standard diffusion. In the standard setting phase, either a single firm or multiple firms draw up a draft standard, which typically includes interface specifications, communication protocols, technical guidelines and investment roadmaps. The draft standard is then made openly available to other firms, which initiates the standard diffusion phase. The published standard is tried and tested by firms in the market, which spend some time evaluating it to decide whether or not to adopt it. These phases are modeled as either market or non-market.

1.1.3.1 Standard Setting Models

The models for standard setting are theoretically categorized into market and non-market, depending on the direction of information exchange. In the market model, the draft-writing firms unilaterally propose their draft standards and the other firms simply either accept or reject them. This process is similar to that of the stock exchange, where sellers set the stock price and buyers decide whether or not to purchase the stocks. No negotiation takes place in this case.

In contrast, the non-market model is based on bilateral information exchanges. When a system is complex and large in scale, firms want to exchange information about it and discuss its details to draw up a draft standard. In this model, the firms involved organize a committee to create a standard and meet several times for mutual exchanges of information.

[1] The terms *standardization* and *standard setting* have different meanings: standardization specifically refers to a combination of standard setting and standard diffusion. Nevertheless, the two expressions are often used interchangeably in scientific studies. Typically, European studies employ the term *standardization*, whereas US studies prefer *standard setting*. This is most likely because Europeans think of standards as de jure standards, while Americans think of them as de facto standards.

The three types of standards tend to be different in how they use the market or non-market model during the drafting process. The market model is most often adopted for de facto standards. In this model, firms do not need to communicate or reach agreements with other firms before they propose their own draft standards. This means that they unilaterally provide their opinions about the target system, while the other firms just accept or reject them, without any negotiation.

Conversely, de jure and consensus standards usually employ the non-market model during the drafting process. In the non-market model, committees or working groups are organized, in which member firms share information, discuss how to address the problems that they face and eventually reach an agreement about the draft standard. In this process, information flows bilaterally rather than unilaterally.

Both the market model and the non-market model have pros and cons for draft-writing firms, which put in a great deal of effort in drawing up draft standards because they want to profit from their adoption. To this end, the market model has a major advantage, in that firms do not need the approval of other firms to establish a standard. If agreement with other firms were necessary, they would have to wait for a long time before publishing a draft, since it may conflict with the interests of other players. The market model eliminates this risk by ignoring the other firms' will and allows the draft-writing firms to publish their draft standard as they see fit.

However, the market model does not always suffice for large or complicated systems. The development project of a large system involves many firms, and the technological knowledge needed is distributed across all the parties involved. No single firm covers the whole system, so that a common knowledge base must be built for joint development. In this case, the non-market model, in which the parties mutually exchange information for standard setting, is the most suitable approach. Although firms have to continue negotiating until they reach an agreement, the non-market model has a clear advantage, in that it can handle a larger system than the market model.

In summary, draft-writing firms decide to use either the market or the non-market model depending on their reasons for pursuing standardization and the nature of the target system. If the target system is not very complicated, they will naturally choose de facto standards, which increase their chances of monetization by employing the market model. If the target system is large and complex, rather than focusing on the strategic priority of monetization, they will work toward building a common knowledge base with other firms by adopting the non-market model.

1.1.3.2 Standard Diffusion Models

The process of standard diffusion refers to how firms adopt a draft standard and eventually come to perceive it as an industrywide common basis. This process too follows one of two patterns, i.e., the market model and the non-market model, and its classification depends on whether there is competition among similar standards to attain the dominant position.

In the market model, there are multiple competing standards, published by draft-writing firms as their own proposals, and firms in the market choose from among these candidates. The competition lasts until one of the draft standards gains the dominant position and is acknowledged as the industrywide common basis. In brief, the market model of standard diffusion is characterized by competition among similar standards in the market.

The non-market model is quite different, in that it does not have multiple competing standards. If similar draft standards coexist, a draft-writing group initiates talks with another draft-writing group and together they draw up an integrated version, which is then published. Firms in the market cannot choose from among multiple options but simply decide whether to accept or reject the standard. Thus, in the non-market model, there is no competition among similar standards, a feature that becomes even more prominent when the standards are made mandatory by law.

De facto and consensus standards establish themselves as industrywide standards through a process based on the market model. A published standard competes against other similar standards until it eventually becomes the industrywide standard, perceived by most firms as a common basis. On the other hand, de jure standards employ the non-market model, which entails no competition among candidates in the market. If multiple candidate versions coexist before publishing, the standard-drafting committees consolidate them into an integrated one. After publishing the standard, firms in the market are required to adopt it, which may sometimes be made mandatory by law.

So far, we have discussed the two models, i.e., market and non-market, that regulate the processes of standard setting and standard diffusion. In the standard setting process, the two models differ in the direction of information exchange, which is unilateral in the market model and bilateral in the non-market model. In the standard diffusion process, the models differ in whether or not competition occurs. The market model is characterized by competition for the dominant position, while the non-market model bypasses it altogether.

1.1.3.3 Outcomes of Open Standards

The three types of open standards use the market model and the non-market model in different ways. De facto standards rely on the market model in both processes of standard setting and standard diffusion, whereas de jure standards are based on the non-market model in both phases. Consensus standards are eclectic, using the market model in the standard setting process and the non-market model in the standard diffusion phase.

Researchers often mistake the consensus approach for the de facto or the de jure approach, since the former is partly similar to the other two. For example, some investigations have failed to recognize consensus standards and maintained a dichotomous classification including only de facto and de jure standards. Yet, ignoring consensus standards brings academic confusion to the stream of studies on open standards. In strategic terms, it is important to identify the three types of standards because they yield different outcomes.

The combination patterns of the market and non-market models cause the three types of standards to have different outcomes. From the knowledge sharing point of view, the main outcome of standardization is the creation of a common knowledge base, which all firms openly share about the target system.

Through the standard setting and diffusion processes, a target system is divided into two parts. This book defines the first part, the knowledge of which becomes common to all firms, as the open area and the second part, the knowledge of which remains proprietary to a few firms, as the closed area. Standardization expands the common knowledge base about the target system, thus making the open area larger.

All three types of standards create an open area in the target system, but the size of this area varies depending on the standard adopted. Generally speaking, consensus standards are likely to establish a larger open area than de facto and de jure standards because the consensus approach is eclectic, using the non-market model for standard setting and the market model for standard diffusion. This combined use of the two models explains why the open area of a consensus standard is larger.

Specifically, compared with de facto standards, consensus standards can produce a much larger open area because the draft-writing firms set up working groups in which to exchange information to draw up the draft standard. In the case of de facto standards, the draft-writing firms do not form partnerships to discuss the draft with third parties, mainly because agreeing with other firms is not their concern and they only follow their own will. Thus, in terms of knowledge sharing, the bilateral exchange of information results in a larger shared base than the unilateral exchange. This is why consensus standards create larger open areas than de facto standards.

Let us now compare de jure and consensus standards. As both use the non-market model in the standard setting phase, they can build equally large common knowledge bases for draft standards. Nevertheless, they display differences in the standard diffusion phase. The firms producing the draft of a consensus standard know that, once it is published, it will have to compete against various standards proposed by other firms. With such competition in mind, they are motivated to render their standard easier for other firms to adopt by allowing for as large an open area as they can.

In contrast, de jure standards avoid this type of competition by creating an integrated draft standard through coordination among standard development organizations that are likely to publish similar standards. Before publishing it, a comprehensive proposal of the standard is produced to minimize potential competition. The firms in the market are required to adopt these standards, which is often made mandatory by law. Therefore, since competition does not come into play, the draft-writing firms have little interest in providing a larger open area. As a result, de jure standards have smaller open areas than consensus standards.

We have discussed the three types of open standards in terms of how large an open area they create in the target system. Compared with the other two, consensus standards afford a larger open area, which means a wider common basis for inter-firm collaborations. This also encourages new entrants into the market of the target system, since even firms that were unfamiliar with it before its standardization can now develop and/or produce the system based on the knowledge provided by the open standard.

Firms began to adopt open standards during the 1980s. This trend grew in the 1990s as a new form of open standard, i.e., the consensus standard, became increasingly widespread, following the relaxation of antitrust laws and the enactment of the National Cooperative Research Act (NCRA) of 1984 and the National Cooperative Research and Production Act (NCRPA) of 1993, which encouraged firms to undertake joint research and production. As explained in Sect. 1.1.2, the three types of standards have different characteristics and thus complement one another. Due to the success of consensus standards, the traditional de facto and de jure processes have also seen a rise in their utilization.

With more and more firms pursuing an open strategy by employing open standards, larger open areas have appeared in many industries. Open areas have the power to attract new entrants. Indeed, any open standard has this power, which increases proportionally to the size of the open area. In this sense, consensus standards are likely to be the most powerful, since they have much larger open areas than the other two standards. The power of open standards brings about structural changes in an industry, for instance stimulating the entry of new players from emerging countries. This point is discussed in Sect. 1.2.

1.2 Institutional Development of Open Standards

Figure 1.1 presents the evolution of standardization policies in Europe and in the US. The shift in industrial policies in Western countries, which took place in the 1980s, is generally believed to have contributed to the key role played by standardization today. In the 1980s, these countries were confronted with the strong economic growth of emerging nations in East Asia, including Japan, and were forced to implement comprehensive policies to boost their industrial competitiveness. Both the US and many European countries (later, the EU) carried out a variety of institutional reforms to build up their international competitiveness.

The major trends in these institutional reforms include the promotion of joint research among companies to stimulate innovations and the strengthening of intellectual property rights to protect returns on investments in research and development (R&D). Standardization is involved chiefly in the former, i.e., the policies for the promotion of joint research. Amidst these changes in the industrial landscape, companies have learnt how to use standardization as a strategic corporate tool. Sects. 1.2.1 and 1.2.2 describe changes in standardization policies in the US and Europe, respectively.

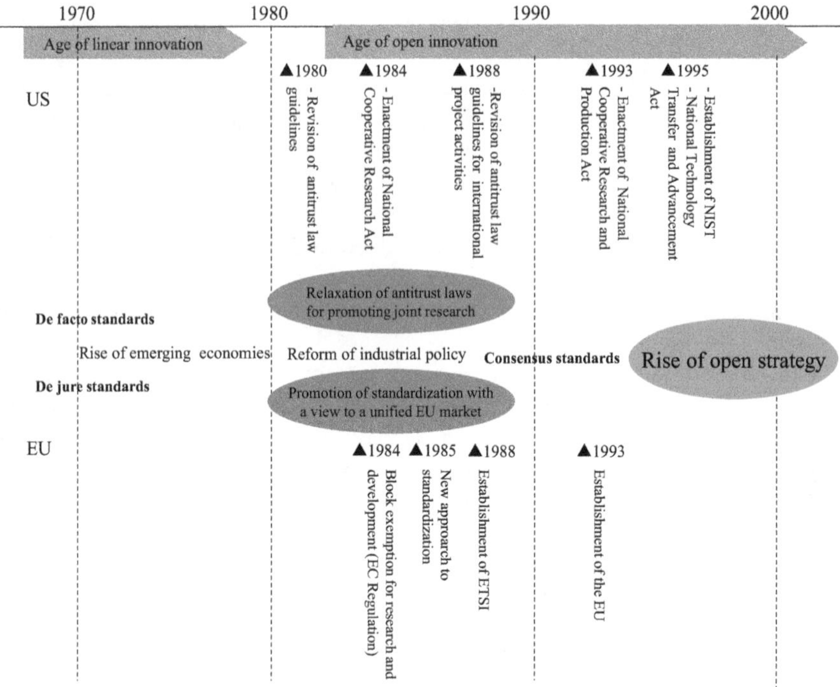

Fig. 1.1 Policies related to open standards in the US and Europe

1.2.1 US Policies Related to Open Standards

In the US, the early 1980s saw a rise in the promotion of joint innovation activities among different firms. This movement boomed partly because the nature of new emerging industries, such as the IT industry, requires connectivity and compatibility among systems. Another reason was that the new industrial policy, which was reformed to revitalize US innovation and gain international competitiveness vis-à-vis emerging economies, encouraged firms to pursue joint innovative activities with other firms. Let us now explore the policy trends related to open standards from the institutional standpoint.

In 1985, the President's Commission on Industrial Competitiveness issued a report, known as the Young Report, which set out the US industrial policy aimed at boosting innovation. Since the Young Report, the importance of innovation has been the central focus of discussions on competitiveness. In terms of the environment for innovative activities, the US has implemented measures to enhance the quality of innovation, including the promotion of joint activities among firms.

The NCRA was enacted in the midst of this movement to revamp industrial policies, with the purpose of stimulating business collaborations. The act was later modified by the NCRPA of 1993, which made it possible for companies to jointly work not only on research but also on subsequent production. As such, the review of industrial policies in the US around the 1980s placed greater emphasis on joint research.

The development of standardization activities was closely linked to this industrial policy of accelerating joint research. Both imply technological development and standard development through corporate collaboration. Corporate collaboration—particularly large-scale collaboration that may impact on an industry as a whole—was not at one's discretion but controlled by antitrust laws. Therefore, in general terms, whether a country actively embraces corporate collaboration or adopts a negative stance against it largely depends on the operation of antitrust laws.

The US antitrust laws had been rigorously administered prior to 1980, which had posed a major obstacle to any attempt at joint research or standard development through corporate collaboration. In joint research, multiple companies collaborate to develop a technology and they are very likely to eventually monopolize it. Thus, joint research was subjected to antitrust laws, and any joint research project that could infringe antitrust laws was strictly penalized. For instance, when a group of companies performed joint research activities and they occupied a certain market share (say 20% or more, although this may not be clearly specified by law), they were liable to be violating antitrust legislation.

The development of an industrial standard was more sensitive, since formulating any industrial standard inevitably involves collaboration among a greater number of firms than joint research. If companies controlling a certain market share came together and created a standard set of specifications, that could be seen as a move to exclude the other market players (Hirabayashi 1993). This is why the development of industrial standards prior to the 1980s was generally carried out through the de facto or de jure process.

Nevertheless, as the government launched the industrial policy of promoting joint research in the 1980s, the application of antitrust laws was gradually relaxed. In 1980, the Department of Justice released the Antitrust Guide Concerning Research Joint Ventures, setting out guidelines for joint research. The most important aspect defined by the Guide was that the development of standard specifications through joint research would not be subject to antitrust laws, provided that third parties were guaranteed free access to the standard specifications formulated by multiple firms possessing a certain combined market share (outcomes of joint research). This policy was more clearly detailed by the National Cooperative Research Act of 1984.

The deregulation of antitrust laws in the 1980s allowed any consortium or forum to create a standard. Up until then, an industrywide standard meant a de facto or de jure standard but, from then on, consensus standardization took off and utterly transformed the standardization process.

1.2.2 EU Policies Related to Open Standards

In Europe, industrial standardization gathered momentum when the region moved toward unification in 1993. Industrywide standards, which had until then been separately established by individual countries, had to be unified into *European* standards.

As in the case of the US, the formulation of standards through corporate alliances could violate antitrust laws or, more specifically, Articles 85 and 86 of the Treaty of Rome. However, the European Commission (EC) Regulation introduced in December 1984, regarding the block exemption from the application of Article 85(3) to categories of research and development agreements, radically changed the overall approach and acknowledged the carrying out of joint research and joint production under a certain set of rules (Miyata 1997, p. 188).

Moreover, the EC announced a *New Approach* to standardization in 1985, which unequivocally recognized industry-led standardization as a means to develop regional standards across Europe. The promulgation of this document triggered the strengthening of the Comité Européen de Normalisation (CEN) and the Comité Européen de Normalisation Électrotechnique (CENELEC) and the setting up of the European Telecommunications Standards Institute (ETSI). The unification of Europe's regional economy bolstered standardization, and the need to build up the international competitiveness of its industry led to the creation of a new form of standardization process guided by the industry itself, resulting in an increase in consensus standards.

A good example of the successful application of the consensus process is the GSM standard, the most prevalent mobile phone system today. In preparation for the unification of Europe, the GSM Working Group, established by the European Conference of Postal and Telecommunications Administrations (CEPT), started the development of GSM in 1982, following the allocation of frequencies to second-generation mobile communications in 1981. This process was of the classic de jure type.

A major shift occurred in 1985 after the *New Approach* was released. With the setting up of ETSI in 1988, standard development activities were transferred from CEPT to ETSI, which caused a key transformation of the standardization process from the de jure to the consensus approach.

Within the CEPT framework, the standardization process was driven by telecommunications administrators and the state-run telephone and telecommunications corporations of the member nations. Conversely, once it was transferred to ETSI, it enabled the free participation of any enterprises, in addition to administrators and corporations. Hence, the process came to involve many different players with diverse backgrounds, including research institutes, universities, users, operators, government officials and communications hardware providers. Communications hardware providers, in particular, took the lead in the standardization process, although all the participants equally wanted to create a standard that would benefit their own entity the most.

In the market of analogue mobile phones, which was the generation prior to that of digital phones, such as GSM, the European mobile phone industry lagged very much behind that of the US and Japan. The industry feared that, once Europe became a single economy, the market would be taken over by overseas providers and, to avoid this, it intended to develop a standard that would take as much advantage of its competitive edge as possible. Accordingly, the European mobile phone industry strategically developed the standard and led the standardization process, aiming to fortify its industrial competitiveness (US Congress, Office of Technology Assessment 1992, p. 69).

In his study on the standardization of second-generation mobile technology, Funk (2002) pointed out that the European standard (GSM), created through the consensus process, had a wider standardization scope than the US standard (CDMA), based on the de facto process, and the Japanese standard (PDC), relying on the de jure process.

Compared with the US case, the EU's regional standards, involving CEN and CENELEC and following the consensus standard approach, had much closer connections with international de jure standards, such as ISO or IEC. Indeed, agreements on technical cooperation have been concluded between ISO and CEN (Vienna Agreement of 1991) and between IEC and CENELEC (Dresden Agreement of 1996). In addition, the close intermeshing of European and international standardization activities has led to 31 and 76% of all European standards adopted by CEN and CENELEC being technically equivalent or identical to ISO and IEC standards, respectively (SESEC 2019).

This broad uniformity between European and international standards has facilitated the implementation of the WTO Technical Barriers to Trade Agreement (WTO-TBT) on the global market. The WTO-TBT Agreement requires technical regulations, standards and conformity assessments to be non-discriminatory and not to create unnecessary obstacles to trade. As a result, regional standards are now influencing the global market. In other words, developing open standards works as an effective open strategy and becomes an important tool to achieve international competitiveness.

1.3 Transformation of Industrial Structures

1.3.1 Industrial Structures Turning into Business Ecosystems

Open strategies based on open standards were often used in fast-growing industries in the 1990s, which led them to undergo a structural change from the vertical form to the horizontal form, as illustrated in Fig. 1.2. In the computer industry, this change was first reported by Grove, who was the CEO of Intel at that time. In his book (Grove 1996), he stated that the computer industry was transforming from the vertical to the horizontal form. He also stressed that the vertical business model, which he referred to as *vertical silos*, was outdated.

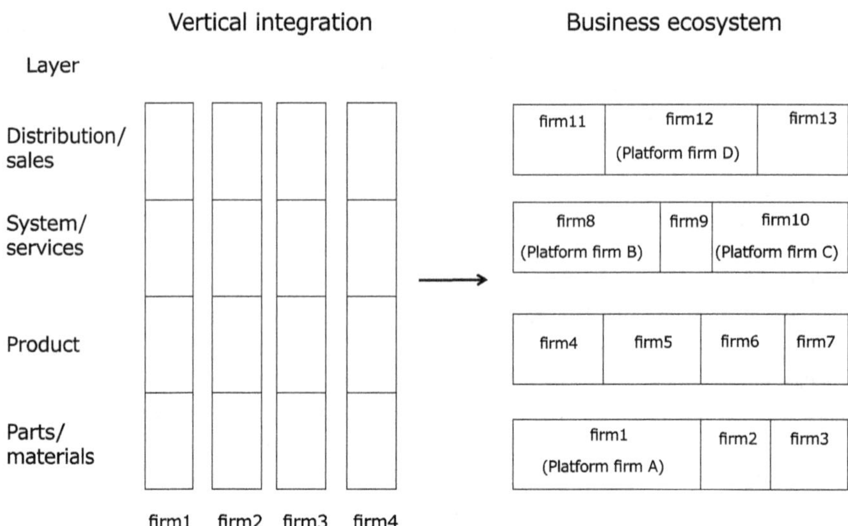

Fig. 1.2 Changes in industrial structure

Firms in the computer industry used to operate in a vertically integrated manner, as shown in the left part of Fig. 1.2. They owned all the functions in the value chain, and kept them inside the firm. For example, IBM directly owned the business divisions of semiconductor chips, computer products, services and sales, increasing its competitive advantage through vertical integration. Its rivals followed the same strategy and retained all of these functions in house.

However, as the computer industry shifted to the horizontal form in the 1990s, firms changed their strategy from vertical integration to specialization in one or more functions. This structural change gave rise to a new approach to business strategy, i.e., the open strategy, thanks to which firms can exploit the horizontal industrial structure by using open standards. In relation to the open strategy, a horizontal industrial structure has at least three noteworthy characteristics.

The first is that the horizontal form consists of multiple layers stacked one on top of the other. Each layer corresponds to a function in the value chain. No firm can deliver its products/services without the other firms' support, and each firm specializes in a certain part of the value chain. Consequently, none of them is able to achieve product innovation by itself, as this is a long sequence spanning many steps from the development of a technology to its delivery to consumers. So, all the players are inevitably interdependent, and this is why inter-firm collaboration is critical to innovation in this type of industry.

The second key feature is that each layer openly connects with the other layers. These open connections among layers mean that a firm in a given layer can trade with any other firm in the other layers. By virtue of the open connections, companies often change suppliers or customers in the process of developing their innovations and delivering them to consumers. As inter-firm connections frequently change, compatibility and connectivity among functions become critical to the smooth delivery of innovations to consumers.

The third characteristic is that a layer leader, i.e., a firm holding a dominant position in the layer, eventually emerges and takes on a powerful role in directing the evolution of the whole industry. The layer leader is referred to as a platform firm. A platform firm exerts a considerable influence not only on the layer in which it operates but also on all the other layers in the industry.

In industries organized according to the horizontal form, firms frequently use open standards as a vital tool for their open strategy. Open standards are effective for the following purposes: (i) building a common knowledge base, (ii) ensuring compatibility and connectivity and (iii) influencing the industry as a whole.

The transition to the horizontal form was first detected in the computer and semiconductor industries. Then, it was also observed in the digital home appliances, cell phones and Internet industries. The Internet, in particular, has a wide range of related industries, resulting in the reproduction of the horizontal form among them. Today, more and more industries have taken on the horizontal form and, to emphasize their typical dynamics, they are customarily referred to as business ecosystems.

1.3.2 Concept of Business Ecosystem

The concept of business ecosystem referring to industrial structure is analogous to the idea of natural ecosystem, yet it differs in how it is understood by researchers. At least three statements hold true in terms of business strategy. Let us analyze them.

First of all, a business ecosystem consists of many firms with different roles, just like the numerous species in a natural ecosystem. A business ecosystem has many economic entities with diverse backgrounds, including not only existing firms but also newcomer firms. Sometimes new entries occur across borders, bringing new technologies and business opportunities and realizing innovations through interactions with existing firms. Diversity is a main driver of the rapid growth of a business ecosystem.

Secondly, the relationships among firms, whether direct or indirect, are complex. A traditional industrial structure is comprised only of firms supplying direct goods, i.e., goods that are directly related to the production of a specific product, such as its parts or materials. An industrial structure featuring exclusively direct goods providers is not a business ecosystem, since the latter typically comprises not only direct goods providers but also complementary goods providers.

A complementary good is a good the sales of which increase the popularity of the good being complemented. The firms selling complementary goods are referred to as complementors. For example, the sales of DVD discs boost those of DVD players. In this case, the DVD disc is a complementary good to the DVD player and a seller of DVD discs is a complementor to that of DVD players.

If the product of a complementor sells well, so does that of the other company, even though they are not trading directly with each other. This relationship, in which the sales of the product of one firm boost those of the other, is caused by a network effect (more precisely, an indirect network effect). By definition, there are two types of network effects. The basic type is referred to as direct network effect, whereby a greater number of users enhances the value of a product, while the other is called indirect network effect, whereby a greater number of users of a certain product enhances the value of a different product. Complementary goods come with indirect network effects.

In a business ecosystem, network effects often arise from the introduction of open standards, resulting in the emergence of complementors. In the above example about the DVD technology, a network effect was generated as the DVD standard, an open standard, was created, followed by the emergence of complementors, i.e., DVD disc providers. Complementors are present because there is a network effect generated in the trade among the firms making up the business ecosystem.

Remarkably, it is very often the case that network effects derive not from the nature of the product but from an intentional arrangement, that is, the setting up of an open standard. In the DVD example, the film industry had begun providing film content long before DVD players were introduced, but it was not yet a complementor to DVD players. Once the DVD standard was established as an open standard, companies in the film industry became complementors to the DVD industry, because the DVD standard undeniably connects DVD players and DVD discs and generates a strong network effect between them. The presence of network effects and the existence of complementors are the two sides of the coin and, as said above, network effects are often generated through the setting up of open standards. As open standards are developed one after another, network effects appear where until then there had not been any and their multiplication within a business ecosystem results in the massive emergence of complementors.

Lastly, natural ecosystems contain some unique species, called keystone species. They exist in very small quantities but, if they were to be removed, the entire ecosystem would collapse (Paine 1966). Drawing an analogy with biology, Iansiti and Levien (2004) argued that some unique firms are able to drive the evolution of an industry. They called such firms keystone firms, even though they are more generally called platform firms in studies on business strategy.

1.3.3 Platform Strategy: A New Type of Competition Strategy Employing Open Standards

The strategic development of open standards has allowed a new firm type to gain competitiveness. These businesses are known as platform firms, or platformers, and they have been actively studied since the 2000s (Gawer and Cusumano 2002; Stango 2004; Gawer 2009; Hagiu and Yoffie 2009; Eisenmann et al. 2011; Rochet and Tirole 2003; Evans et al. 2006).

The typical strategies of platform firms described in these studies appear to be in marked contrast with the traditional strategies focused on products. While the strategies focused on products (product strategies) revolve around enhancing the competitiveness of a company's products, platform strategies aim to actively expand the business ecosystem, consisting of the platformer and its complementary goods companies. Complementors are independent firms, which means that the platform firm is not required to assist them in any way from the standpoint of product strategy. For what concerns platform strategy, however, assisting complementors is logical because the development of complementary goods boosts the demand for the platform products that the platformer provides.

Complementors naturally emerge when an open standard is created, as easily understood from the example about DVD technology. It also becomes obvious that platformers actively engage in standardization activities in order to develop open standards that are advantageous to them.

Section 1.1 explained that consensus standards are a relatively new form of standard and have been ever more widely adopted since the 1990s. As the three types of open standards complement one another, the success of consensus standards has caused the traditional de facto and de jure standards to be more frequently used. Employing a mix of open standards makes a firm's open strategy more efficient, which is why platformers rely on open standards to make their business more competitive.

Platformers quickly become extremely influential in a business ecosystem-type industry. Their influence ripples beyond national boundaries and spreads across the globe, because the open standards that platform firms utilize enable information to spill over irrespective of country borders. This feature of open standards allows a new industry to be created on a global scale, while, at the same time, expanding the influence of platform firms all over the world.

The global presence and operations of platformers have had a large impact on global business ecosystems from the 1990s onwards. Kawakami (2012) noted that the open standard provided by Intel Corporation, a platform leader, underlay the development of the Taiwanese personal computer industry into a world-class industry. Marukawa and Yasumoto (2010) stated that the open standardization of GSM specifications and the platform products provided by semiconductors fabs greatly contributed to the rise of Chinese mobile phone manufacturers. Ogawa (2009, 2014) and Senoo (2009) even argued that strategies based on open standards are indispensable for gaining an international competitive edge from the standpoint of business models. Many of the firms quoted as examples in these studies are those typically called platform owners.

As discussed thus far, the influence of platformers is so pervasive that governments have felt the need to put controls in place. For instance, China and South Korea have accused Qualcomm, Inc. of violating antitrust laws, saying that the semiconductor platform owner operating in the mobile phone market was "abusing its dominant position" in 2015 and 2009, respectively (Wall Street Journal 2015a; Futamata 2013). In addition, the European Commission announced that it would intensify monitoring of the Information and Communications Technology (ICT) industry, where the influence of platformers is particularly strong (Wall Street Journal 2015b). Platform firms are now recognized as a key influence on a nation's industry, as they have the power to both help it develop and make it collapse.

Despite their immense influence, platformers have not yet been thoroughly investigated in existing studies on management strategy. The next chapter (Chap. 2), therefore, explores how industrial structures transformed into business ecosystems as open standards were increasingly developed and explains how platformers gain competitive advantage with the help of theoretical models.

References

Besen SM, Farrell J (1991) The role of ITU in standardization: pre-eminence, importance or rubber stamp? Telecommun Policy 15(4):311–321

David PA, Greenstein S (1990) The economics of compatibility standards: an introduction to recent research. Econ Innov New Technol 1:3–41

Eisenmann T, Parker G, Van Alstyne M (2011) Platform envelopment. Strateg Manag J 32:1270–1285

Evans DS, Hagiu A, Schmalensee R (2006) Invisible engines. MIT Press, Cambridge, MA

Farrell J, Saloner G (1988) Coordination through committees and markets. Rand J Econ 19(2):235–252

Funk JL (2002) Global competition between and within standards: the case of mobile phones, 2nd edn. Palgrave Macmillan, London

Futamata T (2013) Raisensu Keiyaku no Kenkyu: Qualcomm shya Kankoku Dokusenkinshihou Jiken Shoukai (Study on licensing contract: antitrust case on Qualcomm in the Korean market) (in Japanese). http://pari.u-tokyo.ac.jp/column/column101.html. Accessed 01 Sept 2015

Gawer A (2009) Platforms, markets and innovation. Edward Elgar, Cheltenham, UK and Northampton, MA

Gawer A, Cusumano MA (2002) Platform leadership: How Intel, Microsoft, and Cisco drive industry innovation. Harvard Business School Press, Boston, MA

Grove SA (1996) Only the paranoid survive: How to exploit the crisis points that challenge every company and career. Currency/Doubleday, New York

Hagiu A, Yoffie DB (2009) What's your Google strategy? Harvard Bus Rev 87(4):74–81

Harada S (2008) Kokusai hyoujunka Senryaku (Strategy for International Standardization). Denki University Press, Tokyo (in Japanese)

Hirabayashi E (1993) Kyoudou Kenkyu Kaihatsu ni kansuru Dokusen Kinshihou Gaidoraine (Antitrust guidelines for joint research and development). Japan Institute of Business Law, Tokyo (in Japanese)

Iansiti M, Levien R (2004) The keystone advantage: What the new business ecosystems mean for strategy, innovation, and sustainability. Harvard Business School Press, Boston

Jorde TM, Teece TJ (1990) Innovation and cooperation: implications for competition and antitrust. J Econ Perspect 4(3):75–96

Kajiura M (2007) Kokusai Bijinesu to Gijutsu Hyojun (International business and technological standards). Bunshindo, Tokyo (in Japanese)

Kawakami M (2012) Ashuku sareta Sangyo Hatten: Taiwan Note Pasokon Kigyou no Seichou Mekanizumu (Accelerating the growth mechanism of the Taiwanese notebook computer industry). The University of Nagoya Press, Nagoya (in Japanese)

Marukawa T, Yasumoto M (2010) Keitai Denwa Sangyou no Shinka Purosesu: Nihon wa naze Koritsu shitanoka (Evolution in the mobile phone industry: Why does the Japanese mobile phone industry isolate in the global market). Yuhikaku, Tokyo (in Japanese)

Miyata Y (1997) Kyoudou Kenkyu Kaihatsu to Sangyou Seisaku (Joint R&D and industrial policy). Keisou Shobou, Tokyo (in Japanese)

Ogawa K (2009) Kokusai hyoujunka to Jigyou Senryaku (International standards and business strategy). Hakuto Shobou, Tokyo (in Japanese)

Ogawa K (2014) Oupun and Kurozu Senryaku: Nihon Kigyou Saikou no Jouken (Open and closed strategy: conditions for the revival of Japanese companies). Shoueisha, Tokyo (in Japanese)

Paine RT (1966) Food web complexity and species diversity. Am Nat 100:65–75

Rochet J, Tirole J (2003) Platform competition in two-sided markets. J Eur Econo Assoc 1(4):990–1029

Senoo K (2009) Gijutsuryoku de Masaru Nihon ga naze Jigyou de Makerunoka (Why does Japan, with its technological prowess, lose in business?). Diamondsha, Tokyo (in Japanese)

SESEC (2019) Vienna & Dresden agreements. https://www.sesec.eu/vienna-dresden-agreements. Accessed 12 Oct 2019

Stango V (2004) The economics of standards wars. Rev Netw Econ 3(1):1–19

Tatsumoto H, Takanashi C (2010) Competitive strategies on standardization: establishing and exploiting consensus standardization. J Jpn Assoc Manag Syst 26(2):67–81. ISSN: 09188282 (in Japanese)

Tatsumoto H, Ogawa K, Shintaku J (2010) Strategic standardization: platform business and the effect on international division of labor. Ann Bus Adminis Sci 10:13–26. ISSN: 1327-4456

US Congress, Office of Technology Assessment (1992) Global standards: building blocks for the future, TCT-512. US Government Printing Office, Washington, DC

Wall Street Journal (2015a) Qualcomm to pay $975 million antitrust fine to China. https://jp.wsj.com/articles/SB11815783148186973545804580452531974663988. Published 10 Feb 2015, Accessed 1 Sept 2015

Wall Street Journal (2015b) EPA accuses Volkswagen of dodging emissions rules. http://jp.wsj.com/articles/SB10063581187792594737804581241441337997546. Published 19 Sep 2015, Accessed 21 Sep 2015

Yamada H (2007) Hyojunka Sensou heno Riron Busou (Theory for standards wars). Zeimukeiri kyoukai, Tokyo (in Japanese)

Chapter 2
Business Ecosystems and Platform Firms: Theoretical Perspective and Analytical Framework

This chapter reviews studies on the competitive strategies of platform firms and presents the fundamental proposition of this book.

Section 2.1 models the business ecosystem as a prerequisite for platform strategy. In a transaction network, with network effects arising from open standards, firms with new roles emerge: complementors, system users and platform firms.

Section 2.2 uses theoretical models to explain the competitive strategies of platform firms: positioning at the hub, strategic standardization, two-sided market strategy and bundling strategy.

Sections 2.3 points out that existing research mostly disregards the globalization of platform firms. Some Japanese case studies address the phenomenon but lack consistency with theoretical models. Hence, this book tries to bridge this gap by exploring why the competitiveness of platform firms grows as international open standards are created and how their success affects the growth of regional economies.

The fundamental proposition is expressed in Sect. 2.4 as follows: "When an open standard prevails in a global ecosystem, the platform firm gains a dominant competitive position. The success of the platform firm triggers a sudden transformation in the structure of the international division of labor."

Lastly, Sect. 2.5 introduces the case studies illustrated in Chaps. 3–7 and the relationships among them.

H. Tatsumoto, *Platform Strategy for Global Markets*,
https://doi.org/10.1007/978-981-33-6789-0_2

2.1 Business Ecosystem: Open Standard Setting and Transformation of the Industrial Ecosystem

2.1.1 Three Trade Patterns: Complementors and Platform Firms

As discussed in Chap. 1, with the proliferation of open standards, the transformation of industrial structures causes significant changes in firm behavior and eventually affects the division of labor in the global economy. Studies about business ecosystems, a new form of industrial structure, look at the impact of frequent open standard setting on transaction networks from the standpoint of industrial evolution (Gawer and Cusumano 2002; Iansiti and Levien 2004a; Negoro and Sugiyama 2011).

In a broad sense, open standards include a variety of items, like technological roadmaps, reference designs, and so on. They are not readily recognized as industrial standards because they are different from traditional standards, such as safety standards. But they are strategically useful for ecosystem management, through which platform firms develop a common basis to stimulate innovation in their industry. Three processes can be followed for the formulation of open standards, as described in Chap. 1. Since all of them work as an industrywide common basis and support open connections among firms, they accelerate the shift of an industry from the traditional vertical form to a new horizontal one, that is, a business ecosystem.

Researchers have characterized business ecosystems in many different ways. This book defines a business ecosystem as "a community of companies trading direct goods and complementary goods through flexible inter-company networks and public bodies, including standardization organizations, regulators and justice authorities, which support that trade network, in order to provide complicated system products to end users" (Teece 2007; Baldwin 2011). What is noteworthy is that this definition incorporates within its scope not only direct goods but also complementary goods and regards entities that support transaction networks (i.e., standardization organizations) as being part of business ecosystems.

Traditional business-to-business transactions essentially relied on straight-chain-type trade networks. A business ecosystem, on the other hand, encompasses firms that did not exist in any straight-chain-type network: complementors, system users and platform firms.

To clearly show the nature of each of these types of firms, Fig. 2.1 depicts the three trade patterns that can constitute a business ecosystem. In this figure, solid lines represent trade flows, whereas dashed lines represent the presence of network effects.

In the vertical chain model, i.e., the traditional type of business without network effects, the mainstream trade pattern is (a) straight-chain, and all other trade patterns are minor. In this case, Firm X's competitive strategy is to reduce the influence of Upstream Firm U and increase its own bargaining power toward Downstream Firm

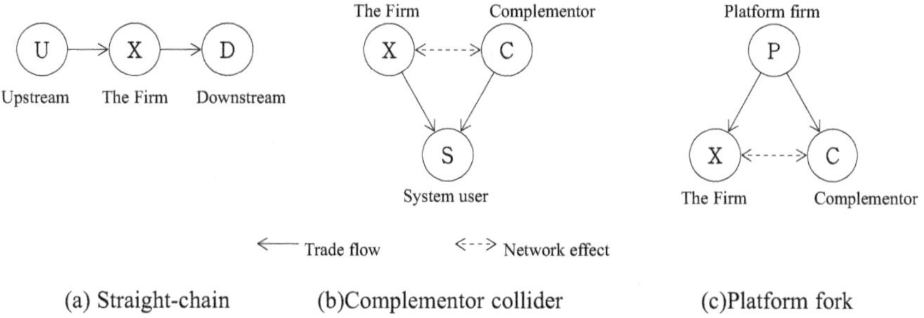

Fig. 2.1 Tri-partite trade patterns

D, so as to maximize the added value to be obtained. The three basic elements in the straight-chain model are the Firm, the Upstream Firm and the Downstream Firm.

On the other hand, in the business ecosystem of an industry that deals with complex products, trade patterns other than the straight-chain pattern are often present, due to network effects. These are (b) complementor collider and (c) platform fork, and they represent the new trade patterns that appear in business ecosystems. Within these patterns, firms with roles that had not existed in the value chain model come into the picture, namely complementary goods suppliers, system users and platform firms.

Complementors (Complementary Goods Suppliers): The (b) complementor collider model presents a scenario in which the goods (products or services) provided by Firm X are complemented by the goods provided by Firm C. Firm C does not trade directly with Firm X, so it is positioned neither downstream nor upstream of Firm X, unlike the case of the straight-chain model. Nevertheless, when more goods provided by Firm C are available, the demand for Firm X's goods also increases. In this sense, the two firms have a certain relationship. One good example of this relationship is the one between DVD player manufacturers and DVD content providers. In this trade pattern, Firm C is called a complementor.

Brandenburger and Nalebuff (1996) made a significant contribution to studies on complementors through their research on these firms' role in the context of competitive strategy. In the value chain model, Firm X was thought to be able to enhance its added value only by reducing the influence of other firms. Nalebuff and Brandenburger, however, pointed out that in a business ecosystem, where network effects occur, the firm's profits may increase more when collaborating with other firms than when competing against them.

The existence of complementors was an epoch-making discovery that subverted the classic value chain model. The idea of competing and collaborating at the same time imposed a paradigm change in how researchers analyzed the capability of corporations to gain competitive advantage; also, this notion was categorized as part of dynamic capability studies, which attach importance to network effects and the role of complementors (Teece et al. 1997, 2007). In the meantime, the stream of studies on regional clusters and national innovation systems, which had been based on the classic theory of industrial organization, shifted its focus toward exploring how combinations of complementors develop to promote innovation through collaboration and competition (Porter 2000; Lundvall et al. 2002).

System Users: In the (b) complementor collider model, users (corporations or individuals) make use of the goods provided by Firm X and of the complementary goods supplied by Firm C together. These corporations or individuals are called system users. For example, the situation where Firm X is a provider of personal computer hardware and Firm C is a supplier of software is regarded as a complementor collider case.

Complex products requiring a large number of complementary goods are known as system products, and their presence has been constantly growing in recent years. Like in the case of personal computers cited above, most products comprising hardware and software are system products. Furthermore, solutions based on the Internet of Things (IoT) and systems based on artificial intelligence (or machine learning) are very likely to involve complementary goods. As discussed in greater detail later, these system products are affected by direct and indirect network effects (Katz and Shapiro 1994) and business-ecosystem-type industrial structures are very frequently created.

Platform Firms: In the (c) platform fork pattern, Firm X trades with Firm P, whereas Firm P and Firm C trade with each other; a network effect exists between Firm X and Firm C. In this case, Firm P is called a platform firm.

Because Firm X trades with Firm P, the relationship between the two may seem like an upstream-downstream relationship, but it is not as simple. When trade with Firm C increases, Firm P will benefit from a proportional network effect increase as an increment in trade with Firm X. On the contrary, if trade with Firm X increases, Firm P will benefit from a proportional network effect increase as an increment in trade with Firm C. In other words, the platform firm can benefit most from network effects in this model.

Incidentally, Iansiti and Levien (2004a), who officially advocated the concept of business ecosystems for the first time, called the firm that plays the central role in a business ecosystem a keystone organization. The nature of keystone organizations is essentially the same as that of platform firms discussed here.

An industrial structure of the business ecosystem type comprises a combination of the three trade patterns shown in Fig. 2.1. Hence, in this model of industrial structure, platform firms may be present, but this is not always the case. Figure 2.2i portrays a trading structure combining patterns (a) and (b) in Fig. 2.1, and no platform firm is involved in this structure (Fig. 2.2).

In Fig. 2.2ii, on the contrary, the structure involves patterns (b) and (c) and features the presence of a platform firm. An entity is regarded as a platform firm not only due to its positioning in the transaction networks. Indeed, as described in Sect. 2.2, the entity becomes a platform firm only when it implements a competitive strategy that is unique to platform firms. That being the case, the firm in Fig. 2.2ii should technically be called a potential platform firm.

Moreover, the description in (ii) may suggest that platform firms are component providers only. This is not correct, because a platform firm may sometimes bundle

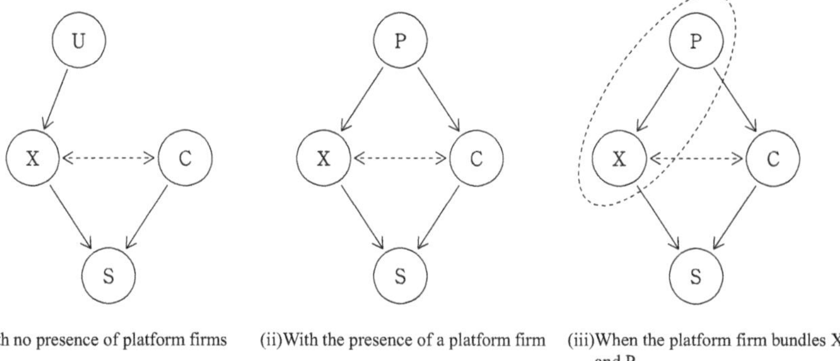

Fig. 2.2 Presence of platform firms

X and P together, which is the instance shown in (iii), and sell products to system users. As discussed in detail later, bundling is one of the major factors providing the foundations for a platform strategy. Apple Inc. is a good example: its iPhone bundles the product, X, being the smartphone, with the management of an app market, P. In this scenario, app providers serve as Firm C. It is possible to identify countless situations in which firms appear to be simple product manufacturers, but they actually turn out to be platform firms when analyzed in greater depth.

2.1.2 From Value Chains to Business Ecosystems

Figure 2.3 illustrates the substantial difference between the business ecosystem model and the classic value chain model. Diagrams (a) and (b) both depict transaction networks with Firm X at the center; specifically, (a) represents the value chain model and (b) the business ecosystem model. The former was introduced by Porter in 1980 and has remained a classic model for studies on competitive strategy. The latter is essentially what was once called the value network (Brandenburger and Nalebuff (1996), but it is more commonly called the business ecosystem model these days.

While (a) and (b) have the same transaction networks, (b) alone carries network effects. For instance, in the field of products that had an industrial structure like (a) in the past, if some standardization takes place and associated network effects emerge, there will be a shift to an industrial structure resembling (b). It must be noted that a business ecosystem like (b) is characterized by the appearance of complementors and a platform firm, which were completely absent in the value chain model.

The two complementors, C_1 and C_2, which first appear in (b), do not have a trade relationship with Firm X. The growth of these two companies, however, determines whether the two system users, S_1 and S_2, to which Firm X provides goods, will grow. Firm X, therefore, cannot ignore the business climate of C_1 and C_2, and, depending on the situation, might even have to support them in some way.

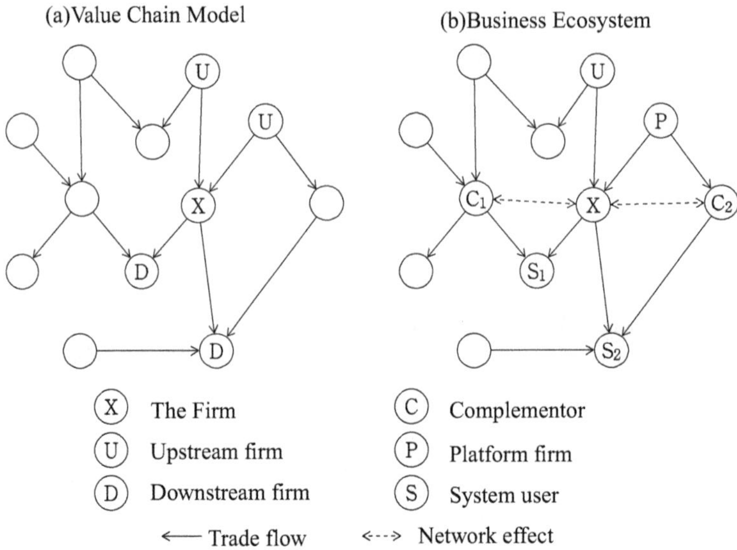

Fig. 2.3 Comparison between the value chain model and the business ecosystem model

Furthermore, Firm P, which first appears in (b), is a source of worry for Firm X. As Firm P grows, it will provide larger quantities of platform products to Firm C_2. This is welcome in itself because it will accelerate Firm C_2's growth. On the other hand, if Firm P becomes disproportionately big and influential, it will start exerting its power over Firm X. If so, Firm X may be deprived of its added value by Firm P.

These changes result from network effects; hence, they become more evident as the number of users rises or, simply, as time passes. In case (b), the competitive advantage of Firm X may be quite large at the beginning; over time, however, it inevitably becomes shakier and shakier. Firms C_1 and C_2, which have network effects on their side, and Firm P, which has network effects on its side and reaps the greatest benefits within the transaction network, will strengthen their competitive advantage. In conclusion, because of the changes in competitiveness resulting from network effects, dynamic competitive strategies are needed in a business ecosystem, and these must be adjusted according to the rise in the number of users.

2.1.3 Direct Network Effects and Indirect Network Effects

Network effects are characterized by the fact that the benefits from a good multiply as the number of users of that good increases. Katz and Shapiro (1985) noted that there are two kinds of network effects: direct effects and indirect effects. Network effects are considered direct when an increased number of users augments the benefits derived from a certain good, whereas they are classed as indirect when an increased number of users expands the quantity and variety of goods complementary to a certain good and, in turn, augments the benefits derived from that good.

Katz and Shapiro illustrated the two types of network effects by taking a system product composed of hardware and software as an example. This book takes smartphones as its example. In detail, with more people adopting the same communication protocol, smartphone users can make calls at a lower cost and exchange data with more people. This is a direct effect. Apps that run on smartphones, on the other hand, are independent products. Nonetheless, they share network effects with smartphones, since the number of compatible apps sold will increase as the number of smartphones sold increases; likewise, the number of smartphones will increase as the number of app products increases. This is an indirect effect. Smartphone units and applications are two different goods to the users' eyes, yet their two markets share the same indirect network effect.

Cases (b) and (c), shown in Fig. 2.1, are triangular trade patterns involving indirect network effects. Since Firm X and Firm C do not trade directly, the pattern is not *triangular* by definition; however, it is generally regarded as *triangular* because the two Firms are affected by the same network. This pattern is markedly different from the traditional industrial structure of the value chain type, since it involves an obvious complementary goods supplier, i.e., a complementor.

Also in trade pattern (a) of Fig. 2.1, the upstream firm, that is the component provider, benefits from direct effects. In the example of smartphone units above, as the consumption of smartphone units using a certain protocol expands, so does the demand for smartphone components. The upstream firm is not a complementor, but it benefits from (direct) network effects. The competitive strategy of platform firms, which will be discussed later, is intended to make effective use of various network effects such as the one described.

2.1.4 Platform Firm and Symbiont Firms

As explained in Sect. 2.1.3, when a platform firm adopts a strategy based on open standardization, direct and indirect network effects will be generated, so that upstream firms (component manufacturers) and complementors will reap benefits. For the purposes of this book, these entities are called *symbiont firms*. Symbiont firms operate at the periphery of the platform firm, yet their roles are not necessarily peripheral.

The concept of business ecosystems originated from the concept of ecosystems in ecology.[1] A natural ecosystem comprises predation, a direct relationship, and

[1] Iansiti and Levien (2004a), who formulated the notion of business ecosystem, borrowed the concept of ecosystems from the science of ecology, as an analogy to industrial structures. They also referred to the special species known as keystone species. The discovery of keystone species dates back to Paine (1966). He partitioned an inshore area into smaller areas and observed what would happen to the other species if a certain species living in each of the areas were removed. His findings confirmed the presence of critically important species, for which he coined the term keystone species.

symbiosis, an indirect relationship; in addition, it is a complex system. An ecosystem in which such codependent relations exist involves very special species, unique in that, though small in terms of population, the complete removal of any of them would result in the extinction of other species in the community. According to Paine (1966), who first introduced the concept, these are called *keystone species*.

Iansiti and Levien (2004b) pointed out that a business ecosystem likewise involves an entity acting as keystone species. They called such entities keystone firms and argued that the source of their competitive advantage lies not only inside the firms themselves but also in their external relations with symbiont firms operating at the periphery. Lastly, they observed that these keystone firms establish relations with symbiont firms, thereby promoting the sound growth and expansion of the industry as a whole. They referred to the examples of Microsoft Corporation providing development tools, so that software developers can design Windows-compliant applications using them, and of Walmart's procurement system, in which suppliers have access to real-time information on Walmart customers' demand. Keystone firms create a platform, hence building up relationships with symbiont firms, in order to establish their competitive edge. In the context of this book, therefore, keystone firms, as identified by Iansiti and Levien (2004b), are termed platform firms.

Platform firms and symbiont firms have a common destiny, in the sense that they share the same business ecosystem and grow together. The growth of the business ecosystem cannot be achieved by the platform firm alone but requires active innovation activities by symbiont firms.

Gawer and Henderson (2007) offered a similar perspective. A platform firm often enters the business arena of symbiont firms and takes their profits away. This behavior deprives the symbiont firms of motivation for active innovation activities in the business ecosystem. Through in-depth interviews (for a total of 72 h) with Intel Corporation, one of the most representative platform firms, Gawer and Henderson collected data concerning 27 projects in which the platform leader planned to enter peripheral markets, out of which it actually carried out 17. These results suggest that Intel carefully decided whether or not to enter the complementary markets because it did not want its symbiont firms to be discouraged from participating. Intel only entered those complementary markets that had implications for control of the platform architecture, so as to minimize the risk of ex-post squeezing of symbiont firms.

Gawer and Henderson also found that Intel Corporation had an effective policy to share its intellectual property, or IP, when it welcomed symbiont firms into the market. Sharing IP worked as a sign that it would refrain from engaging in ex-post squeezing. Decisions about sharing IP were made by Intel Architecture Labs (IAL), an organization independent of business units. Based on this evidence, they reported that the platform firm promoted new entry into complementary goods markets as an enterprise-wide initiative in order to boost the healthy growth of the ecosystem.

The fight between Microsoft Corporation and Netscape tells us exactly the same story from the opposite point of view (Cusumano and Yoffie 1998). Microsoft won the game against Netscape by making use of the relationship between the operation software (OS) market and the web browser market and by implementing strategic bundling. Consequently, Microsoft's Internet Explorer occupied over 70% of the browser market. In terms of innovation, however, this exclusion behavior deprived complementary goods suppliers of motivation, and the platform firm failed to take advantage of the over 70% share that it had fought to win. Despite maintaining high profits, Microsoft has actually stepped away from the center of innovation since 2000 and has ended up allowing Apple Inc. to resurge.

All of these studies and examples indicate that platform firms and symbiont firms share the same destiny and that the healthy growth of a business ecosystem cannot be attained by a platform firm alone. Platform firms are expected to strategically manage their relationships with symbiont firms in order to facilitate the sound development of the business ecosystem.

Platform firms are now a hot topic, actively studied by many researchers, due to their role in driving the evolution of business ecosystems. The next section analyzes the competitive strategy of platform firms, which are central to industrial evolution and to the development, with other players, of business ecosystems.

2.2 Competitive Strategy of Platform Firms

In a business ecosystem, a wide variety of firms and entities play active parts and, among these, the platform firm has the central function. In the personal computer industry, for instance, Microsoft and Intel, which provide core components, lead industrial evolution as platform firms. In the world of Internet communication systems, Cisco played a critical role, while Ericsson, Nokia, Qualcomm and a few others supported the second generation mobile phones as platform providers. When open standards are established, the platform firms obtain competitive advantages in these ecosystems, which rapidly grow to a global scale. Given these circumstances, the number of studies on platform firms suddenly increased in the 2000s.

Figure 2.4 shows the main trends in studies on the competitive strategy of platform firms. Two chief streams can be identified: studies in the context of management of technology and studies in the context of business economics. Recently, there have also been contributions from the standardization and intellectual property strategy sphere and the innovation sphere. These lines of inquiry combine to form a large mainstream of platform strategy studies in the interdisciplinary arena.

2.2.1 *Definition of Platform Firms and Their Competitive Strategies*

Platform firms are defined as firms that conduct platform business and the strategy of building competitiveness through platform business is called platform strategy. Yet, this definition is somehow tautological and fails to clarify what platform business actually is and the key factors for platform strategy.

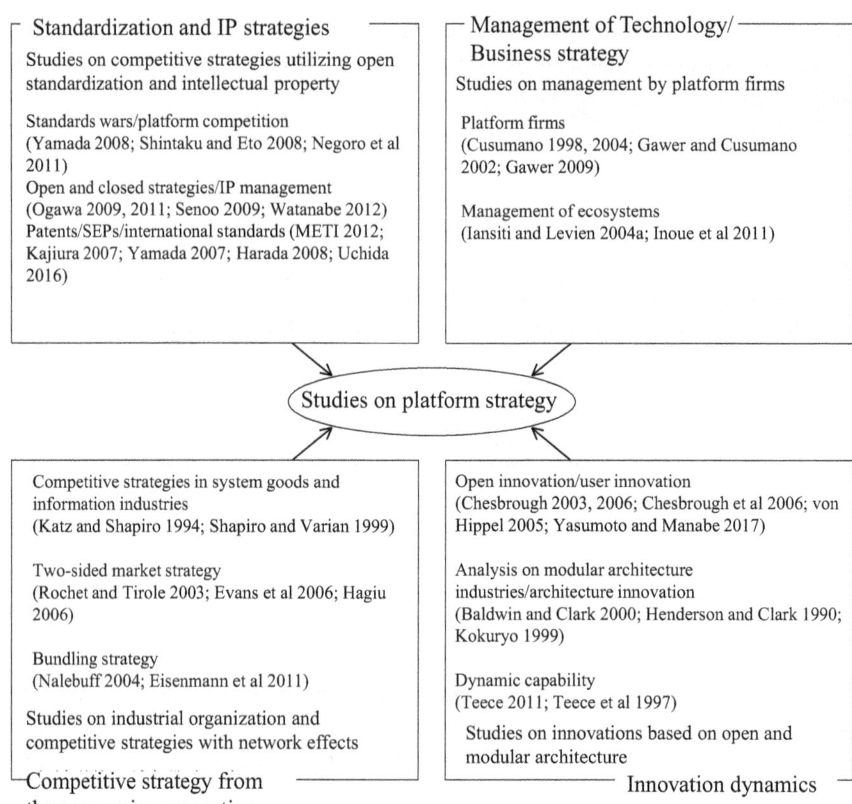

Fig. 2.4 Trends in studies on platform strategy

Previous studies have given different definitions of platform business. Some research has focused on the nature of the products that firms provide. Other works have explored the nature of their business models or the distinctive features of their market positioning. Hence, there is little consensus around the definition of platform business, and a review of prior studies may prove useful to develop a theoretical framework for the following sections.

Platform firms are actively studied from the management and economics perspectives. These works are of two kinds: (i) applied business strategy studies based on the management of technology, focusing on the organizational response of platform firms to business ecosystems (Gawer and Cusumano 2002; Cusumano 2004; Gawer 2009; Baldwin 2011) and (ii) applied business economics studies based on the theory of industrial organization, including positioning in transaction networks, pricing strategy and bundling (Rochet and Tirole 2003; Nalebuff 2004; Hagiu 2006; Eisenmann et al. 2006, 2011). The first group of studies regards a platform as the foundation that connects other layers and components in an industry or system product comprised of multiple layers or complementary components. In the other group of studies, a platform is defined as the foundation that deals with multiple user groups and is used for matching and interacting among different groups.

What is common between the two approaches is that the term *platform* is used to mean the foundation for constructing a network by connecting different elements or groups. In other words, platform business can be described as business that puts in place infrastructures and rules for promoting interactions among multiple different user groups by providing products (Maruyama 2011, p. 235). It is worth noting that the platform is described as the method of providing products and not as the product itself. That is, the categorization of a firm as a *platform firm* is based not on the product provided by the firm but on the method of providing the product, regardless of whether or not the firm intentionally implements a platform strategy.

For example, a *mobile phone firm* means a firm that develops and provides mobile phones. In this case, the firm is defined according to the type of product that it provides. On the other hand, Apple Inc., which provides the mobile phone called iPhone, is not a simple mobile phone firm. It does provide the iPhone but, at the same time, it manages the iTunes Store, which provides the infrastructure and rules for connecting content providers and users; hence, Apple Inc. is a platform firm. The higher the number of iPhones sold, the more content providers there are. The more content providers there are, the higher the growth of iPhone users. In sum, what matters to platform firms is not the product itself but the profit gained through brokering and facilitating exchanges among different groups using the product as a basis.

In their study on two-sided markets, Rochet and Tirole keenly pointed out that the essence of platform business resides in the brokering among different groups (Rochet and Tirole 2003, 2004). They explicitly defined platform firms as "corporations that deal with both of the two markets that share network effects." Such a definition gave great momentum to theoretical research on the strategies of platform firms (Evans et al. 2006; Hagiu 2006; Parker and Van Alstyne 2005; Hagiu and Yoffie 2009), which revealed that platform firms are characterized by unique pricing strategies.

Applied studies based on the management of technology also underlined that the essence of platform strategy is to promote the growth of the industry as a whole, with consideration given to balance among several markets. Gawer and Cusumano (2002) explored the behavior of platform firms using case studies in their pioneering work. They carried out interviews with providers of foundational products in the process of forming business ecosystems, including Intel and Cisco, regarding what kinds of corporate strategies were being implemented. Their investigation showed that platform firms (i) have a proactive attitude toward industrial standardization, (ii) help complementary goods suppliers grow, (iii) always think about their own position in the business ecosystem and iv) adopt a strategic and organizational approach to strategies (i)–(iii).

Similar findings also come from Iansiti and Levien (2004a). They introduced the notion of keystone strategy as the pursuit of monetization, achieved by promoting connections among complementary goods markets in a business ecosystem, which consists of several complementary goods markets, and by facilitating the growth of all of these markets. Platform firms can attain sustainable competitiveness by implementing such a keystone strategy. In other words, the essence of strategy in platform business is to leverage relations with multiple markets.

As seen above, platform business refers to the management and strategic use of relations with complementary goods markets. The following subsections present the theoretical perspectives used in this book to shed light on how the competitive advantage of platform firms is developed.

2.2.2 *Positioning at the Hub*

The first step to understand the competitive strategies of platform firms is to examine the concept of transaction structure (network) as a presumption. The essence of platform business, as described in Sect. 2.2.1, is to broker among different groups. This brokering function is studied in depth in social network investigations, which model transaction networks with a hub, as shown in Fig. 2.5.

The argument that brokering among different networks can be a source of competitive advantage for firms is extensively discussed in recent studies on complex networks, as well as in social network analyses. Brokering is called *bridging* in these academic works, as the firms in question act as bridges among different users.

Classic studies on bridging include "The Strength of Weak Ties" by Granovetter (1973), Freeman's work on betweenness centrality (Freeman 1977), Cook and Emerson's research on bargaining power in exchange networks (Cook and Emerson 1978), and "Structural Holes" by Burt (1992). All of them stated that taking position at a place regarded as a *bridge* in transaction networks gives firms competitive advantage.

A *hub*, or *bridge*, is a junction between two networks, as shown in Fig. 2.5. A hub emerges when networks have structural holes, i.e., areas where no connections exist (Burt 1992; Newman 2010, p. 202). In the case of Fig. 2.5, there are two structural

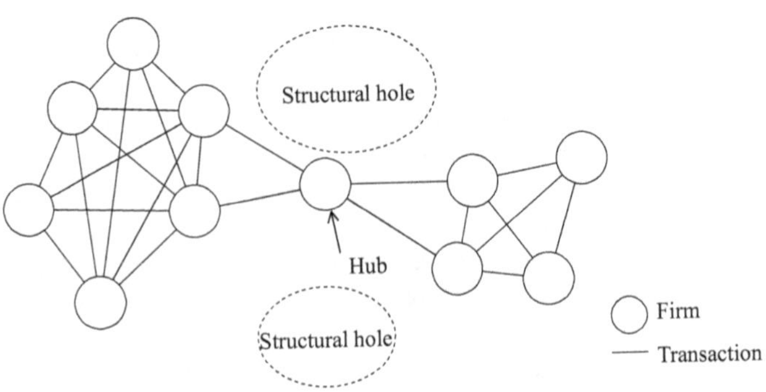

Fig. 2.5 Networks with a hub

holes, creating a junction through which information has to pass in order to flow all over the networks. This junction is called a hub.

A hub is a node with high information betweenness,[2] and any transaction resulting from this betweenness is called brokering. Platform firms, which broker between different networks, are equivalent to firms that are positioned at the hub between transaction networks.

According to Burt (1997), the reason why positioning at the hub serves as the source of a firm's competitive advantage is twofold, from the standpoint of information flow: information benefit and control benefit.

Information benefit gives the firm an advantage because it is able to detect a flow of information between two networks very early on, being on the shortest path between the two networks, and to take various measures accordingly. Assume that a firm in Network A is going to lower its prices. The firm situated at the hub can access this information ahead of any firm in Network B and devise counteractions.

Control benefit, meanwhile, gives the firm at the hub another crucial advantage. It enables it to either add information advantageous to itself to a piece of information flowing from one network to the other or block any information disadvantageous to itself, thereby spreading the collective recognition of the firm's positive image across the network. When a business ecosystem is developing an industrywide standard, all the participants need to share information to set the direction of the industry's evolution. If a firm is positioned at the hub, it can spread information advantageous to its purposes and promote the collective sharing of its positive image, which will reinforce its competitive advantage.

To summarize what has been discussed thus far, the competitiveness building mechanism of platform firms can be described as follows: a platform firm is a firm that positions itself at the hub between two networks to act as a broker between them. This positioning at the hub gives the firm information benefit and control benefit, or competitive advantage based on information flows. It can thus be concluded that taking position at a place with high betweenness in networks strengthens a firm's market performance.

2.2.3 Strategic Standardization

The explanation of competitive advantage as resulting from bridging is derived from the classical theory of social networks. On the other hand, studies on the competitive advantage of platform firms, carried out after 2000, highlight that these firms do not simply mediate between two networks but do so more strategically, by making full use of network effects.

---

[2]In the field of social network analysis, betweenness centrality is an indicator that represents the information betweenness function of a node; nodes are the vertices that form a network. A hub can be described as one of the nodes with the highest information betweenness.

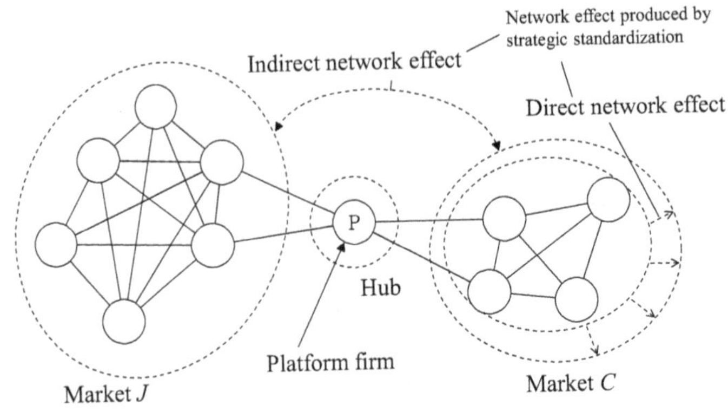

Fig. 2.6 Network effects resulting from strategic standardization

In a business ecosystem consisting of a large number of complementors, network effects produced by open standards are generated very often. Platform firms are the entities that make the most of such effects. This book models the two-sided market strategy and the bundling strategy as their typical competitive strategies. The former uses the firm's function as a broker between two markets, and the latter relies on the influence exerted by the firm on the neighboring market. Both strategies make use of network effects, as far as network effects exist between two markets, allowing the platform firm to enhance its competitive advantage. Incidentally, as the network effects discussed here are between two goods, these are technically indirect network effects and are sometimes called *cross-side network effects*. They are, however, referred to simply as *network effects* in the remainder of this book.

It may happen that network effects are produced in the natural course of events; yet, strategically speaking, it is more desirable to artificially produce network effects between two specific goods according to a firm's strategic intention. To do so, open standard setting is a widely adopted tool. When an open standard is set between two goods, *artificial* network effects are generated between them.[3]

Figure 2.6 illustrates how strategic standardization produces network effects. The diagram shows that both direct and indirect network effects are generated as a result of strategic standardization. Whether direct or indirect, network effects carry strategic value. Yet, from the standpoint of platform strategy, network effects that go beyond two goods markets, i.e., indirect network effects, are more important. Let us verify this notion by taking the DVD industry as an example.

[3]The fact that open standardization is a way to artificially produce network effects is extremely important from a strategic point of view. Traditional studies on platform strategy contained a chicken-and-egg argument regarding the generation of network effects and the effectiveness of the platform strategy. On the contrary, the three patterns of open standardization outlined in Chap. 1 allow network effects to be generated strategically in any target area of transaction networks. In this way, the chicken-and-egg argument can be avoided. Open standardization drastically improves the effectiveness of the platform strategy.

DVD players and DVD content have network effects between them since they are both defined by the DVD standard. A platform firm may strategically determine the scope of compatibility in standardization activities, thereby strategically deciding between which goods network effects should be shared.

This decision is strategic because the firm can determine whether machines able to play DVD content should be confined to DVD players or include DVD drives on laptops and, perhaps, anything that can read the DVD format, like playback software. This exemplifies the generation of network effects based on strategic standardization.

Assuming that the platform firm can generate network effects in an area convenient to itself, the result is an increase in the effectiveness of the two-sided market and bundling strategies, which make use of the relationship between the two markets. The platform firm employs this mechanism as a strategy. Sections 2.2.4, 2.2.5, 2.2.6, and 2.2.7 describe the two strategies in greater detail.

2.2.4 Two-Sided Market Strategy

The theory of two-sided markets sheds light on the platform firms' competitive strategy based on network effects. While ordinary firms can make strategic use only of direct network effects, the platform firm, being in the position of dealing with both markets, can make strategic use of both direct and indirect network effects, thus placing itself in an advantageous position compared with the other firms, from the perspective of competitive strategy.

Assume that a standard for compatibility is established as a communication protocol for mobile phones. If the number of users using the same protocol increases, each of them will have access to more people on the other end of the line, consequently enjoying more benefits. Hence, the establishment of a compatibility standard effectively pushes up the market demand for mobile phones compliant with that protocol. This benefit of direct network effects allows mobile phone firms to boost demand.

Next, let us look at a case in which a compatibility standard is established more extensively. Assume that a compatibility standard is established as a data format to be used in mobile phone applications. In this case, two markets, the mobile phone market and the application market, need to be taken into consideration.

Similarly to the communication protocol case mentioned above, the app market may well see increased demand, since it benefits from direct network effects. A larger number of users adopting the same application causes a growth in demand; this is the direct network effect.

Demand in the application market will grow even further as the prevalence of mobile phones using the same data format expands. Seeing as mobile phones are hardware, while applications are software, then the wider coverage of hardware leads to a growth in demand for software. This growth in demand is the indirect network effect, thanks to which the expansion of the mobile phone market leads to the expansion of the app market.

In this case, the app firms cannot make strategic use of the indirect network effect, because they operate only in the application market. The platform firm, on the other hand, can make *strategic* use of this indirect network effect because it deals with both the mobile phone market and the application market. This is the two-sided market strategy.

Think of a business ecosystem composed of Market *J* and Market *C*, as shown in Fig. 2.7. In this business ecosystem, both direct and indirect network effects are generated. The direct network effect is derived from the fact that an increased number of users in Market *C* further increases the number of users in Market *C*. If the number of users in Market *J* increases and, in turn, the number of users in Market *C* also increases, this is the indirect network effect (Katz and Shapiro 1994).

Assume that a product is offered at the price of P_i^{old} in the quantity of Q_j^{old} on Market *J*, as shown in Fig. 2.8. Assume, likewise, that a product is offered at the price of P_c^{old} in the quantity of Q_c^{old} on Market *C*. The solid line represents the

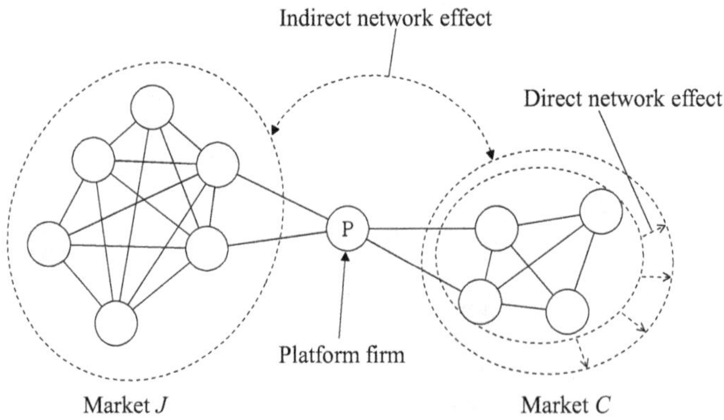

Fig. 2.7 Two-sided markets

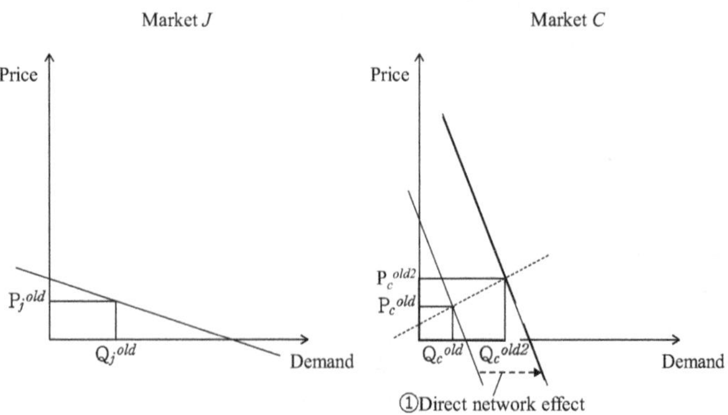

Fig. 2.8 Creation of demand in two-sided markets (direct effect)

demand curve and the dashed line the supply curve. Now, if a compatibility standard is developed in Market *C*, the market experiences an upward push in demand, as shown by the dashed arrow (①) in Fig. 2.8. This effect is a direct network effect. Demand grows from Q_c^{old} to Q_c^{old2}. As the graph illustrates, $P_c^{old} \times Q_c^{old2}$ is greater than $P_c^{old} \times Q_c^{old}$. This demand growth is the result of the direct network effect.

Next, let us look at strategic pricing when the indirect effect comes into play, on top of the direct effect. Figure 2.9 shows price changes in Markets *J* and *C*. Applying the earlier example, let us assume that Markets *J* and *C* are the mobile phone market and the application market, respectively. In the application market (*C*), the common interface established brings about enhanced data compatibility, hence boosting user convenience. Demand in Market *C* is pushed upward accordingly, as shown by the dashed arrow (①) in Fig. 2.9. This is a direct network effect. Demand grows from Q_c^{old} to Q_c^{old2}. This demand growth achieved by the network effect is derived from the establishment of the compatibility standard.

The impact of the standard setting is not limited to the direct effects observed in the application market. As the number of users adopting mobile phones compatible with the data format goes up, the number of users using standard-compatible applications should also increase. This demand creation effect is applicable across the two markets (*J* and *C*); thus, it is an indirect network effect. The dashed arrow (②) in Fig. 2.9 indicates the upward push in demand achieved as an indirect effect.

The indirect effect here depends on the size of the user base in Market *J*; that is to say, by lowering the price of the product on Market *J*, the user base of the mobile phone expands, augmenting the indirect network effect. In more practical terms, the firm can amplify the indirect effect on Market *C* by providing the Market *J* product at lower prices to increase the number of users of that mobile phone.

The application firm mentioned earlier can only make use of the direct network effect, because it only operates in the application market. On the contrary, the platform firm, which operates in the two markets, may take advantage of not only the direct effect but also the indirect effect. More specifically, if the firm sells the mobile phone units at discount prices on Market *J*, this will accelerate the expansion of Market *C*,

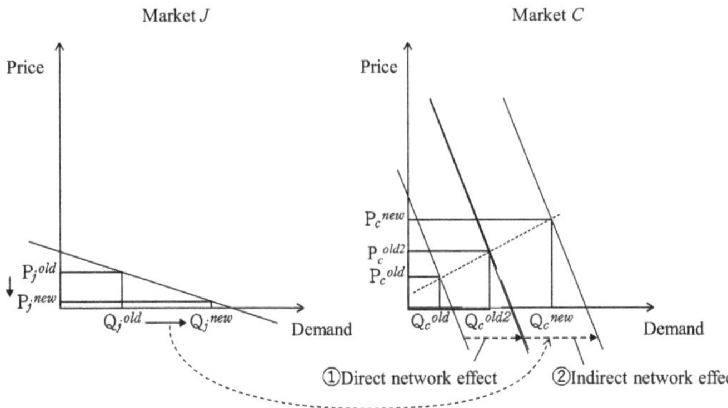

Fig. 2.9 Demand creation due to two-sided markets (direct effects combined with indirect effects)

where it sells applications at premium prices; in sum, the firm will have an overall increased revenue from the two markets combined.

The platform firm can make the most of network effects by setting strategic prices based on the uniqueness of two-sided markets.[4]

2.2.4.1 Demand Creation Effects of Two-Sided Market Strategy

Theoretical studies on two-sided markets emphasize that, when a platform firm adopts a pricing strategy of discount prices in one market and premium prices in the other, the effect produced will go beyond simple grabbing of the surplus (value added), actually accomplishing dynamic demand creation (Rochet and Tirole 2004).

With the direct network effect alone, the demand creation effect accomplished on Market C would be capped at the demand increase from Q_C^{old} to Q_C^{old2}. Total demand

---

[4]The pricing conditions that maximize the sum of the profits from the two markets can be calculated as follows, based on Maruyama (2011):

When U_j and U_c are the per-capita user benefits in Markets J and C, respectively:

$$U_j = \theta_j n_c - p_j$$
$$U_c = \theta_c n_j - p_c$$

where n_j and n_c are the numbers of users in Markets J and C, respectively, θ_j and θ_c represent the per-capita indirect network effect from the other market and p_j and p_c are the prices (platform usage fees) that the platform firm imposes on Markets J and C, respectively.

U_j becomes larger when the indirect network effect, $\theta_j n_c$ becomes larg. er, and it becomes smaller when the platform price, p_j, becomes higher. It must be noted that the indirect network effect, $\theta_j n_c$ becomes larg. er as the number of users in the other market (Market C, in this case) grows. The revenue that the platform firm gains, Π would be described as follows:

$$\Pi = n_j(p_j - c_j) + n_c(p_c - c_c)$$

where c_j and c_c are the costs per user.

Therefore, n_1, n_2, p_j and p_c can be expressed as a function of U_j and U_c:

$$n_j = f(U_j), \quad p_j = \theta_j n_c - U_j$$
$$n_c = g(U_c), \quad \theta_c n_j - U_c$$

When substituting p_j an. d p_c in the equation for Π.

$$\Pi = n_j(\theta_j n_c - U_j - c_j) + n_c(\theta_c n_j - U_c - C_c)$$

The first-order condition for maximum revenues is derived as:

$$\frac{\delta\Pi}{\delta U_j} = (p_j - c_c)f'(U_j) - n_j + \theta_c n_c f'(U_j) = 0$$

in Markets J and C combined would then be the sum of $P_j^{old} \times Q_j^{old}$ in Market J and $P_c^{old2} \times Q_c^{old2}$ in Market C.

On the other hand, when the platform firm implements strategic pricing, though the price falls from P_j^{old} to P_j^{new} , the number of users in Market J goes up and the increased number of users in Market J gives rise to an increase in the number of users in Market C. The total demand in Markets J and C combined will then be the sum of $P_j^{new} \times Q_j^{new}$ on Market J and $P_c^{new} \times Q_c^{new}$ on Market C.

Equation (1), given below, summarizes the above discussion.

$$P_j^{old} \times Q_j^{old} + P_c^{old2} \times Q_c^{old2} < P_j^{new} \times Q_j^{new} + P_c^{new} \times Q_c^{new} \quad (2.1)$$

The left side of Eq. (2.1) is the total demand resulting from the direct network effect alone, whereas the right side is the total demand resulting from both the direct and indirect network effects. As indicated in Eq. (2.1), Fig. 2.9 shows that the right side is greater than the left side. More specifically, the combination of the direct and

---

$$\frac{\delta \Pi}{\delta U_c} = (p_j - c_j) f'(U_c) - n_c + \theta_j n_j f'(U_c) = 0,$$

and the solutions to p_j and p_c are obtained as:

$$p_j = c_j - \theta_c n_c + \frac{f(U_j)}{f'(U_j)} \quad (a1)$$

$$p_c = c_c - \theta_j n_j + \frac{f(U_c)}{f'(U_c)} \quad (a2)$$

Based on Eqs. (a1) and (a2), the basic rules for. pricing that maximizes total revenues from the two markets are summarized as follows:

(i) Offer users discount prices in the market under larger indirect network effects. For example, the price offered to users in Market J, P_j, may be described as Eq. (b):

$$\begin{aligned} P_j &= C_j + \theta_c n_c + \frac{f(U_j)}{f'(U_j)} \\ &= C_j + \theta_c n_j \frac{n_c}{n_j} + \frac{f(U_j)}{f'(U_j)} \end{aligned} \quad (b)$$

The second term of this equation, $\theta_c n_j$, is the indirect network effect per user of Market J on Market C, while $\theta_c n_j n_c$ represents the total indirect network effect of Market J on Market C. When $\theta_c n_j n_c$ is divided by n_j, the resulting $\theta_c n_c$ represents the indirect network effect on each user in Market J. In Eq. (b), the price for Market J, P_j, is lowered by $\theta_c n_c$. This means that the users of a market that has a larger indirect network effect will enjoy discount prices.

(ii) Set low prices in a market that has a user expansion effect.

The third term of Eq. (b) is

$$\frac{f(U_j)}{f'(U_j)} = \frac{n_j}{\Delta n_j}$$

indirect network effects is greater than the direct effect alone. This is the demand expansion effect of a firm's platform strategy.

For Eq. (2.1) to hold true, the following two conditions must be met: (i) price elasticity is higher in Market J than in Market C—the effect of lowering prices on an expanded user base is higher—and (ii) a greater number of users in Market J increases the probability that the number of users in Market C will rise—the indirect network effect is strong.

2.2.4.2 Strategic Significance of Indirect Network Effects

The strategic use of indirect network effects—and not direct effects—carries a crucial meaning from the strategic point of view. With the direct network effect, the firm deals only with one market or user group. With the indirect effect, on the other hand, the firm deals with two markets or two different user groups.

A classic example of the use of direct network effects is the shaving razor, which consists of a holder and replacement blades. These two components share a network effect, because the demand for replacement blades compatible with a certain holder grows as the number of users who have that holder increases. The shaving razor provider, therefore, devises sales plans based on providing the holder at a low (penetration) price, in order to promote it and expand its user base.

The issue encountered by the firm is that the purchasers of the holder and replacement blades are actually the same person. Any rational user would easily understand that, if they bought the inexpensive holder, they would then have to keep buying expensive replacement blades. As a consequence, they might well hesitate to purchase the holder. In actuality, a large number of firms producing shaving razors struggle greatly until the number of users of their holder exceeds a certain level, called critical mass.

Conversely, a typical platform firm deals with two different markets or user groups, as shown in Fig. 2.10. Markets A and B share a network effect, meaning that if the user base of Market A expands, the user base of Market B will follow suit. In many such cases, the price elasticity or the potential market size of Market A is greater than that of Market B. When dealing with such two markets, the platform firm may make money by offering its product at a discount price on Market A, to expand the user base of Market A, while selling its other product at a premium price, commensurate with the user base of Market A, on Market B.

What is important here is that the users of Market A, where discount prices are offered, will not have to compensate for such discount for good, since it is the users of Market B who are paying for it. Thus, users in Market A can buy the product at a discount without hesitation. Market A, where discount prices are offered, is called a subsidy market, because it is subsidized for the purposes of promotion, and Market

---

or the inverse of the delta in the number of users in Market J (expansion rate); so the price, Pj, becomes smaller when the user expansion rate is large, and vice versa.

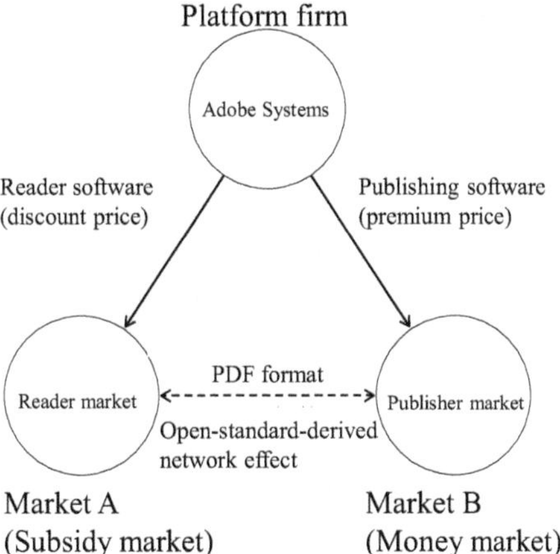

Fig. 2.10 Two-sided markets and platform firm

B, where premium prices are applied, is called a money market, as it is the market for monetization (Eisenmann et al. 2006).

The business case of Adobe Systems Inc. is a good example. The company is very well known for its software for digital document files. Adobe distributes its reader application, which opens digital document files, free of charge in order to expand its user base; meanwhile, it offers publishers the digital document publishing software at high prices. Because reader software users are sensitive to prices, the user base will not expand unless the software is provided free of charge. Publishers, on the other hand, will willingly pay high prices for the digital document publishing software, in accordance with the size of its user base, since their mission is to sell documents. The reason why the platform firm can simultaneously create demand by offering discount prices on one hand and holding out on the other with premium prices is that it takes advantage of the network effects generated between the two markets and of its role as broker mediating between them.

In this example, Adobe deals with both the reader market and the publisher market. Even though the reader application is provided free of charge in the reader market, its users will never have to pay any sort of compensation for this. They will, therefore, use the application without hesitation, which leads to an expansion of the user base. The cost of the reader application is borne by the publishing market, in which the digital document publishing software is provided at high prices. Such premium prices, however, are legitimate in view of the number of readers (reader application users); hence, the publishers purchase the publishing software, though at premium prices. The indirect network effect is attractive because it ripples across different user groups, allowing a firm to quickly expand its market.

The source of the indirect network effect on which two-sided markets rely is the development of a far-reaching open standard. Especially when a standard extending beyond the boundaries of the existing industry is created, indirect network effects are generated among multiple markets. By leveraging these indirect effects, platform firms mediate between markets, thereby achieving demand creation and monetization at the same time.

The prevalence of an open standard means that the interface information is widely shared, so that a variety of complementary goods is developed and supplied. The more the open standard prevails, the stronger the network effect among the system good components becomes. A stronger network effect provides a platform firm with a perfect opportunity to build up its competitive advantage, because the firm may implement a competitive strategy based on the network effect generated between two goods, as discussed earlier.

2.2.5 Bundling Strategy

A number of mechanisms exist for building competitive advantage based on the fact that a business ecosystem comprises many complementary goods. Section 2.2.4 explained the two-sided market strategy, which makes use of the network effect generated between complementary goods markets. Here, we explore what the bundling strategy is. Bundling is the act of combining a product with complementary goods as a package, so that the firm can keep the network effect to itself and expand its competitiveness.

In other words, bundling is a package deal in which the firm either adds complementary goods to its product and sells them as a set or couples complementary goods with its product and sells them as one product. In the sphere of architecture studies, a similar phenomenon is called integralization, as it integrates two functions. Other terms with nearly the same meaning may be used, such as demodularization, systematization, and turn-keying.

Previous studies have pointed out that platform firms frequently enter complementary goods markets by means of bundling and earn competitive advantage (Gawer and Henderson 2007; Nalebuff 2004). This entry into complementary goods markets with the help of bundling is regarded as a new method of market entry, different from the Schumpeterian approach, which is the market entry with new, innovative products. The bundling that platform firms execute, in particular, is actively studied under the name of *platform envelopment* (Eisenmann et al. 2011).

A typical example of product bundling implemented by a platform firm is MS-Office, Microsoft's package product coupling together Word and Excel. The firm added PowerPoint to the package when it advanced into the presentation software market. Also, Apple Inc. entered the music content distribution market by providing the iTunes software onboard its music player product, the iPod, and made further progress by setting up the iTunes Store, an online store of music content. In the mobile phone sector, Google and other platform firms are trying to enhance their competitiveness by bundling (integrating) the marketing function, through which applications are assembled and presented on the smartphone, and the billing function, through which the firm collects payment for the application(s) from the users.

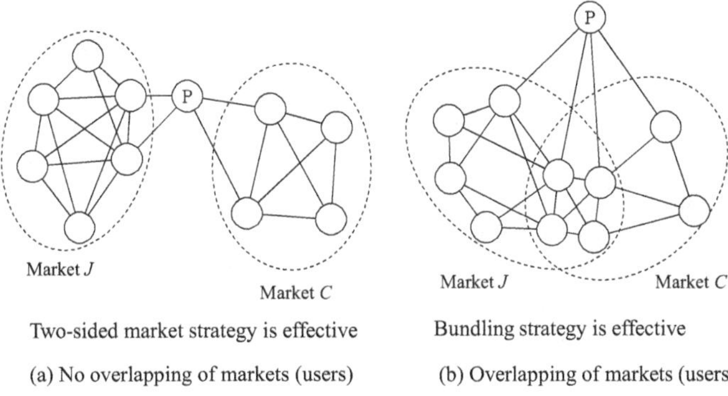

Fig. 2.11 Overlapping of users

This bundling strategy and the two-sided market strategy previously discussed constitute the two major strategies that platform firms pursue in order to construct competitive advantage. Which is more effective? It depends on the relationship between the two markets. Figure 2.11 depicts the relationship between two markets according to the two strategies.

In Fig. 2.11a, the users of Good *J* and Complementary Good *C* do not overlap. In this case, the two-sided market strategy is more effective, since it utilizes the network effect (indirect effect) between the two markets. Conversely, if the users of Good *J* and Complementary Good *C* do overlap, meaning that many users of Good *J* also use Complementary Good *C*, as shown in Fig. 2.11b, the bundling strategy, which sells Good *J* and Complementary Good *C* as a package or integrates the two into one product, is more effective. The bundling strategy is effective as long as there is a network effect between two goods. A business ecosystem, which is composed of multiple complementary goods, provides abundant opportunity for bundling.

Platform firms pursue the two strategies in parallel, by taking one approach under certain circumstances and the other under different conditions. Let us now investigate how platform firms develop competitiveness using bundling.

2.2.5.1 Types of Bundling

There are two types of bundling: pure bundling and mixed bundling. Both provide a way of selling products as a package when there are multiple complementary goods. The difference lies in whether the products are sold exclusively as a package (pure bundling) or are available both as a package and as individual products (mixed bundling). Discount prices are usually offered for product packages.

If a mobile phone firm always sells its unit bundled with the mobile services, this is pure bundling. In this case, a consumer cannot buy the mobile phone unit and sign up for another mobile service separately. The unit and the mobile service always come together. In this sense, the pure bundling approach is a powerful competitive strategic means of taking shares away from competitors.

On the contrary, mixed bundling allows consumers to choose, for instance, whether to buy a hamburger and a drink as a combo or any unbundled menu item when they are at a fast-food restaurant. They can decide to purchase a hamburger from McDonald's and a drink from anywhere else that they like.

From the perspective of a firm's lock-in strategy, mixed bundling, which allows for both package sales and unbundled sales, has a limited effect compared with pure bundling. It provides, however, price discrimination to several consumer groups with different preferences by setting differentiated prices for unbundled products and package deals, as described later. The price discrimination method is used to maximize the amount of total sales. Considering the example of McDonald's, its restaurants sell a menu item at a cheaper price when purchased as part of a combo and at a relatively higher price when unbundled. Unbundled sales are excluded from discount pricing. This is a typical approach to utilizing the mixed bundling concept.

Whether pure or mixed, bundling produces a price discrimination effect and/or a lock-in effect. These effects are studied according to the motivation behind bundling from the economic and strategic points of view.

2.2.5.2 Motivations Behind Bundling: Economic Context and Strategic Context

There are two kinds of motivations for implementing bundling, those linked to the economic context and those having to do with the strategic context. In the economic context, bundling maximizes total revenues. In the strategic context, it gives a firm control over market entries (entry into new markets and/or lock-in of existing markets). The economic context involves the relations between the firm and the users/consumers, whereas the strategic context involves the relations between the firm and its competitors.

Traditional studies on bundling mainly explored the economic context. Price discrimination is a typical economic motivation for bundling. More recent studies, on the other hand, have focused on the strategic context, where bundling is used to gain competitive advantage over one's competitors. For example, bundling helps firms build barriers to the entry of competitors into their market (Nalebuff 2003, 2004).

Bundling in the economic context, economic bundling, typically takes on the mixed form, whereas bundling in the strategic context, strategic bundling, typically takes on the pure form. That said, the two are not rigorously differentiated, since the firms that implement bundling essentially have both economic and strategic motivations and both the mixed and the pure method have similar inherent effects. In actuality, mixed bundling easily becomes almost pure bundling if the supply volume is constrained. In this sense, mixed bundling may be regarded as a general form of pure bundling (Nalebuff 2003, p. 14).

2.2.6 *Economic Bundling*

Several factors come into play in the economic context of bundling: cost reduction, quality enhancement, efficient pricing, etc. Bundling-based cost reduction and quality enhancement are achieved by being able to efficiently develop and manufacture products with overlapping components and sell different products through the same distribution channel. Quality enhancement here also includes reducing the users' learning curve by having different products in the same product line share a common interface. These examples essentially concern achieving higher cost efficiency by reducing diversity in the product types and interfaces based on bundling.

Bundling contributes not only to efficiency on the cost side but to efficient pricing for users/consumers in different segments. It provides a pricing approach so as to earn maximum profits from the product portfolio at hand. Sect. 2.2.6.1 introduces the bundling-based price discrimination strategy as an example.

2.2.6.1 Price Discrimination Strategy Based on Bundling

Let us discuss efficient pricing based on mixed bundling as an example of economic bundling. Efficient pricing is the materialization of price discrimination based on bundling.

Price discrimination means that the firm changes sales prices according to the consumers' willingness to pay, i.e., it sets discount prices for price-sensitive customers and premium prices for non-sensitive customers. It is generally difficult to sell the same product at different prices but, by means of bundling or more strictly, mixed bundling, price discrimination between package deals and unbundled items can be achieved. Figure 2.12 illustrates bundling-based price discrimination by presenting two products, Products 1 and 2, and four users, Users A to D. All four

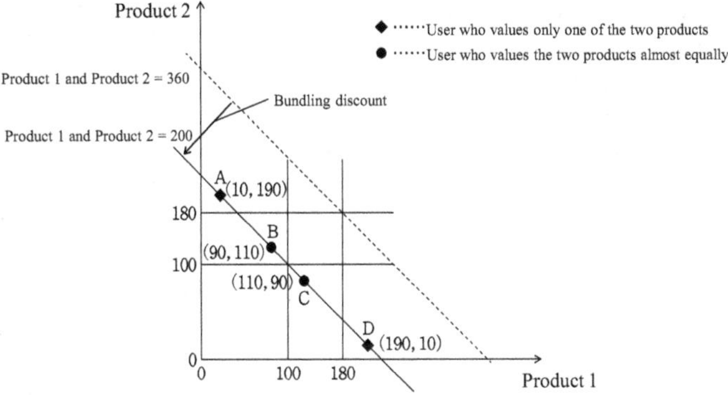

Fig. 2.12 Bundling-based price discrimination strategy

users think that they can pay up to 200 in total for the two products. They have exactly the same budget ceiling but different preferences as regards the two products.

User A is willing to pay up to 190 for Product 1 but does not want to pay more than 10 for Product 2. User D, on the contrary, is willing to pay no more than 10 for Product 1 but up to 190 for Product 2. User B is ready to pay up to 90 for Product 1 and 110 for Product 2. User C wants to pay up to 110 for Product 1 and 90 for Product 2. Users A and D (Group ◆) value one of the two products very highly, whereas Users B and C (Group ●) value the two products almost equally.

2.2.6.2 Pricing System and Total Revenue

What would be the ideal price setting in this situation? The first option is to set high prices for both products to increase total revenue (high-price approach). If Products 1 and 2 are equally priced at 180, User A will purchase Product 1 only and User D Product 2 only. Users B and C will buy neither of the two. The total revenue in this case will be 180 times 2 (360). If high prices are set, only two out of the four users make a purchase; in addition, the two users who make a purchase buy only one of the two products. The total revenue, as a result, is not very high.

Now, let us look at the second option, i.e., setting low prices for both products to encourage all four users to make a purchase (discount approach). If the two products are equally priced at 100, Users A and B will buy Product 2 only and Users C and D will buy Product 1 only. All the users will buy either Product 1 or 2. The total revenue in this case will be 100 times 4 (400). The discount approach certainly gives higher total revenue than the high-price approach (360), but the increment is small despite the fact that the number of buyers goes up from two to four. This is because the product prices are lowered.

The high-price approach prices the two products equally at 180; however, the high prices keep two users from buying any of the products. The discount approach, on the other hand, which prices the two products at as low as 100, succeeds in convincing all four users to buy one of the products. The total revenue, however, does not go up as much as expected, since the discount prices are available to everybody.

A package deal would increase the total revenue further. Let us call this mixed bundling. Mixed bundling allows Products 1 and 2 to be sold together as a package and unbundled as individual products. When sold unbundled, the prices for the high-price approach are applied: each is sold at 180. When sold as a package, the set comprising Products 1 and 2 is sold at 200. With this price setting, User A has a choice between (a) buying Product 1 only at 180 or (b) buying a package priced at 200. User A is willing to pay 190 for Product 1 and 10 for Product 2. Both choices, (a) and (b), satisfy these conditions. More specifically, however, the user has to exhaust all the available budget to buy the package in case (b) but can have 10 extra in hand when buying Product 1 at 180, 10 cheaper than 190, in case (a). Consequently, (a) would be the reasonable choice for User A. Likewise, buying Product 2 only at 180 is most reasonable for User D. On the other hand, Users B and C will not choose option (a), which allows them to buy products individually, but option (b), the package deal, will satisfy their preferences. The total revenue from the mixed bundling approach amounts to 180 (User A) plus 180 (User D) plus 200 (User B) plus 200 (User C), thus 760.

Table 2.1 summarizes the total revenues from the three different approaches. Compared with the high-price approach (360) and the discount approach (400), mixed bundling yields the highest revenue (760). The mixed bundling approach is successful because it leverages the fact that the four users have the same budget constraints but different preferences. The users who value only one of the two products highly (Users A and D) are led to buy individual products at high prices, whereas the users who assign almost the same value to the two products (Users B and C) are led to buy the discounted package. The package is priced at 200, which is much cheaper than the sum of the two individual products ($180 \times 2 = 360$). This discount pricing is called bundling discount and, at first glance, it may appear to give a discount based on the package deal. As a matter of fact, it is intended to maintain the premium prices of the individual products, even after offering discount pricing for the package deal.

Bundling discount is available only to users who purchase the package deal (Users B and C). In a normal discount approach, discount prices are applicable to all users, which does not drive up total revenue by much. In the bundling discount approach, discount prices are available only to those who purchase the package, and anyone who wants to buy a product unbundled has to pay the high price. The mixed bundling approach achieves the highest total revenue because it enables selective pricing according to user preferences.

Platform firms that sell two products typically adopt this mixed bundling approach. For instance, a firm may simultaneously offer a console and game software as a bundled package and as unbundled individual products. This is a typical example of mixed bundling. In other words, the mixed bundling approach allows implementing price discrimination by setting discount prices for consumers purchasing a package and by not applying discount prices to consumers purchasing unbundled products.

The mixed bundling approach is often employed in combination with standardization and its efficacy is maximized when a network effect exists between two products. This is self-explanatory when considering that (a) bundling discount in Fig. 2.13 virtually corresponds to (b) standardization-derived complementarity (i.e., network effect) in the same diagram.

Assume that a user has a personal computer (Product 1) and a smartphone (Product 2). If a standard specifying a format that allows music files to be mutually exchanged is established, the value for money of buying the two products together increases. The value for money, in this sense, corresponds to the change, δ', in the real bundling price in Fig. 2.13b. It functions just like bundling discount δ in Fig. 2.13a. This maximization of the value for money based on standardization has the same effect as bundling discount.

When bundling and standardization are combined, as in the above example, price discrimination is easy to implement. Mixed bundling is frequently used for products that share a network effect—resulting from standardization—between them, such as the video console and game software mentioned above.

Table 2.1 Pricing approaches and total revenues

	Price			User A		User B		User C		User D		Total revere
	Product 1	Product 2	Set of Products 1 and 2	Product 1	Product 2	Product 1	Product 2	Product 1	Product 2	Product 1	Product 2	
High price	180	180	–	×	○	×	×	×	×	○	×	360
Discount	100	100	–	×	○	×	○	○	×	○	×	400
Mixed bundling	180	180	200	×	○	◎		◎		○	×	760

○ = Purchase; × = No purchase; ◎ = Purchase as a set

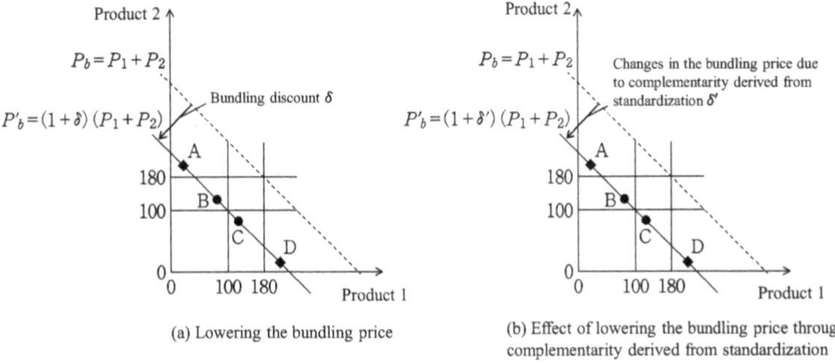

(a) Lowering the bundling price

(b) Effect of lowering the bundling price through complementarity derived from standardization

Fig. 2.13 Changes in the real bundling price resulting from open standardization

The motivation behind the mixed bundling approach described above is to maximize total revenue, so it is an economic reason. Pure bundling, which only provides a package deal and not the option of unbundled purchases, is also often used by platform firms for strategic reasons, such as entering a new market or creating a barrier against newcomers, as described next.

2.2.7 *Strategic Bundling*

Studies on bundling have traditionally focused on the economic context, rather than on the effect of implementing price discrimination through bundling, described above. More recent studies, however, have investigated the strategic motivation in greater depth (Nalebuff 2003, 2004; Eisenmann et al. 2011). The strategic motivation is linked to the control of market entry, i.e., entry into new markets and/or lock-in of current markets, and bundling based on the strategic motivation is called strategic bundling.

As reported in previous research, platform firms enter complementary goods markets, where they bundle and sell their platform products and complementary goods together. Microsoft Corporation bundles its platform product, the Windows operating system (OS), with its complementary goods, software applications. Apple Inc. bundles its Mac personal computer with its iPhone/iPod/iPad mobile devices. In addition to hardware products, Apple also bundles together its iTunes and AppStore, which are software and content distribution services.

Yet, the concept of peripheral markets is actually more complex. The after-sales service market of a product, which the manufacturer enters, is also a peripheral market. A specific example is that of an automaker starting repair and maintenance services. In such a case, if the product is compatible with an open interface, the effect of entering the peripheral market will be greater, as described later, because network effects will be generated. The firm needs to make a strategic decision as to whether to make the open interface accessible to users/consumers only or to competing firms as well.

If it decides to allow its competitors to use the interface, the firm has to share future profits with its rivals, but it can anticipate the effect of market expansion. This kind of entry into a peripheral market at a different layer (products versus solution services) is also part of strategic bundling. The scope of strategic bundling is so large that it includes combinations of products and installation services, products and replacement parts, products and solution services, as well as many other.

Sections 2.2.7.1, 2.2.7.2, 2.2.7.3, and 2.2.7.4 introduce examples of strategic bundling. There are two purposes of strategic bundling: (a) entry into neighboring markets and (b) construction of entry barriers. This book calls the former *offensive bundling* and the latter *defensive bundling.* Incidentally, strategic bundling typically takes on the form of pure bundling.

2.2.7.1 Offensive Bundling: Platform Envelopment

Unlike unbundled sales, bundling restricts the users' freedom, thereby modifying their purchasing behavior. The platform firm takes advantage of these changes in order to take market shares away from its competitors (selling unbundled products). This is called *offensive bundling*. When referring to platform firms, offensive bundling is called *platform envelopment* by Eisenmann et al. (2011). Offensive bundling is a type of user lock-in strategy based on package deals, but it is characterized by the use of bundling to enter a new market.

Apple's entry into the smartphone market is a good example. The firm launched the iPod in 2001 and soon gained a dominant share in the mobile music player market. Then, in 2007, it first entered the mobile phone market. The users of the iPod were able to play music data stored on their iPod units exclusively on the iPhone—and on no other smartphone. The success of the iPhone stems partly from this locking in of iPod users to the iPhone. That is to say, the firm succeeded in making an entry into the smartphone market, until then completely new to it, by taking advantage of the dominant share that it had earned in the mobile music player market. The quality of the iPhone product itself is, needless to say, one of the most significant factors behind its success, but Apple's effective use of the bundling strategy in entering the smartphone market cannot be ignored.

Figure 2.14 illustrates the effects of offensive bundling. The diagram shows how Firm α, which sells Product 1, stages an offensive bundling campaign in order to enter the market of Product 2. In Pattern (a), Firm α sells Product 1 only, but it sells Products 1 and 2 bundled in Pattern (c). Firm β is an existing provider of Product 2 (competitor), which sells the product unbundled.

To make things simpler, let us assume that users are uniformly distributed and that, when Firm α implements bundling, it is pure bundling, meaning that Products 1 and 2 are always sold as a bundle and are not available unbundled.

Revisiting the above example of Apple's mobile music player (iPod) and smartphone (iPhone), Product 1 is the mobile music player and Product 2 is the smartphone.

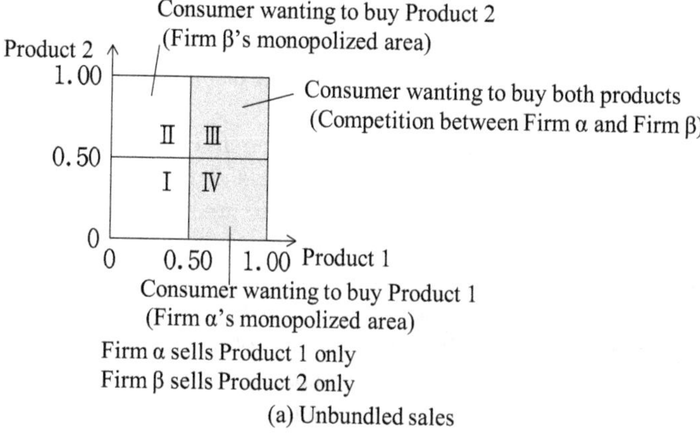

(a) Unbundled sales

The consumer purchases the products even if the total price of Products 1 and 2 is 1 or greater.
Product 2
1.00
Target consumers of Firm α (package deal)
0.50
Total price of Products 1 and 2 = 1
0
0
0.50
1.00
Product 1
The consumer does not purchase the products when the total price of Products 1 and 2 is 1 or greater.

Firm α sells a package deal of Products 1 and 2
(Product 1 is not sold on its own)

(b) Bundling

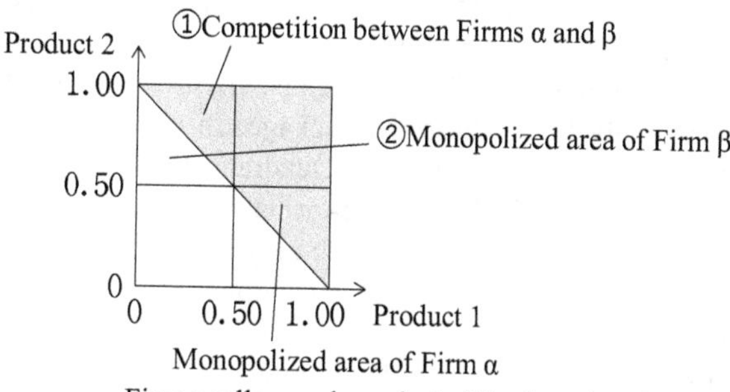

Firm α sells a package deal of Products 1 and 2
Firm β sells Product 2 only

(c) Unbundled sales together with bundling

Fig. 2.14 Unbundled sales and bundling

Firm α is Apple and Firm β is a competing smartphone manufacturer. Apple sells the iPod and the iPhone as a package, with a view to entering the smartphone market; the iPhone is not available as an individual product. Note that this is merely a hypothetical example and does not reflect reality.

In the initial state, (a), Firm α sells Product 1, whereas Firm β sells Product 2. Firm α then decides to launch Product 2, or an equivalent, and it chooses to always provide it as a bundle with Product 1. Products 1 and 2 are not available individually. The market thus moves to state (c), with Firm α staging an offensive bundling campaign against Firm β. Let us take a closer look at each of these steps.

In state (a), Products 1 and 2 are sold individually, or unbundled. Firm α sells Product 1 and Firm β Product 2; both products are sold at the price of 0.50. Quadrant IV in (a) represents consumers who wish to purchase Product 1 only and not Product 2. Quadrant II represents consumers who want to purchase Product 2 only and not Product 1. Quadrant III refers to consumers who wish to purchase both Products 1 and 2; here Products 1 and 2 are competing. Lastly, Quadrant I refers to consumers who want to buy neither of the two products.

In state (b), Firm α introduces a package deal combining Products 1 and 2 and ceases to sell unbundled products (Firm β's situation is not indicated). It is clear that the distribution of consumers who are likely to purchase the package has changed. With the introduction of a package deal, 1.00 is the total price of Products 1 and 2. Thus, consumers who have a total reservation price for Products 1 and 2 of 1.00 or higher only purchase the package. These consumers correspond to the large triangle shown in state (b).

In state (c), Firm α offers Products 1 and 2 as a package, while Firm β sells Product 2 unbundled. Firm α gains a wider consumer distribution area in state (c) compared with (a), whereas Firm β's consumer distribution area grows smaller. This is because Firm α has acquired the consumers in Quadrant III, those who are attracted to Products 1 and 2 alike. These consumers used to separately buy Products 1 and 2 from Firms α and β, respectively. In state (c), however, they have no such option. The choice is between the package (a combination of Products 1 and 2) provided by Firm α and Product 1 provided by Firm β. Because these users are attracted to both products, they are likely to purchase the package. In turn, Firm β loses the opportunity to sell Product 2 to the consumers in Quadrant III.

Furthermore, in Quadrant II in (c), Firm α is bearing down on Firm β. In area ① of Quadrant II, the two firms are competing, which only leaves area ② of Quadrant II as a consumer distribution area that Firm β may occupy.

It is obvious that the consumer distribution area available to Firm β is smaller in (c) than in (a). This is because Firm α sells a bundle of Products 1 and 2 only and not the two products separately, which means that consumers cannot selectively purchase Product 1 or Product 2 according to their preferences. Consumers who want to buy both Products 1 and 2 (Quadrant III of (c)) are enveloped by Firm α, which provides the two products as a package. Hence, the offensive bundling campaign causes a kind of lock-in and boosts Firm α's competitive advantage.

2.2.7.2 Defensive Bundling: Entry Deterrent Effects of Bundling

Bundling also works to erect an entry barrier against potential competitors. Here, the bundling-based lock-in effect is used as a barrier against new entrants. In detail, when a firm sells Products 1 and 2, it can deprive competitors of the incentive to enter the market by lowering the price of the package of Products 1 and 2. This bundling effect is called an *entry deterrent effect* (Nalebuff 2004). For the purposes of this book, this strategy is referred to as *defensive bundling*.

At first glance, this bundling may not seem to differ much from bundling discount, designed to implement price discrimination, which was discussed above; the strategic intention of the two kinds of bundling, however, is completely different. Bundling discount is intended to maximize total revenue by putting in place price discrimination. Defensive bundling, on the contrary, is intended to deprive competitors of profits and reduce entry incentives.

This bundling-based entry deterrent is unique in that it hardly undermines the firm's profits and may even increase them, as discount prices are applied to the product, while drastically slashing the potential profits of competitors. Let us further explore this point in line with Nalebuff (2004).

Figure 2.15 shows the potential size of the user base that can be gained by a new entrant trying to access a market in which bundled products are sold. In state (a), the existing firm sells Products 1 and 2 as a bundle. What if another firm offering exclusively unbundled products tries to enter that market? The new firm will have a certain user base, which corresponds to the potential user base size. This potential size grows larger or smaller depending on the price setting by the entrant (entry price P_e).

What can the existing firm do in response to such an entry? The simplest approach is to lower the bundle price (P_b), so as to reduce the potential size of

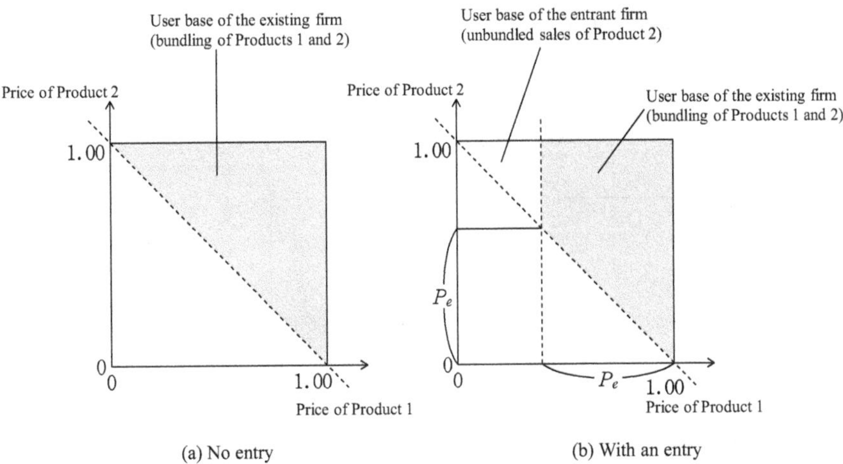

Fig. 2.15 Potential size of the user base of the entrant firm

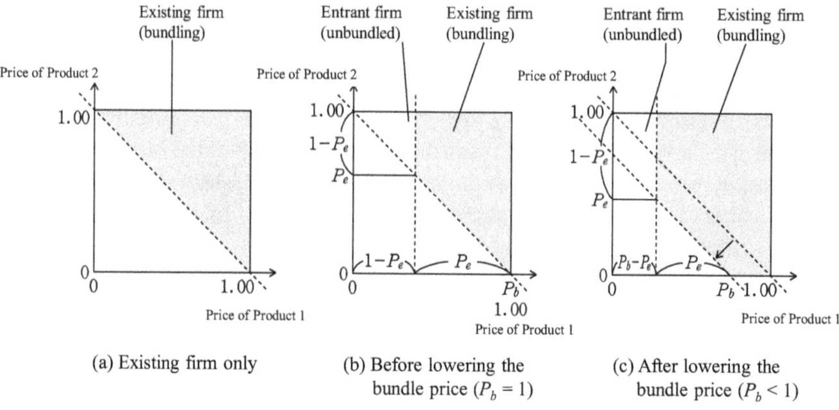

Fig. 2.16 Defensive bundling (1)

the user base that the new firm can gain. Figure 2.16 illustrates the effects of lowering the bundle price. Case (b) refers to the situation where the existing firm decides to sell Products 1 and 2 together at a bundle price of 1 (P_b). Since P_b is lowered, as shown in (c), the potential size of the newcomer's user base is described by $(1 - P_e)(P_b - P_e)$, while the potential size of the existing firm's user base is represented by $1 \times \{1 - (P_b - P_e)\} - \frac{1}{2}P_e^2$.

2.2.7.3 Bundling Prices and Open Standards

Before discussing defensive bundling, it is worth pointing out that standardization is virtually the same as lowering bundle price P_b. As long as a network effect resulting from standardization exists between Product 1 and Product 2, the relationship between the two is complementary (Fig. 2.17).

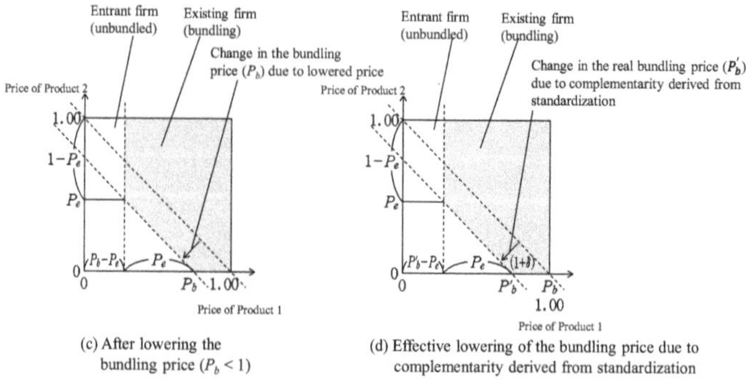

Fig. 2.17 Defensive bundling (2)

When Products 1 and 2 are complementary, the benefit of using the two products together exceeds that of using them separately—and this increment in benefit can be utilized only by the platform firm that offers the two products on the market.

The complementary relationship between Product 1 and Product 2 can be described as follows:

$$V_{1+2} = (1 + \delta)(V_1 + V_2), \delta \geq 0,$$

where V_1, V_2, and V_{1+2} are the values of Product 1, Product 2 and the bundle of Products 1 and 2, respectively, and δ represents the increment in benefit brought about by bundling.

If users are to pay prices P_1 and P_2 for potential values V_1 and V_2, respectively, the following is true. Here, $P_b^{'}$ is the real bundle price.

$$\begin{aligned} P_b &= P_1 + P_2 \\ &= (1 + \delta)P_b^{'}\delta \geq 0 \end{aligned}$$

When δ is 1, the products are perfectly complementary. When δ is 0, no complementarity exists. When $0 < \delta < 1$, they are partially complementary. Whenever a network effect is generated outside of an open standard, they are partially complementary in most cases. A comparison between (c) and (d) in Fig. 2.17 reveals that (d), where a network effect arises from an open standard, has a similar effect as (c), where the bundle price is lowered. Thus, lowering the bundling price and establishing an open standard between Product 1 and Product 2 mean the same, from the point of view of bundling strategy. As far as the network effect exists, lowered bundling prices will further enhance the effectiveness of the firm's bundling strategy (Nalebuff 2004, p. 178).

2.2.7.4 Strategic Effectiveness of Defensive Bundling

Going back to the topic of defensive bundling, let us look at how an entrant firm's best entry price, P_e, and revenue, R_e, as well as the existing firm's revenue, R_i, change when the existing firm lowers the bundle price, P_b, as shown in Fig. 2.16. Nonetheless, the case of the newcomer deciding to enter the market and the other case, i.e., the newcomer deciding not to enter, have to be dealt with separately, since the existing firm's revenue greatly changes in the two situations. Indeed, the existing firm's revenue is represented by $R_{i|entry}$ in the former case and by $R_{i|noentry}$ in the latter case.

A higher bundle price P_b makes it easier for the existing firm to maximize its revenue. However, this pushes up R_e, the potential revenue of newcomers, which sell unbundled products, thus increasing the entry incentive. Once newcomers enter the market, competition begins. On the other hand, a lower bundle price means smaller

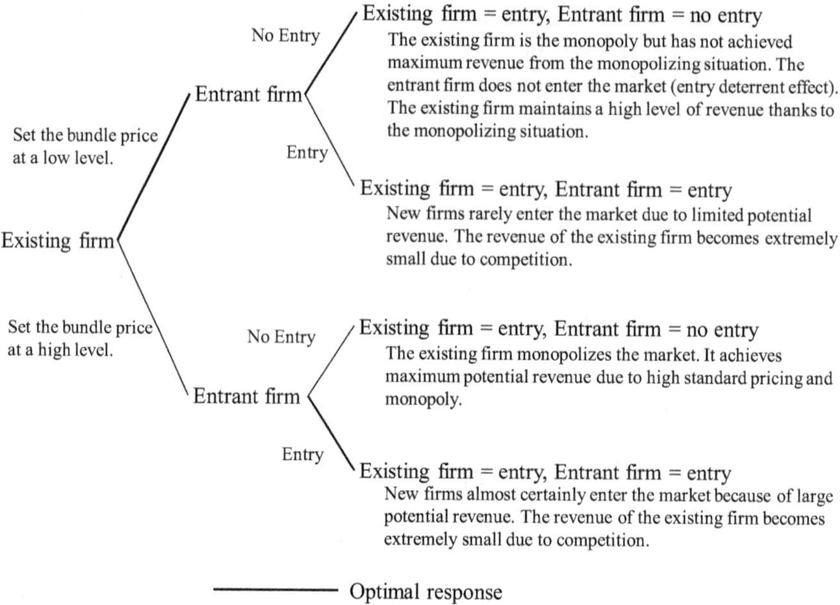
Existing firm
Set the bundle price at a low level.
Set the bundle price at a high level.
Entrant firm
No Entry
Entry
Existing firm = entry, Entrant firm = no entry
The existing firm is the monopoly but has not achieved maximum revenue from the monopolizing situation. The entrant firm does not enter the market (entry deterrent effect). The existing firm maintains a high level of revenue thanks to the monopolizing situation.
Existing firm = entry, Entrant firm = entry
New firms rarely enter the market due to limited potential revenue. The revenue of the existing firm becomes extremely small due to competition.
Entrant firm
No Entry
Entry
Existing firm = entry, Entrant firm = no entry
The existing firm monopolizes the market. It achieves maximum potential revenue due to high standard pricing and monopoly.
Existing firm = entry, Entrant firm = entry
New firms almost certainly enter the market because of large potential revenue. The revenue of the existing firm becomes extremely small due to competition.
Optimal response

Fig. 2.18 Defensive bundling price setting strategy

potential revenues for newcomers, hence reducing the likelihood of their entry. In this way, the existing firm can maintain its monopoly (Fig. 2.18).

Let us use the stages illustrated in Fig. 2.16 to analyze this situation. The first stage is when market entrants have not appeared yet.

The function to express the revenue of the existing firm when no new firms try to enter the market is as follows:

$$R_{i|noentry} = P_b\left(1 - \frac{P_b^2}{2}\right).$$

The function to express the potential revenue of a new firm in this case is defined as follows:

$$R_e = P_e(1 - P_e)(P_b - P_e).$$

To derive P_e, the price setting for the new firm to earn maximum revenue upon market entry, it is necessary to find the first-order differentiation condition for R_e with respect to P_e:

$$(1 - 2P_e)(P_b - P_e) - P_e(1 - P_e) = 0.$$

The above equation is solved to find P_e, and obtain P_e^*.

Table 2.2 Defensive bundling prices and resulting changes in revenue

Bundle price by existing firm (P_b)	Price that allows the entrant firm to maximize its revenue (P_e)	Revenue of the existing firm with no entry by new firms ($R_{i\|noentry}$)	Revenue of the existing firm with entry by new firms ($R_{i\|entry}$)	Potential revenue of the entrant firm (R_e)
1.00	0.333	0.500	0.278	0.148
0.80	0.290	0.544	0.361	0.105
0.68	0.270	0.523	0.374	0.081
0.41	0.180	0.375	0.309	0.034

Note Figures based on Nalebuff (2004)

$$P_e^* = \frac{(1 + P_b)}{3} - \frac{\sqrt{1 - P_b + P_b^2}}{3}$$

P_e^* is the price that allows a newcomer to earn the maximum revenue on the condition of a specific P_b. Table 2.2 shows how P_e and R_e change when P_b is lowered step by step.[5]

According to footnote 5, $P_b = 0.80$ is the monopoly price that achieves the maximum revenue for the existing firm when no new firm enters the market, $R_{i|noentry}$. The existing firm's revenue $R_{i|noentry}$ changes to 0.523 and to 0.375 as the bundle price P_b is lowered to 0.68 and to 0.41. Accordingly, the growth from the revenue prior to lowering the bundle price is 105 and 75% over 0.500, respectively. In this case, the new firm earns a potential revenue, R_e, of 0.081 or 0.034, corresponding to 55 or 23% of the pre-lowering revenue, 0.148. That is to say, a bundle price cut from 1.00 to 0.68 contributes to boosting the existing firm's revenue ($R_{i|noentry}$ improving from 0.500 to 0.523), but almost halves the revenue of the entrant firm. A markdown of the bundle price effectively reduces R_e, a new firm's potential incentive to enter, while maximizing the existing firm's own revenue, $R_{i|noentry}$.

Let us move on to the revenue of the existing firm when a new firm enters the market, which is expressed as follows:

---

[5]The monopolized revenue of the existing firm when no new firm makes an entry is:

$$R_{i|noentry} = x\left(1 - \frac{x^2}{2}\right)$$

The monopolizing price can be obtained by solving the following equation using the first-order condition:

$$-\frac{3x^2}{2} + 1 = 0$$

$$x = \sqrt{\frac{2}{3}} \fallingdotseq 0.80.$$

The monopolized revenue with this price would be $R_{i|noentry} \fallingdotseq 0.544$.

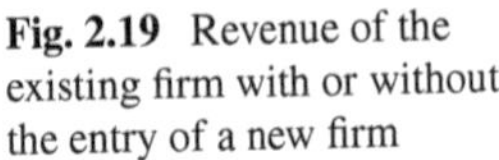

Fig. 2.19 Revenue of the existing firm with or without the entry of a new firm

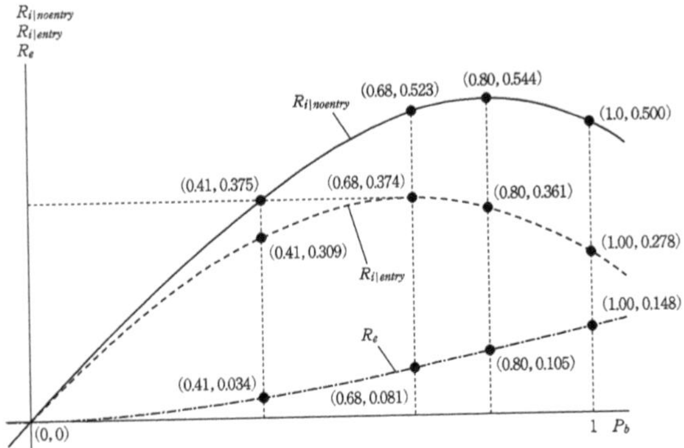

$$R_{i|entry} = P_b\left\{1 \times (1 - P_b - P_e)) - \frac{1}{2}P_e^2\right\}.$$

Columns $R_{i|noentry}$ and $R_{i|entry}$ in Table 2.2 compare the revenues of the existing firm when a new firm enters the market and when it does not, where P_b, the price allowing the existing firm to earn maximum revenue after a newcomer's entry, is 0.68 and $R_{i|entry}$, the firm's maximum revenue, is 0.374.[6]

The maximum revenues of the newcomer either making an entry or deciding against it can be visually understood by looking at Fig. 2.19. The potential revenues of the entrant firm, R_e, drop as the existing firm lowers its bundle price P_b from 1 to 0. Suppressed potential revenues mean a more limited incentive to enter, implying that a barrier to entry is built.

The excellence of defensive bundling in strategic terms is demonstrated by the changes caused by P_b being cut from 1.00 to 0.80. Even though the bundle price is lowered, the revenue of the existing firm, $R_{i|nonentry}$, rises by 8.8%, from 0.500 to 0.544, while the potential revenue of the entrant firm, R_e, falls by 29%, from 0.138 to 0.105.

If P_b is lowered from 1.00 to 0.68, $R_{i|nonentry}$ stands at 0.523, still higher than the pre-lowering level. At the same time, the potential revenue of the entrant firm, R_e, is reduced from 0.148 (when P_b is 1.00) to 0.081 (when P_b is 0.68). Since 0.081 is equivalent to 55% of 0.148, it is clear that the entrant firm loses a large portion of its potential revenue.

[6] If the new firm is to respond to P_b in such a way as to maximize its revenue, $P_e = P_e^*$; the above equation $R_{i|entry}$ can be rewritten as follows:

$$R_{i|entry} = P_b\left((1 - (P_b - P_e^*)) - \frac{1}{2}P_e^2)\right).$$

The maximizing condition is obtained based on the first-order differentiation of $R_{i|entry}$, as follows: $P_b \fallingdotseq 0.68$. Thus, $R_{i|entry} \fallingdotseq 0.374$.

In other words, the existing firm may enjoy greater total revenues while also significantly suppressing the potential revenues of the entrant firm. This is the true power of defensive bundling as a strategic tool.

Lastly, let us consider the existing firm's revenue with and without the entry of a newcomer. Maximum revenue $R_{i|entry}$ is 0.374 (when P_b is 0.68), which is essentially equivalent to the revenue of the existing firm without a new entry, $R_{i|nonentry} = 0.375$ (when P_b is 0.68). This means that the existing firm can decrease the bundle price to 0.41 if it is comfortable, as long as it secures the maximum revenue to be attained when its market is entered by a new player. In this situation ($P_b = 0.41$), its revenue with a new entrant is 0.034, less than a half, or 42%, of what it would have gained with $P_b = 0.68$ ($R_e = 0.081$).

Lower revenues upon entry make new firms less motivated to try and access a market. When P_b is 0.41, the revenue of the existing firm, $R_{i|nonentry}$, is 0.375, 75% of the original revenue (0.500 with $P_b = 1.00$) and 69% of the maximum revenue (0.544 with $P_b = 0.68$). The firm can thus slash the other firms' incentive to enter by half or more with a mere 30% reduction in its revenue from the maximum level.

The above discussion reveals that the existing firm can successfully create an entry barrier against new firms by adjusting its bundle price. In addition, this entry deterrence multiplies when a network effect exists between the two goods. In conclusion, defensive bundling proves to be an extremely effective tool for platform firms that make strategic use of open standards.

2.2.8 Conclusions

So far, we have introduced the business-ecosystem-type industrial structure and described the theoretical models used to analyze the competitive strategies of platform firms, which play a central role in such a structure. An industrial structure of the business ecosystem type encompasses various complementary goods and is often subjected to network effects. In many cases, open standardization, described in Chap. 1, serves as the source of such network effects.

The platform strategy takes advantage of the relationships among multiple markets to build competitive advantage. By positioning themselves at the hub between transaction networks, platform firms gain information benefit and control benefit, which allow them to make the most of inter-market relationships. The typical strategies employed by platform firms are the two-sided market strategy and the bundling strategy, both of which leverage the relationships between two markets and become even more effective when a network effect exists between the two markets. Platform firms, therefore, frequently undertake open standardization, which produces network effects.

2.3 Issues Regarding Earlier Studies on Platform Firms

Existing studies on platform business, particularly those focusing on competitive strategies, are advanced in how they model the competitive strategies of platformers. This is partly because the industrial organization-based approach has given ample consideration to the application of competition laws to platform firms. The case study-based approach is also advanced, but the relationship between the behavior of platform firms and their market performance is not necessarily clear, since this stream of research is performed mainly from the organizational management standpoint (Gawer and Cusumano 2002; Gawer and Henderson 2007; Cusumano 2010).

Whether following the industrial organization-based approach or the case study-based approach, previous investigations around the platform business have chiefly explored market competition and structural changes within domestic markets, while hardly touching upon international competitiveness or international division of labor. These works have looked at business ecosystems without considering any elements of the global economy, such as national borders and the nationality of firms.

A business ecosystem is very likely to produce technical spillovers beyond national borders since it is based on an open standard, which is an explicit form of technological knowledge and is easy to transfer internationally. Therefore, the firms involved in a business ecosystem are not limited to those in developed countries. Research conducted thus far in this field has assumed that the firms making up a business ecosystem must necessarily be based in developed countries only because this is where research on platformers was first carried out.

In the real world, however, global ecosystems, i.e., business ecosystems formed globally by firms from both developed and developing countries, are a regular occurrence. The foundations for such global ecosystems are international open standards. As described in Chap. 1, since the 1990s, when open standard setting was made a flexible process, international open standards have been developed with increasing frequency. The presence of global ecosystems became remarkably obvious in the mid-1990s and their impact has been growing across the world, in terms of both industrial expansion and international competitiveness.[7]

Unlike prior studies on platform business in Europe and the US, those in Japan have paid attention to the development of industries and international competitiveness; yet, the researchers carrying them out have not necessarily intended them to be platform business studies.[8] Accordingly, they are not linked with the theories about the competitive strategies of platform firms, as described later. The following paragraphs outline Japan's main platform business studies.

Two major streams of research can be identified: studies on international standardization and studies on the development of the regional economies of Taiwan,

[7] Against this backdrop, emerging countries liberalized their markets in the 1990s and started entering the global economy (Hoskisson et al. 2000).

[8] Some pioneering studies, such as Kokuryo (1995, 1999) and Negoro et al. (2011), regarded platform business as an industrial structure issue. These, however, covered network businesses only and did not touch upon the issue of global competitiveness.

South Korea and China, all of which are Japan's neighboring countries. The latter fall under the umbrella of platform studies because those regional economies have developed owing to impacts generated by platform business.

Let us begin by exploring the first group of studies. International standardization means that firms come together and share technical knowledge to draft a standard set of specifications that are compatible among them.[9] An international standard is a kind of open standard because it is shared among multiple firms. Shintaku and Eto (2008), Ogawa (2011) and Kajiura (2007) are representative contributions from this stream. They all acknowledge that the method of setting open standards changed from the 1980s or earlier to the 1990s and onward.

Before and during the 1980s, the de facto and de jure standardization processes were the norm. In the 1990s, however, consensus standardization, a new process for the development of standards through the creation of consortia, emerged mainly in the IT and electronics sectors. Shintaku and Eto (2008) and Ogawa (2009) argued that this third approach is completely different from the conventional de facto and de jure processes. They also pointed out that the strategic use of open standardization, whether de facto, de jure or consensus, is crucial to the building of international competitiveness.

Intel Corporation, Qualcomm and Ericsson were among the firms discussed in these works—today known as platform studies—that made strategic use of open standardization processes. It is rare for Japanese firms to pursue strategies based on open standards, and this is why Japanese platform studies usually look at foreign companies. When platformers make strategic use of open standards, they typically become the subject of research on the standardization activities of firms. In fact, many US and European scholars deem the platform strategy to be one of the competitive strategies for standardization (Stango 2004). Therefore, the Japanese studies mentioned so far correspond to the platform strategy studies branching off from standardization competition studies in the US and Europe.

The second group of studies revolves around the regional economic development of Japan's neighboring nations. East Asian countries, particularly Taiwan and South Korea, have achieved remarkable economic development since the 1990s, followed by China from 2000 onwards. The scholars working in this stream have investigated the rapid growth of these economies in conjunction with the platform business in the US and Europe.

The economic growth pattern exhibited by these fast-developing economies is different from the traditional industrial development of the region, analyzed in regional economic studies, and this peculiarity has drawn much academic attention. In the past, this region owed its economic development to the international transfer of industries, propelled by foreign direct investment (FDI) coming from developed countries. Firms based in developed countries directly invested in Taiwan, South

---

[9]Research on open standards in Japan is seen as being part of architecture studies. When a system has an open standard, it means that the firms producing the modules of the system, if modularized, share information about the interfaces connecting such modules; the interface information is open. These studies on open standards have been carried out as studies on open interfaces.

Korea and China, which generated technological knowledge spillovers, leading to the growth of the regional economy over time. Major research of this type includes works on the Flying Geese Model and the international product lifecycle (PLC) theory (Akamatsu 1961, 1962; Vernon 1966; Kojima 2004).

In the Flying Geese Model and the PLC theory, the trigger of international industrial transfer is FDI in emerging markets by firms from developed countries. FDI means, for example, setting up subsidiaries in foreign countries as production and sales strongholds in those markets. When firms from developed countries implement FDI and manufacture products in emerging countries, both tangible and intangible assets accumulate there. Over time, these assets cause spillovers, which, in turn, allow manufacturers funded by local firms in the emerging markets to come into being and grow. At first, these firms produce only for their local markets, but they eventually start exporting their products to developed markets as well.

International industrial transfer, both in the Flying Geese Model and in the PLC theory, is thought to stem mostly from FDI into emerging countries, technical spillovers, and the scale of the emerging countries' local economies. Research on regional economies in East Asia detected a clear shift in pattern for the first time in the 1990s. The most notable difference was the overwhelmingly faster speed of international industrial transfer. The international PLC theory assumes that technical development occurs in a developed country first. The firm from the developed country then sets up a site to produce the completed product in an emerging country through FDI, and the technology or industry gradually takes root in the emerging market. The PLC theory explains that the technical spillovers involved in this process take time. The so-called Theory of Internalization argues that technical know-how and other intangible assets are essentially difficult to propagate beyond borders under market mechanisms, and they barely roll out to other countries through the internal organizations of multinational firms (Buckley and Casson 1976; Teece 1977, 1986).

The international transfer of industry observed in and after the 1990s, however, achieved the processes described above within a very short period of time. Besides, it did not actually involve FDI from developed countries to developing countries. Kawakami (2012) called this phenomenon *compressed industrial transfer* and underlined that the presence of the *ability to absorb* on the developing end makes international transfer, predicated on international platform business and global ecosystems, happen with remarkable speed.

This new form of rapid international transfer of industry has often been observed in the electronics industries of not only Taiwan but also mainland China. Marukawa and Yasumoto (2010) carefully examined the growth of the Chinese mobile phone industry and noted that a key factor behind its success was the platform business of semiconductor manufacturers. Marukawa (2007) characterized this unique industrial growth in emerging countries by using the term *vertical disintegration* within the framework of the theory of industrial organization. The concept of vertical disintegration is equivalent to the general expression *horizontal division of labor*.

Scholars have emphasized that, in this industrial transfer pattern, business growth is based on horizontal division of labor, or a layered structure, rather than on vertical integration. Imai and Kawakami (2007) presented similar arguments based on their findings from a survey on the personal computer industry in East Asia. Economic development relying on vertical disintegration commonly features the presence of platform business as a prerequisite. Platformers sell core components as general-purpose products (platform products) to a wide range of firms. Intel is a perfect example, since it is a platform firm that supplies the core component (central processing unit, CPU) of personal computers and has developed its business according to a vertically disintegrated industrial structure (Grove 1996).

Looking at these two streams of research, the studies carried out in Japan appear to be original and different from their Western counterparts on platform competitive strategy, in that they focus on international competitiveness and international division of labor. As mentioned earlier, US and European scholars in the field of platform strategy studies have tended to disregard these two aspects, preferring to concentrate instead on changes in the domestic industrial structure. This absence was a clear limit of earlier inquires performed in the US and Europe.

Japanese studies, on the other hand, are aimed at exploring standardization strategies and regional economic development, meaning that platform firms are outside their scope of investigation. As a result, they are not correlated with the theory of platform competitive strategy in the US and Europe, introduced in the previous section, and lack a systematic understanding of platform strategy and an analysis of success factors. For example, they make no mention of the strategic use of open standards and the management of relations with symbiont firms as invaluable tools to foster the growth of the business ecosystem as a whole, both of which are unique to the platform strategy. These features have often been indicated in US and European research as an integral part of a firm's platform strategy and are therefore indispensable for a systematic understanding of it.

2.4 Fundamental Proposition

Platform firm studies in the US and Europe have links with the theory of industrial organization and research on corporate strategies in the field of management. They are concerned with domestic businesses and seldom touch upon the international expansion of platform firms. Japanese studies, on the other hand, look at many cases of international expansion of platformers, since they recognize the significance of their impact. These firms, however, are not their main topic of investigation, as research done in Japan focuses on international standards or regional economic development. Accordingly, it lacks consistency with existing theories and a comprehensive understanding of the competitive behavior of platform firms.

In sum, the international expansion and global business of platform firms have not actually been examined. This is rather peculiar considering the scale of the impact that platform firms have on global ecosystems. Therefore, in this book, I present a series of studies based on the following fundamental proposition.

2.4.1 Fundamental Proposition and Subordinate Propositions

This book sets out to verify the following proposition.

Fundamental Proposition: When an open standard prevails in a global ecosystem, the platform firm gains a dominant competitive position. The success of the platform firm triggers a sudden transformation in the structure of the international division of labor.

A global ecosystem here means a business ecosystem that grows beyond national borders or, more specifically, a business ecosystem that involves firms from both developed and developing countries. Such an ecosystem encompasses general business categories, like product firms, components firms, etc. On top of these, there exists a new type of firm that is called platform firm in competition models, as described in the modelling of business ecosystems.

When an open standard to be used internationally is created, network effects are generated in the global ecosystem. Platform firms know how to artificially and strategically produce and make use of network effects. This approach may take on the concrete form of the two-sided market strategy or bundling strategy. Thanks to these strategies, platform firms enjoy enhanced competitiveness, resulting from the development of an open standard in the global ecosystem. Hence, the competitiveness of platform firms derives from network effects. The network effects increase as the ecosystem grows, which makes it more likely for platform firms to attain dominant competitiveness.

Meanwhile, which firms, other than platform firms, have opportunities for growth within this process, those in developed countries or those in emerging countries? According to the findings of the regional economic studies referred to in Sect. 2.3, firms in emerging countries have greater opportunities for growing or catching up with those from developed countries. Thus, the success of a platform firm in a global ecosystem is regarded as a booster for the catch-up of firms from emerging countries and, in addition, it induces a reversal of competitiveness between firms in developed countries and those in developing countries.

This is the essence of the fundamental proposition put forth here, which is, however, rather difficult to verify as it is. Therefore, this book breaks it down into the following four subordinate propositions to be verified. The first three concern the mechanisms put in place by platform firms to gain international competitiveness, and are thus about the main effects of the platform strategy. The fourth one concerns the impact of a platform firm enjoying international competitiveness on the international division of labor, and is thus about the side effects of platform strategy.

Subordinate Proposition (1)

Platform firms make strategic use of open standards to gain competitive advantage.

Subordinate proposition (1) focuses on strategic standardization, which serves as the trigger for the platform strategy. Platform firms exploit network effects as the source of their competitiveness. Strategic standardization means that platform firms strategically and intentionally produce network effects through open standardization, as explained in greater detail in Chap. 3. Strategic standardization allows a platform firm to produce a network effect anywhere it wishes. This is why it is often the first step in the competitive strategy of platform firms.

In the early days, the development of international open standards was not easy. In the 1980s, however, a new standardization process, the consensus process, was introduced, which made it possible to flexibly utilize any of the three approaches to standardization, as seen in Chap. 1. Platform firms, in a sense, do not wait for network effects to accidentally happen but artificially generate them by promoting the creation of open standards, in order to gain competitiveness. Subordinate proposition (1), which denotes this argument, is examined and verified in the case study on the introduction of GSM mobile phones into the Chinese market in Chap. 3.

Subordinate Proposition (2)

Platform firms gain competitive advantage by positioning themselves at the hub of transaction networks and by passing on information among multiple markets.

Subordinate proposition (2) represents the conditions that were unstated assumptions in earlier studies. These works asserted that platform firms expand their competitiveness by passing on information among multiple markets. To act on multiple markets, platformers need to position themselves at their juncture, or hub. Early research regarded this as a basic strategy of platform firms.

Platform firms positioning themselves at the hub may seem obvious; yet, none of the prior studies have provided demonstrative evidence of such an occurrence. This is because empirical work based on inter-firm transaction network data is difficult in the first place. Chapter 4 aims to verify this proposition by showing an empirical study based on transaction network data for the semiconductor manufacturing equipment industry.

Subordinate Proposition (3)

Platform firms gain competitive advantage by implementing two-sided market and bundling strategies, managing relations with suppliers of complementary goods and adopting other strategies based on market structure.

Subordinate proposition (3) concerns ecosystem management by platform firms. As described in the theoretical model, a business ecosystem involves symbiont firms and user firms, as well as platform firms. Since a platform firm provides only one part of a complex system, it cannot expand the ecosystem through its investments alone and needs to encourage symbiont and user firms to willingly make investments. As a consequence, platform firms must strategically manage the value network based on the structure of the market, instead of concentrating solely on their own business.

As outlined in the theoretical model, the management of business ecosystems by platform firms is characteristic, in that it takes the structure of two-sided markets into account and involves direct and indirect strategic actions. As observed, *direct* actions include the bundling strategy, which is used as a tool for entering a peripheral market in the ecosystem. *Indirect* strategic actions include supporting openness within the network in order to promote potential entries into the ecosystem. This behavior is observed in the management of inter-firm relations with symbiont and user firms. Subordinate proposition (3) abstracts the management of the business ecosystem by platform firms.

This book verifies this proposition by discussing the following case studies: Intel's entry into peripheral markets in the ecosystem of personal computers (Chap. 5), Intel's management of inter-firm relations with Taiwanese motherboard manufacturers as symbiont firms (Chap. 6) and Bosch's and Denso's management of inter-firm relations with user firms in the ecosystem of Chinese car electronics (Chap. 7).

Subordinate Proposition (4)

The rise of a platform firm during the formation of a global ecosystem triggers a sudden transformation in the structure of the international division of labor.

Subordinate proposition (4) zeroes in on the second half of the fundamental proposition. This book attempts to establish what kind of impact the success of platform strategies by platform firms has on the international division of labor. Specifically, the goal here is to explore the side effects of the platform strategy.

This proposition presents a paradoxical relationship that may seem counterintuitive. For the time being, global open standards are created in developed countries and most, if not all, platformers are from developed countries. It might, therefore, be logical to conclude that, as a result of the international rise of platform firms, it is firms from developed countries that occupy the global ecosystem in the end. The above proposition, however, argues otherwise, by stating that the international rise of platform firms boosts the catch-up of firms from developing countries with those from developed countries.

The reasons are as follows. As seen in Subordinate Propositions (1)–(3), the competitive strategy of platform firms comprises the use of market structure and of open standards, passing on information among markets. What kind of impact are symbiont firms and user firms in the ecosystem subject to when platform firms implement this strategy package? The exploitation of open standards is expected to accelerate the growth of entrant firms rather than that of existing firms. The new firms in an ecosystem are often those from emerging countries that are trying to catch up with their counterparts from developed countries. Subordinate proposition (4) argues that the success of platform firms, therefore, accelerates the catch-up of the industry of emerging nations and ultimately triggers a sudden transformation in the structure of the international division of labor.

Subordinate proposition (4) is tested in Chap. 8 against the ecosystems discussed in Chaps. 3–7. Each of the four subordinate propositions is verified in a dedicated chapter and all of them are discussed together in Chap. 8.

2.4.2 *Industrial Structure Assumed in This Book*

This book assumes a model of industrial structure, shown below, that is much simpler than the business ecosystem model cited in Chap. 1. The players in the structure are

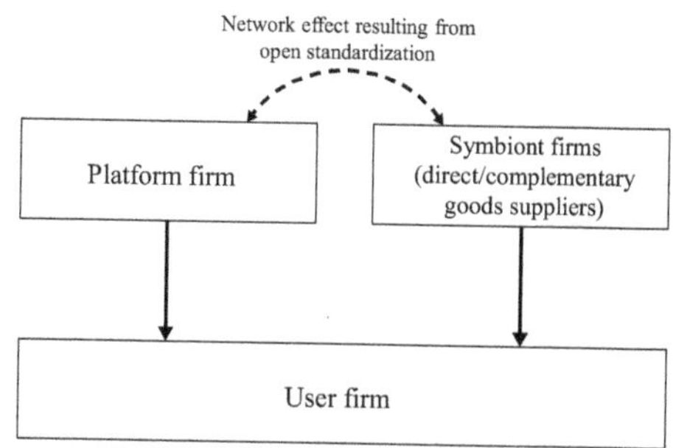

Fig. 2.20 Industrial structure assumed in this book

platform firms, symbiont firms and user firms, and all of these different types of firms are inter-related, as shown in Fig. 2.20. The arrows in the diagram represent the flows of products and services and the dotted line indicates the network effects arising from open standards.

2.4.3 Criteria for Cases to be Studied

The main purpose of this volume is to analyze platform firms' global strategic behavior in an industrial structure of the business ecosystem type. There is great variation among researchers in how the concept of business ecosystem is defined. As illustrated in Sect. 2.1, the present work conceives it as an industry in which an open standard is developed and resulting network effects have an impact on its evolution into a business ecosystem. If the open standard is created at the international level, the ecosystem in question is a global one. This book focuses on the strategic behavior of platform firms in the process of formation of a global ecosystem.

In line with the stated purpose, Chaps. 3–7 examine the ecosystems of mobile phones (Chap. 3), semiconductor manufacturing equipment (Chap. 4), personal computers (Chaps. 5 and 6) and car electronics (Chap. 7). All these ecosystems involve the development of international open standards, namely the GSM mobile phone system in Chap. 3, the global 300 mm specifications in Chap. 4, open interface standards in Chaps. 5 and 6 and, lastly, emissions control regulations and the AUTOSAR standard in Chap. 7. Open standards have affected the behavior of firms in each of these ecosystems.

Another commonality among these ecosystems is their rapid growth in the 1990 and 2000s. The timing of such growth, however, differs among them: the personal computer industry and mobile phone industry grew in the mid-1990s and early 2000s, while the semiconductor manufacturing equipment market and the car electronics market have expanded since the 2000s.

The systems involved are also markedly different. The largest one is the mobile phone system, which covers a whole country, whereas the semiconductor manufacturing system covers one plant and the car electronics system one vehicle. The smallest in size is that of personal computers. As for their similarities, these ecosystems may be described as deeply affected by digitalization and computerization. In addition, all the systems discussed in the various chapters consist of hardware and software and usually have well-defined interfaces.

Chapters 3–7 report on case studies and empirical studies regarding the global ecosystems of these system products. Key data used in the chapters are shown in Table 2.3.

While completing the case studies for Chaps. 3, 6 and 7, special caution was exercised in the handling of the interview data gathered since, as is well known, information obtained from interviews can often be biased. Each case study carried out involved roughly 20–40 interviews. When it comes to an ecosystem-like industrial structure, firms tend to have different views depending on where they are positioned within the market. To minimize such biases, we interviewed representatives from several firms, each characterized by different market positioning in relation to the overall market structure. Specifically, a global ecosystem is an ecosystem in which firms of various nationalities coexist, and the nationality of the firms interviewed may also cause biases. Thus, we intentionally interviewed firms at different bases in different countries. We then verified the information gathered during the interviews against evidence given in the literature (statistical and technical information).

Special care was also taken while performing the empirical study in Chap. 4, which presents an empirical analysis based on panel data of transaction networks in the semiconductor manufacturing equipment industry. Research on this topic tends to look at cross-sectional data (i.e., one point in time), but this approach is not suitable for processing heterogeneity among individuals. An industrial structure of the business ecosystem type, however, takes the inclusion of heterogeneous firms for granted. This is why we used panel data, which allowed us to statistically control for the heterogeneity of individual firms.

In brief, we paid careful attention to preventing any bias from creeping in wherever possible. The details of the data used are given in each chapter.

2.5 Composition of Chapters

Figure 2.21 illustrates the relationships among the chapters of this volume.

Chapter 1 raises key questions, followed by this chapter, which illustrates the theoretical models discussed in prior studies and presents a series of propositions to be analyzed in this book. In brief, Chap. 1 and this chapter argue the following points.

Chapter 1 explains that international open standards became prevalent following the shifts in the standardization policies of governments around the world during the 1980s. It also points out that the influence of platform firms grew substantially in such circumstances.

This chapter explores the theoretical models of competitive strategies in platform business discussed in prior studies. The first step is to define the environment of

Table 2.3 List of data used

Chapter	Heading	Data used
3	Strategic Standardization and Global Ecosystem: GSM Mobile Phone Diffusion in China	21 interviews with 21 European and Chinese entities (2007–2008), including communication equipment providers, a standardization organization, communications operators, mobile phone unit manufacturers, etc. (Hillebrand 2001) on the GSM standard
4	Key Factors in the Success of Platform Strategy in Global Ecosystems: An Empirical Study on the Semiconductor Manufacturing Equipment Industry	Panel data created from 13 years' worth of data gathered from 26 manufacturing equipment providers from (1) to (3): (1) Transaction data: deliveries of equipment to major semiconductors fabs in Asia (ED Research 1998, 2007) (2) Market performance (sales prices): sales value per equipment model in the manufacturing equipment market (Nikkei BP and Global Net 1999, 2001; Global Net 2005, 2009) (3) Plant data (SEMI 2005, 2009): 20 interviews with 20 manufacturing equipment providers
5	Ecosystem Management and Entry into Peripheral Markets: The Platform Strategy of Intel	Intel Corp.'s annual reports Industrial magazines: Microprocessor Report, Electronic Buyers' News Statistics (Prices and quantities between 1995 and 2003) HDD: Techno System Report, Memory: iSuppli, CPU: Microprocessor Report Technical magazines as to product information
6	Relationship Management with Symbiont Firms: Case Analysis of Intel and Taiwanese ODM Vendors	Interviews with Intel and Taiwanese motherboard manufacturers (2006–2008) and with Japanese and American PC providers A total of 31 interviews with 31 firms based in Taiwan, Japan and the US
7	Management of the Relationship with User Firms: A Comparative Case Study of Bosch and Denso	Interviews mainly with Bosch and Denso. 46 interviews with 29 firms, including automotive manufacturers, suppliers, development tool and software providers and semiconductor manufacturers in Japan, Europe, India, China and other ASEAN nations (firms outside China are included to ascertain the global R&D strategies of the above two firms)

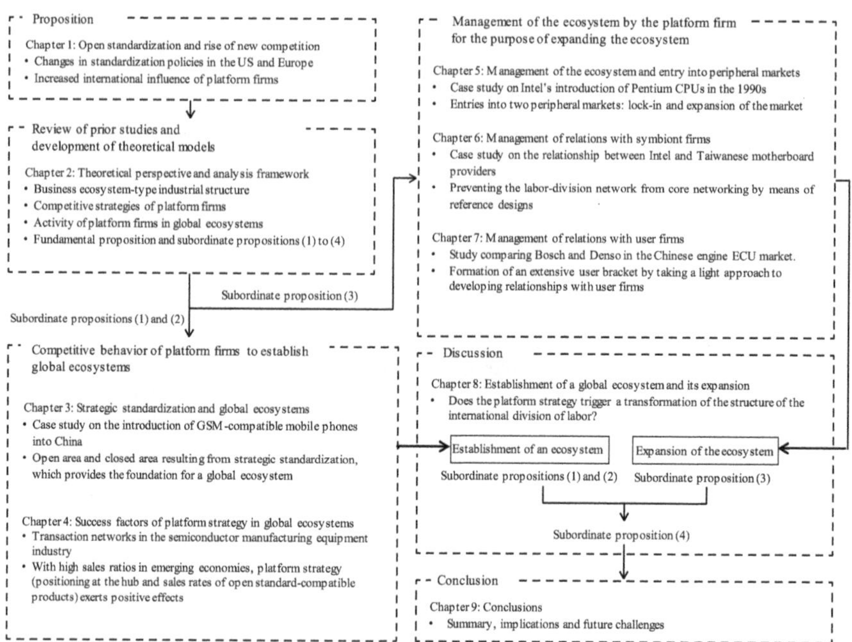

Fig. 2.21 Composition of chapters

business-ecosystem-type industries and understand the relationship between ecosystems and open standards. This is followed by a description of the theories concerning the competitive behavior of platform firms, which implement characteristic competitive strategies in an ecosystem-like industry. The main elements of the competitive strategy of platform firms are identified as their positioning at the hub in transaction networks, the generation of network effects based on strategic standardization, as well as the two-sided market strategy and the bundling strategy. The last portion of this chapter is devoted to the fundamental proposition ("When an open standard prevails in a global ecosystem, the platform firm gains a dominant competitive position. The success of the platform firm triggers a sudden transformation in the structure of the international division of labor"), to be verified through the complete set of case studies reported here, together with some subordinate propositions, to be verified through individual case studies.

Chapters 3–7 present case studies and empirical analyses to assess the validity of the fundamental proposition. Chapters 3 and 4 examine the period when an ecosystem first develops, focusing on the management approaches adopted by platform firms in order to establish global ecosystems. Chapters 5–7 look at the following stage, that of ecosystem expansion, and discuss how platform firms succeed in expanding the global ecosystems established while, at the same time, maintaining, or even strengthening, their competitiveness. The content and main conclusions of each chapter are summarized below.

The core concept of Chap. 3 is strategic standardization and its aim is to reveal how open standardization, which platform firms often pursue, influences global ecosystems. The theoretical models outlined in this chapter alone do not demonstrate that platform firms gain competitiveness in global ecosystems because of open standardization. To shed light on the matter, a detailed case study is presented on the expansion of the GSM mobile phone industry into the Chinese market. Since the mid-1980s, the consensus standardization process has consistently been used as a method to achieve international open standardization. This standardization dichotomizes a system into an open area and a closed area, the former being the part of technology for which standard specifications are defined and the latter being the part for which standard specifications remain essentially undefined. The open area provides the industries of emerging countries, whose accumulation of technological expertise is small, with a perfect opportunity for catching up with developed countries, whereas platform firms, the promoters of standardization, take advantage of the closed area to exert their competitive influence. Focusing on the industries of emerging countries, Chap. 3 identifies the mechanism allowing platform firms to increase their market performance through this dichotomization of architecture based on strategic standardization.

The core concept of Chap. 4 is the relationship between the expansion of markets in emerging countries and the platform strategy. The theoretical models regarding the competitive strategy of platform firms examined in this chapter do not take geographical conditions into account. Hence, Chap. 4 is designed to illuminate the relationship between the expansion of the markets of emerging countries and the platform strategy. The empirical analysis is performed on panel data derived from transaction data and in-market sales values of firms in the semiconductor manufacturing equipment industry between 1994 and 2007. In the world of semiconductor manufacturing, production machines of various kinds must be of the same technological generation. Accordingly, there were repeated attempts at standardization, but they all resulted in failure. The rise of consensus standardization during the 1980s, however, made the open standardization of the 300 mm wafer generation a success and the standard became highly influential.

The empirical analysis shows that high sales ratios in emerging countries are indispensable for the platform strategy of platform firms to be effective in global ecosystems. Platform firms, it is argued, can be successful only when they achieve positioning at the hub, high sales rates of open standard-compatible products and high sales ratios in emerging countries, all of which are to be attained together as a strategy package.

The core concept of Chap. 5 is the entry into peripheral markets. The example analyzed is that of Intel, one of the most well-known platform firms, and its platform strategy in the 1990s, when it turned its ecosystem into a global ecosystem. Intel took advantage of open standardization as a trigger to create an ecosystem. Though its core business was central processing units (CPUs) in personal computers, the firm entered peripheral markets, i.e., the chipset market and the motherboard market, in the process of expanding its ecosystem. Intel's entry into these two markets had different strategic purposes. The entry into the chipset market was intended to be a lock-in strategy, with features similar to strategic bundling (covered in the current chapter), and it reinforced Intel's competitiveness against firms providing compatible CPUs. The entry into the motherboard market, by contrast, was short-lived, but it came as a big blow to the Taiwanese motherboard industry. Although Intel soon withdrew from this market, the Taiwanese motherboard industry reacted by revitalizing its business and large investments went into development and production capacity building.

The core concept of Chap. 6 is the management of relations with symbiont firms. Platform firms are unique in that they cannot deliver a complete product or service on their own, which makes collaboration with symbiont firms vital. As a platform firm continuously incorporates the latest technology into its platform product, a process of joint problem-solving with symbiont firms becomes necessary. Consequently, the value network is limited to a certain group of core symbiont firms, which prevents the ecosystem from expanding. This is called the *dilemma of core networking* and, to avoid it, platform firms develop reference designs and manage their relations with symbiont firms in order to secure openness.

The core concept of Chap. 7 is the management of relations with user firms. After analyzing the relations between platform firms and symbiont firms in the previous chapter, Chap. 7 turns to the relations between platform firms and user firms. Two case studies are introduced to compare the corporate behavior in the Chinese market of Bosch and Denso, core component providers in the electronic control units (ECUs) sector for automotive engines. Bosch followed the typical strategy of platform firms, as seen in Chap. 6. Denso, on the other hand, adopted the typical strategy of traditional product manufacturers. The comparison made between the two case studies on inter-firm relations with user firms reveals that the platform firm, Bosch, successfully developed a larger user base thanks to its simpler inter-firm relations approach.

Chapter 8 makes an argument based on the findings of the preceding chapters. More specifically, it verifies if the case studies and empirical studies in Chaps. 3–7 support subordinate propositions (1)–(4), presented in this chapter. The argument is made building on an analysis framework consisting of the types of firms in the business ecosystem (platform firms, symbiont firms and user firms) and the development phases of the ecosystem (establishment and expansion periods).

The four subordinate propositions are found to be true and it is further established that subordinate proposition (4) involves relatively complicated conditions, i.e., (i) and (ii): (i) a transformation of their international industrial structure occurs more easily in symbiont firms than in user firms; and (ii) when the user industry has market entry regulations in place or undergoes an immediate shift between existing and new firms, a transformation of the international division of labor does not take place in the user industry. In this case, the industries of symbiont firms gather the momentum for a transformation of their international division of labor and experience a deeper structural change.

The transformation of the international division of labor is seen, for example, in the personal computer industry, where the rise of platform firms resulted in the expanded competitiveness of American emerging personal computer firms in the user industry. As for the industries of symbiont firms, in this case, Taiwanese Original Design Manufacturers (ODMs) rapidly emerged, triggering a large-scale transformation in the international division of labor. The rise of platform firms inevitably engenders a new form of international bond between symbiont firms and user firms—symbiont firms in emerging countries and user firms in developed countries or symbiont firms in developed countries and user firms in emerging countries—and, consequently, brings about a transformation of the international industrial structure.

The last chapter summarizes all the findings gathered in this book and discusses their academic and business implications, along with their significance in today's context. It concludes by presenting future challenges and visions.

References

Akamatsu K (1961) A theory of unbalanced growth in the world economy. Welwirtschafliches Archiv 86(2):196–217

Akamatsu K (1962) A historical pattern of economic growth in developing countries. Dev Econ 1:3–25

Baldwin CY (2011) Bottleneck strategies for business ecosystems. Paper presented at the MIT Sloan School, MIT, Cambridge MA, 21 January 2011. http://www.people.hbs.edu/cbaldwin/. Accessed 1 Aug 2011

Baldwin CY, Clark KB (2000) Design rules: the power of modularity. MIT Press, Cambridge, MA

Brandenburger AM, Nalebuff BJ (1996) Co-opetition. Doubleday Business, New York

Buckley PJ, Casson M (1976) The future of the multinational enterprise. Macmillan, London

Burt RS (1992) Structural holes. Harvard University Press, Cambridge, MA

Burt RS (1997) The contingent value of social capital. Adm Sci Q 42:339–365

Chesbrough HW (2003) Open innovation. Harvard Business School Press, Boston, MA

Chesbrough HW (2006) Open business models: How to thrive in the new innovation landscape. Harvard Business School Press, Boston, MA

Chesbrough HW, Vanhaverbeke W, West J (2006) Open innovation: researching a new paradigm. Oxford University Press, Oxford

Cook KS, Emerson RM (1978) Power, equity and commitment in exchange networks. Am Sociol Rev 43:712–739

Cusumano MA (1998) Microsoft secrets: How the world's most powerful software company creates technology, shapes markets, and manages people. Free Press, New York

Cusumano MA (2004) The business of software: What every manager, programmer, and entrepreneur must know to thrive and survive in good times and bad. Free Press, New York

Cusumano MA (2010) Staying power: six enduring principles for managing strategy and innovation in an uncertain world. Oxford University Press, Oxford

Cusumano MA, Yoffie DB (1998) Competing on internet time: lessons from Netscape and its battle with Microsoft. Free Press, New York

ED Research (1998) Tokubetsu Riputo Nichi Kan Tai Shuyou Handoutai Koujou no Seizou Souti '98 (Special report on semiconductor manufacturing equipment in Japanese, Korean, Taiwanese Foundry 1998). ED Research, Tokyo (in Japanese)

ED Research (2007) Tokubetsu Riputo Nichi Kan Tai Shuyou Handoutai Koujou no Seizou Souti 2007 (Special report on semiconductor manufacturing equipment in Japanese, Korean, Taiwanese Foundry 2007) ED Research, Tokyo (in Japanese)

Eisenmann T, Parker G, Van Alstyne M (2006) Strategies for two-sided markets. Harvard Bus Rev 84(10):92–101

Eisenmann T, Parker G, Van Alstyne M (2011) Platform envelopment. Strateg Manag J 32:1270–1285

Evans DS, Hagiu A, Shmalensee R (2006) Invisible engines. MIT Press, Cambridge MA

Freeman LC (1977) A set of measures of centrality based upon betweenness. Sociometry 40:35–41
Gawer A (2009) Platforms, markets and innovation. Edward Elgar, Cheltenham, UK and MA, USA
Gawer A, Cusumano MA (2002) Platform leadership: How Intel, Microsoft, and Cisco drive industry innovation. Harvard Business School Press, Boston, MA
Gawer A, Henderson R (2007) Platform owner entry and innovation in complementary markets: evidence from Intel. J Econ Manag Strategy 16(1):1–34
Global Net (2005) Sekai Handoutai Seizousouchi Shiken Kensa Souchi Shijou Nenkan 2005 (Yearbook of semiconductor manufacturing and testing equipment in the global market 2005)
Global Net (2009) Sekai Handoutai Seizousouchi Shiken Kensa Souchi Shijou Nenkan 2009 (Yearbook of semiconductor manufacturing and testing equipment in the global market 2009)
Granovetter MS (1973) The strength of weak ties. Am J Sociol 78(1):1360–1380
Grove SA (1996) Only the paranoid survive: How to exploit the crisis points that challenge every company and career. Currency/Doubleday, New York
Hagiu A (2006) Pricing and commitment by two-sided platforms. RAND J Econ 37(3):720–737
Hagiu A, Yoffie DB (2009) What's your Google strategy? Harvard Bus Rev 87(4):74–81
Harada S (2008) Kokusai hyoujunka Senryaku (Strategy for International Standardization). Denki University Press, Tokyo (in Japanese)
Henderson RM, Clark KB (1990) Architectural innovation: the reconfiguration of existing product technologies and the failure of established firms. Adm Sci Q 35(1):9–30
Hillebrand F (ed) (2001) GSM and UMTS: the creation of global mobile communication. Wiley Inc., Hoboken, NJ
Hoskisson RE, Eden L, Lau CM, Wright M (2000) Strategy in emerging economies. Acad Manag J 43(3):249–267
Iansiti M, Levien R (2004a) The keystone advantage: what the new business ecosystems mean for strategy, innovation, and sustainability. Harvard Business School Press, Boston
Iansiti M, Levien R (2004b) Strategy as ecology. Harvard Bus Rev 82(3):68–78. https://doi.org/10.1108/eb025570
Imai K, Kawakami M (2007) Higashiajia no IT kikisangyou: Bungyou Kyousou Sumiwake no Dainamizumu (The IT equipment industry in East Asia: Dynamics of division of labor, competition and segregation). Institute of Developing Economies, Japan External Trade Organization, Chiba (in Japanese)
Inoue T, Maki K, Nagayama S (2011) Bijinesu Ekosisutemu ni okeru Nitti no Koudou to Habu Kigyou no Senryaku – Kateiyou Gemu Gyoukai ni okeru Fukuganteki Bunseki (The behaviors of niche and hub firms in the business ecosystem: multifaceted analysis on consumer game industry). Organiz Sci 44(4):67–82 (in Japanese)
Kajiura M (2007) Kokusai Bijinesu to Gijutsu Hyojun (International business and technological standards). Bunshindo, Tokyo (in Japanese)
Katz ML, Shapiro C (1985) Network externalities, competition, and compatibility. Am Econ Rev 75(3):424–440
Katz ML, Shapiro C (1994) Systems competition and network effects. J Econ Perspect 8(2):93–115
Kawakami M (2012) Ashuku sareta Sangyo Hatten: Taiwan Note Pasokon Kigyou no Seichou Mekanizumu (Accelerating growth mechanism of Taiwanese notebook computer industry). The University of Nagoya Press, Nagoya (in Japanese)
Kojima K (2004) Gankou Gata Keizai Hatten Ron: Nihon Keizai, Azia Keizai, Sekai Keizai (Wild geese theory of economic development: Japanese economy, Asian economy, and global economy), vol 1. Bunshindo, Tokyo (in Japanese)
Kokuryo J (1995) Open Network Keiei: Kigyou Senryaku no Shin Chouryuu (Open network management: New trend in business strategy). Nikkei Inc., Tokyo (in Japanese)
Kokuryo J (1999) Open Architecture Senryaku: Network Jidai no Kyoudou Moderu (Open architecture strategy: Collaboration models for network era). Nikkei Inc., Tokyo (in Japanese)
Lundvall B, Johnson B, Andersen ES, Dalum B (2002) National systems of production, innovation and competence building. Res Policy 31:213–231

Marukawa T (2007) Gendai Chugoku no Sangyou: Bokkou suru Chuugoku Kigyou no Tsuyosa to Morosa (Modern industries in China: The strength and fragility of rising Chinese companies). Chuoukoron-Shinsha Inc., Tokyo (in Japanese)

Marukawa T, Yasumoto M (2010) Keitai Denwa Sangyou no Shinka Purosesu: Nihon wa naze Koritsu shitanoka (Evolution in the mobile phone industry: Why does the Japanese mobile phone industry isolate in the global market). Yuhikaku, Tokyo (in Japanese)

Maruyama M (2011) Keiei no Keizaigaku Shinban: Business Economics (Economics in management new edition: Business economics). Yuhikaku, Tokyo (in Japanese)

METI [Ministry of Economy, Trade and Industry] (2012) Hyoujunka Senryaku ni Renkei shita Chizai Manejimento Jireishuu (Case studies on intellectual property management in connection with standardization) Ministry of Economy, Trade and Industry, Tokyo (in Japanese)

Nalebuff B (2003) Bundling, tying and portfolio effects. DTI Economics Paper no. 1, Department of Trade and Industry, UK. http://www.bis.gov.uk/files/file14774.pdf

Nalebuff B (2004) Bundling as an entry barrier. Q J Econ 119:159–187

Negoro T, Sugiyama Y (2011) Tokushu Ekosisutem no Manejimentto Ron ni Yosete (Comments on special issue on ecosystem management). Organiz Sci 45(1):2–3 (in Japanese)

Negoro T, Kamaike S, Shimizu Y (2011) Fukusuu no Ekosisutemu no Renketsu Manajimento – Parareru Purattofomu no Senryaku Ron (Management for connecting plural ecosystems: Strategy of parallel platforms) Organiz Scie 45(1):45–57 (in Japanese)

Newman MEJ (2010) Networks: an introduction. Oxford University Press, Oxford

Nikkei BP, Global Net (1999) Nikkei LSI database Sekai Handoutai Seizou Souchi Shiken Tesuto Souchi Shijou Nenkan 1999 (Nikkei LSI database—Yearbook of manufacturing and testing equipment in the global semiconductor market 1999). Nikkei BP, Tokyo (in Japanese)

Nikkei BP, Global Net (2001) Nikkei LSI database Sekai Handoutai Seizou Souchi Shiken Tesuto Souchi Shijou Nenkan 1999 (Nikkei LSI database—Yearbook of manufacturing and testing equipment in the global semiconductor market 2001). Nikkei BP, Tokyo (in Japanese)

Ogawa K (2009) Kokusai hyoujunka to Jigyou Senryaku (International standards and business strategy). Hakuto Shobou, Tokyo (in Japanese)

Ogawa K (2011) Kokusai Hyoujunka to Hikaku Yuui no Kokusaibungyou Keizaiseityou (International standardization, international division of labor and economic growth). In: Watanabe T (ed) Global Biziness Senryaku (Business strategy for global market). Hakutou Shobou, Tokyo (in Japanese)

Paine RT (1966) Food web complexity and species diversity. Am Nat 100:65–75

Parker G, Van Alstyne MW (2005) Two-sided network effects: a theory of information product design. Manage Sci 51(10):1491–1504

Porter ME (2000) Location, competition, and economic development: local clusters in a global economy. Econ Dev Quar 14(1):15–34

Rochet J, Tirole J (2003) Platform competition in two-sided markets. J Eur Econ Assoc 1(4):990–1029

Rochet J, Tirole J (2004) Two-sided markets: an overview. IDEI University of Toulouse, Toulouse, Mimeo

Senoo K (2009) Gijutsuryoku de Masaru Nihon ga naze Jigyou de Makerunoka (Why does Japan, with its technological prowess, lose in business?). Diamondsha, Tokyo (in Japanese)

Shapiro C, Varian HR (1999) Information rules: a strategic guide to network economy. Harvard Business School Press, Boston, MA

Shintaku J, Eto M (2008) Konsensasu Hyojun Senryaku (Strategy for consensus standards). Nikkei Inc., Tokyo (in Japanese)

Stango V (2004) The economics of standards wars. Rev Netw Econ 3(1):1–19

Teece DJ (1977) Technology transfer by multinational firms: the resource cost of transferring technological know-how. Econ J 87(2):242–261

Teece DJ (1986) Transaction cost economics and the multinational enterprise. J Econ Behav Organ 7(1):21–45

Teece DJ (2007) Explicating dynamic capabilities: the nature and microfoudations of (sustainable) enterprise performance. Strat Manag J 28:1319–1350

Teece DJ (2011) Dynamic capabilities: a guide for managers. Ivey Bus J 75(2):29–34

Teece DJ, Pisano G, Shuen A (1997) Dynamic capabilities and strategic management. Strat Manag J 18(7):509–533

Uchida Y (2016) IoT no Shinten to Kokusai Bijinesu no Kankei ni tsuite – Gijutsu Hyoujun no Gyousaika heno torikumiwo Chushin ni (The connection of the development of IoT and international business: inter-sector initiatives in Technology Standards). Toyama University Working Papers 304, Toyama (in Japanese)

Vernon R (1966) International investment and international trade in the product cycle. Q J Econ 80(2):190–207

von Hippel E (2005) Democratizing innovation. MIT Press, Cambridge, MA

Watanabe T (ed) (2011) Bijinesu Moderu Inobesyon (Business model innovation). Hakuto Shobo, Tokyo (in Japanese)

Yamada H (2007) Hyoujunka Sensou eno Riron Busou (Theorizing for standard wars). Zeimu Keiri Kyokai, Co Ltd, Tokyo (in Japanese)

Yamada H (2008) Defakuto Sutandado no Kyousou Senryaku (Competitive strategy for de facto standards) Hakuto Shobo, Tokyo (in Japanese)

Yasumoto M, Manabe S (eds) (2017) Oupunka Senryaku – Kyoukai wo Koeru Inobesyon (Strategy for open business: innovation across boundary). Yuhikaku, Tokyo (in Japanese)

Chapter 3
Strategic Standardization and Global Ecosystem: GSM Mobile Phone Diffusion in China

After the late 1980s, US and EU platform firms employed strategic standardization and frequently developed international standards. This chapter opens the black box of how a platform firm creates network effects by focusing on strategic standardization, tapping into international standards to create network effects and making them stronger by connecting firms from developed countries and firms from developing countries in a global ecosystem.

To provide an in-depth analysis, a case study was conducted on the GSM mobile phone standard, the most successful mobile phone standard in the 1990s–2000s. GSM was developed through the consensus standard approach in the early 1990s and it was introduced to the Chinese market at the end of that decade.

The case study shows that a strategic standardization initiative by platform firms divides the architecture of a system into an open area and a closed area. The former attracts new participants from developing countries and drives market expansion, whereas the latter allows platform firms to maintain their market shares. Our evidence reveals that the GSM international standard created a global ecosystem and brought about economic growth by helping developed-country firms and developing-country firms work together in the same ecosystem.

3.1 Introduction

Thirty years ago, the development of international standards was just a dream and had rarely been achieved. As the history of length and weight measurements testifies, efforts to establish global standards often failed.[1]

In contrast, after the 1990s, the development of international standards quickly took off in several sectors. The arrival of the Internet led to the establishment of

[1] Some countries use the imperial system (yards and pounds), whereas other countries prefer the metric system (meters and kilograms).

H. Tatsumoto, *Platform Strategy for Global Markets*,
https://doi.org/10.1007/978-981-33-6789-0_3

international standards for text communication, or email, in just a decade. People were soon able to use their mobile phones anywhere in the world thanks to the international standard of global roaming. The DVD format contributed to the rapid diffusion of movie content beyond national borders.

The flourishing of global standards has significantly affected industries across the world. This chapter concentrates on the most recent standardization approach, i.e., the consensus standard, which plays a central role in the development of global standards today, and then analyzes the impact of such standards on the evolution of industries.

Many scholars have carried out theoretical and empirical studies to look into the standardization process as an important element of industrial evolution and competitiveness (David and Greenstein 1990; Shintaku et al. 2000). It has become evident that the international standardization process affects the establishment of a dominant design and determines the growth trajectory of an industry (Anderson and Tushman 1990).

Past research extensively explored the de facto and de jure standardization processes. Since the 1990s, however, a new standardization approach has become more influential across industries. For example, concerning the recording method for the DVD format (Ogawa 2009) and the interfaces used in personal computer designs (Gawer and Cusumano 2002), large numbers of organizations have established consortia to develop standards for the diffusion of their own innovations. This new approach, called the consensus standardization process, has been investigated in recent academic studies (Shintaku and Eto 2008; Tatsumoto and Takanashi 2010).

Table 3.1 compares the three standardization processes. A de facto standard is based on the market process and established thanks to the diffusion of the product. When it secures a dominant position through market trade, the product, or the technology used in the product, is perceived as the de facto standard. On the other hand, a de jure standard is based on the non-market process and, being developed by a public standardization organization, it has legal effects. Typically, this is applied to mandatory or compulsory standards, such as the ones for energy efficiency, safety and security.

The third type, i.e., the consensus standard, is provided for through a non-market process (e.g., voluntary consortium) and is diffused through the market mechanism. In other words, the consensus standard is a hybrid of the de facto and de jure approaches. In formulating consensus standards, firm develop draft standards

Table 3.1 Comparison of the three standardization approaches

Standardization approach	Standard setting	Standard diffusion
De facto standard	Market approach	Market approach
De jure standard	Non-market approach	Non-market approach
Consensus standard	Non-market approach	Market approach

by consulting with one another, similarly to what happens in the de jure process. The diffusion of a consensus standard, however, takes place through market trade, or the market process. It eventually becomes perceived as the industry standard. This situation, in which the market diffusion of a standard establishes it as the industrywide standard, is similar to what occurs in the de facto process.

There are several factors behind the increasing usage of consensus standards. Firstly, collaborations among firms have grown in importance, as the technology of products has become more complex, requiring investments that a single firm cannot afford. In addition, changes in industrial policies have given momentum to this shift, as exemplified by reforms of competition laws introduced by the governments of the US and European nations in the 1980s and their support for consortium- or forum-based efforts to develop open standards relying on firms' voluntary contributions and willingness (Miyata 1997; Tatsumoto and Ogawa 2010).

Academic research reports that consensus standards were frequently established in the 1990s whenever innovations were brought to market (Shintaku and Eto 2008). However, in many cases, the implementation of consensus standards caused firms in developed countries, which led the standardization efforts, to lose competitiveness and allowed firms from emerging countries to gather strength. In the case of the DVD standard, for example, Japanese firms took the lead in the standardization process, but today the DVD player market is mostly occupied by Chinese firms.

Standing by the principles of traditional competitive strategy, standardization processes should provide the firms that initiate them with sources of competitive advantage. The question is, then: why did the power of those leading companies wane? At the same time, what was happening in terms of industrial evolution behind the scenes? Firms have naturally learnt to use these new tools to create business opportunities and gain competitiveness. This chapter defines the process by which firms make strategic use of standard setting and exploit the resulting opportunities, and identifies strategic models and key factors through a case study dealing with the introduction of the GSM mobile phone standard to the Chinese market.

3.2 Concept Development

3.2.1 Standardization and Establishment of Global Standards

Standardization is defined as the process of selecting a certain technology in the industry. Selecting a compatible standard benefits firms and users. When the technology has network effects, the benefits of the compatible standard become greater because a larger number of users of the compatible standard multiplies the utility of that technology.

There are two types of network effects: direct network effects and indirect network effects. The former are observed within the user group of the target good itself, whereas the latter are observed across different user groups, mediated by complementary goods to the target good. Considering both the direct and indirect type, a significant portion of any system is influenced by network effects. When the system is composed of hardware and software, it is subject to network effects arising from the compatibility standard. In this sense, even languages and legal systems have network effects (Katz and Shapiro 1994).

When network effects are present, as the number of users of a standard grows, so do user benefits. This is the reason why the establishment of cross-border compatibility, or international standards, occurs ever more frequently. In the IT and electronics industries, the impact of network effects is considerable and there have been a number of efforts to establish international standards. As the examples of the Internet and the mobile phone industry show, the firms that have adopted open standards enjoy the benefits of these globally available standards.

However, the process of establishing a global standard is not without difficulties. The fundamental issue is that, even though the benefits of a unified compatibility standard are widely recognized, there are multiple options to develop a standard, and the preferences of those involved are often different. This situation is called *Battle of the Sexes* in game theory (Besen and Farrell 1994).

In order to resolve the battle of the sexes problem, a certain coordination process is required. After the Second World War, the de facto and de jure standardization processes were used as the coordination process for developing major international standards.

De facto standards result from a simple, yet powerful, international standardization process. Individual firms offer their products on the market based on their own strategy, and the technology that eventually becomes prevalent is regarded as the standard. In the case of products with strong network effects, a certain technology autonomously establishes itself as the standard through market trade, thanks to the bandwagon effect.

Standard setters may instead choose the de jure approach to establish global standards. Typically, the creation of a de jure standard is initiated by an international Standard Developing Organization (SDO), such as the International Organization for Standardization (ISO), the International Electrotechnical Commission (IEC) and the International Telecommunication Union (ITU). The creation of such a standard is a formal process that has the legitimacy to require firms to adopt it and, in extreme cases, this may be made mandatory by law. For example, de jure standards for safety or energy efficiency are often enforceable by law.

De jure standards are successful when applied domestically, since they are rooted in the legal system of a country. In the case of international application, however, there is no organization that has the authority to require firms to adopt a standard. Without legitimate power, international SDOs cannot exert strong leadership to coordinate those participating in the standard setting process. This is why de jure standards have been criticized for being just a "rubber stamp", implying that their implementation simply acknowledges what is already there as de facto standard (Besen and Farrell 1991).

Worse still, the formal process of de jure standardization lacks flexibility in the draft-writing phase. When an international SDO holds meetings to write a draft standard, there is great variation among participants in terms of nationality, technological level and market position; hence, they often need a long while to reach an agreement on the draft. By the time it is finalized and published, the resulting standard is already outdated and worthless to the firms in the market.

Since international SDOs did not have enough legitimate power and often failed to publish standards in a timely manner, some researchers voiced concern that the de jure standardization process alone might not be sufficient to form global standards (Besen and Farrell 1991; Harada 2009). Even though two standardization approaches existed, only the de facto one was efficient in establishing global standards—that is, until consensus standards gained prominence.

3.2.2 Creation of Open Standards for Complex Systems: Emergence of the Consensus Standard Approach

Historically, the de facto standardization process was the most realistic approach to creating open standards in a global ecosystem. The usage of de facto standards, however, has a limitation. Since a de facto standard is introduced by the unilateral action of a dominant firm, it is difficult to apply this approach to a system that exceeds a certain level of complexity. Prior research has demonstrated the benefits of consensus standards, rather than de facto standards, when the system requires the involvement of a greater number of participants (Farrell and Saloner 1988). Compared with de facto standards, consensus standards are characterized by consultation, or bilateral communication, during the standard setting process, which allows for the mutual exchange of information among participating firms. The consultation process has a number of clear benefits, described below.

The first is expectation of market growth. If firms have to invest massively in the target technology, they should have the prospect of achieving a vast installed base in the future to justify that investment. The non-market approach, in which firms gather to discuss the technology and share an investment roadmap, contributes to developing such a prospect among participating firms.

The second is close coordination. When technologies with numerous elements are involved, the participating firms may have different preferences as regards the available technologies. In this case, the de facto process, in which firms invest individually depending only on their own preferences and do not consult with one another, is inefficient to achieve harmonization. Conversely, when developing a consensus standard, the participating firms exchange technological information and negotiate until they agree on a draft standard; thus, this process is more suitable for a complicated system than the de facto approach.

The consensus approach relies on the non-market process, or consultation, in the standard setting phase. The mutual exchange of information among participating firms during the draft-making process helps build up robust expectations in terms of market growth, while also facilitating agreement on the target technology in detail. In the standard diffusion phase, instead, the consensus approach employs the market process, or arbitrary investment. After the standard is published, the firms invest in their compatible technology solely based on their own will. This means that they invest more if they see other technologies competing against their own. Such massive investments speed up the diffusion of the standard.

The consensus standardization process, which combines both the market approach and the non-market approach, is effective in building up expectations, strengthening coordination and diffusing the target technology. Besides, it works particularly well for large systems. Hence, it is no surprise that, after the 1990s, firms began to prefer consensus standards over the other two approaches.

3.2.3 Nature of the Consensus Standardization Process: Making the Open Area Larger

To examine the impact of consensus standardization on industrial structure, let us now look at the nature of the output from the consensus standardization process, i.e., the consensus standard.[2] The process of consensus standardization is defined as the process of designing an artifact based on consultation prior to entering the market process. Participating firms produce a draft standard according to their common notion of the product and target technology; then, they develop their own versions of the product individually. In a way, the standard serves as the basic product design.

Vast research has been conducted on the basic designs of complex artifacts in the stream of architecture studies (Baldwin and Clark 2000; Fujimoto et al. 2001; Garud et al. 2002), and the following two points have emerged.

Firstly, thanks to the process of standard setting, the target system has clearly defined interfaces. The firms involved define the component-to-component relations prior to the development of the product. These interfaces are openly shared to ensure compatibility and connectivity among the subsystems, which allows the target system to have a modular architecture.

Secondly, even though the architecture of the product is modularized, not all the modules have clearly defined interfaces. They actually come in two types: (1) modules with clearly defined interfaces, plainly indicating the product's dependency on the modules and (2) modules with vaguely defined interfaces, characterized by ambiguity in the product's dependency on the modules. The former is called the *open area* and the latter the *closed area* (Tatsumoto et al. 2009).

The two areas are associated with the business strategies of the firms setting the standard. Typically, the firms combine open and closed strategies depending on their business strategy. An *open strategy* is a policy to cooperate with other firms in

[2]See Tatsumoto (2011) for a survey of the literature on standardization, including the consensus approach.

order to expand the market of the standardized product. A *closed strategy* is a policy to exclude other firms in order to monopolize profits (Asaba 1998; Brandenburger and Nalebuff 1996). The open area becomes larger when firms emphasize the open strategy, whereas the closed area becomes larger when firms place more importance on the closed strategy.

The three approaches to open standards have different tendencies in demarcating open and closed areas. A consensus standard is more likely to produce a larger open area than the other two standards. The reason behind this is explained by the strategic behavior of the firms taking part in its drafting.

Compared with a de facto standard, for which firms unilaterally propose their ideas and other firms choose which one to accept, a consensus standard is established based on multilateral information exchanges and consultation among the entities involved. In the consultation process, the participating firms disclose their technological information, which never happens in the case of de facto standards. Since the consensus-based standard setting process requires agreement among all participants, it needs to ensure clear understanding of the technology and process by disclosing a wider range of technological information. Otherwise, the firms involved cannot reach an agreement on the draft standard. Therefore, consensus standards tend to establish larger open areas than de facto standards.

The distinction between the de jure standard and the consensus standard lies in the diffusion process. The diffusion of a de jure standard is accomplished through legal legitimacy or mandated by law. By contrast, a consensus standard does not have such legitimacy. Therefore, standard setting firms carefully consider the diffusion of their consensus standard and are motivated to establish larger open areas, so as to promote the adoption of the standard across the industry. This is why consensus standards have larger open area than de jure standards, even though both involve consultation during the draft-writing process.

While all types of standards divide a product into an open area and a closed area, consensus standards are likely to produce larger open areas. Tatsumoto and Takanashi (2010) reported that firms usually define larger open areas to promote the adoption of their standard when they choose to create a draft standard following the consensus approach.

In sum, the standardization process divides a product's architecture into two areas, open and closed. This architectural transformation leads to a new industrial environment and market growth. The firms involved, which see standardization as a strategic tool, carefully produce a draft standard, prepare their business to fit the new environment and exploit the market growth caused by standardization. This study analyzes the strategic process through which standard setting firms cause architectural transformations and exploit the resulting environment.

3.2.4 Separation of the Open and Closed Area: Impact on the Industry

When firms conduct strategic standardization, the architecture of the product in question is divided into an open area and a closed area by setting a standard. In a global ecosystem, the division of product architecture often influences the international division of labor. That is to say, international standards change industrial structures on a global scale. Let us now look in greater detail at how standardization impacts the global ecosystem.

Standardization has two types of effects in terms of market entry and rivalry, i.e., pro-competition effects and anti-competition effects (David and Steinmuller 1994). The two types of effects change the industrial structure through firm behavior.

Pro-competition effects are caused by the fact that the standardization process transforms tacit knowledge into explicit standards and discloses them to the public. Standardization reduces the cost of access to information. By referring to the standard, any firm can avail itself of technological information that was previously reserved to a handful of firms. The industry is subject to three kinds of pro-competition effects.

Firstly, the number of market entries increases, since new entrants can easily obtain the technological information that they need thanks to standardization. The presence of more firms results in intensified price competition in the market. Secondly, the variety of products becomes limited because of standardization, which further intensifies price competition. Thirdly, in the case of products with many components, the clear definition of component-to-component interfaces accelerates the development of such components and encourages complementors to provide tools and services. Improvements in the development environment contribute to cost reductions for the entire product.

The first two are direct pro-competition effects, brought about by lowering the cost of access to information. Reduced access costs increase the number of participants and intensify price competition. On the other hand, the third is an indirect pro-competition effect, caused by the diffusion of components and complementary tools/services sold by the complementors, which are called symbiont firms in the context of business ecosystem studies.

In contrast, anti-competition effects are caused by internalizing or hiding the information in a black box during the standard setting process. There are three factors which affect the industry.

Firstly, by avoiding the disclosure of sufficient technical specifications, the development of products and complementary goods compatible with the standard becomes difficult; thus, the number of new entrants in the market is limited. Secondly, an expanded installed base implies excessive switching costs for users, who might not be able to switch to other technologies. This is known as technological lock-in and limits competition among rival technologies. Third, due to the incorporation of the relevant patents into the standard and the setting of high license fees, the number of new entrants does not increase.

In light of these pro- and anti-competition effects, the nature of the open and closed area is explained as follows. The open area has more pro-competition effects, with more clearly defined and detailed interface specifications. Pro-competition effects encourage new entries and competition in the open area. In contrast, the closed area has more anti-competition effects because interface information is not sufficiently disclosed. Anti-competition effects limit new entries in the closed area.

Here, we consider a global ecosystem, which consists of firms from both developed countries and developing countries. International standardization transforms the architecture of a product and divides it into an open area and a closed area. The separation of the two areas influences the global ecosystem, comprised of developed-country firms and developing-country firms.

The open area entices new entries and fierce price competition soon starts, due to the direct competition effect. Subsequently, since the variety of product types is limited, price competition is further intensified. For the firms in developed countries, the source of differentiation is eliminated and they are exposed to price competition. Thus, many of them leave the industry altogether or explore new forms of business.

On the contrary, firms from emerging countries gain access to information that used to be owned exclusively by firms from developed countries. Since the diffusion of complementary goods is also promoted, firms from emerging economies have the opportunity to enter the market by utilizing the technology information and complementary goods obtained. Generally, firms from developing countries have the advantage of low-cost operations and can gain competitiveness vis-à-vis firms based in developed countries.

In addition, the indirect competition effects brought about by symbiont firms in the ecosystem stimulate developing-country firms to participate in the competition. The symbiont firms provide complementary goods (components, tools and services) to the developing-country firms. As symbiont firms compete against each other, they come to provide more sophisticated and advanced goods, supporting the catch-up of developing-country firms with their counterparts in developed countries. Their goods help to fill the technological gap between the developed-country firms and the developing-country firms. Consequently, more developing-country firms become members of the global ecosystem.

In the closed area, on the other hand, interface definitions remain unclear; thus, the number of new entrants to the market is limited. The technological know-how and industrial context remain tacit knowledge that potential entrants can hardly learn. Existing firms are still able to technologically differentiate themselves from their competitors, and they exploit their technological assets and competitive advantage over their rivals.

The behavior of symbiont firms also contributes to the competitive advantage of existing firms in the closed area. Without clearly defined industrywide interfaces, component providers, a type of symbiont firm, have to develop their items with customized interfaces to fit their customers' products. Their investments become their relation-specific assets, and this benefits the existing customer firms, while acting as a barrier to prevent potential new entrants from accessing the product and components markets.

In a global ecosystem, it is often the case that new entrants are firms from developing countries and incumbent firms are from developed countries. The developing-country firms try to catch up with their competitors, the developed-country firms, but it is usually hard for new entrants to prevail over the incumbents. However, international standards generate a new industrial climate, inducing the breakdown of the product architecture into two parts, the open area and the closed area. In the open area, entrant firms can easily learn the technology based on the knowledge that has been made open; on the contrary, in the closed area, existing firms retain their competitive advantage using their technological know-how and relation-specific assets. Consequently, within a global ecosystem, developing-country firms emerge as new entrants in the open area, whereas developed-country incumbents keep their competitive advantage in the closed area.

When firms conduct strategic standardization, the resulting open area entices new entrants by offering explicit knowledge, whereas the closed area allows existing firms in advantageous positions to exploit their tacit knowledge as an entry barrier. In the context of a global ecosystem, this means that international standards help developing-country firms, i.e., the new entrants, to easily catch up with developed-country incumbent firms in the open area. It also means that developed-country firms are able to maintain their competitive advantage by using their technological knowledge in the closed area. The arguments above are summarized in the following hypotheses:

Hypothesis 1: Architectural transformation driven by strategic standardization

Strategic standardization separates a product architecture into an open area and a closed area.

Hypothesis 2: Industrial growth in the open area

Hypothesis 2-1:

The increased entry of developing-country firms in the open area boosts the growth of the ecosystem.

Hypothesis 2-2:

In the open area, symbiont firms provide goods and services to developing-country newcomers and assist them in catching up with developed-country firms.

Hypothesis 3: Industrial growth in the closed area

In the closed area, platform firms from developed countries retain their competitiveness and grow.

Hypothesis 4: Effect of the interaction between the open and closed area

The market growth of the open area stimulates that of the closed area, and vice versa. In this growth process, developing-country firms gain power in the open area, whereas developed-country firms keep their advantage in the closed area. This pattern of growth creates a new form of international division of labor.

Hypothesis 1 means that a product is separated into two areas when strategic standardization by platform firms takes place. One is the open area, which is, as intended by platform firms, thoroughly standardized and its technological information is widely shared. The other is the closed area, where most elements are kept out of the standardization process and the technological information is not disclosed.

Hypotheses 2-1 and 2-2 concern market growth in the open area, where technical information and industrial context information are widely shared. Hypothesis 2-1 examines the remarkable growth of developing-country firms in the open area. The wide sharing of technical information stimulates new entries into the ecosystem. These new entrants are mainly firms from developing countries that would have previously renounced entering, since they had no access to the relevant technical information, which was internalized by the incumbent firms in developed countries. Since developing-country firms consider the open area an opportunity for catching up with developed-country firms, they rush to join the ecosystem.

Hypothesis 2-2 examines the role of symbiont firms, which provide developing-country firms with goods and services that assist them in catching up with developed-country firms. As technical information is widely shared in the open area, symbiont firms utilize it to deliver various products and services. With an increase in entries by developing-country firms, symbiont firms have the opportunity to offer turnkey systems[3] and/or core components to assist such entries. These advanced goods and services provided by symbiont firms accelerate the technological catch-up of developing-country firms.

Hypothesis 3 examines industrial growth in the closed area. Here, technical information is kept confidential, so as to discourage any new entries. The original owners of the technology maintain competitiveness and continue to grow. These existing firms are platform providers located in developed countries that carry out strategic standardization. In the closed area, therefore, platform firms from developed countries enjoy competitive advantages and maintain steady growth.

Hypothesis 4 tests the interdependence between the open area and the closed area. After the two areas are separated, the ecosystem firstly starts to grow in the open area, with new entries from developing countries. The growth of the open area stimulates that of the closed area; this is because the two areas originally constituted a single system and have retained strong network effects even after architectural separation based on standardization. In the closed area, platform firms from developed countries remain competitive and benefit from market growth.

This growth process makes the global ecosystem expand, with developing-country firms in the open area and developed-country firms in the closed area, leading to a new form of international division of labor.

Hypotheses 1 to 4 do not simply claim that the establishment of an international standard enhances the competitiveness of the standard-writing firms, which come mainly from developed countries. Rather, they point to the rise of a new form of

---

[3] A turnkey system is a system that can be operated by simply turning a key. All the know-how required to operate it is already embedded in the system, so that the user does not need to have any advanced know-how.

international division of labor, with developing-country firms growing in the open area and developed-country firms gaining greater power in the closed area, respectively. These hypotheses are tested in Sect. 3.3 below using a case study that explores the introduction of the GSM mobile phone standard to China.

3.3 Case Study

3.3.1 *Data and Methodology*

A case study was conducted to test the hypotheses proposed in the previous section. The study collects data regarding the standardization of the GSM mobile phone standard and its introduction to China. This case was chosen with the aim to investigate the impact of international standards on global ecosystems. The GSM standard is the most widely used standard among mobile phone systems, and its introduction to China played a critical role in its diffusion process. The case also reveals how strategic standardization works in the diffusion phase and how it impacts on the growth of a global ecosystem.

Data were collected following the survey method used by Yin (1984). They mainly consist of interviews (as primary sources) conducted from September 2007 to August 2008 and market statistics from literature survey (as secondary sources).

The interview survey comprises twenty interviews with eighteen organizations, including European firms and Chinese firms, over three periods. The sessions with the European organizations were conducted in September 2007, involving telecommunications infrastructure providers, a standard developing organization and European subsidiaries of Japanese telecommunications operators. A total of six interviews were carried out with five organizations, each session taking about two hours. The survey of the Chinese market took place in August 2007 and it targeted local mobile phone producers, local mobile phone design companies and semiconductor manufactures. It featured seven sessions with seven organizations, i.e., one interview per company. In June 2008, four organizations in China were interviewed, including telecommunications infrastructure providers and telecommunications service providers (one interview per company). In addition, I interviewed two Japanese telecommunications infrastructure providers, for a total of three interviews.

The secondary sources included industrial magazines, academic journals, analyst reports and technical guides and manuals by specialized publishers, namely all the issues of the NTT DoCoMo Technical Journal published by NTT DoCoMo between 1992 and 2006 and Hillebrand (2001). The latter volume, compiled by the European Telecommunications Standards Institute (ETSI), discusses the GSM standard setting process.

Our analysis consists of two steps that look at the state of industrial evolution at the industry level (Sect. 3.3.3) and at the corporate competition level (Sect. 3.3.4), by comparing the growth of the open area and the closed area of the GSM mobile communications system in China. In the second step, a firm-level analysis is performed by describing firm competition in the open area and the closed area. Finally, the hypotheses are revisited and discussed based on the case study findings (Sect. 3.4).

3.3.2 Standardization of the GSM Mobile Communications System

3.3.2.1 Process of GSM Standard Setting

GSM, a digital mobile phone technology that originated in Europe, was the most widely used mobile technology in the global market in the 1990s. The standard setting process for GSM was initiated in 1982 by the European Conference of Postal and Telecommunications Administrations and transferred to the ETSI in 1989. Importantly, this transfer symbolized the shift of the standardization process from the de jure approach to the consensus approach.

The GSM standard was supposed to become a unified standard for digital mobile phones across all European countries. However, there was no legitimate body to enforce its implementation in the EU, and each country had domestic standards for mobile communications. These standards had been established through the de jure approach; thus, they were mandatory by law, as they were closely connected to the domestic communications and industrial policies of each country. Since countries typically prioritize domestic industrial development over international compatibility, there was little chance of establishing a compatible standard all over Europe using the de jure approach. This was the reason why European mobile phone systems lacked international roaming functionalities at that time. The standard championed by the two major powers in Europe, Germany and France, and the one put forward by the Nordic countries, including Sweden and Finland, fiercely competed against each other, which raised concerns over the consolidation of the proposed specifications into a unified GSM standard. In the end, the specifications favored by the Nordic countries actually became the GSM standard.

To implement a compatibility standard for mobile phones in Europe, a new approach, the consensus approach, was introduced in 1988, when ETSI was first set up. In this new approach, great importance was attached to consensus building, because the adoption of the standard was not enforced by the European Commission but left entirely up to each of the member countries and their operators (Hillebrand 2001, Chap. 2).

In order to ensure the widest possible adoption of the published standard by the member countries, ETSI invited all European bodies related to mobile communications to participate in its development. This open policy promoted vigorous information exchanges and achieved concessions and agreement across several areas in the standard setting process. Participating bodies included operators, telecom equipment manufacturers, mobile phone makers, and semiconductor and software suppliers. Considerable emphasis was placed on the diffusion of the standard, and active entries into the market were actually observed after its publication.

As described above, the GSM standard followed the consensus approach. Firms came together and consulted with one another on a draft standard and later competed against each other over standard-compatible products. The market competition accelerated the diffusion of the standard. The standard setting activities were based on the non-market process, while its diffusion was based on the market process. The outcome of standardization, i.e., the GSM standard, has the typical features of consensus standards (Funk 2002). Indeed, it has a larger open area than other mobile phone standards developed using the de facto or de jure approach.

3.3.2.2 GSM System Architecture: Open Area and Closed Area

The GSM standard consists of three subsystems: the mobile station, the base station and the network equipment (Fig. 3.1). Each of these subsystems has a corresponding product: the mobile phone unit, the base station and the network switch. The present study defines the mobile phone industry as the supplier of mobile phone units and the infrastructure industry as the supplier of both base stations and network switches.

The GSM standard sets forth the specifications for the three subsystems and the interfaces between them. Whereas the interfaces between the subsystems are clearly defined, the interfaces inside each subsystem are not explicitly standardized. More specifically, the interfaces between the subsystems, such as the A interface and the Um interface, are open interfaces, meaning that their protocols are clearly defined and published. Conversely, the A-bis interface between the base station and the base

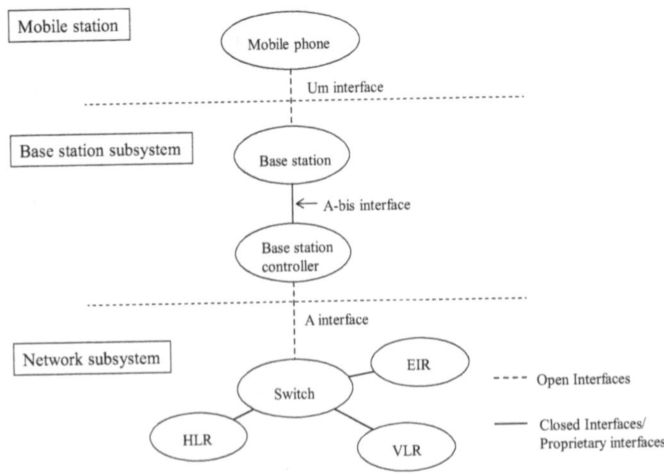

Fig. 3.1 GSM mobile phone system architecture

station controller inside the base station subsystem, for example, merely has a name but is not standardized in detail, meaning that it is a closed interface (Mi and Yin 2005, p. 70; Bekkers 2001). Since closed interfaces are proprietary, they are a source of anti-competition effects.

As far as telecommunications systems are concerned, the purpose of setting a standard is to provide reliable connectivity for mobile phones, which geographically move around and need to connect to base stations managed by different manufactures. Therefore, the mobile phone unit itself is far more standardized than the other two subsystems.

The different levels of standardization of the three subsystems also reflect the will of the entities involved in the standard setting process. The firms that led the draft-writing activities were telecom infrastructure firms, such as Ericsson and Nokia. Because their main business was providing base stations and network switches, they were motivated to keep these subsystems closed, as black boxes. On the contrary, they wanted to openly share the details of the mobile phone unit itself, an integral part of compatibility for international roaming. Indeed, they strategically guided the GSM standardization process to their advantage.

The GSM specifications for mobile phones include protocols and technical guidance, explaining the details of the communication process that a GSM-compatible mobile phone unit has to implement. Mobile phone makers and semiconductors and software suppliers refer to these specifications for their product designs. The in-depth explanations help in product development and enhance the compatibility of mobile phones. Comprehensive descriptions of the mobile phone system account for a large portion of the GSM standard documentation.

In contrast, the GSM standard documentation features limited information on the infrastructure (base station and network switch). Infrastructure systems have important functions in terms of compatibility, such as the base station control method or the caller authentication algorism of the network switch. These technologies are retained as proprietary knowledge and excluded from standardization.

In the GSM standard, the mobile phone subsystem is the open area, where technological information is sufficiently disclosed, compared with the infrastructure subsystems (base station and network switch), which are the closed area, where most of the information remains proprietary. This derives from the product architecture breakdown occurred during the GSM standardization process. To shed light on the matter, openness indices were calculated based on the GSM Phase 1 standard and compared among the subsystems, as reported in Table 3.2 below.

Openness draws a distinction between the open area and the closed area. The basic concept of openness is how much firms openly share information about design elements in the entire system. Design elements information concerns design factors, like interfaces, protocols, modules and product architecture. A high level of openness means that a large portion of the information about the design elements is shared industrywide. The idea of openness has frequently been mentioned by researchers (Garud et al. 2002; Baldwin and Clark 2000; Fujimoto et al. 2001). Nevertheless, at present, no clear definition is available to precisely quantify the concept. For the purposes of this book, openness is defined as follows:

Table 3.2 Openness of subsystems in the GSM standard

Subsystem	Main modules	Description	Openness (%)
Mobile station	– Mobile phone	Handy units carried by the users of the mobile communications system, i.e., mobile/cellular phone devices	83.60
Base station subsystem	– Base station – Control system of the base station	A group of devices that constitute a telecommunications unit (cell), i.e., telecommunications base station	9.30
Network subsystem	– Switch – HLR – VLR – EIR	Equipment which relays the location of the mobile caller to the database in real time and searches for the counterparty in response to a call, i.e., telephone exchange in general	3.80
Other	– SIM card – Instructions, etc.	How to operate the entire telecommunications network	3.30

$$Openness = \frac{Number\ of\ shared\ design\ elements}{Number\ of\ total\ design\ elements} \tag{3.1}$$

Hence, openness is the ratio of how much information is shared considering all the design elements. Shared design elements are the elements specified in the standard. The number of elements was measured as the number of sections in the standard documentation and also as the product of the number of design elements per module and the number of pages dedicated to that module. The number of design elements assesses the qualitative aspect (a larger number of elements means a wider range of technical information shared), whereas the product of the number of elements and the number of pages assesses the quantitative aspect (a larger number of pages means a higher level of detail in the information shared).

Total design elements are all the design elements in the entire system described in the standard documentation, and they are measured by counting how many modules make up the system. Following this methodology, openness is operationalized as shown in Eq. (3.2). Here, the numerator represents the number of design elements shared and the denominator the total number of design elements.

$$Openness = \frac{\sum_{i=1}^{nModules} Items_i \times Pages_i}{nModules} \tag{3.2}$$

Table 3.3 Openness matrix

Subsystem	Items	Pages	nModules	Openness	Openness (%)
Mobile station	58	1,421.5	1	82,447	83.6
Base station subsystem	41	1,184.8	2	9,174	9.3
Network subsystem	42	838.8	4	3,708	3.8
Other	18	477.8	2	3,287	3.3
Total	159	3,923.0	9	98,617	100.0

Source Calculated by the author based on Mouly and Pautet (1992)

The variables were calculated based on the "List of GSM Specifications" in Mouly and Pautet (1992), as explained below:

Items (number of sections in the standard documentation):

The standard documentation categorizes the content of the standard into sections according to the categories of the design rules. The number of sections represents the qualitative coverage of the information shared; it is measured by counting the number of sections dedicated to the subsystems of the GSM system per module, in accordance with Mouly and Pautet (1992).[4]

Pages (number of pages in the standard documentation):

The standard documentation provides numeric values and mechanisms to be followed in conjunction with the design rules. The level of detail of the descriptions varies, as some sections thoroughly specify the design rules, while other sections just roughly explain the mechanisms. The different extents of the descriptions may be regarded as the quantitative size of the design rules.

The specifications of the standard consist of two types of information. One is the description of the modules themselves (standard specifications for how the modules behave), while the other is the description of their connections with other modules (standard specifications for the interfaces among the modules). Since the latter involves multiple modules, pages were allocated equally among the relevant modules. Thus, the values in the Pages column of Table 3.3 include decimal numbers.[5]

---

[4]In the latter half of the 1990s, the GSM standard was upgraded in order to support data communication, and the impact of this revision should be taken into consideration. Newer versions of the GSM standard, however, have always ensured upward compatibility, and GSM Phase 1 has remained influential in all versions. Therefore, this book refers to GSM Phase 1 to calculate openness.

[5]Assume Subsystem A, which is comprised of two modules. Module 1 has ten sections, with 20 pages in total. The sections, however, can concern either the module itself or the interface between the two modules. When 15 pages are dedicated to the module itself and five pages to the interface, the number of pages allocated to Module 1 is adjusted as $15 + 5/2 = 17.5$. Likewise, when Module 2 has five sections and 5.5 pages after adjustment, its openness is calculated as $(17.5 + 5.5)/2 = 11.5$.

nModules:

For the total design elements, the number of modules composing each subsystem was counted based on the GSM architecture diagrams.[6]

GSM features three subsystems. Table 3.2 illustrates the variables described above and the openness of each subsystem, while Table 3.3 shows the openness matrix.

The mobile phone subsystem displays the highest level of openness (83.6%), as opposed to the limited openness of the base station and network switch (9.3% and 3.8%, respectively). These results confirm that the main area of standardization was the mobile phone, which is also in line with the evidence gathered from the interviews. Hence, in the analyses performed in the following subsections, the mobile phone is regarded as the open area and the base station as the closed area.

3.3.3 Growth of the GSM Mobile Phone Industry in China

3.3.3.1 Introduction of the GSM Mobile Communications System into China

Two years after the commencement of Europe's commercial GSM service, China introduced the GSM mobile communications system into its market. China Unicom, established in 1994, predicted that future demand for second-generation (2G) mobile phones in China would grow and decided to introduce the GSM system, which had already been put in place in Europe. China Telecom, a branch of the Ministry of Posts and Telecommunications, followed suit. China Telecom was later split and restructured as China Mobile. The real expansion of the mobile phone market began in 1999. At that time, the number of mobile phone users was 43,300 thousand and it reached 393,420 thousand in 2005 (Marukawa 2007). This book analyzes China's mobile phone industry in and after 1999.

3.3.3.2 Growth of the Market and Number of Suppliers

Figure 3.2 shows the size and number of suppliers of China's GSM market. The size of the base station market in 2002 displayed a sharp rise, which, however, does not reflect a general trend. Due to data availability constraints, Chinese local suppliers were counted as mobile phone suppliers, whereas both foreign and Chinese suppliers were counted as base station suppliers. This proves sufficient to understand the global trend regarding market participation.

The size of the mobile phone market was 17,530 thousand units in 1999 and rapidly grew to 138,940 thousand units in 2006, through fierce price competition arising from

[6]The number of patents was also taken into consideration as a potential total number of design elements, but it was concluded that it would be heavily biased due to, for instance, a concentration of patent applications in a certain area.

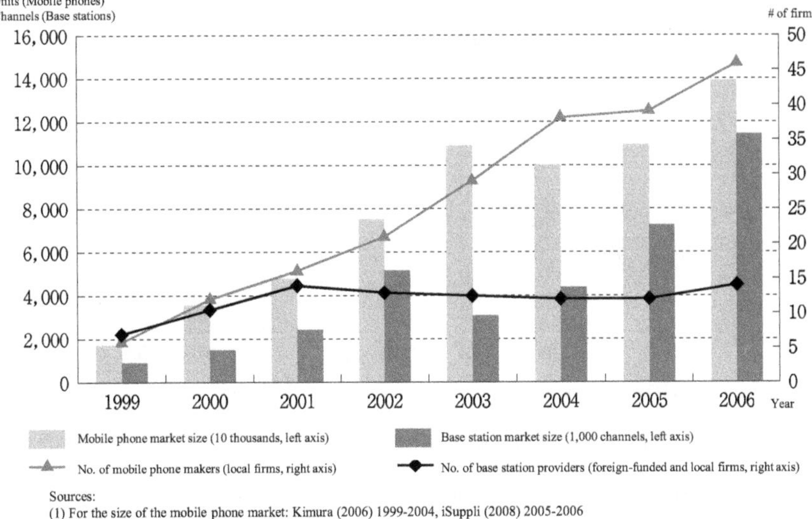

Fig. 3.2 Size and number of suppliers in the mobile phone market and the base station market

the launch of various products. This rapid market expansion required an increase in communication capability, which led to the growth of the base station market. The size of the base station market was 932 thousand channels in 1999 and increased to 11,450 thousand channels in 2006. The mobile phone and the base station originally made up a single product system. The two subsystems, therefore, are complementary to each other; when either market grows, the other market grows accordingly. In the case of GSM, the expansion of the mobile phone market stimulated the growth of the base station market.

The number of participating firms indicates that there were active entries into the mobile phone market, while entries into the base station market were very limited. The mobile phone market included fewer than ten firms in 1999, which steadily went up to more than 40 Chinese domestic suppliers by 2006. The base station market, in the meantime, saw only limited new entries, with a total of around 15 providers involved.

3.3.3.3 Mobile Phone and Base Station Market Shares

Figure 3.3 shows the market shares of domestic suppliers and foreign suppliers in China's mobile phone market. Foreign suppliers are multinational enterprises based in developed countries, whereas domestic suppliers are Chinese-funded businesses. The former include Nokia, Motorola and Samsung, while the latter include both

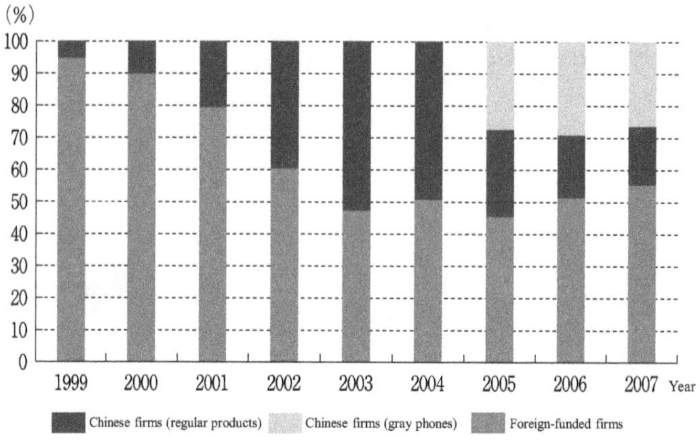

Fig. 3.3 Market shares of mobile phones in China

firms with government permission and unauthorized firms. The devices manufactured by these unauthorized suppliers are called *guerrilla mobile phones* (shānzhàijī, in Chinese) or non-regular products.[7] This book refers to them as *gray mobile phones.*

In 2005, the Chinese government relaxed its regulations on the manufacture and sale of mobile phones and completely abandoned them in 2007. As a result, today there is no distinction between authorized products and non-regular products, but they are still reported separately in statistics, based on the identity of the suppliers. Gray mobile phones, which rapidly expanded their market share after 2005 and are ubiquitous across China, are produced exclusively by domestic suppliers.

Figure 3.4 shows the market shares of base station suppliers in China, providing a different picture than that of the mobile phone market. After 1999, the base station market expanded, but with very few new entries, and foreign suppliers retained large shares. These foreign suppliers included Ericsson and Nokia, which had played an important role in the GSM standard setting process. However, China also has major telecommunications equipment companies that are top-ranking in the global market, such as Huawei and ZTE. They succeeded in technological development and secured large shares in the global market at that time. However, even these top-ranking companies were unable to occupy a substantial share of the base station market in their own homeland.

[7]Both unauthorized mobile phones and counterfeit mobile phones are collectively called guerrilla mobile phones (shānzhàijī, in Chinese). As explained in this book, this definition is applied to phone devices manufactured without government permission. It also refers to phone devices released onto the market without paying the due license fees or without passing the GSM Association's compatibility test.

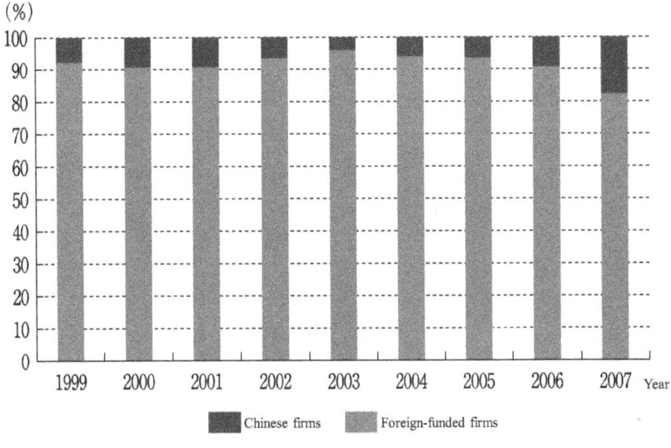

Fig. 3.4 Market shares of base stations in China

3.3.4 Comparison Between Competition Patterns in the Open Area and the Closed Area

3.3.4.1 Competition Patterns in the Open Area: Mobile Phone Market

Right after its introduction (1994), the mobile phone was used only by the wealthy class, and this remained the case until the end of the 1990s. In that period, the market was dominated by foreign mobile phone suppliers. The real expansion of the Chinese mobile phone market started in 1999, and many Chinese domestic suppliers have since entered this arena. From 2000 to 2005, in particular, Chinese domestic suppliers rapidly gained market shares and achieved substantial economic growth, but fierce competition triggered price erosion. Low mobile phone prices led to an additional increase in users and, as a consequence, the market expanded further.

This section examines the market entry of Chinese mobile phone suppliers. Through standardization, the mobile phone became the open area product of the entire GSM architecture, and this transformation caused pro-competition effects in the mobile phone industry.

Firstly, Chinese mobile phone suppliers technically caught up with developed-country suppliers by adopting the GSM standard. Since the functions of GSM mobile phones were widely standardized, they accomplished this catch-up in a very short time. In accordance with the 8th five-year plan (1991–1995), the Chinese government and the Ministry of Electric Industry's Research Institute No. 7 conducted in-house development of the mobile phone, and the development team provided the Ministry of Posts and Telecommunications with a prototype in 1996. The accumulated know-how and expertise were transferred to TV manufacturers in Xiamen, such as Xoceco and Soutec, and the development team members moved to these firms and contributed to further advances in the Chinese telecommunications industry. Since the interfaces were standardized, it was easy for domestic suppliers to fill the knowledge gap and catch up with developed-country suppliers.

Secondly, component suppliers played an important role in the catching-up efforts of Chinese mobile phone makers. Attracted by the prospect of a huge GSM market, many suppliers of parts, materials and services entered the Chinese market. Among these, semiconductor manufacturers were instrumental in supporting the catch-up of Chinese mobile phone suppliers, since they provided chips (a core component of mobile phone devices) as an integrated solution. As Chinese mobile phone suppliers were new entrants and, thus, lacked technical expertise, they greatly benefited from this turnkey solution, which included a chipset, protocol stack and reference design.

For example, Lucent (now renamed Agere) started to supply core components to the government-owned telecommunications company Eastern Communications Co., Ltd. in 1997 and to appliance manufacturer Konka Group Co., Ltd. in 1998. Analog Devices Inc. (ADI) supplied core components to ZTE, Kejian, TCL and Amoi Technology Co., Ltd., and these Chinese mobile phone makers adopted ADI components for their own development activities. Eventually, the core components of Taiwanese semiconductor manufacturer MediaTek became the industrial standard. After 2004, MediaTek integrated almost all the electronic components used in a mobile phone and provided them as a turnkey solution, compatible with the GSM standard. By using integrated components, new entrant suppliers from China developed and manufactured mobile phones without extensive technical expertise. MediaTek eventually gained a market share greater than 50%.

Other complementors, such as design and manufacturing providers, also entered the Chinese market. Because they offered mobile phone design services, they were called *design houses*. Around 1999–2000, Korean and Taiwanese design houses started to provide design and manufacturing services to Chinese mobile phone suppliers.

For example, Firm A, a Korean design house, was established in 1999 as an outsourcee providing design and manufacturing services. In the industry, this form of outsourcing is called Original Design Manufacturing (ODM), by which a service provider designs and manufactures products that are sold under the brand of the outsourcer firm. Firm A increased its sales from 2001 to 2003 and delivered mobile phone products to Chinese suppliers, such as Amoi, Bird and Panda Electronics.

After 2000, Taiwanese firms, including Compal, Arima, Quanta, Inventec and Wistron, started to provide ODM services to Chinese mobile phone suppliers. Stimulated by the success of these Korean and Taiwanese firms, Chinese design houses were also established between 2001 and 2002, mainly by Chinese engineers who had worked for foreign mobile phone suppliers.

In brief, component suppliers and design houses assisted new Chinese mobile phone suppliers, which lacked in-house technical know-how and expertise, to gain market shares over a short period of time.

3.3.4.2 Competition Patterns in the Closed Area: Base Station Market

In contrast with the mobile phone market, the base station market, which remained in the closed area of the GSM standard, featured a limited number of new entries by Chinese firms. This resulted from the absence of technical information and from the fact that the interfaces associated with the base stations were internalized and concealed.

The base station consists of two elements, i.e., the base transceiver station (BTS) and the base station controller (BSC). The interface between these two elements remained proprietary (A-bis interface) (Bekkers 2001). Since the BTS needs to work with the BSC, a newly-constructed BTS has to be connected to an existing BSC. Yet, because the interface between the BTS and the BSC is not disclosed, only the supplier that previously installed the BSC in an area can supply BTSs in that area. Such infrastructure providers were mostly the European telecommunications companies that had led the GSM standard setting initiative. These platform firms, therefore, had a competitive advantage in the additional base station market and, thus, occupied dominant positions. During the phase of GSM diffusion all over China, the closed interface (A-bis interface) brought great advantages to these pioneers (Fig. 3.5).

In the mobile phone market, or the open area of the GSM standard, various affordably priced products were released by new entrants, which attracted first-time mobile phone users. The investments made by mobile phone suppliers were fueled by the rapid growth of mobile phone users, resulting in a flourishing of new products and a constant increase in new users. The positive cycle between product investments and user expansion led to an explosion of the mobile phone market in China.

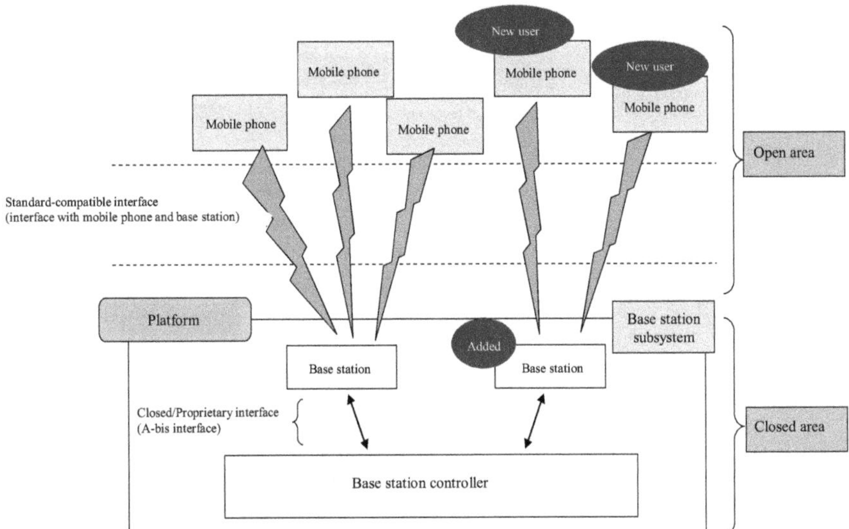

Fig. 3.5 GSM system platform structure

As the mobile phone market grew, the installed base stations required more capacity to process increasing numbers of calls and text messages and, to enhance the existing capacity, additional stations were needed. In such a case, an additional base station must have connectivity to the existing base station controller. The interface with the existing base station was, however, closed and kept proprietary. Thus, any new station had to be provided by the very same supplier that had originally installed the base station system in a given area. This meant that the pioneering equipment suppliers were in an advantageous position in the capacity enhancement investment market. These firms were mostly EU or US telecom system suppliers that had conducted strategic standardization as leading players in the GSM standard setting process.

Because of the concealment of the connection interface (A-bis interface), Chinese suppliers could neither enter the market nor increase their market shares (Mi and Yin 2005, p. 70). Even though China itself had top-ranking domestic telecommunications system providers, like Huawei and ZTE, they failed to gain market shares. This mechanism, particularly beneficial to the pioneers, was embedded in the standard and assured the advantageous position of European telecommunications system providers even in non-EU markets, such as China.

Figure 3.6 explains the development of the GSM telecommunications system in China by comparing the mobile phone and base station markets. Both markets (that is, both the open and the closed area) boomed after the end of the 1990s, with the mobile phone market expanding 9.7 times and the base station market 6.0 times (TRX represents the number of channels, which is used to measure the total amount of base stations).

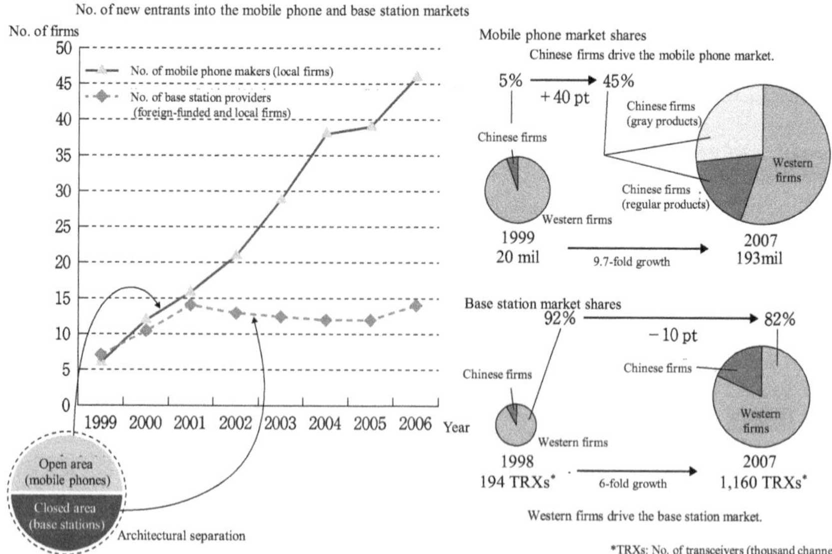

Fig. 3.6 Development of GSM mobile telecom systems in China

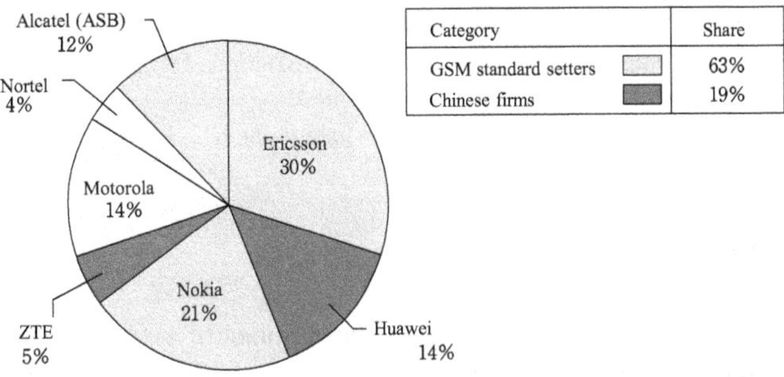

Source: Created by the author based on iSuppli (data on the numbers of units)

Fig. 3.7 GSM base station market shares in China (2007)

These two markets are clearly distinct from each other in terms of the number of market entrants. The mobile phone market, being the open area, is subject to frequent entries and the number of players increased continuously in the course of market expansion. This phenomenon is discernible in Fig. 3.2. As illustrated in Fig. 3.6, prior to its expansion (i.e., in 1999), the market was dominated by developed-country suppliers. In 2007, however, after its expansion, about half of the market was occupied by Chinese suppliers, which reveals that its growth was driven by Chinese suppliers.

The base station market also grew in conjunction with the expansion of the mobile phone market. Compared with the situation in 1998, by 2007 its size had undergone a six-fold expansion. Yet, developed-country telecommunications firms still held a dominant position. The market share of Chinese telecommunications system providers increased slightly between 1998 and 2007 but, in spite of this, Western suppliers retained strong competitiveness in the base station market.

Figure 3.7 shows the shares held by telecom system providers in China's base station market in 2007. Chinese local providers, such as Huawei and ZTE, were indeed present. Huawei, in particular, is a gigantic organization that ranks third in the global market and is also known for its strong competitiveness in the telecommunications systems market. Nonetheless, even in their own country, these providers struggled to gain certain market shares against the firms that had taken the lead in the standard setting process.[8]

Both the mobile phone and the base station are part of the GSM ecosystem. However, their growth trajectories differed substantially depending on the openness of their reference markets, meaning the level of open sharing of technical know-how. The GSM ecosystem displayed contrasting patterns of market growth in the open area and in the closed area. In the open area, or the mobile phone market, growth was

[8] With respect to the base station market in China, the present analysis focuses on the GSM system. The next-generation LTE system was introduced into China in 2014, which may cause major changes in the market shares of the base station market as a whole, including all systems.

driven by new entries of Chinese local firms. In the closed area, or the base station market, existing Western telecommunications providers remained competitive and led the market expansion.

3.4 Discussion and Conclusions

This chapter examined the difference in the number of new market participants between the mobile phone and base station markets in view of the openness provided by the GSM standard.

The process of standardization of the GSM mobile phone system was initiated by telecom infrastructure suppliers in Europe and later joined by their US counterparts. During this process, they strategically laid out a draft standard to exploit the resulting market growth; in other words, they carried out strategic standardization.

When comparing the openness of the subsystems shown in Fig. 3.2, it is evident that the overall system is divided into an open area, i.e., the mobile phone unit, and a closed area, i.e., the base station and network switch. This separation derives from the fact that the main business of the Western telecom system providers was infrastructure systems, such as base stations and exchangers. This argument confirms the validity of Hypothesis 1.

As for Hypotheses 2-1 and 2-2, the former is related to industry growth in the open area, and is supported by the substantial number of new firms that entered the mobile phone market, with Chinese newcomers eventually occupying more than half of it. Referring once again to Fig. 3.2, the track record of the firms involved in the mobile phone market further validates Hypothesis 2-1.

Concerning Hypothesis 2-2, an in-depth examination of competition patterns in the mobile phone market reveals that semiconductor manufactures and design houses played an important role in assisting the market entry of China's domestic mobile phone manufactures. These so-called symbiont firms helped Chinese mobile phone firms to catch up technologically. The semiconductor manufacturers did so by delivering their products as turnkey solutions, while the design houses offered design and manufacturing services. Both facts support Hypothesis 2-2.

Hypothesis 3 is related to industry growth in the closed area. It is supported by the number of participants in the base station market (Fig. 3.2) and their market shares (Fig. 3.7). The Western telecom system providers that led the international standardization of GSM kept specific subsystems in the closed area during the standard setting process, strategically embedding a mechanism that would give them advantages in terms of GSM system architecture. They did not standardize the A-bis interface in the base station, meaning that they wished the base station to remain a black box. Because the interfaces of the subsystems in the closed area were internalized and kept confidential, Chinese local firms could not enter that market or increase their market share.

As demonstrated by data on the GSM base station market, shown in Fig. 3.7, the firms that had initiated the GSM standard setting process, including Ericsson and

Nokia, were able to occupy a vast share of that market (63% in total). In contrast, the combined market share of Chinese local firms was merely 19%.

In the GSM standardization example, telecom system providers initiated the standard setting process. They kept the telecom infrastructure (i.e., base stations) in the closed area, excluding it from the scope of comprehensive standardization and concealing the details of the connection interfaces. These black boxes served as entry barriers against Chinese local firms, such as Huawei and ZTE.

The leadership of Western telecom infrastructure providers in the GSM standardization initiative brought the mobile device side into the open area and the infrastructure side into the closed area. Subsequently, Chinese firms were able to enter the mobile phone market and expand their shares, while Western telecom companies maintained their shares in the base station market.

This interpretation of the GSM case might be criticized, as some might point out that the number of Chinese firms entering the base station market was low because telecommunications equipment requires much larger development investments than mobile devices. In actual fact, however, there are several major telecom infrastructure providers in China. They have been highly competitive in the telecom market since the beginning, yet they could not secure a share in the GSM infrastructure market, which can only be explained by the unique structure of the GSM standard.

The above becomes even more evident when the GSM and CDMA standards are compared. China introduced two telecom systems as second-generation mobile technology, namely GSM and CDMA. CDMA is of the same generation as GSM and was standardized in the US. The standard setting of CDMA was initiated by Qualcomm, which, at that time, was a star-up company specializing in the provision of telecom semiconductors and technological licenses. Since Qualcomm's competitive edge was in digital signal processing and it produced baseband processors (the main chipset used for communication) for mobile phone makers, it wanted to keep the chipset of the phone unit confidential, whereas it did not intend the infrastructure side to be the closed area. Thus, in comparison to GSM standardization, CDMA standardization was carried out following a very different approach, based on Qualcomm's priorities.

The differences between the two systems resulted in remarkable differences in the infrastructure market. JETRO (2011, pp. 7–8) offers comprehensive data on China's telecom system market in 2009, as given in Fig. 3.8. In the GSM infrastructure market, Ericsson had the largest market share (31.6%), followed by Siemens (21.5%), Alcatel-Lucent (16.8%), Huawei (14.7%), ZTE (11.7%) and other firms (3.7%). In the CDMA infrastructure market, ZTE had the largest market share (39.2%), followed by Huawei (23.7%), Alcatel-Lucent (17.3%), Nortel (10.2%), Motorola (8.5%) and other firms (1.2%).

The combined share of Chinese firms in the GSM infrastructure market was only 26.4%, as opposed to 62.9% in the CDMA infrastructure market. In the GSM standard, the base station was placed in the closed area, which blocked the entry of Chinese local firms.

Lastly, Hypothesis 4 concerns the interactions between the open area and the closed area. Figure 3.2 shows the market share trends of both the mobile phone

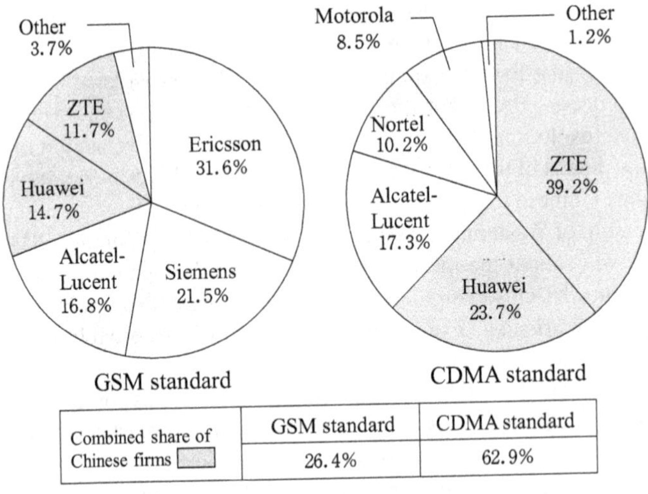

Combined share of Chinese firms	GSM standard	CDMA standard
	26.4%	62.9%

Source: JETRO (2011) pp. 7–8

Fig. 3.8 Market share trend of base stations (2009): GSM and CDMA

and the base station market. Figures 3.3 and 3.4 display the ratios between non-Chinese and Chinese suppliers in the two markets. These figures demonstrate that the market growth of the open area (mobile phone market) stimulated the growth of the closed area (base station market). The market shares in the open area confirm the rise of Chinese local firms, whereas Western telecom system providers, which led the standard setting efforts, maintained dominant market shares in the closed area. This evidence underpins the legitimacy of Hypothesis 4.

The present chapter has focused on the frequent establishment of international standards in recent years and explained their impact from the viewpoint of the standard setting process. The consensus standard approach is a new and hybrid process combining the market approach and the non-market approach, so that standard setting firms flexibly develop the standard draft that is most desirable for their business.

Since the consensus approach tends to create a larger open area, consensus standards promote the active entry of developing-country firms in the context of a global ecosystem. At the same time, the consensus approach is often influenced by the draft-writing firms, which strategically exploit the resulting market growth through their platform business. During the standard setting process, they try to configure their source of profit as a black box. Their platform business gains global competitiveness as the standard spreads to many parts of the world.

Developing-country firms grow by entering the open area, while developed-country firms remain competitive in the closed area. This can be interpreted as a new global division of labor. The Chinese GSM mobile telecommunication process is a prime example of this new international division of labor.

3.4.1 Strategic Standardization as a Platform Strategy: Defining the Open and Closed Area

Strategic standardization is a convenient tool for platform firms. The core of their business model is to make the most of strong network effects, and open standards are a powerful source of such effects. In recent years, open standards have been influential not only in the domestic sphere but also in the international sphere, as they have become global standards. The case study presented here investigates how strategic standardization impacts on global ecosystems.

During the standard setting process, platform firms identify the portion of the target system that is closely tied to their core business and keep it as a closed area, so as to ensure their own profitability. On the other hand, they set up an open area outside their core business and circulate an open standard in an effort to guarantee the growth of the entire ecosystem, of which they themselves are part. In this way, both areas, open and closed, are established within the overall architecture of the system.

Platform firms often use consensus standards to strategically transform the system architecture. By means of the consensus approach, many firms come together and exchange ideas in consortia or forums, thus achieving a more flexible and wider-scope standard setting process compared to the other standard approaches. Furthermore, they can apply the consensus standard to any part of the system, as long as they build consensus around it. This means that consensus standards are not bound by technological restrictions.

During strategic standardization, the part earmarked for the open area is standardized in detail. The technological information associated with it is openly shared, allowing new entrants to easily access the market. An increase in entries intensifies competition in the open area, consequently changing the value curve. Figure 3.9 explains this transformation.

The standardized area (standardized layer) becomes an open area, where all the players have access to the information and knowledge included in the standard. Such open access to information that was previously inaccessible to firms outside the area offers new opportunities to provide products and solutions.

The open area induces new entries, thus driving the rapid growth of the market thanks to an ever-increasing number of newcomers. After some time, the added value of that area starts to decline due to fierce competition among firms, as shown by α in Fig. 3.9. As continued entries further intensify competition, the firms that are good at cost-efficient operations survive. In the context of a global ecosystem, these firms are often based in developing countries, and the key benefit that they derive from open standards is the opportunity to catch up with existing firms.

In contrast, the firms whose core business is inside the closed area avoid competition from the outside. They take advantage of the changed environment and concentrate on the closed area, by shifting their organizational scope from the whole product to a core component, while still utilizing their knowledge of the entire system. This knowledge helps them to retain an advantage over rival firms. They exploit the growth

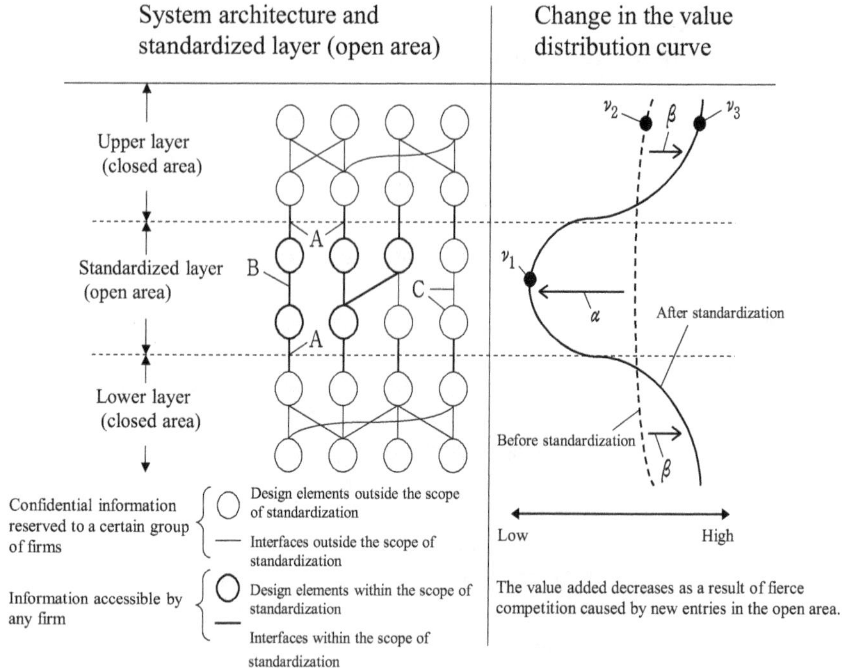

Fig. 3.9 Open area and closed area generated by strategic standardization

of the market by developing a new business model that profits from an increase in newcomer entries into the open area. Their business still resides in the closed area, but they benefit from the growth of the open area.

The corporate behavior adopted by these firms enhances profitability in the closed area. This effect, which modifies the value distribution curve, is shown by β in Fig. 3.9. Special attention must be paid to the fact that the effect of β is brought about by the new business model, which was planned during the standard setting phase. Previous studies have focused only on changes in the open area and mostly disregarded what happens in the closed area. Leading firms developing open standards also devise strategies to exploit their new environment, as demonstrated by the GSM case.

For what concerns the GSM standard, leading firms kept the base station interface confidential and secured their own competitiveness in the capacity expansion market. Once the open standard was published, the architecture of the GSM system was decoupled into an open area and a closed area. As a result, the industry grew at remarkable speed.

In the open area, frequent market entries were observed, which led to market expansion. Accordingly, telecom capacity needed to be strengthened. In other words, an increase in the installed base stations was required to boost telecom capacity. Since the interfaces in the closed area remained proprietary by virtue of the GSM standard setting activity, additional base stations could be provided only by those firms that had supplied the base stations at the outset. In this way, the telecom infrastructure market grew along with the expansion of the mobile phone market.

Both markets grew quickly but in different ways. The mobile phone market grew thanks to increased entries and intense rivalry. In the telecom infrastructure market, on the other hand, a mechanism was in place to secure the competitiveness of its forerunners. This mechanism was strategically established during standardization by the platform firms that took the lead in the standard setting process.

Figure 3.9 corroborates this mechanism. A comparison between the value of the open area after standard setting (ν_1 in Fig. 3.9) and that of the closed area before standard setting (ν_2 in Fig. 3.9) reveals that the profitability of the closed area becomes naturally higher than that of the open area if no special strategy is put in place. That said, the decline of the open area value, as shown by α, is caused by intensified competition deriving from the entry of new firms, mainly from developing countries, into the global market. The firms that make strategic use of these changes can enjoy the benefits of an increase in value added in the closed area, as indicated by β (ν_3 of Fig. 3.9). Most typically, such a strategy takes on the form of international business expansion by entering emerging countries through the use of strategic standardization. Accordingly, assuming that there are two enterprises in the closed area, if one adopts an international expansion strategy and the other does not, the former gains a competitive advantage over the other. The winner is successful because it makes use of the environmental change brought about by the effect of α, i.e., new entries from emerging countries, so that it can sustainably benefit from the effect of β.

This platform strategy utilizing the standardization principles can be modeled as follows. Platform firms design the architecture not only of the standardized layers (the areas that are standardized in detail) but also of the whole system, including the surrounding layers. They decide which area should be open or closed in such a way as to gain profitability, while the ecosystem as a whole continues to expand. Taking into account the expansion of the ecosystem in addition to their own profits means developing a new concept of division of labor, involving their suppliers as well as new market participants.

When platform firms use international standardization, they consider a new form of international division of labor. They spare no effort to identify potential market participants because the expansion of the ecosystem is achieved by new entries. With respect to the global market, incumbent firms mainly come from developed countries, whereas newcomers are from developing countries, so that platform firms naturally try to connect these two groups and form a global ecosystem.

Strategic standardization is a powerful tool for platform strategy and it is very different from the traditional practice of standard setting. The purpose of standard setting used to be to establish common interfaces in the target system, as indicated by A in Fig. 3.9, and make them publicly available. However, strategic standardization targets not only the interfaces but also the surrounding areas (e.g., layers). This is because attracting new entrants implies disclosing technological information in relevant areas. As depicted by B in Fig. 3.9, strategic standardization has an area where design elements and connecting interfaces are standardized in detail.

On the other hand, as represented by C in Fig. 3.9, there are portions of the system where design elements and technical information are not fully disclosed, even in the standardized layers. These are regarded as the closed area, where openness is limited. Unsurprisingly, platform firms single out their main business area as the closed area. The greater the degree of detail in standardization, the easier the sharing of information becomes; in other words, the openness of the standardized layers grows. The openness of an architecture can be expressed as the ratio between B and C, and a higher ratio of B to C means greater openness. In turn, greater openness has a stronger effect on the expansion of the ecosystem.

Symbiont firms might have to react to the platform firms' strategic standardization if their core business is included in the open area, since it might be seriously affected by strategic standardization. From the standpoint of new entrants, the open area provides the best opportunities for business expansion. On the other hand, existing firms in the open area might have to transform their business. In both cases, these symbiont firms need to carefully observe the course of strategic standardization and thoroughly assess standardized area B and closed area C, because the type of area determines profitability in the post-standardization phase. Strategic standardization and the resulting shifts in the value distribution curve give symbiont firms and user companies the opportunity to access the market or rethink their business to achieve increased profitability.

3.4.2 Separation Effect of the Platform: Impact of Strategic Standardization on Global Ecosystems

Figure 3.10 illustrates how strategic standardization by platform firms affects global ecosystems, i.e., the international division of labor, and how emerging firms from developing countries attain growth opportunities. Within this process, three steps can be identified in chronological order. The separation into the open and closed area and the collaboration between developed countries and emerging economies are the two strategic elements that platform firms exploit.

As discussed above, the strategic standardization carried out by platform firms splits the architecture of a single product system into two areas, i.e., the open area and the closed area.

In the first step, platform firms clearly identify the open area and the closed area. As leaders in the standard setting process, they can envisage the architectural transformations and resulting environment, once the standard is published.

In the second step, platform firms draw new participants into the open area. At the same time, they transform their own business model into one that provides a platform to help the new entrants operate in the market. Such a business model change inevitably entails organizational reforms; hence, it requires strong leadership and a strategic mindset. Platformers do their best to identify likely ecosystem entrants. Many of these new entrants are typically new players in the industry and firms from emerging economies.

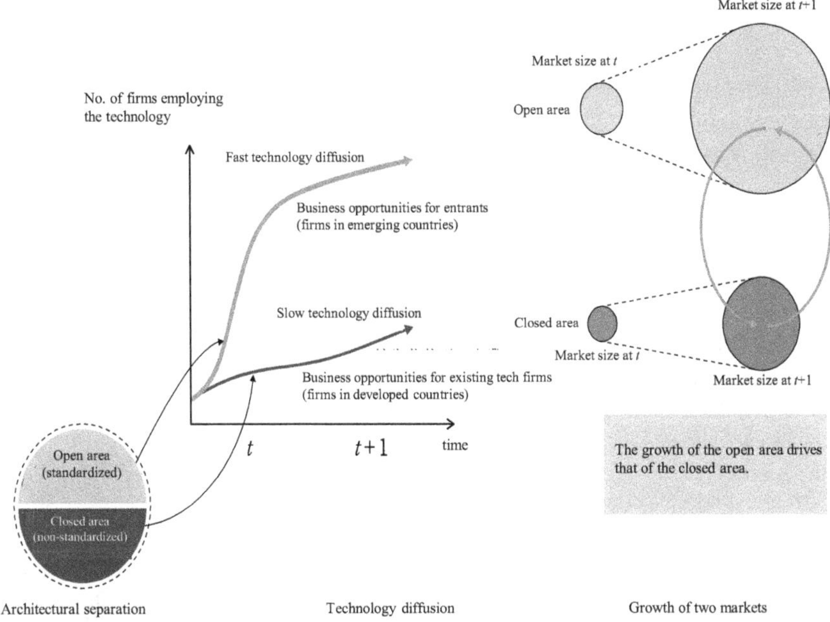

Fig. 3.10 Architectural separation and growth of entrants from emerging countries

Since the technological information concerning the open area is fully disclosed, technical expertise no longer plays a crucial role in competition. Competitive advantage is brought about by the enhancement of production capacity, based on flexible investment strategies and cost-efficient operations. In this regard, developing-country firms are relatively better off than their counterparts from developed countries.

In the third step, developing-country newcomers seize the available growth opportunities by quickly embracing the platform and investing massively in production capacity enhancements. Meanwhile, the platform firms stay in the closed area and profit from the growth of the open area by leveraging their main goods, i.e., platform products. They connect the growth of the open area and of the closed area by forming a global ecosystem that comprises both developed-country firms and developing-country firms. This new form of international division of labor generates demand in both arenas, leading to economic development.

In short, a platform strategy based on strategic standardization divides the product architecture into an open area and a closed area, which allows developed-country firms and developing-country firms to work together. On top of this, further demand is created by lower costs and larger investments made by newcomers. This effect is called *separation effect of the platform* and its impact on global markets has attracted much attention (Tatsumoto et al. 2009).

3.5 Summary

This chapter examined the introduction of the GSM mobile system into China as a case study and explained how strategic standardization by platform firms separates a single product system into two areas, i.e., the open area and the closed area.

Since the technical information is widely disclosed to the public as an open standard, this market provides newcomers with a golden opportunity. In the context of a global ecosystem, they are typically developing-country firms. These new entrants are further supported in their endeavors by the goods and services that symbiont firms can offer.

In the closed area, new entries are not promoted, since the technological information is not disclosed. However, as the open area grows, the market of the closed area also grows. Therefore, the platform firms, which supply goods and services for the closed area, can expand their business, while also maintaining strong competitiveness in the market.

This chapter shed light on how strategic standardization, as a platform strategy, encourages architectural separation (into the open area and closed area) and assists new entrants from emerging countries in joining the ecosystem, thereby helping platform firms themselves increase their profits. The next chapter explores how the strategic standardization practices by platform firms described in this chapter are aligned with the competitive strategies of platform firms explained in Chap. 2. The semiconductor equipment industry is investigated by means of an empirical quantitative analysis, using datasets from transaction network data.

References

Anderson P, Tushman ML (1990) Technological discontinuities and dominant designs. Adm Sci Q 35:604–633

Asaba S (1998) Kyousou to Kyouchou network gaibusei ga hataraku shijou deno senryaku. Organ Sci 31:44–52 (in Japanese)

Baldwin CY, Clark KB (2000) Design rules: the power of modularity. The MIT Press, Cambridge MA

Bekkers R (2001) Mobile telecommunications standards: GSM, UMTS, TETRA, and ERMES. Artech House, Boston MA

Besen SM, Farrell J (1991) The role of ITU in standardization: Pre-eminence, importance or rubber stamp? Telecommun Policy 15(4):311–321

Besen SM, Farrell J (1994) Choosing how to compete: Strategies and tactics in standardization. J Econ Perspect 8:117–131

Brandenburger AM, Nalebuff BJ (1996) Co-opetition. Doubleday Business, New York

David PA, Greenstein S (1990) The economics of compatibility standards: an introduction to recent research. Econ Innov New Technol 1:3–41

David PA, Steinmuller WE (1994) Economics of compatibility standards and competition in telecommunication networks. Inf Econ Policy 6:217–241

Farrell J, Saloner G (1988) Coordination through committees and markets. Rand J Econ 19(2):235–252

Fujimoto T, Aoshima Y, Tateishi A (2001) Business architecture seihin soshiki process no senryakuteki sekkei. Yuhikaku, Tokyo (in Japanese)
Funk JL (2002) Global competition between and within standards: the case of mobile phones, 2nd edn. Palgrave Macmillan, London
Garud R, Kumaraswamy A, Langlois R (2002) Managing in the modular age: Architectures, networks, and organizations. Blackwell, Malden MA
Gawer A, Cusumano MA (2002) Platform leadership: how Intel, Microsoft, and Cisco drive industry innovation. Harvard Business School Press, Boston MA
Harada S (2009) Kokusai hyoujunka senryaku. Denki University Press, Tokyo (in Japanese)
Hillebrand F (ed) (2001) GSM and UMTS: the creation of global mobile communication. John Wiley & Sons Inc., Hoboken NJ
JETRO (Japan External Trade Organization) (2011) Senshin Kigyou Kenkyu Sin Enerugi Bunya ni okeru Sentan Kigyou Kenkyuu (Advanced enterprise research: Research on advanced companies in the new energy field). JETRO Intellectual Property Department, Beijing (in Japanese)
Katz ML, Shapiro C (1994) Systems competition and network effects. J Econ Perspect 8(2):93–115
Marukawa T (2007) Gendai chuugoku no sangyou bokkou suru chuugoku kigyou no tsuyosa to morosa. Chuokoron-Shinsha Inc., Tokyo (in Japanese)
Mi Z, Yin S (2005) Zhong Xing Tong Xun-Quan Mian Fen San Qi Ye Feng Xian De Zhong Yong Zhi Dao (ZTE: the golden mean of comprehensively dispersing enterprise risks). Contemporary China Publishing House, Beijing (in Chinese)
Miyata Y (1997) Kyoudou kenkyuu kaihatsu to sangyou seisaku. Keiso shobo, Tokyo (in Japanese)
Mouly M, Pautet MB (1992) The GSM system for mobile communications. Telecom Publishing, Washington DC
Ogawa K (2009) Kokusai hyoujunka to Jigyou Senryaku (International standards and business strategy). Hakuto Shobou, Tokyo (in Japanese)
Shintaku J, Eto M (eds) (2008) Consensus hyoujun senryaku. Nihonkeizai shinbunsha, Tokyo (in Japanese)
Shintaku J, Konomi Y, Shibata T (2000) Defact standard no honshitsu. Yuhikaku, Tokyo (in Japanese)
Tatsumoto H (2011) Kyousou senryaku to shite no Consensus hyoujunka senryaku. MMRC Discussion paper 346, Manufacturing Management Research Center, University of Tokyo (in Japanese)
Tatsumoto H, Ogawa K (2010) Oushuu no innovation seisaku oushuu gata open innovation system. Akamon Manag Rev 9:849–872 (in Japanese)
Tatsumoto H, Takanashi C (2010) Hyoujun kikaku wo meguru kyousou senryaku Consensus hyoujun no kakuritu to rieki kakutoku wo mezasite. J Jpn Assoc Manag Syst 26:67–81 (in Japanese)
Tatsumoto H, Ogawa K, Fujimoto T (2009) Platforms and the international division of labor: a case study on Intel's platform business in the PC industry. In: Gawer A (ed) Platforms, markets and innovation. Edward Elgar, Northampton MA, pp 345–369
Yin R (1984) Case study research. Sage Publications, Beverly Hills CA

Chapter 4
Key Factors in the Success of Platform Strategy in Global Ecosystems: An Empirical Study on the Semiconductor Manufacturing Equipment Industry

This chapter examines the effectiveness of the competitive strategies of platform firms using transaction data from the semiconductor manufacturing equipment industry. For a long time, the firms in this industry had secured their competitive advantage by means of product strategies. However, when an open standard was established for the 300 mm wafer technology around the year 2000, some companies started using platform strategies. We look at the relationships among the key competitive strategies of platform firms—i.e., *positioning at the hub*, *sales rate of open standard-compatible products*, and *sales ratios in emerging markets*—by presenting an empirical analysis of these competitive actions, based on transaction data for the period considered.

Our evidence shows that the three components of platform strategy, namely, positioning at the hub, high sales rates of open standard-compatible products and high sale ratios in emerging countries, have strong interactions, so that the platform strategy is not effectual in a global ecosystem unless sales ratios in emerging countries stand at, or are higher than, a certain level. Another main takeaway is that the function of community-to-community mediation has been taken over by platform firms, as shown by the network analysis results.

4.1 Introduction

Platform firms have attracted considerable interest in academic and practitioners' circles, as they often play a central role in a business ecosystem. Eisenmann (2007) reported that 60 companies in Forbes magazine's list of the 100 Most Innovative Companies relied in some way on network effects to run their business, which is considered a platform strategy from the strategic point of view. That being the case, a substantial amount of research on platforms has been produced, including Gawer and Cusumano (2002), Rochet and Tirole (2003), Hagiu and Yoffie (2009), Hagiu (2006), Evans et al. (2006), Eisenmann et al. (2011), Gawer and Henderson (2007) and Gawer (2009).

H. Tatsumoto, *Platform Strategy for Global Markets*,
https://doi.org/10.1007/978-981-33-6789-0_4

These studies have in common such concepts as *network effects*, *companies providing complementary products or services* and *open standards* and explain the importance of managing the whole business ecosystem. Japanese investigations on strategic standardization and the open and closed area strategy (Asaba 1998; Shintaku et al. 2000; Shintaku and Eto 2008; Yamada 2008; Senoo 2009; Ogawa 2009, 2014; Watanabe 2011) also feature the notion of leading platform firms and companies pursuing platform strategies. Their conclusions are mostly similar to those of the above European and American analyses, which suggests that this area is at the center of international attention.

Yet, the above research presents some problematic aspects. First of all, it mostly consists of case studies or theoretical studies, whereas quantitative empirical analyses are notably absent. This means that there is still little empirical evidence as to whether the strategies adopted by platform firms, like *positioning at the hub* and *strategic standardization*, mentioned in Chap. 2, are actually effective and under what conditions they are effective. Given the significant influence of platform firms today, it is truly remarkable that hardly any empirical studies have been undertaken. More recently, especially in the field of econometrics, quantitative analyses measuring the extent of network effects have been performed (Clement and Ohashi 2005; Corts and Lederman 2009). Nonetheless, these investigations focus mainly on pricing strategy, without offering a broader, clearer perspective on the effects of, and conditions for, platform strategies. Another little understood issue is what kind of interactions occur between platform firms' business expansion into emerging countries and their platform strategies, although several reports point out that platform firms become more influential as they penetrate the markets of emerging countries, as shown by the case of the telecommunications industry described in Chap. 3.

To examine the effectiveness of platform strategies, this chapter presents an empirical study using semiconductor manufacturing equipment transaction data from around the year 2000, when the generation of the technology shifted to the 300 mm wafer.

Semiconductor manufacturing equipment includes various kinds of machines, such as exposure machines, coater developers and etchers, which are orchestrated to constitute one production line. Since the machines in a production line have to come from the same generation, defined by the miniaturized size and the wafer diameter, the industry develops roadmaps for semiconductor manufacturing and sets forth open standards for compatibility among different devices. These activities intensified in the late 1990s, when the prices of semiconductor manufacturing equipment increased sharply. Under such circumstances, the standard for the 300 mm wafer diameter was established. The 300 mm standard prescribed a wide spectrum of standardization elements associated with fabs, including specifications for the wafer diameter, for the shapes of semiconductor materials and for automatic transfer systems and CIM software.

The 300 mm standard is said to have had a great impact on the global ecosystem of semiconductor manufacturing. This empirical study explores the competitive actions of semiconductor manufacturing equipment providers in the process of establishing open standards. Traditionally, these equipment firms most actively implemented product strategies, which measure competitiveness based on the technological level of products. However, as mentioned above, when open standards became more important, some of them shifted to platform strategies.

This chapter focuses on the *positioning at the hub* strategy, one of the basic strategies of platform firms. In addition, it examines the relationship between this strategy and the other platform strategies, like *sales rates of open standard-compatible products* and *sales ratios in emerging markets*, from an empirical perspective.

A panel dataset was prepared for the empirical analysis, based on a combination of data on semiconductor manufacturing equipment transactions between equipment providers and semiconductor manufacturers and sales amounts in the equipment market. To estimate the effectiveness of each strategy, a multiple regression analysis was performed, using both models with and without interactions among the strategies. To compensate for heterogeneity among individual firms, firm dummies, company size (number of employees) and variety of process tools offered were included in the models as control variables. The sales value of manufacturing equipment per company was used as the dependent variable.

Our empirical study estimated how the positioning at the hub strategy affects sales amounts in relation to the other two competitive strategies regarding sales ratios. In sum, the three components of platform strategy, i.e., positioning at the hub, high sales ratios of open standard-compatible products and high sales rates in emerging countries, have strong mutual interactions.

The most interesting finding from our analysis was that high sales ratios in emerging countries are an essential prerequisite to make the platform strategy work. Positioning at the hub and high sales ratios of open standard-compatible products have both positive and negative effects on sales amounts, depending on the level of sales in emerging countries. In a model that considers the three competitive strategies, high betweenness centrality has a positive effect on sales when the ratio of sales in emerging countries is about 40%, while it has a negative effect on sales when the ratio is lower than 15%; its effect is unclear when the ratio is in between. This model further suggests that, for a firm whose ratio of sales in emerging countries is average or lower than average, high betweenness centrality has a negative effect on sales as the sales ratio of open standard-compatible products increases. In contrast, for a firm whose ratio of sales in emerging countries is higher than the average, high betweenness centrality has a positive effect on sales as the sales ratio of open standard-compatible products increases. A position with high betweenness centrality in the transaction network means a hub node. In summary, the positioning at the hub strategy, a basic pillar of any platform strategy, is estimated to have a significantly negative effect on sales amount, unless the ratio of sales in emerging countries is above a certain threshold.

4.2 Previous Studies on Platform Strategy and Hypothesis Building

4.2.1 Previous Studies on Platform Strategy

Positioning in Transaction Networks

As explained in Chap. 2, the most fundamental strategy for platform firms is positioning at the hub in a transaction network. Both theoretical research and case studies support the idea that positioning at the hub enhances the competitiveness of a platform firm (Kokuryo 1995, 1999; Fujitsu Research Institute and Negoro Lab 2013). By positioning itself at the hub, a platform firm can acquire *information benefit* and *control benefit* in the transaction network. These advantages are based on the classic social network theory.

The *information benefit* is an advantage by which the firm positioning itself at the hub obtains faster access to relevant information than the other companies in the network. The *control benefit* is an advantage by which the firm positioning itself at the hub can select, or even partially modify, the information transmitted to the other companies in the network for its own benefit.

Gawer and Cusumano (2002) examined the concept of platform leadership by illustrating how Intel built relationships with other firms in peripheral industries (including providers of complementary products or services), collected information from them and set up open standards by consolidating the information collected. These behaviors are regarded as exploiting the advantages arising from positioning at the hub.

In order to prove that a firm is placed at the hub of a transaction network in terms of information betweenness, betweenness centrality, an indicator for network structures, is used in the field of social network research (Freeman 1977; Wasserman and Faust 1994). Betweenness centrality focuses on information transmission within a network and assesses how essential a node (i.e., a company) is to information transmission in that network. A node company that acts as an intermediary among several groups or between two groups with large numbers of members has high betweenness centrality. See Appendix 1 to this chapter for further details about betweenness centrality.

Positioning at the hub in transaction networks, particularly with high betweenness centrality, enables a firm to mediate among multiple markets, giving it a fundamental advantage in implementing the two-sided market strategy. The two-sided market strategy can be applied to a broader scope when an open standard is widespread throughout the industry, exerting network effects across several markets. This is why the platform firm positioning itself at the hub becomes more competitive.

Attitudes Toward Open Standards

Researchers have reported that platform firms proactively pursue open standards that involve the whole industry. As mentioned in Chap. 1, depending on their standardization approach, open standards are divided into three categories: de facto, de jure and consensus standards. A de facto standard is established by a single firm, which directly determines its profit, often resulting in a fierce standards war with rival companies advocating other, non-compatible standards. The war over video game console standards, which is frequently cited in reports and dissertations, is a typical standards war about selecting a de facto standard (Ikuine 2012). Platform firms, of course, actively respond to open standards.

De jure standards, which are established by public organizations, are known to rely on formal steps. Leading public standardization organizations include the International Organization for Standardization (ISO) and the International Electrotechnical Commission (IEC). While de facto standards indicate *standards in actual fact*, de jure standards mean *legal standards*, since standardization is carried out by public bodies and diffusion may be forcibly implemented by means of legislation. This is why de jure standards are most often used for safety standards. Although platform firms deal with this type of open standards as well, international de jure standards suffer from the lack of an enforcement body having authority to spread them beyond national borders; as a result, they are criticized for being mere rubber stamps for de facto standards (Besen and Farrell 1991). It is considered difficult to establish international standards solely through the de jure approach, because no public standard setting organization has enough authority to legally acknowledge a technology as a single, unified international standard (Besen and Farrell 1991; Harada 2009).

In recent years, consensus standards have been increasingly employed to create international open standards (Shintaku and Eto 2008). Consensus standardization is a way to set standards through a consortium or a forum established by several companies. As seen in Chap. 1, this approach has gained popularity since the mid-1980s. In order to establish a large-scale open standard that covers a whole business ecosystem, platform firms frequently utilize the consensus approach (Shintaku and Eto 2008). A consensus standard is not formed by a single company but involves collaboration among platform firms, symbiont firms and user firms. The Universal Serial Bus (USB) standard (Gawer and Cusumano 2002) and the 300 mm wafer standard, the subject of this chapter, are categorized as consensus standards.

A consensus standard is quite different from a de facto standard, in that it is unclear whether platform firms can expect significant profits directly from the diffusion of the standard. In spite of that, there are two reasons why platform firms routinely utilize the consensus approach. First of all, the consensus approach can create an open standard for a vast and complex system through discussion with various companies. Without the platform firms' coordinating function, establishing a unified standard for a complex system would prove impossible. Secondly, the spread of an open standard develops the ecosystem and, in turn, increases the chances of boosting profits, even though profiting directly from the standard may not be expected. For these two reasons, platform firms recurrently opt for the consensus approach and utilize open standards for their products and services.

Attitudes Toward Emerging Markets

Not many empirical studies thus far have focused on the attitude of platform firms toward emerging markets, and the ones that have done so simply report facts based on case studies. These investigations have been performed mostly by Japanese researchers.

Kawakami (2012) described the detailed process by which Intel, a leading platform firm, actively supported the notebook computer industry in Taiwan and eventually developed global demand for personal computers. Imai and Kyo (2009) and Marukawa and Yasumoto (2010) showed that MediaTek of Taiwan, a semiconductor platform firm, provided the mobile device industry of China with vast amounts of platform products, which led to the growth of that industry. Needless to say, various open standards related to PCs and the GSM standard must have contributed to this growth too, but their role was not discussed in these works.

Very few studies explicitly explored the relationship between international standardization and the business expansion of firms into emerging markets. A noteworthy exception is Ogawa (2009), which did not specifically refer to platform firms, but pointed out that international standardization promotes the division of labor for system products in such manners that are acceptable to industries in emerging countries; in addition, it explained what corporate behaviors are observed among firms utilizing standardization. In more recent research contributions, these behaviors have been regarded as consistent with those of platform firms utilizing strategic standardization.

The above studies argued that platform firms enhance the success of the market by providing industries in emerging economies with products as turnkey solutions, thus helping them catch up with the developed world. As they have already accumulated enough technologies, industries in advanced countries do not necessarily need turnkey solutions, which might rather deprive them of their differentiating factors. On the other hand, turnkey products are welcomed by industries in emerging economies, which have not accumulated enough technologies, because they provide a good opportunity for them to catch up with developed nations. In addition, it was pointed out that such turnkey solutions are bound to thrive even more once open standards are widespread, because the diffusion of standards makes it easier to develop and provide turnkey solutions compatible with them (Imai and Kyo 2009; Ogawa 2009).

Following the setting of an open standard, common understanding regarding its gigantic and complicated system is established within the industry, which makes it easier to identify the parts of the system that should be provided as turnkey solutions. Imai and Kyo (2009) noted that MediaTek, a Taiwanese semiconductor company, provided semiconductor chips and electronic boards as turnkey solutions to Chinese mobile phone makers when the GSM standard was introduced into China. Ogawa (2009) also reported that Sanyo Electric Co, Ltd. offered turnkey solutions consisting of optical components and mechanical components to Chinese manufactures of DVD players compatible with the DVD standard. As these examples suggest, when platform firms develop and provide turnkey products based on open standards, they tend to gear them toward industries in emerging countries, with fewer accumulated technologies, since those firms are most likely to actively embrace the products. Against this backdrop, platform firms are thought to expand their sales of open standard-compatible products in emerging markets.

The following sections use transaction data on the semiconductor manufacturing equipment industry to conduct an empirical analysis around the effectiveness of the competitive strategies implemented by platform firms. In this industry, firms used to rely on product strategy to secure their competitive advantage but, once an open standard was created for the 300 mm wafer technology around the year 2000, some of them began pursuing a platform strategy. The effectiveness of this platform strategy is analyzed below using transaction network panel data from that period.

4.2.2 Research Design

The analysis was performed primarily on transaction network data in the semiconductor manufacturing equipment industry. A semiconductor manufacturer purchases manufacturing equipment to manufacture semiconductor devices. Most of the providers of semiconductor manufacturing equipment are independent; they have close relationships with certain semiconductor manufacturers but, from time to time, they also enter into opportunistic transactions with other fabs. This makes the transaction networks between semiconductor manufacturers and equipment providers particularly complex. In the field of semiconductor manufacturing processes, open standardization started to gain ground in the 1990s, in order to keep up with increasing technology complexity and soaring investments. As a result, network externalities were frequently generated among several fields and complex business ecosystems were developed one after another.

Our statistical analysis was preceded by a preliminary survey, which was performed based on interview data and the available literature. The interviews took place over two time periods, between 2005 and 2008. The interviewees included 20 companies (30 people in total and, specifically, six device makers, three equipment providers, six transfer equipment providers, two material companies and one software developer), as well as two trade associations. The Interview List provided at the end of this book offers more information about the organizations interviewed. The interviews were carried out with such a variety of entities to avoid any strong information bias, which would have been inevitable if a single field (e.g., manufacturing equipment companies) had been covered, since a business ecosystem consists of a variety of entities.[1] An empirical analysis was performed, building on the preliminary survey, to test the hypotheses stated in Sect. 4.2.4.

---

[1]The interview results are summarized in Tomita and Tatsumoto (2008), which also includes additional sessions of the 2008 survey.

4.2.3 Research Subjects and Hypothesis Building

This study examines the process of 300 mm standardization in the semiconductor manufacturing equipment industry. Since its name comes from the diameter of the silicon wafer, the 300 mm standard refers to a generation of technology characterized by a larger diameter than before, specified as 300 mm. Semiconductor devices are manufactured by forming fine electric circuits on a silicon wafer. The generation of semiconductors is defined by two factors: minimum linewidth of the electronic circuit (called design rule or process rule) and diameter of the silicon wafer (wafer size). The finer the design rule, the more semiconductor devices can be obtained from the same area of silicon wafer. Likewise, the bigger the wafer size, the more semiconductor devices can be obtained from a single wafer. While the design rule was in the order of micrometers in the 1990s, it entered into nanometers around 2000, reaching as little as 32 nm in the latest generation (1 nm is one billionth of a meter). Regarding the wafer size, although 6–8 inches was a popular size in the 1990s, a bigger diameter of 12 inches (300 mm) has been widely adopted in modern fabs produced after 2000.

Semiconductor manufacturing involves various technological elements, such as lithography machines (exposure machines), which perform patterning of electric circuits, coater developers, etchers, which shave off silicon in accordance with the pattern, sputters, which form various membranes, heating furnaces, cleansing equipment, automatic transfer equipment for transferring the silicon wafers and construction techniques for clean rooms. These wide-ranging technologies all need to be integrated together in every generation. Open standards, which define the wafer diameter and other parameters to be used by the different machines, are beneficial to all the parties involved thanks to their shared roadmap and specifically selected generation.

4.2.3.1 History of Open Standards in the Semiconductor Industry

In the 1970s and 1980s, firms individually selected technology generations depending on their own investment strategy (Space 2000). Since the 1990s, however, the semiconductor industry and the semiconductor manufacturing equipment industry have been sharing and jointly circulating information on semiconductor generations, based on a plan describing target generations developed by the International Technology Roadmap for Semiconductors (ITRS) or through consortia for semiconductor technology development, such as the Semiconductor Manufacturing Technology (SEMATECH) (Tarui 2008). Several factors led to this shift. In particular, the complication and diversification of semiconductor manufacturing processes and equipment made it difficult for a single company to cover all the processes on its own. Also, the players in the industry needed to reduce risks and eliminate duplication in research and development (R&D) investment by sharing R&D milestones with each other, since process development and R&D in manufacturing equipment required

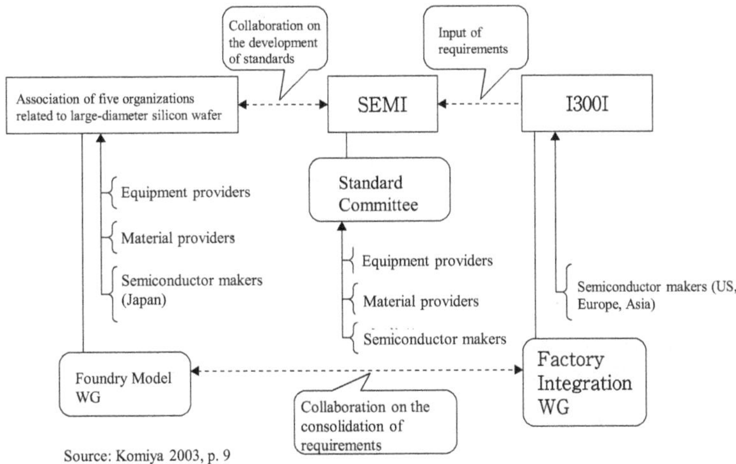

Fig. 4.1 Parties involved in 300 mm standardization activities and SEMI

massive amounts of investments. As a consequence, information was actively shared and standardization was strongly encouraged at the industrial level.

At that point, however, firms were still competing over the wafer diameter and open standards were still arising from de facto standardization. For example, the line adopted by IBM became the de facto standard for the 6-inch generation, while the one adopted by Intel became the de facto standard for the 8-inch generation.

When the next generation (300 mm generation = 12-inch generation) was being discussed in 1994, the firms involved realized that the amount of capital investment for that generation would rise sharply and started highlighting the importance of formal standardization. Various consortia, alliances, and initiatives were established to this end. It is worth noting that the 300 mm line standardization was carried out according to the consensus approach, rather than the conventional de facto approach.

The standardization of the 300 mm wafer began in 1994, with the involvement of Japanese and overseas industry players (Fig. 4.1). In Japan, five organizations concerned with semiconductors and their manufacturing equipment, i.e., JEIDA, JSNM, SIRIJ, EIAJ and SEAJ,[2] joined hands to organize J300 and, in the US, SEMATECH played a leading role in organizing I300I. J300 and I300I featured repeated meetings and workshops and promoted standardization organizations. However, as semiconductor companies using semiconductor manufacturing equipment were the main members of J300 and I300I, their activities mostly consisted in compiling a list of requirements for 300 mm fabs. The actual standardization activities were carried out by SEMI, Semiconductor Equipment and Materials International, a consortium of semiconductor material and manufacturing equipment providers, based on user specifications.

[2]JEIDA stands for Japan Electronic Industry Development Association, JSNA for Japan Society of Newer Metals, SIRIJ for Semiconductor Industry Research Institute Japan, EIAJ for Electronic Industries Association of Japan and SEAJ for Semiconductor Equipment Association of Japan.

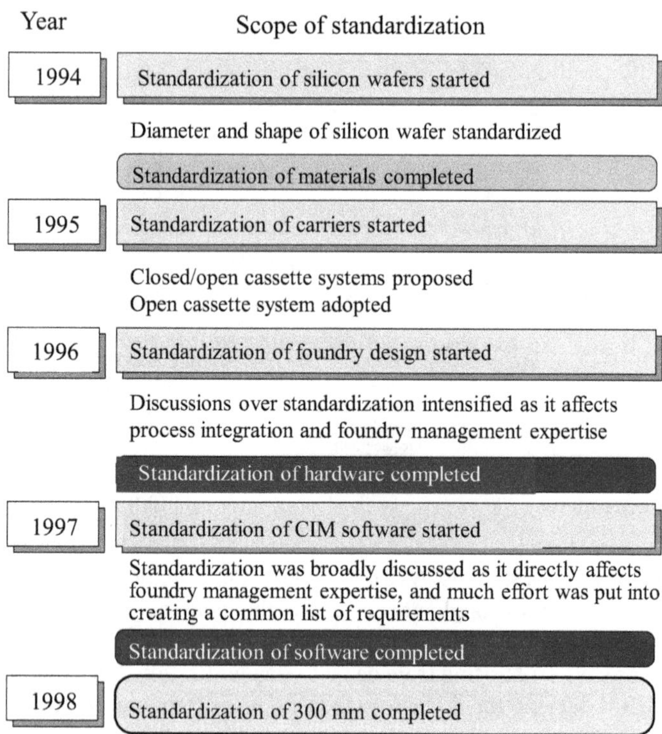

Fig. 4.2 Timeline of 300 mm standardization activities

SEMI, which had a great impact on the interface standards for 300 mm manufacturing equipment, began the process of standardizing the shape of the silicon wafer in 1994, standardized automatic transfer equipment and its data protocol and completed its standardization efforts in 1998 (Komiya 2003). Products (semiconductor manufacturing equipment) compatible with the 300 mm standard first appeared on the market in the early 2000s.[3]

4.2.3.2 History of 300 Mm Standardization Activities

The activities regarding 300 mm standardization began in 1994. As shown in Fig. 4.2, the first step was to establish standards for the geometry of the wafer. The carriers that convey the wafers, fab design and CIM (Computer Integrated Manufacturing) were standardized stepwise in 1995, 1996 and 1997, respectively. The reason why the wafer was standardized first was that wafer size, quantity and pitch (interval

[3]According to annual reports published by Tokyo Electron, a major semiconductor manufacturing equipment provider, its sales of products compatible with the 300 mm standard exceeded 50% of the total revenue of its semiconductor equipment division in 2003 (Tokyo Electron 2003).

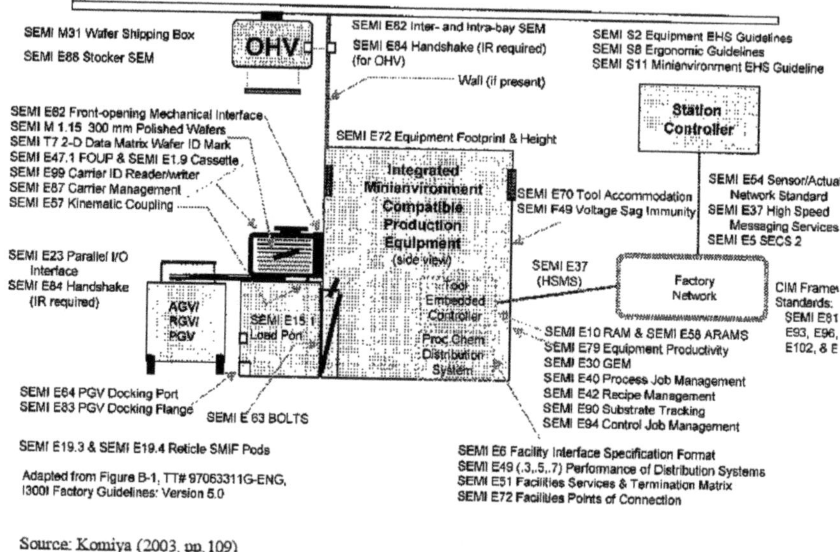

Fig. 4.3 SEMI international standards developed for 300 mm fabs

between wafers) would influence the interfaces between carriers, transfer machines and manufacturing equipment.

Although there were phases in which building consensus among the stakeholders was difficult, during each step of system development standardization, in-depth discussions were held to reach broad agreement.

The greatest standardization efforts were devoted to the production system, which serves as the preparatory step for the whole semiconductor manufacturing process. Figure 4.3 outlines the standardized transfer system, in which all the components constitute the standard governing wafer transfer. They include the physical shape of the wafer, the carrier for containing and conveying the wafer, the transfer machine for conveying the carrier, the load port that receives the carrier from the transfer machine, the manufacturing equipment that receives the wafer from the load port and micro-processes it and the software controlling the entire production system (CIM software).

The two biggest differences are detected between the foundry compatible with the 300 mm standard and the conventional foundry. The first is the introduction of localized clean technology. As localized clean technology was introduced into the 300 mm foundry, the design capacity for the clean room became less critical than before. Moreover, since many specifications were standardized for the transfer system and the machines could be evaluated by Selete (a joint venture of ten Japanese semiconductor companies) and I300I, the start of operation of the system was achieved much more easily, with fewer communication issues than ever before. The significantly shorter time for the ramp-up of a 300 mm foundry—the time from construction to

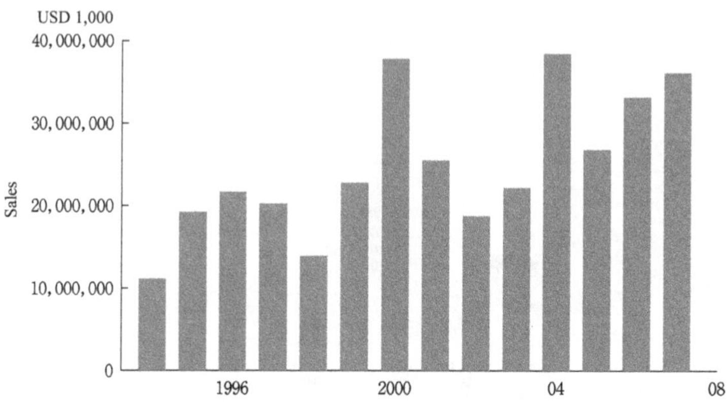

Source: Created from Nikkei-BP/Global Net (1999, 2001) and Global Net (2005, 2009). Original data extracted from the Semiconductor Equipment Test/Inspection Worldwide Annual Issues.

Fig. 4.4 Sales of semiconductor manufacturing equipment (all regions)

the start of mass-production—owes to the effects of standardization. In addition, the use of a closed carrier no longer requires intangible know-how on fab management.

The second unique aspect of the 300 mm standard is the intelligent foundry. By networking the different pieces of equipment on the floor, the system automatically and intelligently manages the recipe and the stock level of each process. Some advanced 200 mm foundries had already adopted intelligent operations, but this was only partially implemented and did not cover all the equipment. As the new 300 mm foundry has a unified standard framework in place, the system automatically calculates optimal material handling. Systems that support the 300 mm framework came to be sold as CIM systems.

Figure 4.4 shows sales trends in the semiconductor manufacturing equipment industry (in USD1,000). Capital investment peaked in 2000 and 2004. It was initially believed that the 300 mm generation manufacturing equipment would become widely adopted by 2001. Nevertheless, after the IT bubble burst in 2001, semiconductor manufacturers started to slash their investments and full-scale adoption of 300 mm-compatible equipment began only in 2003–2004.

4.2.3.3 Changes Brought About by the 300 mm Standard in the Semiconductor Industry and the Semiconductor Manufacturing Equipment Industry

To enhance the understanding of the hypothesis building and empirical analysis presented in the following sections, this subsection briefly describes what the semiconductor industry and the semiconductor manufacturing equipment industry were going through during the period under investigation.

The 300 mm standard, which was standardized in the 1990s, became popular in and after 2000. For the 300 mm generation, the open standardization process was carried out using the consensus approach, in response to a steep rise in capital investment costs.

Prior to the 300 mm generation, semiconductor manufacturers in advanced countries individually purchased the equipment that they needed based on a dyadic (one-to-one) relationship with equipment providers. In this scenario, the semiconductor firms asked for customization and then, to protect their technological know-how, performed adjustments to the interfaces between machines by themselves, thereby accumulating technical expertise.

For what concerns the 300 mm generation, however, this kind of advantage in technical know-how declined due to two key factors: (i) the adoption of closed carriers eliminated the need for foundry management expertise in dealing, for example, with clean rooms, which had been crucial for semiconductor manufacturers until then; and (ii) foundries became more and more intelligent, so that recipe management and inventory control were integrated into the equipment itself and even overall foundry management know-how was provided as part of the CIM software.

Despite this reduction in technical advantage, foundries in advanced countries, particularly in Japan, were not very willing to switch to the 300 mm open standard. As a consequence, they had to fight an uphill battle against foundries in emerging nations, which were quickly bridging the competitiveness gap.

The equipment industry also experienced major changes. Equipment providers that continued to exclusively supply foundries in Japan and other advanced nations failed to increase their sales. Those that succeeded in improving market performance were the providers that strategically sold 300 mm-compatible machines and interface adjustment know-how as a package to foundries in emerging nations. Semiconductor manufacturers in emerging countries did not have sufficient levels of foundry operation know-how but were keen to improve their technical endowment to reach advanced-country standards.

Japanese semiconductor firms across the board struggled in the competition with semiconductor makers from emerging nations, which were taking advantage of their position as followers. On the other hand, the semiconductor manufacturing equipment providers that proactively focused on sales in emerging economies successfully developed, together with the foundries there, as platform firms.

Hardly any entity involved in the 300 mm standardization effort had anticipated such industrial changes. The consortium blindly believed that the machines compatible with the 300 mm standard would be used by foundries in advanced nations. The semiconductor manufacturers and semiconductor manufacturing equipment providers of advanced countries had devoted a great deal of effort to establishing the 300 mm standard; hence, they uniformly thought that the foundries of the developed world would be using 300 mm-compatible equipment. In hindsight, however, the 300 mm-compatible equipment was mostly installed in the foundries of emerging countries.

4.2.4 Hypothesis Building

Regarding the shift to the 300 mm generation of semiconductor manufacturing equipment that occurred around 2000, this study proposes four hypotheses about the actions taken by semiconductor manufacturing equipment providers. These all reflect corporate behaviors resulting from the strategy of platform firms.

The first hypothesis has to do with positioning in transaction networks. As seen in Sect. 4.2.1 on previous studies, one of the basic strategic policies of platform firms is to position themselves at the hub of transaction networks. They enhance the impact of their overall strategy not only through positioning at the hub but also by making use of open standards and by entering into emerging markets. Examining these strategic actions requires that a hypothesis on positioning strategy be constructed first.

In a previous study (Wasserman and Faust 1994), the hub in transaction networks was expressed as betweenness centrality of the indicators representing the network structure. Betweenness centrality is a network indicator characterizing nodes on a network in such a way that it becomes larger when the two networks bridged are both larger or the number of nodes to be bridged is lower.

Hypothesis 1: Hypothesis about the actions of platform firms regarding positioning in transaction networks

Semiconductor manufacturing equipment providers positioned in a place with high betweenness centrality in transaction networks achieve greater market performance than others.

This hypothesis assumes that platform firms increase their competitive edge through positioning at the hub. This might seem too straightforward, but it has been pointed out by a number of studies on platform firms (Iansiti and Levien 2004; Negoro and Ajiro 2011; Kokuryo 1999; Inoue et al. 2011); nevertheless, it has hardly been verified empirically. Besides, Hypotheses 2 and 3 below are grounded in the positioning strategy, which makes it particularly important to formulate Hypothesis 1.

Next, building on Hypothesis 1, Hypothesis 2 about the strategy of platform firms regarding open standards is constructed. The 300 mm standard of the semiconductor manufacturing equipment industry is an open standard. Active adoption of products compatible with an open standard boosts the spread of a new technology, which results in the growth of the ecosystem for the platform firm(s). The spread of the open standard brings about complementarity among several manufacturing equipment markets, generating network effects across them. The platform firm(s) positioned at the hub can enjoy increased opportunities to pursue the two-sided market strategy and the bundling strategy, which makes it easier to improve market performance, compared with other average players in the industry.

Hypothesis 2: Hypothesis about the actions of platform firms regarding open standards

Semiconductor manufacturing equipment providers in positions with high betweenness centrality achieve greater market performance than other providers by selling equipment compatible with open standards.

The processes of the semiconductor industry started to be provided as a platform in the late 1990s, when platform firms focused their efforts on offering manufacturing equipment in the form of turnkey solutions (Shintaku et al. 2008; Tatsumoto et al. 2009). The manufacturing of semiconductor devices requires a variety of manufacturing equipment, and semiconductor manufacturers combined the different pieces of equipment to build a device production process. It would be ideal if a production line could be designed by verifying all process machines one at a time, which obviously costs too much. The provision of the processes as a platform is the solution to this challenge.

Hypothesis 3 deals with business expansion into emerging markets. Previous studies have suggested that platform firms provide markets with turnkey solutions when a large-scale open standard is established, citing emerging countries as the most promising customers for such turnkey solutions. Industries in advanced countries that have already accumulated enough technology find these solutions not only unnecessary but likely to take away their outstanding advantage. On the other hand, turnkey solutions greatly benefit industries in emerging countries, which have accumulated only a limited amount of technology, by providing them with a golden opportunity to catch up with the developed world.

Hypothesis 3: Hypothesis about the actions of platform firms regarding emerging countries

Semiconductor manufacturing equipment providers in positions with high betweenness centrality achieve greater market performance than other providers by selecting industries from emerging countries as customers.

Finally, Hypothesis 4 on the relationship between expansion into emerging countries and strategic use of open standards is developed. Hypotheses 2 and 3 addressed the strategic use of open standards and the business expansion into emerging countries pursued by platform firms. Now let us look at the interaction between these two components. Open standardization refers to the process of describing technical information in the form of a set of standard specifications, so that the information is widely shared. Equipment that is compatible with such an open standard is advantageous to firms in emerging countries, willing to catch up with the developed world, while firms in advanced countries have limited use for it. Hence, when implemented together, strategic use of open standards and business expansion into emerging countries are expected to exert a combined effect. This concept is expressed as Hypothesis 4 below.

Hypothesis 4: Hypothesis about the relationship between expansion into emerging countries and strategic use of open standards

Semiconductor manufacturing equipment providers in positions with high betweenness centrality successfully increase their sales of manufacturing equipment compatible with open standards by selecting industries from emerging countries as customers.

The following empirical research examines and verifies Hypotheses 1 to 4 proposed above.

4.3 Empirical Analysis

4.3.1 Data

The purpose of this empirical study is to clarify the effectiveness of the platform strategies implemented by semiconductor manufacturing equipment providers, which are used as our unit of analysis. The subject of the investigation are the transaction networks between semiconductor manufacturers and semiconductor manufacturing equipment providers.

More specifically, the transaction networks in the semiconductor manufacturing equipment industry of East Asia (Japan, South Korea and Taiwan) are considered, since this region is the global center of semiconductor manufacture and large capital investments are made there. The dataset used for the empirical study was prepared by combining the following three types of data, along with financial information on the firms covered in the study (business reports and public information from their websites):

(1) Transaction data between semiconductor manufacturers and semiconductor manufacturing equipment providers (data on delivery of manufacturing equipment to each foundry);
(2) Sales data of each equipment provider in each machine market;
(3) Profile data of each foundry.

Data on delivery to major semiconductor foundries in Asia were used as (1) transaction data (ED Research 1998, 2007). Sales data in the semiconductor manufacturing equipment market (2) were used to assess market performance (Nikkei BP and Global Net 1999, 2001; Global Net 2005, 2009). Data on each foundry (3) comprised information about foundries (SEMI 2005, 2009), such as the generation to which the introduced manufacturing equipment (design rules and wafer size) belonged. (1) Transaction data and (2) sales data are panel data by year and by equipment provider.

The transaction data used cover 8,798 manufacturing equipment transactions carried out by major foundries in Japan, Korea and Taiwan between 1994 and 2006. They include 37 semiconductor manufacturers in Japan, Korea and Taiwan and 26 semiconductor manufacturing equipment providers in Japan, the US and Europe. The combined sales of these 26 firms account for about 70% of the worldwide total sales over 10 of the 13 years covered by the manufacturing equipment sales data to be provided later. While equipment providers vary from very small to large firms, the 26 providers examined in this study can be classified as large-sized firms engaged in global business.

The transaction data were available as bipartite graphs showing the relationships between the semiconductor makers and the equipment providers, and the transaction networks were derived and rebuilt from these data on an annual basis. The networks involve both the semiconductor manufacturers and the equipment providers. A network variable, betweenness centrality, to be explained later, was calculated from the transaction networks and was regareded as each firm's network feature. Using betweenness centrality, panel data about the 26 equipment providers were prepared for the 13 years between 1994 and 2006. Then, performance variables, such as market shares and strategy variables, were added to the dataset to be analyzed.

Market sales data contained figures for eight kinds of manufacturing equipment, such as exposure machines and coater developers. These eight different kinds of machines cannot constitute a production line unless they are all of the same generation, which is why roadmaps and open standards are needed. In the period from 2000 to 2003, the semiconductor technology transitioned to the 300 mm generation. Open standards strongly affected sales data for the period covered by this dataset. Although market sales data were added by region, the sales data for Japan, South Korea and Taiwan were used in order to match the areas with the transaction data.

To assess overall sales of 300 mm-compatible equipment, whether a firm delivered equipment to a foundry compatible with the 300 mm standard was determined based on transaction data (delivery data) and foundry profile. Delivery to a 300 mm-compatible foundry suggests that the firm delivered manufacturing equipment compatible with the 300 mm standard.

Hence, the dataset needed for the analysis was prepared from transaction data, sales data, and foundry profile data. Using this dataset, several regression models were developed for comparison; performance was adopted as the dependent (objective) variable, whereas network, platform strategy, etc. were used as the independent (explanatory) variables. The models were built as linear additive models and regression models with interaction effects, as described later.

4.3.2 Variables

The following variables were created and inserted into the regression models.

4.3.2.1 Performance Variable

Sales amount of manufacturing equipment (jtk_sales):

The sales amount was selected as the performance variable because it accounts for a firm's competitive edge in the equipment market. Based on sales data, the sales amounts of the Japanese, Korean, and Taiwanese markets, the three regions investigated here, were calculated. IMF yearly exchange rates were used to adjust currencies and the values were standardized to US dollars (USD1,000).

4.3.2.2 Competitive Strategy Variables

Betweenness Centrality (bts):

As explained in the theoretical discussion of Chap. 2, a platform strategy relies on using a bridging position within a network of firms that connects several markets. In order to represent the properties of a network, several network centrality indexes have been devised (Wasserman and Faust 1994; Newman 2010), among which betweenness centrality is known to represent the bridging property that connects two groups of firms (Freeman 1977).

The betweenness centrality index emphasizes how well a firm mediates or transfers information within a network. Firms that make up a network are regarded as exchanging information via the network. If a firm is in a position where no information can be disseminated across the network without its presence, this means that it plays an important role in terms of information transmission. Without this firm, the other firms in the network would be completely cut off from each other and would not be able to mutually exchange information. Such a position in a network is called a hub. A hub may be formed either by a single firm or by a group of firms. In actuality, the criterion of being cut off from the network is too strict and bts can be assessed by how a node is positioned on the shortest path between other nodes. Simply put, bts grows when (1) a firm mediates between larger networks or (2) the networks consist of fewer firms.[4,5]

---

[4]This study used the igraph package of statistical software R (Csardi and Nepusz 2006) to create transaction networks for each year, consisting of semiconductor manufacturers and semiconductor manufacturing equipment providers, based on the transaction data previously mentioned. Betweenness centrality was then calculated assuming the transaction networks to be nondirectional graphs, after deleting duplicated ties.

[5]While transaction networks themselves are unidirectional, information networks created along with them are bidirectional (nondirectional). This is why the transaction networks were regarded as nondirectional data in this research. Importantly, though it is a small issue, I deleted duplicated ties, which are regarded as giving weighting to the exchanged information. Hence, betweenness centrality can take duplicated ties into account in some models. In this study, however, betweenness centrality was calculated based on networks with duplicated ties removed considering that (i) betweenness centrality should explain only the arrival of information and (ii) another variable (nProc) in the regression models gives the weighting function.

Sales ratio of products compatible with the open standard (300 mm standard) (Ro300, Ratio of 300 mm standard-compatible products).

Platform firms make use of the diffusion of open standards as a typical platform strategy. The extent to which platform firms used the 300 mm semiconductor foundry standard in their business was inserted into the regression models as a strategy variable of the sales ratio of open standard-compatible products. The ratio was calculated by looking at the procurement data of semiconductor manufacturers and by extracting the number of transactions for manufacturing equipment delivered to 300 mm semiconductor foundries and to non-300 mm semiconductor foundries. A fractional number was then created, with the former information as the numerator and the sum of the former and the latter as the denominator.

Sales ratio of products in emerging markets (EMSR, emerging market sales ratio).

The sales ratio of products in emerging countries was calculated by dividing the sales amount in emerging economies by the total sales of a semiconductor manufacturing equipment provider, on an annual basis. The sales data concerned Japan, South Korea and Taiwan, with Japan representing an advanced market and South Korea and Taiwan emerging markets.

Control Variables

The following variables were created and inserted into the regression models as control variables, not represented by the network and strategy variables above, to capture firm-specific properties and inter-annual economic changes.

Year Dummies (YEAR DUMMY):

To control for inter-annual economic changes, year dummies were included in all the regression models.

Firm Dummies (FIRM DUMMY):

To capture specific properties of individual firms that cannot be expressed by the network and strategy variables, firm dummies were created and included in all the regression models.

Number of Employees (nEmpl):

Since an alternative hypothesis states that company size has an impact on its market share, the number of employees of each firm was extracted from annual reports and its logarithm was included in some of the regression models.

Number of processes supported (nProc):

The production of semiconductor devices comprises many kinds of processes, such as patterning, etching and heat treatment. These are performed using manufacturing equipment provided by semiconductor manufacturing equipment providers. The larger the number of processes a firm's manufacturing equipment products support, the more it earns. The number of processes supported by the equipment provider was included in some of the regression models.

Statistic	N	Mean	St.Dev.	Min	Max
jtk_sales	182	606, 577.90	733, 778.80	19, 507	3, 939, 386
bts	182	30.598	37.135	0	161.202
nEmpl	182	15, 652.56	35, 319.99	160	323, 827
nProc	182	2.819	1.751	1	8
Ro300	182	0.145	0.235	0	1
EMSR	182	0.328	0.14	0.014	0.702

(a) Descriptive statistics of the created variables

	jtk_sales	bts	*n*Empl	*n*Proc	Ro300	EMSR
jtk_sales	1					
bts	0.743	1				
nEmpl	−0.021	−0.142	1			
nProc	0.534	0.507	−0.181	1		
Ro300	0.132	−0.03	−0.019	0.046	1	
EMSR	0.334	0.222	−0.153	0.08	0.615	1

(b) Correlation table between the created variables

Fig. 4.5 Descriptive statistics and correlation coefficients of the variables

Figure 4.5 illustrates the descriptive statistics and correlation coefficients of all the variables used in this study. The problem of multi-collinearity was disregarded in this regression analysis, since the correlation table exhibits no variables with coefficients equal to 0.8 or greater.[6]

4.4 Results

The analysis was carried out in two stages. In the first stage, a simple linear additive regression model was used with the ordinary least squares (OLS) method for estimation. A linear additive model is a regression model that features only a linear expression and is employed as a generalized approach in empirical studies in the field of business management. On the contrary, a regression model with interaction effects has an interaction term representing the product of two variables.

In linear additive models, we cannot detect the dependence of a variable on the level of the other variables but simply the existence of other variables. This is the reason why the interaction models (regressions with interaction effects) were considered in the second stage. In interaction models, the effect of a variable depends on the level of the other variables. For instance, an interaction model can show that the

[6]Statistics software R was used to estimate the regression models (R Development Core Team 2011).

Impact of the 300 mm standard on the equipment industry (linear additive model)

	Dependent variable					
	jtk_sales					
	ml (1)	m2 (2)	m3 (3)	m4 (4)	m5 (5)	m5.1 (6)
bts	4,705.954*** (1,546.756)	4,614.143*** (1,554.867)	3,743.769** (1,566.500)	3,736.850** (1,586.517)	3,515.084** (1,598.603)	0.178
nEmpl		−0.903 (1.278)	−0.620 (1.260)	−0.622 (1.265)	−0.563 (1.266)	−0.027
nProc			95,858.800** (38,356.380)	96,169.210** (39,671.700)	95,206.060** (39,656.500)	0.227
Ro300				12,428.750 (384,633.800)	−28,289.060 (386,213.600)	−0.009
EMSR					409,382.700 (376,873.500)	0.078
Constant	1,408,612.000*** (202,384.800)	1,418,087.000*** (203,177.500)	971,207.400*** (267,962.200)	969,971.100*** (271,611.000)	882,423.100*** (283,151.700)	0.000
firm dmmy	Yes	Yes	Yes	Yes	Yes	Yes
year dmmy	Yes	Yes	Yes	Yes	Yes	Yes
Observations	182	182	182	182	182	182
AIC	5,166	5,167	5,161	5,163	5,164	5,164
R^2	0.847	0.848	0.854	0.854	0.855	0.855
Adjusted R^2	0.809	0.809	0.815	0.814	0.814	0.814
F Statistic	22.318*** (df=36;145)	21.654*** (df=37;144)	22.016*** (df=38;143)	21.302*** (df=39;142)	20.825*** (df=40;141)	20.825*** (df=40;141)

Note: $p<0.1$;$p<0.05$;$p<0.01$

Fig. 4.6 Estimates of regression models (linear additive models)

effect of positioning at the hub additively increases when the firm positioned at the hub promotes the use of an open standard. This means that the effect of positioning at the hub depends on the level of diffusion of the open standard. In this respect, interaction models depend on the situation of other variables.

Figures 4.6 and 4.7 provide the estimation results based on the linear additive models and the interaction models, respectively.

4.4.1 Results of the Regression Models (Linear Additive Models)

The dependent variable in the regression models is the performance variable (sales in the Japanese, South Korean and Taiwanese markets: jtk_sales), as discussed in Sect. 4.3.2. The regression models from m1 to m5 include 26 firm dummies, year dummies for 13 years and the number of employees (nEmpl) for statistical control, in order to clearly observe any effects. Model m5.1 is the same as m5, except that it is used to estimate standardized partial regression coefficients. The results of the regression coefficients, standard errors and probabilities of statistical significance observed in the regression analysis are provided in Fig. 4.6.

Impact of the 300 mm standard on the equipment industry (interaction model)

	Dependent variable				
	jtk_sales				
	m6 (1)	m7 (2)	m8 (3)	m9 (4)	m9.1 (5)
bts	2,404.475 (1,538.809)	−9,636.307*** (3,589.126)	−9,798.974*** (3,619.599)	−2,330.778 (3,833.895)	−0.118
nEmpl	0.060 (1.209)	−0.231 (1.161)	−0.181 (1.170)	−0.148 (1.103)	−0.007
nProc	104,839.800*** (37,655.920)	114,709.700*** (36,174.650)	117,874.100*** (37,022.720)	152,874.600*** (35,851.920)	0.365
Ro300	−46,163.030 (366,048.400)	137,653.900 (354,221.600)	−39,207.210 (544,054.800)	1,260,631.000** (596,321.800)	0.405
EMSR	326,534.400 (357,736.100)	−304,188.300 (383,195.300)	−396,643.100 (440,570.100)	−103,829.300 (420,969.800)	−0.020
bts × Ro300	16,201.330*** (3,931.131)	4,914.665 (4,857.229)	4,275.438 (5,094.097)	−82,604.430*** (20,889.410)	−1.072
bts × EMSR		33,658.870*** (9,147.659)	33,904.670*** (9,192.474)	13,722.980 (9,869.565)	0.282
Ro300 × EMSR			455,671.800 (1,061,611.000)	−2,325,296.000* (1,193,809.000)	−0.380
bts × Ro300 × EMSR				183,789.000*** (43,006.550)	1.264
Constant	812,588.700*** (268,883.200)	1,132,572.000*** (271,878.500)	1,151,245.000*** (276,128.300)	814,253.600*** (272,006.600)	0.000
firm dmmy	Yes	Yes	Yes	Yes	Yes
year dmmy	Yes	Yes	Yes	Yes	Yes
Observations	182	182	182	182	182
AIC	5,145	5,130	5,132	5,111	5,111
R^2	0.871	0.882	0.883	0.896	0.896
Adjusted R^2	0.833	0.847	0.846	0.863	0.863
F Statistic	23.035*** (df=41;140)	24.823*** (df=42;139)	24.107*** (df=43;138)	26.922*** (df=44;137)	26.922*** (df=44;137)

Note: $p<0.1$;$p<0.05$;$p<0.01$

Fig. 4.7 Estimates of regression models (interaction models)

Model m1 uses betweenness centrality as its network variable and firm dummies (for 26 companies) and year dummies (for 13 years) as its control variables. The coefficient of determination of m1 is 0.809, which clearly demonstrates that betweenness centrality (bts) has a significant positive impact on the sales amount. The bts variable has statistical significance at the 1% level.

Model m2 has three control variables, i.e., number of employees (nEmpl), firm dummies (for 26 companies) and year dummies (for 13 years), to observe how betweenness centrality is influenced. The partial regression coefficient remains positive, though it becomes smaller, with statistical significance at the 1% level.

Model m3 incorporates the number of processes supported (nProc), in addition to betweenness centrality and the three control variables mentioned above. The sign of nProc is positive, with statistical significance at the 5% level. Models m4 and m5 likewise manifest similar levels of statistical significance. This suggests that providing equipment for a greater number of processes has a positive impact on the sales amount.

Model m4 includes the sales ratio of products compatible with the 300 mm standard (Ro300) as a strategy variable, while model m5 also features EMSR, which represents the sales ratio of products in emerging countries. Both variables are proven to have no statistical significance in both m4 and m5.

Interpreting models m1 through to m5 points to the following two findings. First of all, a firm in a transaction network that is in a position with higher betweenness centrality (that is to say, at a hub), tends to generate higher sales. Secondly, firms providing equipment that supports more processes tend to generate higher sales.

The sales ratio of open standard-compatible products (Ro300) and the sales ratio of products in emerging countries (EMSR), on the other hand, are found to be statistically insignificant. This means that these regression models cannot clarify the effects of strategic activities, such as using the spread of open standards as a strategic tool, which is a typical platform strategy, and achieving sales value expansion by promoting sales in emerging countries.

These results might be due to the adoption of simple linear additive models for the regression analysis in Fig. 4.6. The estimations in Fig. 4.6 were carried out by assuming the three firm strategies (taking a position with high betweenness centrality, sales ratio of products compatible with open standards, and sales ratio of products in emerging countries) as independent from each other. However, these strategies are likely to have mutual interactions, as stated in Hypothesis 4.

In order to shed light on this matter, it is necessary to estimate regression models that take the interactions between betweenness centrality and the other strategies into account. Section 4.4.2 extends the estimations above using regression models with interaction effects, i.e., models that feature interaction terms.

4.4.2 Results of the Regression Models (Regression Models with Interaction Effects)

The regression analysis based on simple linear additive models concluded that the impacts of Ro300 and EMSR are not statistically significant. This section re-estimates these effects by expanding the regression models into regression models with interaction effects. The results obtained are provided in Fig. 4.7.

As for the coefficient of determination and Akaike information criterion (AIC) of each model from m6 to m9, their coefficients of determination are all above 0.8, which means that each regression model suitably explains the distribution of the observed values. The F-test statistic is statistically significant in all the regression models. AIC, which indicates the degree of fit of a model with consideration given to the number of parameters, is the lowest in m9, meaning that m9 is best fitting among all the models. The standardized partial regression coefficients based on m9.1 show that the interaction term among bts, Ro300 and EMSR exerts the greatest effect, followed by the one for bts and Ro300. The number of processes, nProc, is significantly positive in all the models.

In regression models with interaction effects, evaluating the variables included is rather complicated, because the impact of a variable changes depending on the magnitude of another variable. This effect cannot be measured based solely on the estimation results in Fig. 4.7. Hence, in order to assess the models, the following paragraphs attempt to plot marginal effect diagrams, with the marginal effect on the vertical axis and the moderator variable on the horizontal axis. Note that the 95% confident interval for the marginal effect is displayed as a dashed line in these diagrams (see Appendix 2 for details on marginal effects and moderator variables).

Model m6 refers to a regression model with an interaction term between bts and Ro300. The interaction term is positive and statistically significant, while the main effect of bts is not significant. The main effect of Ro300 is negative, though also not significant.

As mentioned, regression models with interaction effects are relatively difficult to interpret. The fact that the main effect of bts is not statistically significant does not mean that bts has no effect at all in model m6; rather, it should be interpreted to mean that the effect of bts cannot be statistically significant without dependency on (or interaction with) the effect of Ro300. In other words, when m5 (Fig. 4.6) and m6 (Fig. 4.7) are compared, the effect of bts shown in m5 already encompasses the interaction with Ro300, while the interaction model constructed as m6 produces no statistical significance in the main effect of bts but it does produce significance in the interaction term between bts and Ro300. That is to say, the effect of bts is explained largely by the effect of interaction dependent on the value of Ro300.

Conversely, the strong interaction between betweenness centrality (bts) and the open standard (Ro300) suggests that high betweenness centrality alone cannot exert a positive impact on the sales amount. The reason why betweenness centrality seemed to have a positive impact in m5 is that the model did not properly consider the effect of the open standard. There was in fact a non-negligible interaction between betweenness centrality and the open standard. One way of interpreting this is that betweenness centrality has a positive and statistically significant effect on the sales amount only when the firm with high betweenness centrality takes advantage of the open standard.

The next step is to verify the impact of Ro300 on variations in the effect of bts by drawing marginal effect diagrams. The marginal effect represents the effect of bts, defined as ME(bts) $= \frac{\Delta jtk\_sales}{\Delta bts}$ in a regression model equation. The marginal effect of bts is dependent on the value of the moderator variable, Ro300. The solid line in Fig. 4.8 represents the marginal effect, and its confidence interval (±95%) is

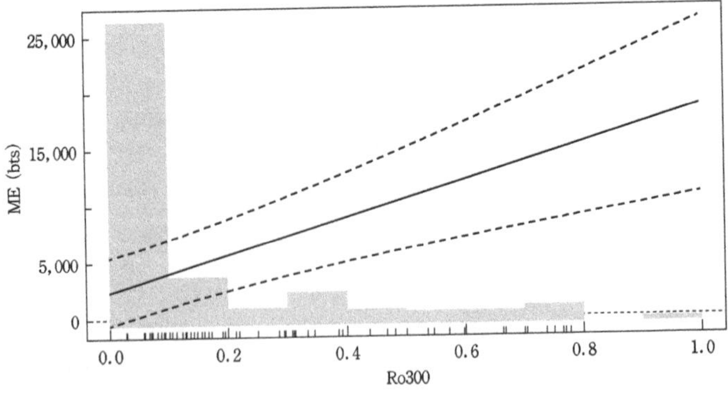

Fig. 4.8 Marginal effects of sales ratio of 300 mm-compatible products and betweenness centrality (model m6)

displayed as a dashed line. In order to express the range of values for the moderator variable, the x axis is given a lag and a histogram is also included to show frequency.

Figure 4.8 demonstrates that the marginal effect of betweenness centrality (bts) becomes greater as Ro300 increases. In other words, firms with high betweenness centrality achieve higher sales when they increase the sales ratio of open standard-compatible products. The marginal effect of betweenness centrality, ME(bts), can be divided into two ranges:

(i) ME(bts) is not statistically significant when Ro300 is smaller than 0.05;
(ii) ME(bts) is significantly positive when Ro300 is greater than 0.05.

This leads to the conclusion that Ro300 has an overall significantly positive effect and no significantly negative effect at any point along its spectrum. The interaction between the strategy variables confirms the presence of effects arising from the use of open standards as part of a firm's platform strategy, as theorized in Hypothesis 2.

Model m7 incorporates an interaction between bts and EMSR. The interaction term between bts and EMSR is found to be positively significant, while the main effect of bts is negatively significant. The main effect of EMSR is also estimated to be negative, but it is not statistically significant. Since the main effect and the interaction effect have opposite signs, the total effect cannot be understood unless it is evaluated on a marginal effect diagram. Model m7 is used to assess the marginal effect of bts and EMSR. The marginal effect of bts in m7 depends on the value of EMSR. Therefore, the diagram has EMSR on the horizontal axis and ME(bts) on the vertical axis, as shown in Fig. 4.9. The solid line is the regression line of ME(bts) with respect to EMSR, while the dotted lines show its 95% confidence interval. The histogram represents the frequency distribution of EMSR.

In model m7, the main effect of bts is significantly negative. This indicates that, when EMSR = 0, ME(bts) is negative and its 95% confidence interval does not include the case of ME(bts) = 0, as shown in Fig. 4.9. The slope of the regression line points to a positive relationship between EMSR and ME(bts), which translates into a positive interaction between bts and EMSR.

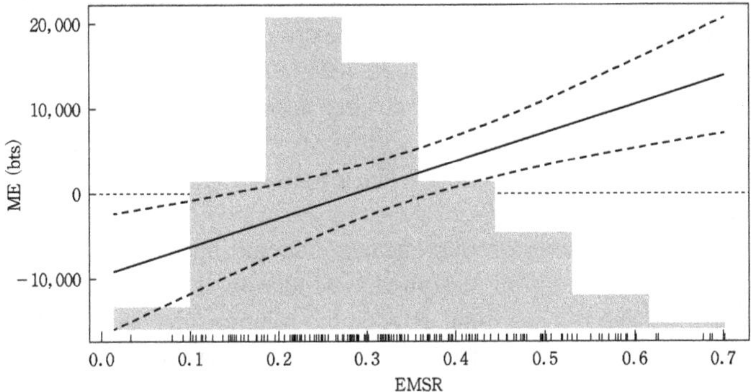

Fig. 4.9 Marginal effects of sales rates in emerging economies and betweenness centrality (model m7)

Figure 4.9 reveals that ME(bts), the marginal effect of betweenness centrality, varies with EMSR and can be divided into the following three ranges:

(i) Within the range EMSR < 0.15, ME(bts) is negative and statistically significant;
(ii) Within the range 0.15 < EMSR < 0.38, ME(bts) is not statistically significant:
(iii) Within the range 0.38 < EMSR, ME(bts) is positive and statistically significant.

Ranges (i) to (iii) can be interpreted as described below.

In the case of semiconductor manufacturing equipment providers with low sales ratios of products in emerging countries, classified as (i), when betweenness centrality goes up, its impact on the sales amount is negative and statistically significant. The more betweenness centrality improves, the less these providers earn. Hence, higher betweenness centrality results in a decline in the sales amount for these firms.

In the case of semiconductor manufacturing equipment providers with average sales ratios of products in emerging countries, classified as (ii), when betweenness centrality goes up, its impact on the sales amount is unclear and not statistically significant. As seen in the histogram, most equipment providers fall into this class.

In the case of semiconductor manufacturing equipment providers with high sales ratios of products in emerging countries, classified as (iii), their sales amount can increase with statistical significance when their betweenness centrality goes up.

The above three cases suggest that improving only betweenness centrality (i.e., positioning at the hub) is not necessarily effective to achieve an increase in the sales amount. Only when the sales ratio of products for emerging countries is high, is the effect of betweenness centrality positive. This result supports Hypothesis 3.

Adding an interaction between bts and EMSR in m7 does not result in the interaction term being statistically significant. This implies that there might be an interaction among bts, Ro300 and EMSR. To address this, model m9 was created with a higher-order interaction term. Incidentally, m9.1 is a conversion of m9 into standardized regression coefficients.

When m6 and m7 are compared, m9 presents itself as the best-fitting model in terms of both the coefficient of determination and AIC. Accordingly, model m9 is chosen to test Hypotheses 1 to 4, keeping the results illustrated thus far in mind.

In m9, the interaction term among bts, Ro300 and EMSR is found to be positive and statistically significant. Model m9 supports the effect of platform strategy explained in Hypothesis 4, which states: "Semiconductor manufacturing equipment providers in positions with high betweenness centrality successfully increase their sales of manufacturing equipment compatible with open standards by selecting industries from emerging countries as customers." The graphs in Fig. 4.10 display the marginal effects in m9.

Model m9 is an interaction model arranged according to three dimensions and having two moderators. Ro300 is assigned as Moderator 1 and EMSR as Moderator 2. In order to illustrate the marginal effects, the relationship between Moderator 1 and the marginal effect is plotted for five cases, each having a different value for Moderator 2, i.e., mean value, values at $\pm$1SD of the mean and values at $\pm$2SD of the mean, where SD stands for Standard Deviation.

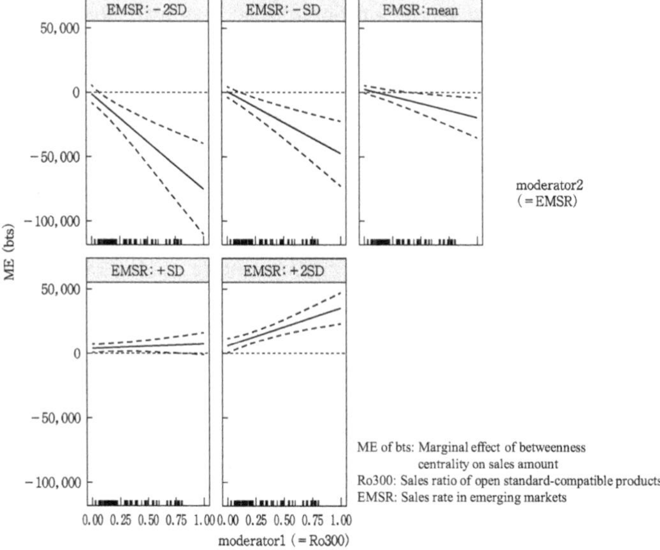

Fig. 4.10 Marginal effects of betweenness centrality, Ro300 and EMSR (model m9)

Figure 4.10 shows how the marginal effect of betweenness centrality changes as the levels of Ro300 and EMSR change, based on m9. The horizontal axis represents the level of Ro300 and the vertical axis refers to ME(bts). Five regression lines are given, including one line for EMSR being at the mean, two for 1 SE and 2 SEs below the mean in EMSR (-SD/-2SD in EMSR) and the other two for 1SE and 2SEs above the mean in EMSR (+SD/+2SD in EMSR).

Each regression line is accompanied by dotted lines depicting the 95% confidence interval. Whether the marginal effect is statistically different from zero at the 5% level can be confirmed by determining if the confidence interval contains ME(bts) = 0 or not. If the confidence interval contains ME(bts) = 0, the marginal effect is not statistically significant at the 5% level. On the contrary, if the confidence interval does not contain ME(bts) = 0, the marginal effect is statistically significant at the 5% level.

The five regression lines can be divided into two groups, i.e., one for EMSR being at and below the mean (Mean, -SD, -2SD) and one for EMSR being above the mean (+SD, +2SD).

As for the first group, the relationship between Ro300 and ME(bts) is nearly always negative across the entire range of Ro300. In other words, firms with EMSR standing at or below the mean experience a negative impact on their sales amount when they improve their betweenness centrality. The fact that ME(bts) decreases as Ro300 increases may be explained by observing that semiconductor manufacturing equipment providers in advanced countries adopt the 300 mm standard less frequently than those in emerging countries. Thus, although bts is supposed to have a positive impact on the sales amount, the forced adoption of the 300 mm standard actually exerts a negative impact.

On the other hand, in the group with higher sales ratios to emerging countries (+SD/+2SD), ME(bts) is positive across the entire range of Ro300; also, the relationship between Ro300 and ME(bts) is positive. This trend is particularly evident in the regression line of +2SD. It can be concluded that the group with higher EMSR has positive MEs(bts) and higher bts has a positive impact on sales for this group. Additionally, the effect can be enhanced by increasing the level of Ro300, and the positive effect of Ro300 on ME(bts) is especially visible for firms with higher EMSR (+2SD).

In sum, model m9 points to strong interactions among bts, Ro300 and EMSR, thus supporting the effect of a firm's platform strategy in Hypothesis 4. Because of the presence of interactions, Hypotheses 1 to 3 are affected by the level of the moderator variables. The marginal effects diagram in Fig. 4.10 shows that Hypotheses 1 to 3 do not hold true when the ratio of sales in emerging countries is low (EMSR < mean), while they do when it is high (+SD < EMSR). In the following explanations, *low* ratios of sales in emerging countries should be interpreted as EMSR < mean and *high* ratios as +SD < EMSR.

When the ratio is low, the marginal effect of betweenness centrality, ME(bts), is significantly negative across all ranges. On the contrary, when the ratio is high, the effect is significantly positive across all ranges. This means that Hypothesis 1 holds true on condition that EMSR is high.

For what concerns the relationship between ME(bts) and Ro300, a moderator variable, the slope is significantly positive when EMSR is high. This means that Hypothesis 2 holds true on condition that EMSR is high.

Lastly, with respect to the relationship between ME(bts) and EMSR, ME(bts) is significantly negative across all ranges when EMSR is low, but it is positive across all ranges when EMSR is high. In other words, the higher EMSR is, the greater the marginal effect of betweenness centrality. This means that Hypothesis 4 holds true.

The results of m9 support Hypothesis 4, which suggests the presence of interactions among bts, Ro300 and EMSR, but they also support Hypotheses 1 to 3 on condition that EMSR is high. These findings are consistent with the results of m6 and m7 described above. High EMSRs are found to be an essential prerequisite to ensure the success of the strategies related to positioning at hub and high sales ratio of open standard-compatible products.

4.5 Network Analysis

4.5.1 Details of the Transaction Network

The regression analysis described above statistically reveals that the interactions among bts, Ro300 and EMSR have a positive effect on sales growth. Although betweenness centrality, one of the network structure indexes representing the transaction network, was found to have an impact on sales in Sect. 4.4, its detailed mechanisms remained unclear. The purpose of this section is to describe what was happening

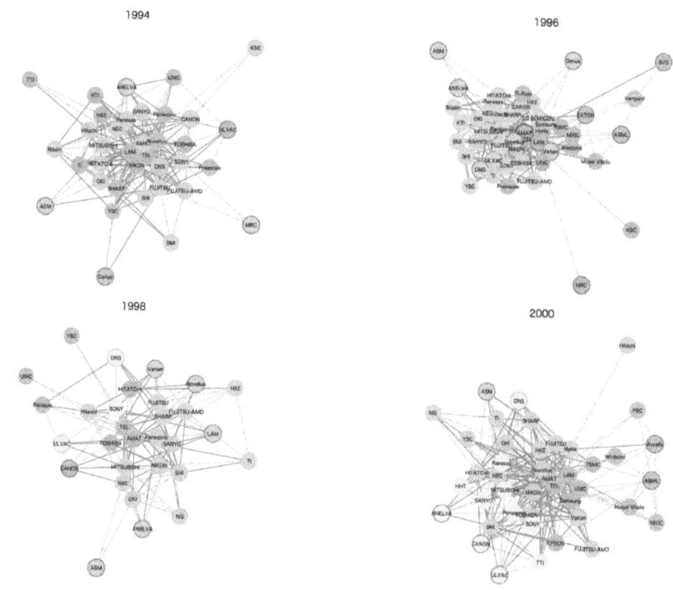

Note: HITACHI represents the semiconductor business unit, and Hitachi represents the semiconductor manufacturing equipment provider.

Abbreviations: HKE for Hitachi Kokusai Electric, YSC for Yasu Semiconductor Corporation, Nisshin for Nisshin Electric, KSC for Kawasaki Steel Corporation, SMI for Sumitomo Metal Industries, SHI for Sumitomo Heavy Industries, NIE for Nisshin Ion Equipment and HHT for Hitachi High Technologies.

Fig. 4.11 Transaction networks of the semiconductor manufacturing equipment industry (1994–2000)

in the transaction networks, by adopting a network analysis method (functional cartography method) and the same data as before for transaction networks.[7]

Firstly, the transaction networks were drawn for every other year from 1994 to 2006, in order to understand what the transaction networks analyzed in the previous section look like, as shown in Figs. 4.11 and 4.12.

The nodes in the charts represent the semiconductor manufacturing equipment providers and the semiconductor manufacturers constituting the transaction network of the semiconductor manufacturing equipment market (nodes with the same color are members of the same community). A procedure based on algorism[8] was implemented to determine to which community each of the firms belonged. It revealed, for example, that the transaction network in 1994 consisted of four communities.

The ties connecting the nodes indicate the presence of transactions (delivery) of semiconductor manufacturing equipment. There are two types of ties: the dashed lines represent transactions within a community, whereas the solid lines refer to transactions between communities. From the viewpoint of the competitive strategies

---

[7]Regarding community clustering, however, the data containing duplicated ties were used, since the information on weighted transaction ties is helpful for a clearer analysis.

[8]The spinglass algorithm was used. Calculations were performed using the igraph package of the statistics software R.

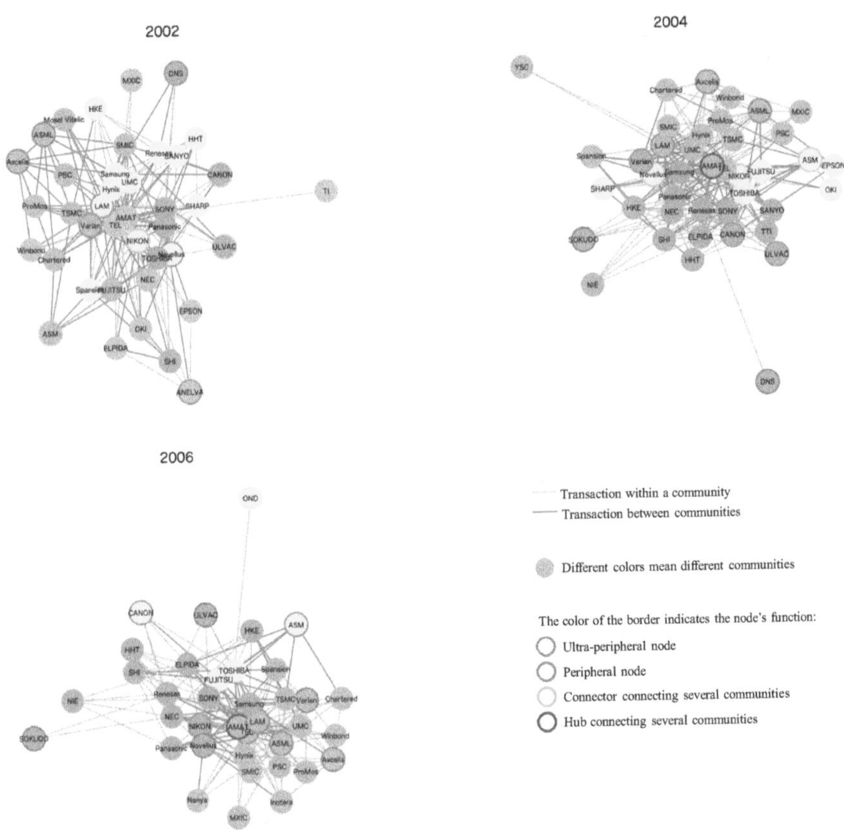

Fig. 4.12 Transaction networks of the semiconductor manufacturing equipment industry (2002–2006)

of platform firms, reviewed in Chap. 2, these inter-community transactions are more important.

The rim (perimeter) of the nodes representing semiconductor manufacturing equipment providers is color coded to account for the roles determined by the functional cartography method. The functional cartography method uses betweenness centrality for calculation. Betweenness centrality is an index indicating how critical each node is (whether it cannot be replaced by any other node) for information betweenness across the entire network. Information betweenness can be further broken down into inter-community betweenness and intra-community betweenness. The functional cartography method determines the functions of the nodes by focusing on the types of betweenness[9] (see Appendix 3 at the end of this chapter for details

[9]Functional cartography is often used for depicting complicated genetic networks in the field of biology (Guimerà and Amaral 2005). For the actual algorithm, the websites by Mr. Takemoto (Takemoto 2013) were used as a reference. See Appendix 3 for details on the nodes function methods.

on the functional cartography method). Incidentally, communities in a transaction network are places where transactions are frequently performed; hence, they are regarded as markets.

All the biannual charts show that there are several communities in the network. A closer look at the network charts for 2004 and 2006 reveals that AMAT (Applied Materials, Inc.) acted as the hub connecting several communities. The firm is a semiconductor manufacturing equipment provider dealing with a wide range of manufacturing equipment, especially coater developers and etchers.

The network chart for 2006 features two major communities. The blue group represents the Taiwanese semiconductor industry, including TSMC and UMC. The red group represents the Japanese semiconductor industry, including RENESAS, ELPIDA, NEC and TOSHIBA. In this chart, Samsung, the leading South Korean semiconductor firm, is part of the Japanese group, while Hynix, another South Korean firm, belongs to the Taiwanese group.

Based on the transaction network for 2006, the functional cartography method estimated that AMAT stood at the hub. This is confirmed by the fact that many ties (mediating between communities) can be seen spreading out from the AMAT node. Most importantly, despite belonging to the Taiwanese group, AMAT had a powerful intermediary role between the Japanese and Taiwanese semiconductor industries. Thus, it can be concluded that, in 2006, AMAT was a platform firm pursuing a platform strategy.

Interestingly enough, exposure machine providers (stepper firms), which are regarded as central in the semiconductor industry, are not at the hub in terms of information betweenness. This means that, from the point of view of platform competitive strategies, they do not follow any platform strategy. The exposure machine is a very important piece of semiconductor manufacturing equipment because it determines the minimum linewidth, which in turn determines the generation of semiconductor technology. Exposure machines are traded at the highest unit prices among all the processes. Nevertheless, AMAT, which is not a provider of exposure machines, is a platform firm rather than a stepper firm in terms of platform competitive strategy. It is also a predominant equipment provider with a product portfolio covering not only manufacturing equipment but solutions for semiconductor manufacturing processes. A Japanese company with a similar business style is Tokyo Electron Company.

A look at the chart for 1994 shows that AMAT was not positioned at the hub then. Also, by reviewing the charts from 1994 through to 2002, it can be seen that the firm was at the hub in 1996 but not in any other year. This means that AMAT was not able to maintain its hub position. On the contrary, the network charts for 2004 and 2006 show that the firm was successfully positioned at the hub in both years, meaning that it was successful in implementing a platform strategy. This can be explained by the wide diffusion of semiconductor manufacturing equipment compatible with the 300 mm standard after 2003.

4.5.2 Changes in Communities Over the Years

Observing the changes in the transaction networks over the years from 1994 to 2006 in Figs. 4.11 and 4.12 makes it clear that the ecosystem—consisting of the semiconductor industry and the manufacturing equipment industry, which comprise several communities—grew in the 1990s. In the 2000s (particularly after 2004), however, the ecosystem appears to be largely divided into two communities. One gathers around the Japanese semiconductor industry and the other around the Taiwanese semiconductor industry. As mentioned previously, the South Korean semiconductor firms, Samsung and Hynix, belong to the Japanese group and the Taiwanese group, respectively.

In order to confirm this interpretation, Fig. 4.13 was created to show how the communities changed over the years, with the horizontal axis displaying the years and the vertical axis referring to the number of member firms in the community. Communities are distinguished from one another by the type of line. Thirteen communities in total were identified in the transaction networks from 1994 to 2006.

Four communities were present in 1994, but they merged into two groups by 2006. In the meantime, some new communities developed and soon disappeared in the space of a single year or just a few years. The most enduring among these communities was community 02, which had already existed in 1994 and lasted until 2006. Companies that were members of a defunct community eventually found a place in another community, while continuing communities sometimes gained or lost members. Therefore, community sizes never remained constant.

As of 2006, community 02 included ASML, TEL, AMAT, LAM, Axcelis, Varian, Spansion, Hynix, TSMC, UMC, Winbond, MXIC, ProMos, PSC, SMIC, Chartered, Nanya and Inotera. Similarly, community 06 included Hitachi Hi-Tech Corporation, Hitachi Kokusai Electric Inc., Novellus, ULVAC, OND, Sumitomo Heavy Industries, Ltd., Nissin Ion Equipment Co., Ltd., NEC, Renesas, Panasonic, SONY, ELPIDA

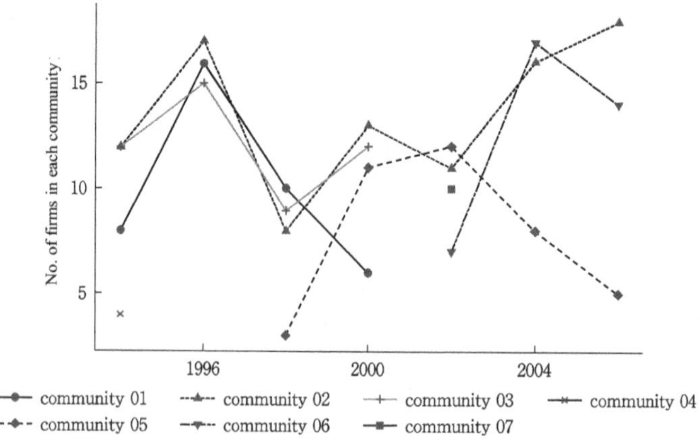

Fig. 4.13 Trends of communities

and Samsung. Firms belonging to communities other than community 02 in 1994 had moved to either community 05 or community 06 by 2006.

All the communities saw a decline in the number of members in 1998. This is probably because the Asian Financial Crisis had occurred in the previous year. Since semiconductor manufacturers had to curb their capital investments due to the crisis, the number of transactions (deliveries) of manufacturing equipment decreased.

In order to assess how the whole picture of the transaction network evolved over the years, network modularity was calculated and plotted, as shown in Fig. 4.14. Network modularity is an index indicating whether the network is integral or modular and it is calculated by dividing the communities using an algorithm. This index becomes smaller when there are more ties among the communities, and vice versa.

Looking at the period from 1994 to 2002, modularity increased significantly in 1998 but remained low in all the other years. Lower levels of modularity mean that the firms in the transaction networks are closely dependent on each other. In other words, the entire transaction network is integral.

Considering that 1998 was a special year due to the Asian Financial Crisis, its remarkable level of modularity is regarded as an outlier. If the modularity trend between 1994 and 2000 is observed by keeping this point in mind, the transaction network can be interpreted as having become more integral during that period.

After 2000, on the other hand, modularity gradually increased. Higher modularity levels mean that the transaction network is divided into multiple communities and the number of ties connecting them is small. Modularity rose significantly in 2005 and 2006, suggesting that the transaction network became more modular.

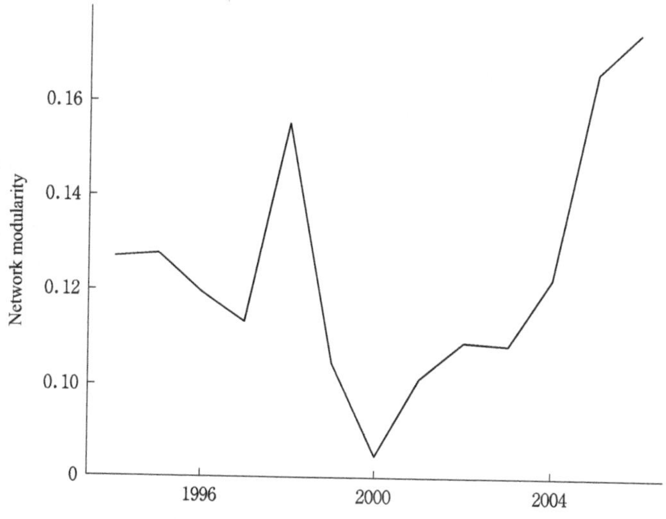

Fig. 4.14 Interannual changes in transaction network modularity

The absolute level of network modularity between 1994 and 2006 remained rather low, ranging from 0.1 to 0.15, but it is difficult to directly interpret the meaning of the absolute level, since it is industry-dependent. In contrast, it is relatively easy to make a comparative assessment of modularity levels in different years, as it reveals chronological changes in the characteristics of the transaction network.

To conclude, judging by the time series changes in network modularity, the ecosystem of semiconductor manufacturers and equipment providers became more integral in the 1990s and more modular in the 2000s.

4.5.3 Positioning of Manufacturing Equipment Providers in Transaction Networks

In order to figure out where each manufacturing equipment provider was positioned within its transaction network, the data were organized following the functional cartography method.

The functional cartography method estimates the function (role) of nodes by calculating the z value and the P value of each node from network data. The z value represents a standardized number of ties from the node to other nodes inside the community to which it belongs. A node with higher z value has a greater influence on the community. The P value becomes higher when the node belongs to a larger number of communities. A P value close to 1 means that the node belongs to the largest number of communities, while a P value close to 0 means that the node belongs to a single community.

A graph with the z value on the y axis and the P value on the x axis, called a z-P chart, was created by plotting all the nodes analyzed here. A node plotted in the upper-right corner is regarded as a hub node. A hub node bridges several communities and mediates a sizable amount of information. A node plotted in the lower-right corner, on the contrary, mediates a limited amount of information, though it bridges several communities. Such a node is called a connector node.

Figure 4.15 provides z-P charts for the years under investigation. Focusing on AMAT, it can be seen that the firm was positioned in the upper-right corner in many of the years, meaning that it started implementing a platform strategy as early as the 1990s.

Since 2001, however, the platform firm has most notably held its position in the upper-right corner. More concretely, in and after 2003, AMAT alone remained in the upper-right corner, while the other companies moved toward the lower-left corner. Tokyo Electron was also positioned in the upper-right corner, but its z value was a little smaller than that of AMAT.

Moreover, in Fig. 4.16, the functions of the equipment providers' nodes are identified and the ratios of the different functions are presented. The functions of the nodes observed in the transaction networks studied include hub nodes, connector nodes, peripheral nodes and ultra-peripheral nodes. Though both connector nodes and hub

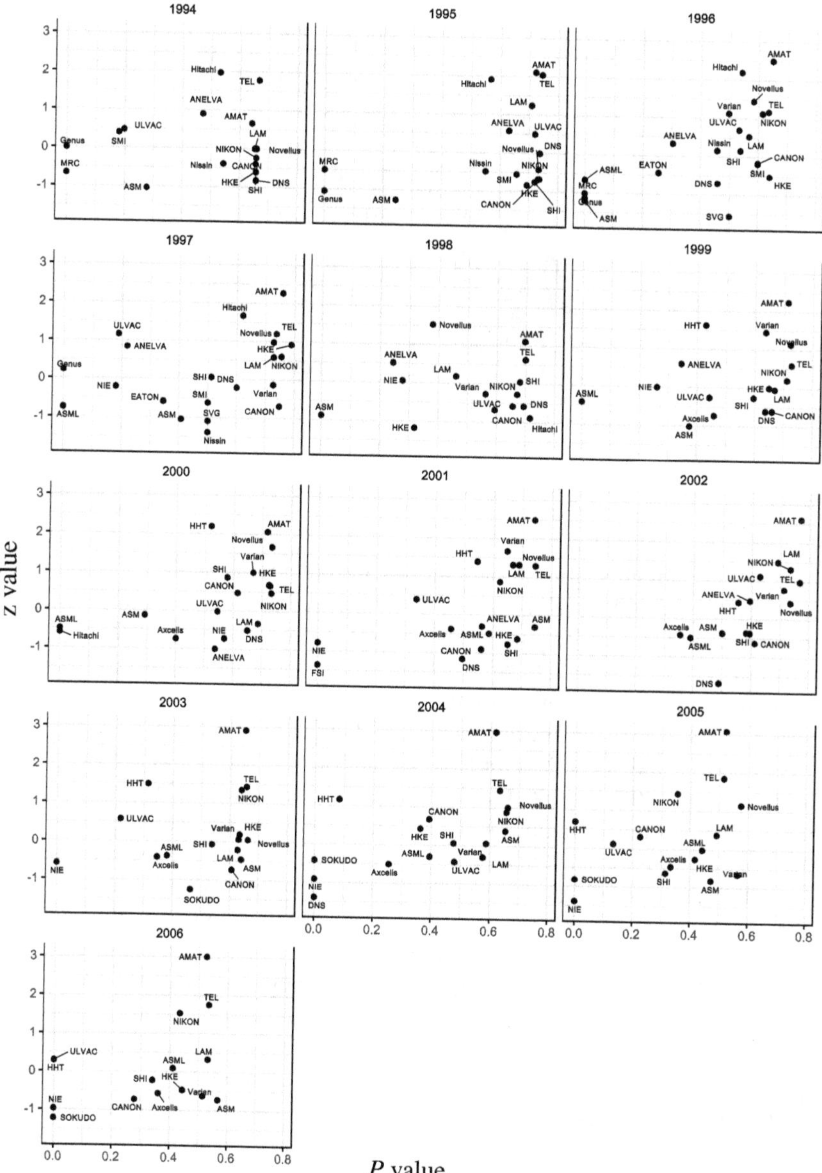

Fig. 4.15 Network positions of semiconductor manufacturing equipment providers (by year)

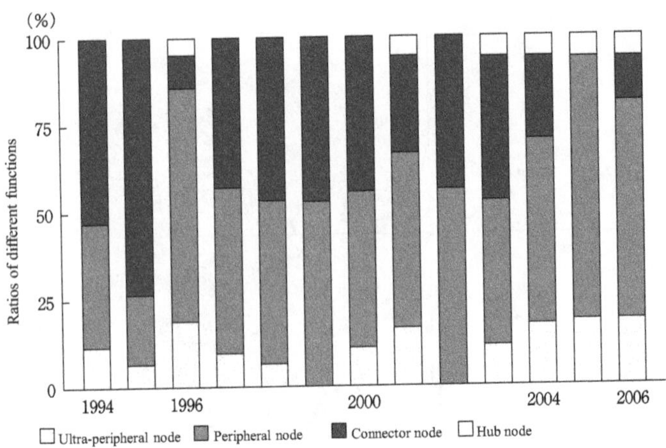

Fig. 4.16 Interannual change in the ratios of nodes functionality

nodes mediate among multiple communities, the latter remarkably excel in betweenness centrality (see Appendix 3 at the end of this chapter for more information on the criteria for distinguishing between hub nodes and connector nodes).

Ultra-peripheral nodes already existed in 1994 and kept growing until 2006, although the change was rather subtle. In contrast, peripheral nodes and connector nodes exhibited drastic changes between 1994 and 2006.

Peripheral nodes accounted for only about 40% of all the nodes in 1994, but they reached roughly 70% in 2006. On the other hand, connector nodes corresponded to more than 50% of all the nodes in 1994, but they drastically decreased to less than 10% in 2006, with the most noticeable drop observed between 2003 and 2006.

The hub position bridging several communities, which platform firms covet the most, first appeared in 1996 but disappeared in the following years. It reappeared in 2001 and was gone again the next year, followed by a permanent presence between 2003 and 2006. Only one semiconductor manufacturing equipment provider, Applied Materials, was identified as a hub node between 2003 and 2006, the same period when the 300 mm standard actually began to spread. According to Tokyo Electron's annual reports, Applied Materials began to deliver manufacturing equipment compatible with the 300 mm standard in 2000 and its sales ratio of 300 mm-compatible products exceeded 50% of its total sales in 2003 (see the process analysis in Appendix 4 at the end of this chapter for further details).

This trend in node functions leads to the following interpretation. Before 2003, when the 300 mm standard was not yet widespread, there were a number of semiconductor manufacturing equipment providers that mediated among communities, which is supported by the fact that a certain amount of connector nodes are observed in the charts for those years. After 2003, however, the diffusion of the 300 mm standard evolved into three main trends, detailed below.

First, a hub mediating among several communities continuously existed. Such a hub node is considered to be a place where a firm implementing a platform strategy is positioned. Second, the number of connector nodes mediating among several communities rapidly decreased, as a platform firm took over this role. Third, while connector nodes became fewer, the number of peripheral nodes and ultra-peripheral nodes grew considerably. In other words, when the function of mediating among several communities was occupied by a platform firm, the other companies tended to move to peripheral positions.

In sum, as open standards began to spread in 2003, connector nodes that up until then had mediated among several communities were pushed out to peripheral positions and the mediating function converged into the hub node. This presumably reinforced the bargaining power of the hub firm. In conclusion, positioning at the hub enhanced the effectiveness of the platform strategy.

4.6 Conclusions and Implications

This study examined the effectiveness of platform competitive strategies using transaction data on the semiconductor manufacturing equipment industry and sales data by product. The semiconductor manufacturing equipment industry consists of firms providing various machines for different processes. To ensure compatibility across these different pieces of equipment, an open standard for the 300 mm generation was developed. Using the diffusion of an open standard as part of one's platform strategy is a typical competitive strategy. In this study, a regression analysis was performed to assess the effectiveness of platform strategies. At the same time, in order to better understand the mechanisms behind it, the transaction network was studied based on the functional cartography method.

By carrying out a regression analysis with consideration given to interactions, the empirical study estimated platform strategy effectiveness. It was found that, although a firm with high betweenness centrality tends to have better market performance, or more sales, this outcome depends not only on positioning at a hub with high betweenness centrality but also on the ratio of sales in emerging countries. Such effects are statistically interpreted as interactions among betweenness centrality, sales ratio of open standard-compatible products and rate of sales in emerging countries.

The empirical analysis revealed that the marginal effect of betweenness centrality (on the sales amount) increased when firms sold semiconductor manufacturing equipment compatible with the open standard to semiconductor companies in emerging countries. Conversely, if the ratio of sales in emerging markets, EMSR, was average or lower, the sales ratio of open standard-compatible products undermined the effectiveness of betweenness centrality.

The following three competitive strategies, when combined as a platform strategy package, were identified as able to bring about interaction effects and achieve the strongest impact:

(i) Positioning at the hub in transaction networks, i.e., achieving higher betweenness centrality;
(ii) Increasing sales ratio of open standard-compatible products, i.e., making strategic use of open standards;
(iii) Increasing the ratio of sales in emerging countries, i.e., promoting sales to new market participants.

The network analysis that followed showed that, as the 300 mm open standard started to gain popularity in 2003, hub nodes, which mediate among several communities, became a permanent feature. At the same time, connector nodes, which had previously fulfilled the same mediating role, were pushed out toward the periphery. Hence, the hub node acquired greater bargaining power by appropriating the mediation role.

In the 1990s, firms placed at connector nodes acted as mediators among communities and the modularity of the transaction network was low. In and after 2003, the function of community-to-community mediation was concentrated into platform firms at hub nodes and the modularity of the network grew. The platform strategy pursued by platform firms caused a structural change in the transaction network, heightening its modularity. Thus, in general, the strategic behavior of platform firms propels the modularization of transaction networks.

The empirical study and the network analysis combined suggest the following conclusions.

Previous research has solely emphasized (i) high betweenness centrality, or positioning at the hub, as an effective competitive strategy. Our empirical study, however, revealed that such high betweenness centrality was supported by high sales rates of open standard-compatible products and high sales ratios in emerging countries. High betweenness centrality alone cannot realize the full impact of platform firms' competitive strategies. Rather, as our study demonstrated, the true mechanism of platform strategy is to combine the three strategy components of high betweenness centrality, high sales ratio of open standard-compatible products and high rate of sales in emerging countries as a package, thereby making use of the interactions among them.

Furthermore, the network analysis based on the functional cartography method shed light on the impact of platform strategy firms other than the platform firm. By positioning itself at the hub, a platform firm completely takes over the inter-community mediating function, which, in turn, pushes firms that used to act as mediators into peripheral nodes, with the consequent risk that they may lose their bargaining power. In sum, the competitive strategies of platform firms are able to drastically change the structure of transaction networks.

In order to ensure the success of the platform strategy in a global business ecosystem, a high ratio of sales in emerging countries is an essential prerequisite. This means that the platform strategy offers emerging economies in the global ecosystem the opportunity to catch up with the technological standard of the developed world. In the case of the semiconductor industry, South Korean and Taiwanese semiconductor manufacturers seized and benefited the most from this opportunity.

Two specific aspects of the competitive strategies of platform firms identified in this study deserve further consideration. Firstly, the competitive strategy of proactively selling open standard-compatible products to emerging countries is closely linked to positioning in the transaction networks of the business ecosystem.

What differentiates this study from other works on platform strategy is that the empirical analysis carried out relied on a clear definition of the basic strategy of platform firms as *bridging several communities*. While previous studies exclusively dealt with the business process of platform firms, the focus here is on positioning in transaction networks and competitive strategies. Thanks to the analytic framework adopted, it was possible to develop a quantitative assessment of the competitive strategies of platform firms in transaction networks. It was found that the competitive strategies of platform firms are effective only when there is an interaction between the positioning at the hub strategy, a high sales ratio of open standard-compatible products and a high rate of sales in emerging countries. Positioning at the hub on its own does not ensure success.

Secondly, this kind of analysis was extended to cross-border transaction networks. Firms in advanced countries and those in emerging economies both collaborate and compete with one another as participants in a business ecosystem. To take international competitiveness into consideration, the transaction networks in a global business ecosystem should be analyzed in greater depth. However, previous research did not fully explore the modeling of transaction networks in a business ecosystem. Accordingly, it failed to unveil the influence of platform firms on global business ecosystems. On the other hand, our empirical study clarifies the impact of the global strategies of platform firms.

A closer look at the results from the network analysis indicates that the platform strategy triggers extensive structural changes in a transaction network. When the inter-community mediating function is taken over by the platform firm, the nodes that used to mediate among communities are pushed out toward peripheral nodes, with less bargaining power. Most of the firms that previously mediated among several communities are established equipment providers in advanced countries, which ultimately lose their competitive edge as the platform firm becomes ever more successful. The platform strategy also encourages newcomers to enter the market, providing them with good opportunities to catch up with the technological standard of the developed world. South Korean and Taiwanese semiconductor manufacturers appear to have made the most of this opportunity by quickly upgrading their technical levels to the latest generation. This implies that the competitive strategies of platform firms are likely to bring about a global transformation in industrial structures.

This chapter elaborated on an empirical analysis regarding transaction data on semiconductor manufacturing equipment in order to examine platform strategy effectiveness. That said, the platform strategies implemented by firms are in actual fact much more complicated. Indeed, platform firms are expected to pursue the expansion of their ecosystem, in addition to boosting their own profits. In this regard, the next chapter reports a case analysis on the Pentium CPU of Intel, one of the most representative platform firms of the 1990s. The analysis in Chap. 5 looks into the strategic significance of Intel's entry into two peripheral markets from the standpoint of ecosystem management.

Appendix 1: Betweenness Centrality

The analysis of transaction networks presented above employed a network index called betweenness centrality. Centrality is typically used in network analysis to express the characteristics of nodes in networks (Wasserman and Faust 1994). There are several types of centrality indices, reported in Fig. 4.17.

Each of these centrality indices indicates that a node is at the center of a network from a certain standpoint. The order-of-magnitude centrality index shows to what extent a node is at the center in terms of the number of ties (or edges) that it has. In Fig. 4.17, nodes C to F have an order of magnitude of 3.000, the highest among all the seven nodes. This does not necessarily mean that they have the highest values also for what concerns the other centrality indices.

The eigen-value centrality index represents a node's order-of-magnitude centrality but after weighting, so as to attach the greatest importance to the tie that connects to a node with the largest number of ties. The proximity centrality index is an inverse number of the average number of steps from a node to the other nodes, so it deals with the aspect of distance. The betweenness centrality index shows how central a node is in a network in relation to information transmission, or whether the node is indispensable for communicating information along the network.

This book assesses network centrality using betweenness centrality. Higher betweenness centrality means that (i) the two networks bridged by the node are larger and (ii) the two networks are bridged by fewer nodes. Because of these two characteristics, network analyses often use the betweenness centrality index to identify the nodes that act as hubs.

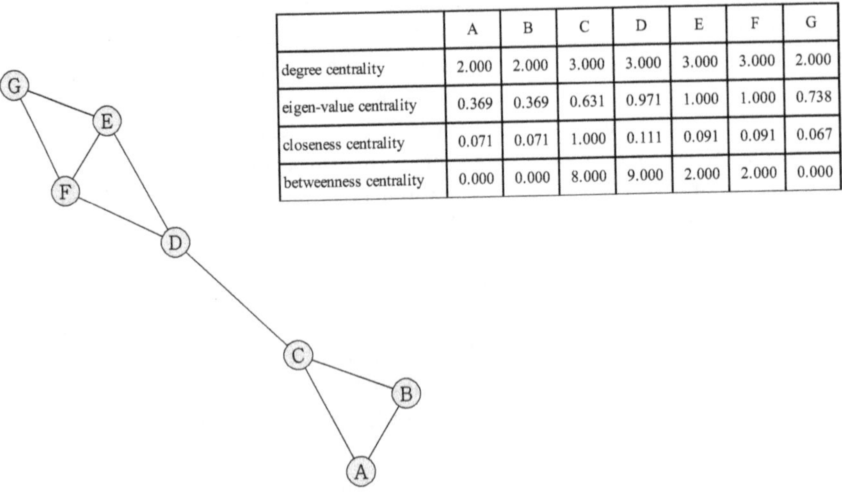

	A	B	C	D	E	F	G
degree centrality	2.000	2.000	3.000	3.000	3.000	3.000	2.000
eigen-value centrality	0.369	0.369	0.631	0.971	1.000	1.000	0.738
closeness centrality	0.071	0.071	1.000	0.111	0.091	0.091	0.067
betweenness centrality	0.000	0.000	8.000	9.000	2.000	2.000	0.000

Fig. 4.17 Network centrality indices

The betweenness centrality of Node i, $C_b(i)$, is derived by using equation

$$C_{b(i)} = \sum_{i \neq j \neq k} \frac{g_{jk}(i)}{g_{jk}}$$

in which $C_b(i)$ is the betweenness centrality of Vertex i, $g_{jk}(i)$ is the number of shortest paths between Vertex j and Vertex k going through Vertex i and g_{jk} is the number of shortest paths between Vertex j and Vertex k.

Appendix 2: Interaction Model

The empirical analysis conducted in this chapter made use of several statistical tools. This appendix provides an in-depth explanation of the interaction model, which was not fully described in Sect. 4.4.

For the purposes of this book, linear regression models with interaction terms are called interaction models. They are routinely employed in empirical analyses in business management and in the social sciences, but they are often misapplied and thus special attention is required in their use. Brambor et al. (2005) surveyed empirical analyses based on interaction models in the field of politics and pointed out that, though regarded as similar, the linear additive model and the interaction model are different and their results are often interpreted wrongly. Here follows a basic explanation of the interaction model.

A typical interaction model is expressed as follows:

$$Y = b_1X + b_2Z + b_3XZ + \epsilon \tag{4.1}$$

where Z is a moderator variable and ϵ is an error term that estimates a normal distribution.

Formula (4.1) can be converted into Formula (4.2), which makes it clearer that the effect of X varies depending on the value of Z.

$$Y = (b_1 + b_3Z)X + \ b_2Z + \epsilon \tag{4.2}$$

Here, the effect on Y when X increases by one unit is called the marginal effect of X on Y. The marginal effect of X on Y in Formula (4.2) is expressed as $\frac{\Delta Y}{\Delta X}$ or $ME(X)$.

$$\begin{aligned} ME(X) &= \frac{\Delta Y}{\Delta X} \\ &= b_1 + b_2Z \end{aligned} \tag{4.3}$$

It is evident that *ME(X)* depends on the value of *Z*, which translates into two important characteristics: (1) the value range of *Z* affects *ME(X)* and (2) the value of *Z* affects the confidence interval of *ME(X)*.

The first characteristic of the value range of *Z* affecting *ME(X)* is evident in Formula (4.3). The second characteristic is evident from the fact that the standard error of *ME(X)* is dependent on the value of *Z*. The standard error of *ME(X)*, $\sigma_{ME(X)}$ is expressed as follows:

$$\begin{aligned}\sigma_{ME(X)} &= \sigma_{\frac{\Delta Y}{\Delta X}} \\ &= \sqrt{var\left(\hat{b}_1\right) + Z^2 var\left(\hat{b}_3\right) + 2Zcov\left(\hat{b}_1\hat{b}_3\right)}\end{aligned} \quad (4.4)$$

where $\hat{b}_1$ and $\hat{b}_3$ represent estimates of b_1 and b_3, $var\left(\hat{b}_1\right)$ and $var\left(\hat{b}_3\right)$ are variances of $\hat{b}_1$ and $\hat{b}_3$, respectively, and $cov\left(\hat{b}\hat{b}_3\right)$ represents the covariance of $\hat{b}_1$ and $\hat{b}_3$. Since the standard error of ME(X), σ, is dependent on the value of Z, the size of the confidence interval of ME(X) changes if the value of Z changes.

Figure 4.18 is provided to give an intuitive understanding of (4.1) and (4.2), by depicting the marginal effect of Formula (4.5) below.

$$\begin{aligned}Y &= X + Z + 0.5XZ \\ &= (1 + 0.5Z)X + Z\end{aligned} \quad (4.5)$$

The marginal effect of *X* on *Y* (= *ME(X)*) in Formula (4.5) depends on the value of moderator Z. Given $Z = 4$, *Y* increases by 3 when *X* increases by one unit. Given $Z = -4$, Y decreases by 1 when X increases by one unit. This clearly demonstrates that the effect of *X* depends on the value of *Z*.

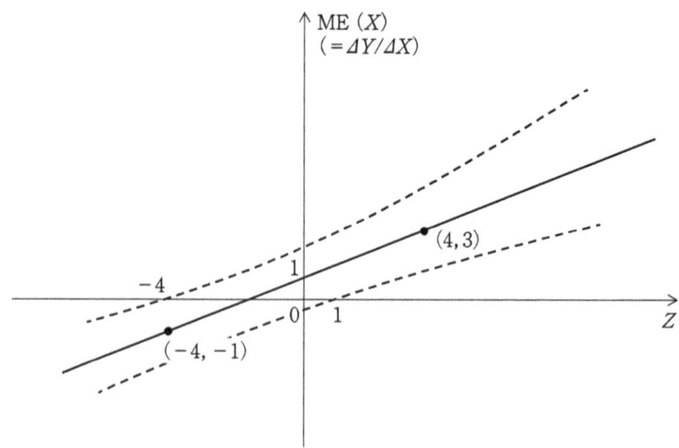

Fig. 4.18 Marginal effect of X on Y when Z is a moderator

Provided that the value of Z is greater than 1, $ME(X)$ is always positive. When Z is smaller than -2, however, $ME(X)$ is always negative. This proves characteristic (1) above, which states that the value range of Z affects $ME(X)$.

Moreover, the statistical significance of $ME(X)$ changes with the value of Z. The confidence interval of $ME(X)$ is indicated by dashed lines. When the interval contains 0, $ME(X)$ is not statistically significant. This means that $ME(X)$ is not statistically significant in cases where Z ranges from -4 to 1 and also that $ME(X)$ is not effectual. With the value of Z being lower than -4, the marginal effect is negatively significant and, with Z being higher than 1, the marginal effect is positively significant.

As mentioned in (4.2) above, in interaction models, the value of Z has an impact on the confidence interval of $ME(X)$. This is the reason why the confidence interval changes along the x axis in Fig. 4.18. As the confidence interval varies with the value of Z, a typical regression table (a matrix showing estimates of regression coefficients) is not sufficient to interpret the estimation results of the interaction models. A marginal effect diagram is needed to see how $ME(X)$ changes along with the value of moderator variable Z.

Appendix 3: Functional Cartography Method

The functional cartography method is an algorithm to estimate the functions of nodes based on information on ties among nodes in a network. The concept was introduced by Guimerà and Amaral (2005), which used this approach to estimate the functions of nodes in joint networks of protein genes. The node functions estimated with this method include hubs, connectors, peripheral nodes, and so on. Since platform firms adopt the strategy of positioning themselves at hubs, the functional cartography method is valuable to establish which firms adopt the positioning strategy, based on data about their transaction network.

The algorithm determining the node functions consists of two steps. The first step divides a transaction network into several communities to identify to which community each node belongs. Modularity Q is used as the criterion for the division. Communities are divided in such a way as to maximize the value of Modularity Q.

The second step calculates the z and P values for each node. Note that these values are completely different from the z and P values often used in statistics. The z value here is a standardized value of the number of ties to the other nodes within the community, using standard deviation. A higher z value means that the node is more influential in the community. The P value represents the extent to which the node mediates among multiple communities. The function of each node is determined based on these two values. Guimerà and Amaral (2005) proposed seven node function, R1 to R7, as shown below.

Fig. 4.19 correlates the seven functions, R1 to R7, with the z and P values. Guimera and Amaral (2005) introduced these seven node functions assuming biological networks; hence, this method does not strictly fit the nodes of transaction networks. Nevertheless, it would still be helpful for this analysis in order to establish whether or not a node is a hub and whether a hub connects multiple communities.

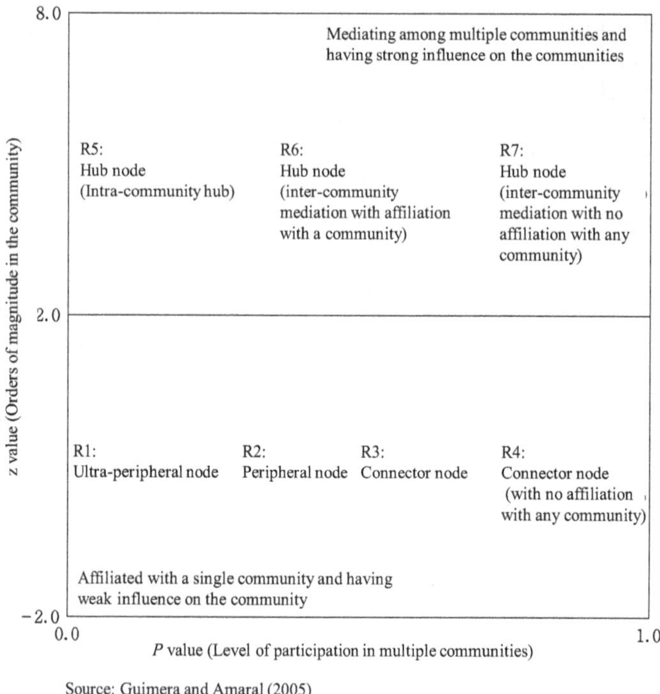

Fig. 4.19 Correlation between the z and P values and the node function

Of the seven functions, two aspects are particularly important from the perspective of platform strategies. The first is to distinguish between a hub and the other nodes. A node with a z value of 2 or higher is deemed to have particularly numerous ties and is identified as a hub. While R1 to R4 may be connected to quite a few nodes and communities, they have fewer ties than hub nodes do. R5 to R7 have a sufficient number of ties to be considered hubs. The second aspect is to determine whether the node identified as a hub above is a hub inside the community or a hub mediating among communities. This is achieved mainly by considering the P value. R5 is an internal hub within a community, whereas R6 and R7 are hubs mediating among communities. Platform firms are regarded as those that take positions in R6 or R7, in the sense that they mediate information among communities.

Appendix 4: Process Analysis (Analysis of Capital Investment in the Lithography Process)

The empirical study based on the regression analysis revealed that platform firms improve their market performance (sales) by making strategic use of open standards and expanding sales in emerging countries. The network analysis suggested that the community-to-community mediating function was absorbed by the hub position in 2003, giving platform firms greater bargaining power.

This appendix conducts a process analysis to understand what changes occurred in emerging economies during the period under investigation in terms of their technical levels, taking the lithography process as an example. The lithography process is an essential part of semiconductor manufacturing, since it determines the basic capacity of a foundry.

Fig. 4.20 shows changes in the per-unit investment amount and the total scale of investment in the lithography process. The x axis displays the years and the y axis indicates the unit price (in USD1,000). The per-unit investment amount is obtained by standardizing the total amount invested in acquiring semiconductor manufacturing equipment for the lithography process to the number of equipment pieces. For example, if exposure machines worth one million dollars in total were sold in South Korea and the number of units sold was four, the unit price is calculated as 250 thousand dollars. Generally speaking, a higher unit price for lithography equipment indicates that the machine acquired is of a more modern generation.

The size of the dots on each line graph represents the total amount of investment. As the total amount of investment is calculated per region, regions with a larger number of semiconductor manufacturers tend to have greater amounts. In other words, the per-unit investment amount reflects which generation of equipment the semiconductor manufacturers in the region were buying, since a greater amount

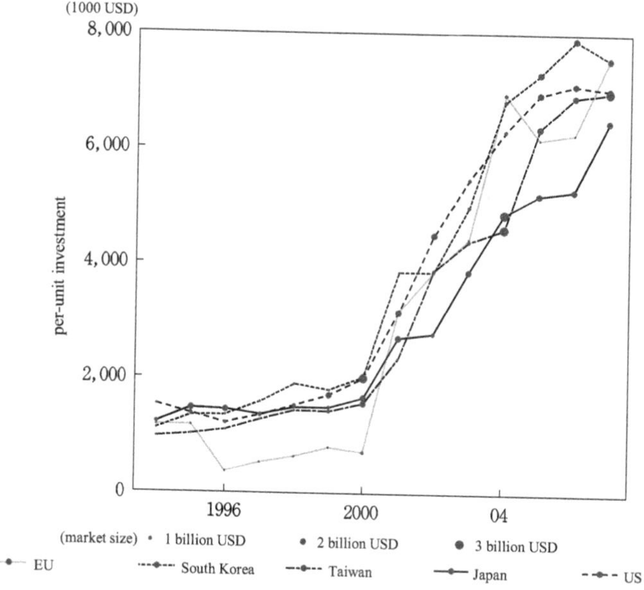

Fig. 4.20 Changes in the per-unit investment amount and total scale of investment in the lithography process

of investment allows manufacturers to purchase equipment of a more advanced technology. Manufacturers spending the same per-unit amounts are considered to have purchased manufacturing equipment of the same generation.

Fig 4.20 suggests the following considerations. First, a comparison among Japan, South Korea and Taiwan, the countries studied in the regression analysis and the transaction network analysis, reveals that Japan and South Korea had similar levels of investment in the lithography process from 1994 to 1996, though the per-unit investment amount of Japan was slightly higher than that of South Korea. Taiwan lagged behind its two neighbors in terms of per-unit investment amount.

In 1997, the per-unit investment amount of South Korea exceeded that of Japan. The difference between the two countries stayed within a certain range until 2000, but it started to grow in 2001 and, since then, it has remained so great that it cannot be ignored. This seems to suggest that average production lines in South Korea have been more advanced than those in Japan since 2001. Note that the per-unit investment amounts given in Fig. 4.20 are very rough figures and accuracy is of no importance here.

Now, let us compare the per-unit investment amounts of Japan and Taiwan. Although Taiwan had a lower level of per-unit investment amount than Japan in 2001, it invested more than its neighbor in the following year. In 2004, Japan was once again in the lead, but it was overtaken again by Taiwan a year later. The per-unit investment amount of Taiwan has since been at higher levels than that of Japan.

What is obvious from Fig. 4.20 is that, as far as lithography equipment is concerned, the per-unit investment amount of Japan and those of South Korea and Taiwan reversed between 2001 and 2004. The semiconductor industry experienced two extraordinary events during that period. The first was the burst of the IT bubble in 2001, while the second was the diffusion of semiconductor manufacturing equipment compatible with the 300 mm standard. In its annual reports, Tokyo Electron, a major semiconductor manufacturing equipment provider, explains the situation in each of these years as follows.[10]

2000

"Due to the tightening of capital investment all around the world, the equipment market for the 200 mm wafer has been shrinking. We have been receiving, however, a favorable number of orders for manufacturing equipment for the 300 mm wafer. All models compatible with the 300 mm standard are now ready, and the sales ratio of equipment for 300 mm-compatible equipment has reached nearly 20%… To us the shift to the 300 mm generation paves the way for a higher market share." (Tokyo Electron 2001, p. 6).

2001.

(In response to the question "How would you describe fiscal year 2001 as a whole?")
"The semiconductor manufacturing equipment industry experienced the worst downcycle since this business began. Although there have been some downward swings in

[10]Note that the situation in a certain year is reported in the following year's annual report.

the past, this year's downcycle has been the most serious in history in terms of both scale and speed… However, it has not been all bad. It has become clear that we are definitely an industrial leader also in the field of manufacturing equipment compatible with the 300 mm generation, which is now replacing the older generations." (Tokyo Electron 2002, p. 8).

2002

"The view that inventories were low for some semiconductor components spread through the industry at the beginning of the year, which motivated semiconductor manufacturers to make capital investment. Unfortunately, however, demand did not continue to rise, resulting in excessive inventories, and the industry could not fully recover… As for the trend in manufacturing equipment… by diameter, manufacturers in the US and South Korea and foundries in Taiwan are spending more on 300 mm-compatible lines and, consequently, the ratio of sales of 300 mm manufacturing equipment is approaching 50%." (Tokyo Electron 2003, p. 21).

2003

"More and more semiconductor manufacturers are currently investing in 300 mm-compatible manufacturing equipment when they make new acquisitions… As a consequence, 300 mm equipment now accounts for more than 50% of our total sales in the semiconductor manufacturing equipment division. According to our survey, we are ranked at the top in the markets for many 300 mm-compatible machines in fiscal year 2003…" (Tokyo Electron, 2004, pp. 2–5).

2004

"In fiscal year 2004, the PC and mobile phone markets saw sound demand and the digital appliances market was likewise very vibrant. Accordingly, the demand for semiconductors for those devices and liquid crystal panels grew, resulting in active capital investment… We were able to significantly improve our business performance." (Tokyo Electron 2005, p. 6).

"In terms of wafer diameter, as many semiconductor manufacturers have started investing in 300 mm-compatible foundries, we have focused on this segment." (Tokyo Electron 2005, p. 24).

Table 4.1 summarizes these developments in the industry.

According to Tokyo Electron's annual reports between 2001 and 2005, although the shift to the 300 mm generation began in 2000, the investment amount plunged in 2001, following the burst of the IT bubble. Semiconductor manufacturers resumed capital investment and started to buy 300 mm equipment in 2002, which already accounted for more than 50% of the total sales of Tokyo Electron's semiconductor manufacturing equipment segment in 2003. This implies that a full-scale shift to the 300 mm generation took place in 2003.

In the meantime, the per-unit investment amount in the lithography process of South Korea by far exceeded that of Japan in 2001, and the per-unit investment amount of Taiwan exceeded that of Japan in the following year. These observations suggest that the generation of technology to be newly introduced became more

Table 4.1 Developments in the semiconductor manufacturing equipment industry from 2000 to 2004

Year	Description in annual reports of Tokyo Electron	Investment in the litho process in South Korea	Investment in the litho process in Taiwan
2000	– Investment increased along with the booming semiconductor market – Shipment of 300 mm equipment started	– In per-unit investment, it exceeded Japan – The difference between the two remained at a certain level	
2001	– Investment suddenly decreased following the burst of the IT bubble	– In per-unit investment, it exceeded Japan by far – The difference between the two narrowed	– Investment level was lower than in Japan – The difference between the two remained at a certain level
2002	– The semiconductor market did not fully recover – Capital investment by semiconductor manufacturers was still weak – 300 mm manufacturing equipment accounted for almost 50% of total sales		– Per-unit investment exceeded that of Japan
2003	– 300 mm manufacturing equipment exceeded 50% of total sales – The scale of capital investment did not catch up with the level in 2000		
2004	– The scale of capital investment returned to the level in 2000 – Most capital investment was made in 300 mm production lines	– Per-unit investment topped that of the US and became the world's Number 1	– Japan overtook Taiwan in terms of the per-unit investment, but only briefly
2005	– Decrease in capital investment again		– Taiwan overtook Japan again – The per-unit amount of investment approached that of the US

advanced in South Korea and Taiwan than in Japan. The per-unit investment amount in the lithography process kept growing in South Korea and Taiwan; South Korea stepped ahead of the US in 2004 and Taiwan came close to US values in 2007. On the other hand, the amount of investment made by Japanese semiconductor manufacturers was much lower than in the other two countries. This examination of investments in the lithography process between 2001 and 2005 proves that the

South Korean and Taiwanese semiconductor industries rapidly increased their technical levels by proactively purchasing manufacturing equipment compatible with the 300 mm standard

References

Asaba S (1998) Kyousou to Kyouchou: Network Gaibusei ga Hataraku Shijou deno Senryaku (Competition and cooperation: Strategies in the market of network externalities). Organ Sci 31(4):44–52 (in Japanese)

Besen SM, Farrell J (1991) The role of ITU in standardization: pre-eminence, importance or rubber stamp? Telecommun Policy 15(4):311–321

Brambor T, Clark WR, Golder M (2005) Understanding interaction models: improving empirical analyses. Political Anal 14:63–82

Clement MT, Ohashi H (2005) Indirect network effects and the product cycle: Video games in the U.S. 1994–2002. J Indust Econ 53(4):515–542

Corts KS, Lederman M (2009) Software exclusivity and the scope of indirect network effects in the U.S. home video game market. Int J Indust Organ 27(2):121–136

Csardi G, Nepusz T (2006) The igraph software package for complex network research. Inter J Compl Syst 1695. http://igraph.sf.net

ED Research (1998) Tokubetsu Riputo Nichi Kan Tai Shuyou Handoutai Koujou no Seizou Souti '98 (Special report on semiconductor manufacturing equipment in Japanese, Korean, Taiwanese Foundry 1998). ED Research, Tokyo (in Japanese)

ED Research (2007) Tokubetsu Riputo Nichi Kan Tai Shuyou Handoutai Koujou no Seizou Souti 2007 (Special report on semiconductor manufacturing equipment in Japanese, Korean, Taiwanese Foundry 2007) ED Research, Tokyo (in Japanese)

Eisenmann TR (2007) Managing networked business: course overview for educators. Harvard Business School, Boston MA. http://www.hbsp.harvard.edu

Eisenmann T, Parker G, Van Alstyne M (2011) Platform envelopment. Strateg Manag J 32:1270–1285

Evans DS, Hagiu A, Schmalensee R (2006) Invisible engines. MIT Press, Cambridge MA

Freeman LC (1977) A set of measures of centrality based upon betweenness. Sociometry 40:35–41

Fujitsu Research Institute, Negoro Lab at Waseda University Business School (2013) Platform Business Saizensen 26 Bunnya wo Zukai to Data de Tettei Kaibou (Frontline of platform business: Anatomy in 26 segments with illustrations and data). Shoei-Sha, Tokyo (in Japanese)

Gawer A (2009) Platforms, markets and innovation. Edward Elgar, Cheltenham UK and Northampton MA

Gawer A, Cusumano MA (2002) Platform leadership: How Intel, Microsoft, and Cisco drive industry innovation. Harvard Business School Press, Boston MA

Gawer A, Henderson R (2007) Platform owner entry and innovation in complementary markets: evidence from Intel. J Econ Manag Strateg 16(1):1–34

Global Net (2005) Sekai Handoutai Seizousouchi Shiken Kensa Souchi Shijou Nenkan 2005 (Yearbook of semiconductor manufacturing and testing equipment in the global market 2005)

Global Net (2009) Sekai Handoutai Seizousouchi Shiken Kensa Souchi Shijou Nenkan 2009 (Yearbook of semiconductor manufacturing and testing equipment in the global market 2009)

Guimerà R, Amaral LAN (2005) Functional cartography of complex metabolic networks. Nature 433:895–900

Hagiu A (2006) Pricing and commitment by two-sided platforms. RAND J Econ 37(3):720–737

Hagiu A, Yoffie DB (2009) What's your Google strategy? Harvard Bus Rev 87(4):74–81

Harada S (2009) Kokusai Hyoujunka Senryaku (Strategies on international standardization). Denki University Press, Tokyo (in Japanese)

Iansiti M, Levien R (2004) The keystone advantage: what the new business ecosystems mean for strategy, innovation, and sustainability. Harvard Business School Press, Boston MA

Ikuine F (2012) Kaihatsu Seisansei no Dilemma–Digital Jidai no Innovation Pataan (Productivity dilemma in development–innovation patterns in the digital era). Yuhikaku, Tokyo (in Japanese)

Imai K, Kyo K (2009) Keitai Denwa Sangyou (Mobile phone industry). In: Shintaku J, Amano T (2009) Monozukuri no Kokusai Keiei Senryaku–Asia no Sangyou Chirigaku (International business strategies of manufacturing companies–industrial geography in Asia). Yuhikaku, Tokyo, pp 111–135 (in Japanese)

Inoue T, Maki K, Nagayama S (2011) Bijinesu Ekosisutemu ni Okeru Niche no Koudou to Habu Kigyou no Senryaku – Kateiyou Gemu Gyoukai ni okeru Fukuganteki Bunseki (The strategies of niche and hub firms in the business ecosystem–Multi-facet analysis on the video game industry). Organ Sci 44(4):67–82 (in Japanese)

Kawakami M (2012) Asshuku sareta Sangyou Hatten (Accelerated industrial growth–Growth process of Taiwanese notebook PC industry). Nagoya University Press, Nagoya (in Japanese)

Kokuryo J (1995) Open Network Keiei: Kigyou Senryaku no Shin Chouryuu (Open network management: New trend in business strategy). Nikkei Inc., Tokyo (in Japanese)

Kokuryo J (1999) Open Architecture Senryaku: Network Jidai no Kyoudou Moderu (Open architecture strategy: collaboration models for network era). Nikkei Inc., Tokyo (in Japanese)

Komiya H (2003) Gurobaru Sutandado he no Chosen – 300 mm Handotai Kojo he muketa Hyojunka no Rekishi (The challenge to the global standard–History of the semiconductor factory of 300 mm wafer). SEMI Japan, Tokyo (in Japanese)

Marukawa T, Yasumoto M (2010) Keitai Denwa Sangyou no Shinka Purosesu: Nihon wa naze Koritsu shitanoka (Evolution in the mobile phone industry: why does the Japanese mobile phone industry isolate in the global market). Yuhikaku, Tokyo (in Japanese)

Negoro T, Ajiro S (2011) Keieigaku ni okeru Puratofomuron no Keifu to Kongo no Tenbou (Reviews and perspectives on the platform studies in management research). Waseda University IT Strategy Research Center Working Paper 39:1–25 (in Japanese)

Newman MEJ (2010) Networks: An introduction. Oxford University Press, Oxford

Nikkei BP, Net Global (1999) Nikkei LSI database Sekai Handoutai Seizou Souchi Shiken Tesuto Souchi Shijou Nenkan 1999 (Nikkei LSI database–Yearbook of manufacturing and testing equipment in the global semiconductor market 1999). Nikkei BP, Tokyo (in Japanese)

Nikkei BP, Net Global (2001) Nikkei LSI database Sekai Handoutai Seizou Souchi Shiken Tesuto Souchi Shijou Nenkan 1999 (Nikkei LSI database–Yearbook of manufacturing and testing equipment in the global semiconductor market 2001). Nikkei BP, Tokyo (in Japanese)

Ogawa K (2009) Kokusai hyoujunka to Jigyou Senryaku (International standards and business strategy). Hakuto Shobou, Tokyo (in Japanese)

Ogawa K (2014) Oupun and Kurozu Senryaku: Nihon Kigyou Saikou no Jouken (Open and closed strategy: Conditions for the revival of Japanese companies). Shoueisha, Tokyo (in Japanese)

R Development Core Team (2011) R: A language and environment for statistical computing. R Foundation for Statistical Computing, Vienna. http://www.R-project.org/

Rochet J, Tirole J (2003) Platform competition in two-sided markets. J Eur Econ Assoc 1(4):990–1029

SEMI [Semiconductor Equipment and Materials International] (2005) WorldFabWatch: Database (Jan, 2005th edn. SEMI, Milpitas CA

SEMI [Semiconductor Equipment and Materials International] (2009) WorldFabWatch: Database (May, 2009th edn. SEMI, Milpitas CA

Senoo K (2009) Gijutsuryoku de Masaru Nihon ga naze Jigyou de Makerunoka (Why does Japan, with its technological prowess, lose in business?). Diamondsha, Tokyo (in Japanese)

Shintaku J, Eto M (2008) Konsensasu Hyojun Senryaku (Strategy for consensus standards). Nikkei Inc., Tokyo (in Japanese)

Shintaku J, Tatsumoto H, Yoshimoto T, Tomita J, Park E (2008) Seihin Akitecuchua kara miru Gijutsu Denpa to Kokusai Bungyou (International technology diffusion and division of labor from the perspective of product architecture). Hitosubashi Bus Rev 56(2):42–61 (in Japanese)

Shintaku J, Konomi Y, Shibata K (2000) Defakuto Sutandado no Honshitsu (Essentials of de facto standards). Yuhikaku, Tokyo (in Japanese)

Space RI (2000) Twenty-five years of SEMI standards 1973-98. SEMI, Milpitas CA

Takemoto K (2013) R seminar on igraph. https://sites.google.com/site/kztakemoto/r-seminar-on-igraph—supplementary-information. Accessed 23 Jan 2015

Tomita J, Tatsumoto H (2008) Handoutai ni okeru Kokusai Hyojunka Senryaku–300 mm wafer Taiou Handoutai Seizousouchi no Jirei (Standardization strategy in the semiconductor industry–the case study of semiconductor manufacturing equipment for 300 mm wafer standards). MMRC Discuss Paper 222:1–28 (in Japanese)

Tarui Y (2008) Sekai wo Rido suru Handoutai Kyoudou Kenkyuu Purojekuto (World-leading joint research projects in the semiconductor sector). Kogyo Chosakai Publishing Co., Ltd, Tokyo (in Japanese)

Tatsumoto H, Tomita J, Fujimoto T (2009) Purosesu Sangyou to shiteno Handoutai Maekoutei (An analysis of semiconductor wafer process as processing foundry business). In: Fujimoto T, Kuwashima K (eds) Nihongata Purosesu Sangyou (Japanese process industries). Yuhikaku, Tokyo (in Japanese)

Tokyo Electron (2001) Annual repoto 2001 (Annual report 2001). http://www.tel.co.jp/ir/library/ar/index.htm. Accessed 01 Sept 2015 (in Japanese)

Tokyo Electron (2002) Annual repoto 2002 (Annual report 2002). http://www.tel.co.jp/ir/library/ar/index.htm. Accessed 01 Sept 2015 (in Japanese)

Tokyo Electron (2003) Annual repoto 2003 (Annual report 2003). http://www.tel.co.jp/ir/library/ar/index.htm. Accessed 01 Sept 2015 (in Japanese)

Tokyo Electron (2004) Annual repoto 2004 (Annual report 2004). http://www.tel.co.jp/ir/library/ar/index.htm. Accessed 01 Sept 2015 (in Japanese)

Tokyo Electron (2005) Annual repoto 2005 (Annual report 2005). http://www.tel.co.jp/ir/library/ar/index.htm. Accessed 01 Sept 2015 (in Japanese)

Wasserman S, Faust K (1994) Social network analysis: methods and applications. Cambridge University Press, Cambridge

Watanabe T (ed) (2011) Bijinesu Moderu Inobesyon (Business model innovation). Hakutou Shobo, Tokyo (in Japanese)

Yamada H (2008) Defakuto Sutandado no Kyousou Senryaku (Competitive strategy for de facto standards) Hakuto Shobo, Tokyo (in Japanese)

Chapter 5
Ecosystem Management and Entry into Peripheral Markets: The Platform Strategy of Intel

An ecosystem can grow only when symbiont firms make the necessary investments. To ensure the smooth expansion of the ecosystem, platform firms willingly collaborate, and sometimes intentionally compete, with symbiont firms. Entry into peripheral markets is the strategic tool that they use for this purpose. This chapter examines Intel Corporation's entry into peripheral markets to promote the adoption of Pentium CPUs in the 1990s. An ecosystem can grow only when symbiont firms make the necessary investments. To ensure the smooth expansion of the ecosystem, platform firms willingly collaborate, and sometimes intentionally compete, with symbiont firms. Entry into peripheral markets is the strategic tool that they use for this purpose. This chapter examines Intel Corporation's entry into peripheral markets to promote the adoption of Pentium CPUs in the 1990s.

Intel is a manufacturer of core semiconductor components for personal computers (PCs) and one of the best-known platform firms. Intel aimed to diffuse a new personal computer architecture when it launched its Pentium CPU in 1995.

The diffusion of the architecture, however, was very slow. Intel successfully formed a new ecosystem but struggled to expand it. To overcome this obstacle, the firm decided to enter the chipset market and the motherboard market, which were peripheral to its own market.

Intel's entry into the chipset market was meant to reinforce its bargaining power and its entry into the motherboard market had the goal to encourage symbiont firms to expand the ecosystem. Our case study confirms that Intel effectively stimulated investments by symbiont firms and achieved the growth of the ecosystem through its entry into peripheral markets.

5.1 Introduction: Research Questions

Intel Corporation, the best-known platform firm in the semiconductor industry, has been extensively examined by researchers (Gawer and Cusumano 2002; Gawer and Henderson 2007). Intel is a semiconductor manufacturer and not a personal computer

H. Tatsumoto, *Platform Strategy for Global Markets*,
https://doi.org/10.1007/978-981-33-6789-0_5

provider, but it plays an important role in the PC ecosystem. How could a semiconductor supplier become a platform firm of the whole PC industry and gain such power over it? This question is the reason behind our study. Indeed, even though the car navigation system has become an important element of the automobile, it is hard to imagine a car navigation supplier turning into a platform firm of the whole automobile industry.[1] Nonetheless, such a phenomenon did take place in the PC industry.

Back in the 1980s, Intel was merely a component supplier. It provided a core component of the PC, i.e., the CPU,[2] but it was still nothing more than a major component supplier. Had Intel remained a pure supplier, it would not have grown into the gigantic corporation that it is today.

As described later in this chapter, Intel was recognized as a platform firm in the PC ecosystem thanks to its success in introducing the Pentium CPU (from now on, referred to as the *Pentium*) in the 1990s. Even before the launch of the Pentium, the firm already had substantial influence on the industry, but PC makers still regarded it simply as a core component supplier. With the success of the Pentium, it established its position as a platform firm and also managed to expand the PC ecosystem across the world.

When pursuing ecosystem expansion, a platform firm needs to set the strategic goal of diffusing its own products/services while maintaining competitiveness. In order to trigger the formation of an ecosystem, platform firms utilize open standards, which is called strategic standardization. That said, an open standard alone does not guarantee the diffusion of a platform product. In fact, the market share of the Pentium was as low as around 3% even two years after its launch on the market. No spread of the platform product means no expansion of the ecosystem and, in such a case, entering a peripheral market might prove invaluable.

Entry into peripheral markets is considered part of the bundling strategy (see Chap. 2). The goal of strategic bundling, as derived from theoretical studies, is to exclude competitors from and control the market. In actuality, however, platform firms develop and implement more complex bundling strategies and lock-in is not their sole purpose. They sometimes enter a peripheral market to motivate symbiont firms to make investments, so as to expand the ecosystem. In the case study presented here, Intel entered the motherboard market with the aim to create the right investment climate for its symbiont firms, i.e., Taiwanese motherboard suppliers. To shed light on how the bundling strategies of platform firms work, this chapter examines the case of the Pentium, by focusing on Intel's strategic entry into the chipset and motherboard markets.

---

[1]As of 2007, it was not plausible that the car navigation system would be a platform component of the automobile. More recently, however, with the introduction of autonomous driving, digital maps have become an important platform of the ecosystem.

[2]The CPU, which stands for Central Processing Unit, is the primary semiconductor component that provides the computation capability of a personal computer.

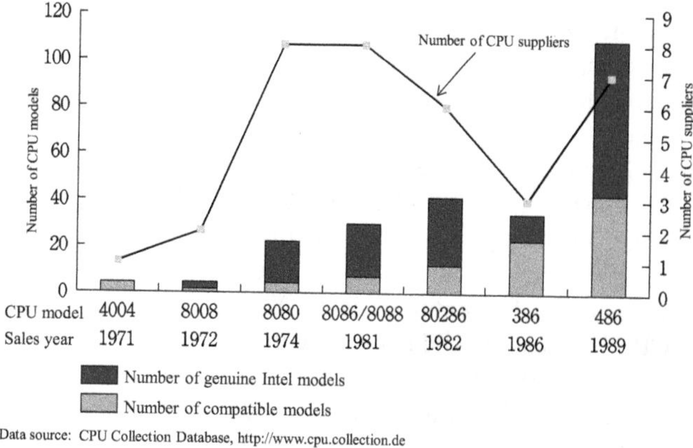

Fig. 5.1 Number of CPU suppliers and CPU models

5.2 Early 1990s: A Tough Time for Intel

Let us begin by looking at the situation in which Intel found itself in in the early 1990s. In 1986, Intel launched the 386 CPU, the world's first 32-bit CPU for the personal computer, and achieved incredible success, which was referred to as *elegant monopoly*. The 486 CPU, the successor to the 386, was also well received in the market, and the firm further increased its sales.

As the PC market continued to expand, the CPU market attracted new entrants, since Intel was the sole supplier at that time. Some firms started manufacturing compatible CPUs and some workstation CPU suppliers started providing CPUs for personal computers. PC manufacturers welcomed this trend since they were always keen on sourcing cheaper CPUs. Thus, in the early 1990s, Intel had to face four major threats, described below.

5.2.1 Rise of Suppliers of Compatible CPUs

Intel's sales came for the most part from CPUs. Therefore, the greatest threat to the firm was to see the x86 CPU[3] market, which it had built from scratch, eroded by other firms marketing compatible CPUs. The term *compatible CPUs* here refers to chips capable of processing the same tasks and running the same software as Intel's x86 CPU series. These chips were developed and sold by Intel's rival semiconductor firms.

Figure 5.1 tracks the number of CPU suppliers in the market and the number of CPU models (derivative models) available. The models provided by Intel are

[3] An x86 CPU is a CPU whose instruction set is compatible with the 8086. CPUs having instruction sets compatible with each other can run the same software and hardware.

counted as genuine CPU models, while the compatible CPUs supplied by competitors are counted as compatible models. The larger the number of suppliers, the fiercer the competition. The larger the ratio of compatible CPU models, the fiercer the competition against Intel.

From the 1970s to the early 1980s, the number of CPU suppliers was quite high, but it had fallen considerably by 1986. This trend was closely related to Intel's CPU business strategy. In the 1970s, its core product was DRAM and Intel willingly licensed CPU production to other makers, since CPU sales amounted to only a relatively small portion of its entire business. Yet, in 1985, Intel shifted its strategic focus to the CPU business and did not license the production of the x86, causing the number of CPU suppliers to fall.

However, Fig. 5.1 also shows an increase in the number of CPU suppliers at the end of the decade, which suggests that several semiconductor manufacturers developed compatible CPUs on their own, without licensing from Intel. These compatible CPU suppliers included Advanced Micro Devices (AMD), Inc. and Cyrix.

Such follower firms made the most of their position as followers to compete against Intel. The key to the success of any CPU business is to assist the growth of third parties developing software and hardware products that a specific CPU supports. CPU suppliers, therefore, provide development environments for software and hardware vendors and organize seminars to circulate technical information about their CPUs. Intel, which pioneered this approach, had to spend vast amounts of money to carry out these actions. Compatible CPU suppliers, on the other hand, did not have to bear any of those costs and just concentrated on the sales of their compatible CPUs.

Because they were designed to be manufactured at a lower cost, compatible CPUs were also advantageous in terms of price competition. For instance, the compatible CPU provided by Cyrix had large cache capacity and executed the instruction set of x86 CPUs using software (microcode) rather than hardware circuitry. Hence, compatible CPU providers supplied cost-effective CPUs to the market, despite inferior performance, consequently expanding their market share in the volume zone.

Intel filed lawsuits against these compatible CPU suppliers for infringing its patents and copyrights in an attempt to beat them off, but it seemed difficult to completely remove them from the market through legal action.

5.2.2 *Price Busting in the PC Market*

After the launch of the IBM PC in 1981, the PC market kept growing steadily, until it started to slow down in the early 1990s. The industry as a whole acknowledged that the PC market had reached the point of maturity and entered the next phase of price competition. The first to respond to this change were emerging PC manufacturers, such as Dell and AST Research. They procured PCs from Taiwanese PC manufacturers (ODM firms) and provided cost-competitive products to the North American market.[4]

On the other hand, experienced PC manufacturers with in-house research and development capabilities, such as Compaq, were heavily impacted by this price busting scenario. At that time, Compaq enjoyed high profitability, by providing mainly high-end models, and was regarded as the BMW of the PC industry. Thus, falling PC prices placed considerable strain on its business.

In 1992, Eckhard Pfeiffer, Compaq's newly appointed CEO, announced a major redesigning of the company's products to provide low-cost PCs. This new strategy involved a different approach to parts procurement and cost reduction efforts targeted the CPU in particular, due to its high price. If Compaq had depended on Intel alone for its core component, it would have been difficult to reduce the cost of purchasing CPUs, which led to the decision to assist other compatible CPU suppliers. Indeed, there was growing willingness among PC suppliers to accept compatible CPUs.[5]

5.2.3 Rise of RISC CPU Suppliers

In the same period, suppliers of workstation CPUs started appearing in the PC market. Workstation CPUs, called RISC CPUs, are designed for higher performance and their architecture is different from that of CPUs for PCs.

The first attempt to apply RISC CPUs to PCs occurred in the early 1990s, exemplified by the formation of the ACE Consortium[6] in 1991. The ACE Consortium planned to use RISC CPUs in high-end PCs, so as to enable them to run 3D CAD and perform other tasks that had previously been exclusive to workstations.

In line with this movement, Microsoft Corporation developed an OS for the RISC CPU, released as Windows NT in 1993. Applications for Windows could also run on Windows NT-based PCs, opening up the possibility that RISC CPUs could become widely adopted across the high-end and mid-range markets.

---

[4]ODM stands for Original Design Manufacturing. Within the scope of their contracts, PC ODM firms not only perform manufacturing but also procure components and sometimes even design the PCs themselves. These Taiwanese ODM firms are described in Chap. 6.

[5]IBM and Compaq initially announced that they would not employ the Pentium. Compaq announced that it would adopt compatible CPUs provided by AMD for its strategically important Presario series.

[6]The ACE Consortium consisted of Microsoft, MIPS Computer Systems, Digital Equipment Corporation, the Santa Cruz Operation, Acer, Control Data Corporation, Kubota, NEC Corporation, NKK, Olivetti, Prime Computer, Pyramid Technology, Siemens, Silicon Graphics, Sony, Sumitomo, Tandem, Wang Laboratories and Zenith Data Systems.

5.2.4 *Long-Standing Legacy Technologies*

At the beginning of the 1990s, a drastic change occurred in the PC market, i.e., the transition of the user operating environment from CUI (character user interface) to GUI (graphical user interface).

In response to the explosive diffusion of GUI-enabled Windows 3.0, launched by Microsoft in 1990, PC suppliers wanted to provide PCs with graphics processing capabilities compatible with Windows 3.0, and a market for graphics accelerators for Windows soon developed. Graphics accelerators suppliers defined an interface called the VL bus, which, thanks to its simple structure, was instantly adopted across the industry.

The VL bus, however, worked with the external bus of the 486 CPU, a fact that was inconvenient for Intel, which wanted to promote the shift to the Pentium. The dependence of the VL bus on the graphics accelerator and the CPU hampered the transition to a higher performance CPU generation. To Intel, which continued research and development to further enhance CPU performance, the VL bus was a legacy technology that prevented evolution in the desired direction.

Once an old technology, such as the VL bus, takes root, end users accumulate assets that are compatible with it, like 486 CPU-based assets in the example above, which makes the diffusion of a new technology (Pentium, in our case) very slow. This market reality was perceived by Intel as nothing but a threat to the evolution of the CPU and was, therefore, unacceptable.

5.3 Transition to a New Generation

5.3.1 *Essential Problem: Lingering of the Old Technology*

Of the four threats faced by Intel in the early 1990s, the most pressing one was growing competition with suppliers of compatible CPUs, but the most essential problem was the legacy technology lingering inside the PC, as described in Sect. 5.2.4.

The performance of a PC is determined not only by its CPU. PC manufacturers buy many kinds of electronic components from parts suppliers and assemble them into their products, which determines the overall performance of their PCs. These electronic components exchange electric signals and, to do so, they need a common protocol. The protocol discussed here is called the bus standard.

The aforementioned VL bus was an extension of the old standard of the former generation and, as a result, it was unsuitable for high-speed processing of bulk data. A new generation, or a new architecture, was needed.

RISC CPU proponents suggested bringing the architecture used in high-speed workstations into the PC industry. Though its adoption would mean sacrificing compatibility with traditional PCs, this architecture could greatly enhance processing speed. To counter this move by RISC CPU suppliers, Intel had to come up with a new-generation architecture dedicated to the PC industry as quickly as possible.

Additionally, the lingering legacy technology had created a desirable market environment for compatible CPU suppliers, which were developing and providing inexpensive CPUs and lost no opportunity to stage a price war against Intel. PC manufacturers, already affected by intense price competition, were inclined to adopt more affordable compatible CPUs. Clearly, that intense price competition was something that Intel had to avoid at all cost.

5.3.2 Inside the PC: Architecture of the PC

In order to explain the transition between technological generations, this section describes the architecture of the PC. Figure 5.2 is a photograph of a motherboard, the core component of the PC. The motherboard is an electronic board, equipped with the CPU, hard disk drive (HDD), dynamic random access memory (DRAM), graphics card and so on. It is connected to the power unit and then placed inside the case to form the personal computer. Figure 5.2 shows how the CPU and the chipset are mounted onto the motherboard.

To gain a better understanding, Fig. 5.3 displays a PC's core electronic components and the interdependencies among them. It is easy to see a shift in the scope of Intel-supplied components between before and after the launch of its platform product (1990 and 1992, respectively). The platform product that Intel developed was an integrated set of CPU and chipsets.

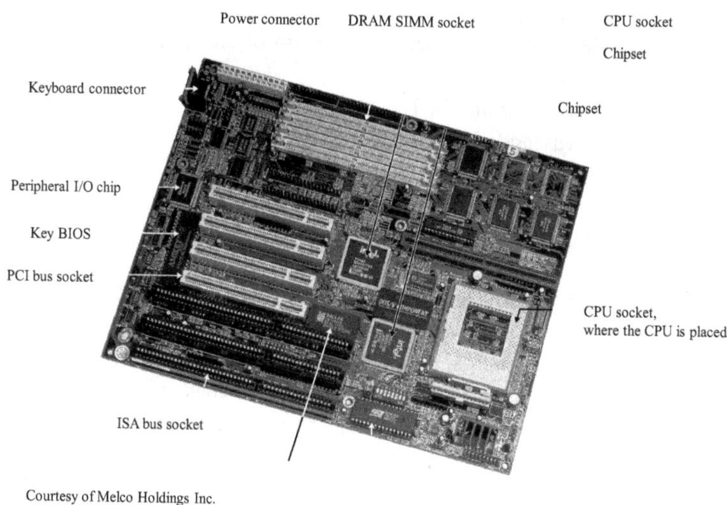

Fig. 5.2 Photo of a motherboard

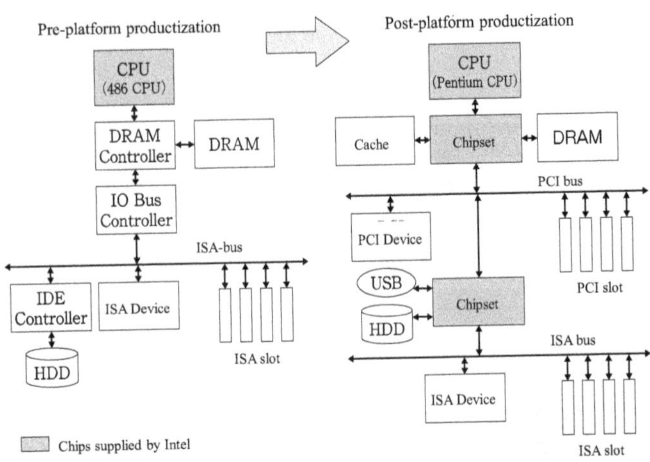

Fig. 5.3 Platform products of Intel

The shaded rectangles indicate semiconductors provided by Intel. Before platform productization, Intel provided CPUs only. After implementing its platform strategy, the platform firm provided two chipsets in addition to the CPU. Chipsets had previously been developed by major PC manufacturers in house. Intel entered the chipset market and started supplying chipsets too, as part of its platform strategy.

The lines between the semiconductors and the electronic components in Fig. 5.3 refer to the signal transmission line, which transfers data. As a single line links multiple components, a protocol is needed to define the rules concerning the use of the line, so as to prevent data collision and congestion. A combination of the physical form of the signal line and the protocol in the form of electronic signals is called a bus standard.

Comparing the two diagrams in Fig. 5.3, it is clear that a new bus standard, called the PCI bus, was added in the post-platform structure. The establishment of the PCI bus standard was the first step that Intel took in pursuit of its platform strategy. Establishing a new bus standard was essentially equivalent to proposing a new architecture of the PC.

Intel's platform strategy was implemented when the Pentium CPU was released in 1993. The launch of the Pentium CPU was not just about putting a new-generation CPU on the market but about setting up a platform business for the first time, which represented a whole new challenge for Intel. The firm introduced various novel concepts, rather than simply drawing on traditional business models. Its first move was to establish a new bus standard for signals between chipsets (PCI bus standard), through a consortium called the PCI Special Interest Group (PCI-SIG). Intel thus engaged in open standardization, paving the way for the creation of a new ecosystem.

5.3.3 *First Step Toward a New Architecture: Establishment of the PCI Bus*

Intel firstly formed a consortium to develop a new ecosystem in which the bus protocol would be standardized as the PCI standard. The bus, as shown in Fig. 5.3, is an electric circuit connecting the chips and the bus protocol is a signal procedure. The PCI is a bus standard; it is not a CPU architecture but a computer architecture. The standardization of bus standards had usually been carried out by PC firms.[7] Hence, the involvement of Intel, a CPU supplier, in the basic design of the PC did not only cross the borders of business segments but was also likely to cause a conflict of interest with its clients.

This is why the initial scope of standardization of the PCI was limited to the local bus of the CPU,[8] i.e., the bus adjacent to the CPU. The data rate between the CPU and the DRAM, which were co-located on the local bus at that time, had reached its limit and a new protocol was needed. The establishment of a new local bus standard was an essential issue for Intel's core business, since the PCI bus was originally positioned between the CPU and the chipset. The first version of the PCI standard (Rev. 1.0) was released by Intel in June 1992 out of sheer necessity as a CPU supplier.

The next version (Rev. 2.0), released with less urgency in April 1993, was naturally quite different. The scope of standardization covered not only the local bus but also the system bus (the bus for the extension IO chip), meaning that the standard no longer concerned CPU suppliers alone but PC firms as well. Hence, Rev. 2.0 was released under the name of PCI-SIG, indicating that it was published not by Intel but by a consortium.

Originally, there were five participants in PCI-SIG, i.e., Intel, DEC, Compaq, IBM and NCR. PCI Rev 2.0 was an important turning point[9] because Intel, a CPU supplier, took the initiative in standardizing a portion of PC architecture, which triggered the commencement of its platform strategy.

---

[7]Traditionally, bus standards were formulated by PC suppliers as de facto standards. The AT bus standard, which was a major standard before the establishment of the PCI, is a good example. It first appeared in the IBM PC/AT personal computer released in 1984 (hence its name) and was defined solely by IBM, making it a de facto standard. For extension devices to be developed, IBM made the AT bus circuit diagram open but kept the signal access timing and other pieces of information confidential, which actually hindered compatibility among extension devices. In 1987, the Institute of Electrical and Electronics Engineers (IEEE) specified the mechanical and electrical properties and released the standard under the new name of ISA (Industry Standard Architecture) bus. However, the name did not catch on and the industry continued to use the expression *AT bus*.

[8]In many cases, the data rate of the local bus is the bottleneck of the processing capability of the CPU.

[9]In June 1995, PCI Rev 2.1, based on the clock frequency of 66 MHz, was published, marking an increase in the signal pin numbers. PCI Rev 2.1 became the most widespread version of the Pentium CPU. PCI Rev 2.2 was released in December 1998, which coincided with the period of transition from Pentium II to Pentium III and the time when PCI-based devices were shifting to the 3.3 V bus system. Hence, this revision took low electricity consumption into consideration.

Table 5.1 CPU diffusion by type in North America at the end of 1994

CPU Type	Number of units (1,000 units)	Share (%)
Intel 486	26,900	38
Intel 386	19,500	28
Intel 286 or older	11,800	17
Motorola 68000	9,200	13
Intel Pentium	2,300	3
Power PC	370	1
Total	70,700	100

Source Uchida (1994), based on data provided by IDC

5.3.4 *Launch of the Pentium CPU and Its Delayed Diffusion*

Before the introduction of the Pentium, every time Intel launched a new CPU, new PC models carrying the latest CPU were released on the market, but always with a substantial time lag. For instance, the 80286, launched in 1982, took two years to become available to end users as the core of the PC/AT, while a full year passed between the release of the 386 CPU and its adoption onboard PCs. Thus, regardless of the time of first release of Intel CPUs, it was entirely up to PC manufacturers to decide whether they would feature in new PC models.

Table 5.1 provides some rough figures about the units present in the North American market by CPU generation at the end of 1994. The Pentium CPU, launched in March 1993, was a strategically important product for Intel to gain competitive advantage vis-à-vis compatible CPU suppliers and RISC CPU suppliers. However, its diffusion was still only around 3% as of the end of 1994.

This time lag in Intel CPU adoption may be ascribed to the rise of compatible CPU suppliers. These suppliers targeted the PC segment of older CPU generations, such as the 386 and 486.[10] The performance of the compatible CPUs developed by them was equivalent to that of the latest Intel CPU, so PC manufacturers simply needed to replace Intel's genuine CPUs with compatible products. These compatible CPUs, therefore, represented an obstacle to market transition to the Pentium generation.

In opposition to this trend, Intel's key strategy at that time was to manufacture and supply a massive number of Pentium CPUs and increase the share of Pentium-based PCs in the market. This mass manufacturing and supply was the only way for the firm to gain profits by providing its Pentium CPUs at reasonable prices, so as to make up for the substantial research and development costs and manufacturing costs

[10]Another reason for the delayed diffusion of the Pentium CPU was the inferior performance of the preceding 486 CPU in terms of integer operations. Compatible CPU suppliers were launching improved 486-based CPUs and users could achieve higher performance by just upgrading their CPU rather than buying a new Pentium-based PC (http://ascii.jp/elem/000/000/915/915669/index-2.html, accessed 07 Feb 2017).

borne. Mass diffusion would also revitalize complementary goods markets. This was the most powerful strategy for Intel to compete against suppliers of RISC CPUs and compatible CPUs.

Nonetheless, because the popularity of CPU and PC models is frequently a chicken-and-egg situation, the practical implementation of the above strategy was by no means easy. A new mechanism that would allow the Pentium CPU to be sold much faster and in much larger quantities had to be created. Intel did so by entering its peripheral markets to manage the ecosystem firsthand and encourage symbiont firms to invest.

5.4 Entry into Two Peripheral Markets: Management of the Ecosystem

5.4.1 Entry into the Chipset Market

Under the circumstances described above, Intel assigned a new role to its chipset business. Intel's chipset business, which had originated from the ASIC business, started in 1986 and was aimed at manufacturing semiconductors for PC peripherals, such as keyboard controllers and timer controllers for the IBM PC/AT. Nonetheless, the firm was not very enthusiastic about the results achieved until then. The chipset business brought in only very low gross margins, unlike the CPU business, and was also subjected to extremely harsh competition. In view of its limited profits, deciding to invest in the chipset business was a bold move. The CPU business, on the contrary, enjoyed much higher gross profits, equal to about 40% (1988–1990).[11]

Around 1991, when the establishment of the PCI standard became a realistic goal, Intel reformed its organizational structure. The chipset business (Integrated Microprocessor Division—IMD) became an arm of the Microprocessor Group and was renamed PCI Division (Yu 1998).

Thus, not only did Intel give a new role to its chipset business but it also engaged in it with determination. The division developed a chipset implementing the PCI standard and also established a development plan for chipsets in line with the CPU development roadmap (Yu 1998).

In 1992, the chipset division built a prototype of the 420TX (Saturn) chipset for the i486. The Saturn chipset was a pilot product designed for the 486 CPU and was presented at Comdex, a large-scale PC tradeshow. The presentation, which advocated

[11]The low profitability of chipset products was always a matter of serious concern to Intel. The chipset division, however, persuaded the management that, without high-performance chipsets, Intel's high-speed CPUs would not be accepted in the market. The argument was convincing, yet the chipset division did not manage to secure the necessary budget and did all that it could to keep the business going, despite extremely low profitability. For example, the manufacturing of chipsets was outsourced to third-party fabs. Later, both in-house fabs and third-party fabs contributed to Intel's chipset production (Burgelman 2002).

Table 5.2 Release history of CPUs and corresponding chipsets

Release	Chipset type	Name	Corresponding processor
1992 Nov	420TX	Saturn	i486/SX2/DX/DX2, Intel DX4
1993 Mar	430LX	Mercury	Pentium 60/66 MHz(P5)
1994 Mar	430NX	Neptune	Pentium(P54C), MMX Pentium
1994 Mar	420EX	Aries	i486/SX2/DX/DX2, Intel DX4
1994 Mar	420ZX	Saturn II	i486/SX2/DX/DX2, Intel DX4
1995 Jan	430FX	Triton	Pentium(P54C), MMX Pentium
1995 Oct	430MX	Mobile Triton	Pentium(P54C), MMX Pentium
1996 Feb	430VX	Triton II VX	Pentium(P54C), MMX Pentium
1997 Feb	430TX	Triton II TX	Pentium(P54C), MMX Pentium

the superiority of the Saturn chipset by comparing the graphics performance of the ISA and the PCI, was very successful and confirmed the significance of planning chipsets following the direction of the CPU roadmap (Yu 1998).

Since CPUs and chipsets were designed and developed according to the same roadmap, the launch of a new CPU was always announced concurrently with the launch of associated chipsets. Table 5.2 provides a release history of CPUs and corresponding chipsets and proves that Intel did develop them based on a coherent plan. Note that the Pentium CPU had some derivative versions, such as P5, P54C, MMX Pentium and Pentium II.[12]

In 1995, Intel released the 430FX (Triton), which became the firm's most popular chipset product of the early days. 1995 was also the year of the *Intel 3-2-1* Project, described below in Sect. 5.4.3. The firm sold four million units of its PCI chipsets in 1994, 20 million in 1995 and 70 million in 1996, making it the largest PC chipset supplier in just a few years' time (Yu 1998, p. 57).

[12]The Pentium CPU had multiple versions. The first version, called P5, used the bipolar CMOS (BiCMOS) process and was thus a large, die-size product. The CMOS process was used in P54C and its follow-ons.

5.4.2 Entry into the Motherboard Market

Since the diffusion of the Pentium CPU was so slow, Intel thought that supplying corresponding chipsets was not sufficient and decided to produce Pentium-based motherboards too (Electronic Buyers' News, 02 Oct 1995). Yet, this meant that it would face serious competition from traditional motherboard suppliers and PC suppliers that developed and provided their own motherboards.

The decision came under fierce criticism even from the inside. The firm was earning over 40% gross profits and entering the motherboard market would definitely lower this margin. Some also said that it would represent a deviation from Intel's business domain, since producing motherboards is essentially about assembling parts, which requires a different set of technical capabilities from that of semiconductor manufacturers. To Intel, however, ensuring a swift transition to the Pentium was what mattered the most.

In order to achieve this goal, it was vital to integrate the CPU with its peripheral chips. In particular, the area related to the extension I/O (the system bus) and the area related to memory (DRAM) had to be adjusted for a PC system with the latest Intel CPU to be developed. The peripheral LSI chips and adjustments with the bus might pose an issue in case the motherboard is not properly designed.

5.4.2.1 PC Firms and Motherboard Suppliers

Traditionally, motherboards corresponding to the latest CPU were first released by PC manufacturers possessing the appropriate technical capabilities, such as Compaq, Hewlett-Packard and IBM. When a new CPU was introduced, these PC firms developed the corresponding motherboard for their own server and PC products. They started by developing a motherboard for servers, which would bring in margins as high as 25–30%, sufficient to recover its development costs. After that, they spent 18 months or so to slowly develop a motherboard for consumer PCs. This strategy was known as the *generation window* concept. It was clear to Intel that the diffusion of the Pentium CPU would be delayed if Intel continued to rely on PC manufacturers like Compaq and IBM.

By contrast, Dell and Gateway2000, the emerging PC manufacturers, were competitive in the volume zone market targeted at consumers and refrained from developing cutting-edge motherboards by themselves. They just waited for specialized motherboard suppliers to develop their own products supporting the latest-generation CPU.

Many of these motherboard suppliers were Taiwanese. They typically developed motherboards only when they were convinced that the latest CPU just released would become popular; otherwise, they deferred the development activities. This was because developing a motherboard compatible with the newest CPU required designing electronic circuitry using new chipsets and new technology; hence, it entailed considerable risks. They understandably hesitated to invest until they became confident that a new motherboard would be profitable.

In such an environment, Intel started producing its original motherboards. In 1993, the firm manufactured them in Oregon, Puerto Rico and Ireland, where industrial board computers used to be made (The Wall Street Journal, 31 Oct 1995). The manufacturing of motherboards for the Pentium in these plants in 1993 was, so to say, a trial in mass production and ended up outputting a million motherboards (Electronic Buyers' News, 30 May 1994). Intel's sales of motherboards soared to approximately 4 to 5 million in the following year (Electronic Buyers' News, 02 Oct 1995).

Nonetheless, the supply volume of Intel's motherboards was still small in the global market. About 80% of PC motherboards were supplied by Taiwan as of 1994. To truly spread the Pentium CPU worldwide, Intel needed to involve Taiwanese manufacturers in developing and supplying motherboards for the Pentium.

5.4.2.2 Reaction of Taiwanese Motherboard Firms

Taiwan saw a swift rise in specialized suppliers of motherboards dedicated to PCs (i.e., motherboard firms).[13] At the dawn of the PC era, PC manufacturers had designed and manufactured their own motherboards, but the emerging makers typically procured motherboards from motherboard suppliers, instead of developing them in house. To meet their demand, specialized motherboard suppliers grew and increasingly gained power. Elitegroup, established in 1987, was one of the first specialized motherboard manufacturers that rose to prominence.

The motherboard manufactured by Taiwanese suppliers were 20% cheaper than those produced by their US rivals. When fierce price competition started in the US PC market in the early 1990s, major PC providers naturally decided to opt for Taiwan-made motherboards. The procurement ratio of Taiwan-made motherboards by US PC manufacturers was 32% in 1992 and 48% in 1993, while it exceeded 50% in 1994 (Mizuhashi 2001).

Taiwanese motherboard firms were responsible for 80% of global motherboard production in the early 1990s. In 1994, 17.5 million motherboards were manufactured in Taiwan (Electronic Buyers' News, 30 Jan 1995) and the market share of Taiwanese manufacturers reached 81% in the same year (Electronic Buyers' News, 04 Mar 1996). It should be noted that these figures refer to outsourced motherboards and most major PC suppliers actually manufactured their own. In any case, these market shares are high enough to emphasize the influence of Taiwanese firms on the market.

[13]The Taiwanese PC industry was established in 1983, when imitations of the newly launched IBM PC/XT started to be manufactured by Taiwanese makers. Since they had been producing imitations of the Apple II, it was only natural for these manufacturers to enter the market for IBM-compatible PCs. In 1984, however, IBM filed a lawsuit against the Taiwanese manufacturers for breaching the BIOS patent and, in 1985, it hunted down the guilty parties together with the Taiwanese government. The following year, IBM and the Taiwanese manufacturers reached a settlement. As time went by, some Taiwanese suppliers started manufacturing original-brand PCs and exporting them to Europe, while others became OEM firms for leading US brands, producing PCs and motherboards.

In 1993, Intel asked Taiwanese motherboard suppliers to manufacture motherboards dedicated to the latest Pentium CPU. The suppliers, however, were reluctant, since Pentium chips accounted for only 3% of processors in North America at that time and the overwhelming majority of motherboards were 486-based. It is thus no surprise that Taiwanese motherboard suppliers were hesitant to embrace the Pentium business.

5.4.3 Intel 3-2-1 Project

In late 1994, Intel announced a plan to substantially increase the production volume of its own motherboards to be released the following year. This was called *3-2-1 Project*. The numbers stood for the 30 million units of the Pentium CPU, the 20 million chipsets and the 10 million Pentium-based motherboards that Intel aimed to ship out in 1995 (Microprocessor Report, Vol. 9, No. 11, 21 Aug 1995).

10 million motherboards were equal to approximately 20–30% of the entire production in Taiwan at that time,[14] and the announcement put a great deal of pressure on Taiwanese motherboard suppliers.

Furthermore, in June 1995, Intel cut the price of its Pentium-based motherboards[15] by 11%. Intel-branded motherboards were recognized as expensive, but the price reduction brought them down to 160 USD/unit, as opposed to 140–160 USD/unit for Taiwanese motherboards with equivalent specifications. Hence, Taiwanese motherboards seemed to retain their competitiveness at first glance but, in marketing its products, Intel smartly offered a combination of motherboard and chipsets. This caused Taiwanese motherboard suppliers to be affected by strong price pressure (Electronic Buyers' News, 26 Jun 1995).

Despite such efforts, Intel could not achieve its target motherboard production volume and production remained in the 5–8 million range in 1995 (Nihon Kougyou Shinbun 1997; Electronic Buyers' News, 04 Mar 1996).

The failure to accomplish the ten million motherboard production target needs to be further scrutinized. Section 5.4.4 looks at this point in detail and tries to determine whether it can be ascribed to a simple lack of capability on the part of Intel or whether it had to do with the firm's strategic behavior.

[14]In 1994, the export of motherboards from Taiwan amounted to about 30 million units, excluding those for Desktop PCs and Note PCs produced in Taiwan.

[15]The name of the product line was Zappa.

5.4.4 Retreat from the Motherboard Market and Standardization Efforts

Intel did not just observe and passively accept the failure of its ambitious motherboard production plan for 1995. In July 1995, it announced the ATX standard (ATX 1.0) for motherboards and, toward the end of the year, it asked Taiwanese motherboard vendors to manufacture ATX-compatible motherboards. The firm switched its strategy to manufacturing the motherboard by itself up to a certain amount and subcontracting the rest to Taiwanese vendors (Nihon Kougyou Shinbun 1997).

The ATX standard meticulously specified the position of the power source and the layout of the CPU and external IO connectors on the motherboard, representing a strong push toward the commoditization of motherboards. Intel designed its motherboards based on the ATX standard, the Taiwanese suppliers dealt with manufacturing and Intel then put them on the market. Since ATX-based motherboards relying on Intel's designs were readily available, PC manufacturers started procuring ATX-based motherboards as well (Electronic Buyers' News, 04 Mar 1996). Subsequently, Intel released motherboard standards in quick succession, as shown in Table 5.3.

In 1996, Intel started licensing its motherboard technology to major Taiwanese motherboard suppliers. The first licensee was Acer (Electronic Buyers' News (10616624), 29 Jun 1996, Vol. 42, Issue 2101, p. 2), followed by various other Taiwanese firms (Electronic Buyers' News, 04 Mar 4 1996, Issue 996, p. 12). In May 1996, the firm concluded manufacturing technology license agreements with five major Taiwanese motherboard suppliers. As mentioned above, Intel limited its own motherboard production to six million units and subcontracted any excess to the Taiwanese firms (Nihon Kougyou Shinbun 1997). The main customers of Intel's motherboards at that time were Dell, Gateway2000, Micron Electronics and other new players in the PC industry (Electronic Buyers' News, 28 Apr 1997).

Table 5.3 Standardization of the motherboard (form factor) and release year

Release year	Form factor	Initiator
1984	AT	IBM
1985	BabyAT	IBM
1995 Jul	ATX	INTEL
1997 Feb	NLX	INTEL, IBM, DEC
1997 Dec	MicroATX	INTEL
1999 Feb	FlexATX	INTEL
2001 Mar	miniITX	VIA

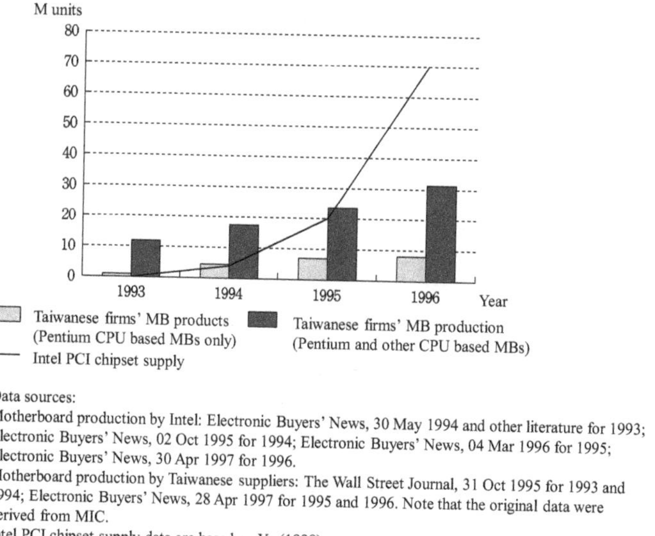

Fig. 5.4 History of motherboard and chipset production

5.4.5 *Mass Supply of Chipsets*

Intel outsourced the production of motherboards to Taiwanese firms, but it continued to provide the chipsets that it manufactured to Taiwanese motherboard suppliers (Fig. 5.4).

Taiwanese motherboard suppliers sometimes used compatible chipsets designed by Taiwanese fabless semiconductor firms, such as SIS and VIA, but they most frequently worked with Intel's chipsets. Intel eventually turned into the world's largest chipset supplier, which came as a severe blow to those Taiwanese chipset makers.

In 1995, the majority of motherboards sold by Taiwanese firms used Intel's chipsets. Thus, Intel had finally succeeded both in establishing a system in which the CPU and the chipsets were combined as a platform and in providing the global market with a massive amount of such platform products.

5.4.6 *Continuous Efforts Toward Open Standardization*

Intel was able to recover the money invested in CPU development and gain high profits thanks to huge sales. Its basic strategy was to move forward in the cycle of mass diffusion of its Pentium CPU, and open standardization would play a vital role in achieving this. For a CPU to be widely diffused, the PC carrying that CPU needs

Category	Name	'90	'91	'92	'93	'94	'95	'96	'97	'98	'99	'00
Local bus	PCI 1.0			■	■	■	■	■	■	■	■	■
I/O bus	PCI 2.0				■	■	■	■	■	■	■	■
Power supply	ACPI 1.0							■	■	■	■	■
MB layout	ATX						■	■	■	■	■	■
Peripheral device (low speed)	USB1.0							■	■	■	■	■
Peripheral device (high speed)	USB2.0											■
HDD I/F	Ultra DMA							■	■	■	■	■
Graphics bus I/F	AGP 1.0							■	■	■	■	■
Onboard sound	AC97							■	■	■	■	■
PC system design	PC98:System Design Guide								■	■	■	■
Memory I/F	PC 100, …									■	■	■

■ Year of release of the standard developed under Intel's leadership

Fig. 5.5 List of open standards developed under Intel's leadership

to be widely diffused. This is why Intel, a CPU supplier, initiated standardization in various PC-related areas. Its involvement in standardization activities was most notable in the mid to late 1990s.

As seen when discussing its participation in the chipset and motherboard markets, Intel frequently initiated the standardization of peripheral parts around the CPU. Figure 5.5 summarizes which technical areas were standardized under the leadership of Intel and when the open standards were released.

Intel's open standardization move had two main objectives. The first was to commoditize entry-level PCs and accelerate the diffusion of PCs in this category. The standardization of the motherboard enabled Taiwanese motherboard suppliers to provide affordable motherboards for the latest CPUs. Activating peripheral markets is often the purpose of standardization; if so, it may not always be necessary for a platform firm like Intel to act by itself. In many cases, however, an open standard is not enough to make the peripheral markets grow at the expected speed and the firm must intervene firsthand, as seen with Intel's entry into the motherboard market. Intel used the combined strategy of setting an open standard and entering a peripheral market to stimulate that peripheral market, from which it often withdrew within a short period of time.[16]

[16]Intel regularly entered peripheral markets and provided products at low prices. It did so in order to revitalize them thanks to its presence and enable the entire ecosystem to expand. This is why Intel's market entries typically lasted only for a short while. Gawer and Henderson (2007) examined the 27 cases in which Intel planned to enter peripheral markets and found that the firm shared and licensed its patents when joining these markets. Sharing patents means allowing competitors to use one's technology, which should have worked against Intel. However, if the purpose is to activate peripheral markets, then this is a reasonable strategy.

The second objective was to expand the PC user base by including as standard functions the PnP function, the multimedia function and other functions that allowed users to take full advantage of high-spec CPUs. At the same time, by standardizing these functions, Intel was also encouraging users to purchase the latest CPUs. Intel defined new applications that required the high processing capacity of its latest CPUs as new standards, which led to the further diffusion of its CPUs. The standardization of new technologies, such as the USB standard, contributed to the market accepting the value added of the latest, high-performance CPUs.

In both standardization cases, Intel's course of action was to keep the technological information related to the CPU confidential, i.e., as a black box. Hence, Intel managed to establish a profitable business by exclusively supplying the product that contained its intellectual property rights, based on the standardized platform.

Table 5.4 provides information on how each standard listed in Fig. 5.4 was established. Three patterns can be identified in Intel's standardization strategy; (i) standardizing on its own (de facto), (ii) standardizing together with a small group of symbiont and/or user firms (de facto or consensus) and (iii) standardizing through a consortium, such as a forum, SIG or large-scale alliance (consensus).

Pattern (i) was typically used in standardizing peripheral interfaces around the CPU, as these were directly related to Intel's key product. The graphics bus I/F and the memory I/F are good examples. Because these elements directly impacted the CPU performance, Intel carried out the standardization on its own. In some cases, Intel took an already existing standard, established by a public standardization organization, added some specifications and released it as its own. In the memory I/F domain, for instance, it established the PC100 standard, made more restrictive by the JEDEC standard. The firm also chose this standardization pattern for the technological elements that had a decisive impact on the diffusion of its CPU, as seen in the case of the ATX standard for the form factor of the motherboard, which was initially established by Intel alone.

The firm sometimes carried out standardization activities together with a few major symbiont and/or user firms, i.e., pattern ii. For instance, the ACPI, a standard for power supply specifications, and the Ultra DMA, an interface with the HDD, were developed by Intel in collaboration with major manufactures in their respective fields.

Examples of pattern (iii) include the PCI and USB standards, which, due to the nature of their technology, necessitated the involvement of many device manufacturers. Nevertheless, membership in the forum or SIG was limited in the early days, and those who joined later utilized the specifications defined by the initial members.

Table 5.4 History of standardization

Category (technical area)	Name	Year of completion	Standard type	Participants	Standardization steps
Local bus (periphery of the CPU)	PCI 1.0	1992	De facto	Intel alone	Initially announced by Intel alone and evolved into a standardization organization, the PCI Initiative
I/O bus (periphery of peripherals)	PCI 2.0	1993	Consensus	Consortium with major symbiont firms and user firms	Announced by the PCI Initiative, initial membership of Intel, DEC, Compaq, IBM and NCR
Power source	ACPI 1.0	1996	De facto	Joint development with major symbiont firms and user firms	Announced on the initiative of Microsoft, Intel and Toshiba
Motherboard layout	ATX	1995	De facto	Intel alone	A standard for motherboards for PC/AT compatible PCs, announced by Intel
Bus for peripherals (low speed)	USB 1.0	1996	Consensus	Consortium with major symbiont firms and user firms	Announced at the USB Forum, initial membership of Compaq, Intel, Microsoft and NEC
Bus for peripherals (high speed)	USB 2.0	2000	Consensus	Consortium with major symbiont firms and user firms	Jointly developed by Intel and Microsoft and evolved into the USB Forum

(continued)

Table 5.4 (continued)

Category (technical area)	Name	Year of completion	Standard type	Participants	Standardization steps
HDD I/F	Ultra DMA	1996	Consensus/De jure	Joint announcement with major symbiont firms and standard released by ANSI	Jointly announced by Quantum and Intel and officially standardized by ANSI as ATA/ATAPI-4 in 1998
Graphics bus	AGP 1.0	1996	De facto	Intel alone	A standard for the dedicated bus (data transfer circuit) between the video card and the main memory, announced by Intel
Onboard sound	AC97	1996	De facto	Intel alone	A standard for the LSI to realize the sound function, promoted by Intel in 1996
Entire PC design	PC98: System Design Guide	1997	De facto	Joint announcement with major symbiont firms	Initially announced as Microsoft's patent (1997) but as a joint patent of MS and Intel in 1998
Memory I/F	PC100	1998	De facto	Intel alone	Intel's proprietary

5.5 Establishment of the Platform Concept

5.5.1 Establishment of the Platform Concept: Open/Closed Areas

Figure 5.4 gives the impression that Intel standardized the whole spectrum of PC elements. In fact, however, a closer look at the target fields reveals that it standardized only the external interfaces of its platform, consisting of the CPU and chipsets.

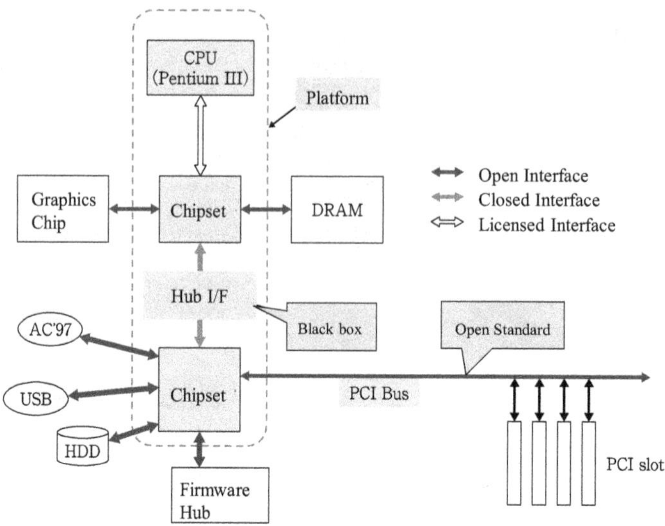

Fig. 5.6 Platform and the open and closed areas

Figure 5.6 illustrates the end state of the PC architecture achieved with the Pentium III generation. The semiconductors in the shaded boxes (the CPU and two chipsets) are the platform provided by Intel. The arrows represent interfaces between the electronics. The black arrows symbolize open interfaces specified by open standards, the gray arrows closed interfaces protected by classified information and the white arrows licensed interfaces, i.e., the patented interfaces that can only be used with a patent license.

As Fig. 5.6 shows, open interfaces were used between the platform and the electronic products just outside it, for instance, the interfaces with the memory and with the HDD. In this way, Intel standardized the external interfaces of the platform very thoroughly.

Conversely, the internals of the platform were kept as a black box. The interfaces inside it were either closed and unstandardized or licensed to a limited number of firms for manufacturing. The licensing was handled based on patents, and Intel very carefully selected potential licensees in order to control its technical information. Whenever a firm without a licensing agreement was found to be using the licensed interface, Intel aggressively initiated an intellectual property dispute. A typical example is the patent litigation between Intel and VIA, detailed in Sect. 5.5.2 below.

This tendency—i.e., keeping the platform internals in the closed area, excluding rivals from entering, and placing the externals in the open area, promoting active transactions in the peripheral markets—grew stronger as the CPU generations progressed.[17]

[17] For the Pentium II CPU generation, the north bridge was renamed the Media Control Hub (MCH) and the south bridge the IO Control Hub (ICH). The PCI bus was placed beneath the ICH chipset

Intel created the black box following the two-pronged approach of licensing and concealing information. Licensing primarily covered the local bus between the CPU and the chipset. The local bus is a bus (signal line) running from the CPU to the chipset, represented by the solid white arrow in Fig. 5.6. The licensed patent was embedded in the bus protocol of the local bus. By supplying the chipset and the CPU together, the firm was able to incorporate the patent into the bus protocol. The licensing agreement prohibited the licensees, i.e., compatible CPU manufacturers, from manufacturing CPUs with a pin configuration compatible with the Pentium (pin-compatible CPUs), at least for some time after the expiration of the license agreement. Thanks to this mechanism, the licensees could not use Intel's chipset on its own.

The information concealment policy was pursued by means of non-disclosure agreements (NDA). The information regarding the CPU interface accessible without an NDA was extremely limited, since it could be exploited to develop compatible CPUs. Intel thus made sure that the information necessary for performance upgrades and production of compatible CPUs would not be disclosed unless an NDA had been concluded.[18] Since the internals of the platform were protected by patents and the information was concealed, there was no way for compatible CPU manufacturers to penetrate into the platform that Intel had built.

The components with connections to the external interfaces of the platform, such as the DRAM and HDD, were exposed to fiercer price competition, since the interfaces had been completely standardized. The end product, or the PC, quickly became commoditized, with substantial drops in prices as the functions provided by the combination of the CPU and chipsets were standardized. Meanwhile, the price of the CPU inside the platform remained stable and its average unit price rarely decreased. In this way, Intel successfully maintained high gross margins and achieved eightfold sales growth during the 1990s.

5.5.2 *Closed Area: Patent Litigation and Prohibition of Pin-Compatible CPUs*

Intel precluded compatible CPU manufacturers from using its platform through the clever use of intellectual property rights. The cases of AMD and VIA Technologies, Inc. are good examples of how Intel behaved in this regard.

---

and the MCH and ICH were connected via a dedicated interface with proprietary specifications. This realignment made the area between the CPU and the chipset a complete black box.

[18]The specification document, Pentium Processor User's Manual, Volume 3: Architecture and Programming Manual, Intel Corp., stipulated that developers had to enter into an NDA with and obtain the manual from Intel in order to access the information needed to achieve the full performance of the Pentium (such as the impact on CPU performance when multiple instruction sets were simultaneously executed). For compatible CPU manufacturers, designing a Pentium-compatible CPU became significantly more difficult than in the case of the 486, for which the necessary information was readily available.

In 1995, AMD and Intel signed a new patent licensing agreement that included two crucial clauses. One prohibited AMD from using Intel's microcode with respect to the 486 CPU and following generations. The other, which was more troublesome for AMD, was a stipulation against repurposing the socket for the generations coming after the Pentium. In other words, Intel prohibited AMD from manufacturing pin-compatible CPUs. AMD would still be allowed to manufacture products with perfect software compatibility with Intel's instruction sets, but it would be barred from developing pin-compatible CPUs. In brief, AMD would not be able to supply any compatible CPUs for the platform that Intel had established by incorporating the chipsets.

Intel pursued a strict policy of preventing compatible CPU manufacturers from using the socket of the Pentium. When it launched the P6 generation CPU, the one after the Pentium, Intel introduced the requirement of a patent license for any party wanting to use the protocol of the local bus of the P6 CPU (P6 bus). This meant that a license from Intel was needed to manufacture pin-compatible CPUs and compatible chipsets.

The litigation between Intel and VIA, a compatible chipset manufacturer, concerned this licensing issue. At that time, Intel was planning to apply the RAMBUS standard to the next-generation memory, but VIA launched chipsets conforming to the synchronous DRAM, which was based on the PC133 specification. This led Intel to assert the invalidity of its license to VIA. Table 5.5 lists the patents infringed by VIA according to Intel's claim.

The above suggests that Intel controlled the market by licensing the local bus and by obtaining patents relevant to the local bus between the chipset and the CPU. Interestingly, the dates of application demonstrate that these patents had not been secured during the technical development phase but were filed after Intel set its platform strategy in motion. This fact implies that the platform firm formulated its patent portfolio with careful consideration given to the designation of the open and closed

Table 5.5 List of patents infringed by VIA based on Intel's claim

US Patent Number	Title	Date of application	Date of granting
5333276	Method and Apparatus for Priority Selection of Commands	1991/12/27	1994/06/26
5548733	Method and Apparatus for Dynamically Controlling the Current Maximum Depth of a Pipelined Computer Bus System	1994/03/01	1996/08/20
5581782	Computer System with Distributed Bus Arbitration Scheme for Symmetric and Priority Agents	1994/03/01	1996/12/03
5740385	Low Load Host/PCI Bus Bridge	1994/12/19	1998/04/14

Source Nikkei Electronics, 26 Jul 1999, p. 36

areas. Owing to its legal actions, Intel successfully eliminated pin-compatible CPU manufacturers from the market of the P6 (Pentium Pro and Pentium II) generation.

5.5.3 *Open Area: Expansion of Peripheral Markets and Enhancement of the Value of the CPU*

Various open standards were incorporated into the chipset, many of which were established and released under the leadership of Intel. To the CPU business, open standardization meant the provision of attractive PC functionalities, requiring high CPU performance. The best example of this is the USB standard.

The widely-diffused USB standard is used in PCs today to connect input devices, such as keyboard and mouse, multimedia devices, such as a microphone or camera, storage devices, such as an external HDD or flash drive, and Internet access devices.

From the viewpoint of the CPU business, the USB standard is essential because a PC with USB capability needs a large amount of CPU power. The USB protocol, i.e., the area defined as the USB standard, consists of three parts: the physical layer, the control layer and the USB control protocol layer in the operating system (OS). The physical layer defines the arrangement and protocol for electrical signals. The control layer interprets the signals sent from the physical layer to a certain extent. The USB control protocol in the OS creates data from the signals coming from the USB device, so that applications can process them.

What makes the USB standard unique is the USB control protocol in the OS. A large portion of the USB standard is dedicated to this protocol, and so a high-performance CPU is needed to operate the OS at high speed. Hence, the performance of a USB device relies heavily on the performance of the CPU. In contrast, the physical layer's performance is quite limited. The semiconductors that have a USB interface rarely conduct logical processing and depend on the OS, which is on the CPU, to perform such tasks.[19]

This means that USB-enabled PCs always need the latest CPUs, with the highest processing capabilities. In fact, in the early days, the communication between USB devices and the PC was most severely hindered by the performance of the CPU. PCs with higher-performance CPUs have faster access to USB devices, and vice versa. The USB standard is ultimately meaningful in terms of providing users with attractive functions enabled by high-performance CPUs.

[19]The data transfer capability of the USB standard was implemented at the semiconductor level and not at the OS level; in other words, the standard setters could have chosen a distributed-processing approach. In that case, the reliance of USB functionality on CPU performance would have been minimized, avoiding the need for users to acquire the latest high-performance CPU.

5.6 Impact of the Platform Strategy

5.6.1 Trend of Average Sales Prices of the PC and Its Main Components

To verify the impact of Intel's platform strategy, Fig. 5.7 displays the changes in the average sales prices (ASPs) of the PC and of its main components along the time axis. Average sales prices were derived by dividing the total value of annual shipment by the total quantity shipped in a given year.

The platform strategy was initiated by Intel with the Pentium generation, which was launched in 1993, but its impact did not become evident until 1995 or later, when the Pentium was adequately diffused. Hence, the ASPs examined here refer to the year 1995 and following years.

The average sales prices (ASPs) of the PC and of its key components, such as the HDD and the DRAM, started declining substantially in 1995. The DRAM saw the sharpest price drop, reaching in 2003 20% of its original 1995 price. Likewise, the HDD fell to 40% of the 1995 price and the PC to 60%.

By contrast, the average sales price of Intel's CPU was quite stable throughout the period studied, except in 2001 and 2002, when price-busting occurred following the burst of the Internet bubble (dot-com bubble). In 2003, it recovered and stood at 90% of its 1995 level.

A closer look at the line graph of the Intel CPU ASP suggests that the platform firm did not only prevent the sales price of the CPU from declining, but it even

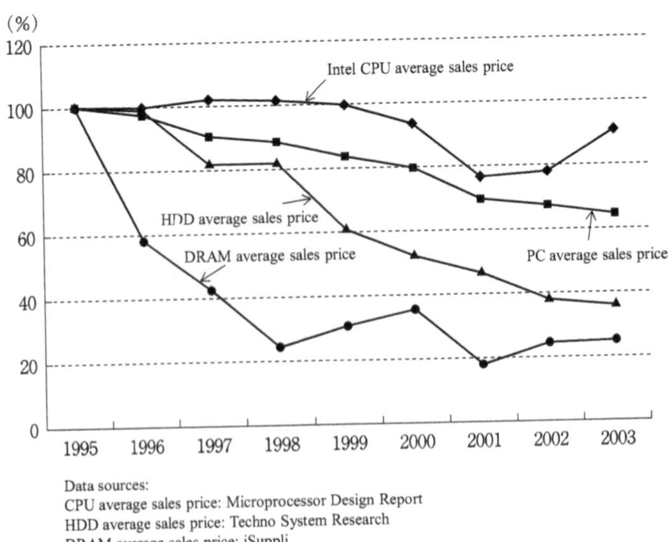

Fig. 5.7 ASPs of the PC and key components

achieved higher prices in 1997 and 1998 compared to 1995. Also, as mentioned, in 2003 its CPU ASP stood at around 90% of the 1995 level. During these eight years, the average sales price of Intel CPUs declined by 10% only. The CPUs provided by Intel, which developed the platform, maintained their price or even fetched higher prices at times, while the price of the HDD substantially dropped, despite it being one of the main PC components as well. These facts clearly demonstrate that the success of its platform strategy gave Intel extraordinary bargaining power.

Now, if we turn to the ASPs of Intel CPUs and PCs, something interesting emerges. Until the year 2000, the ASP of PCs continuously declined, while that of Intel CPUs stayed stable. After the Internet bubble burst, the ASP of CPUs dropped in 2001 and 2002, but it soon recovered in 2003, when the aftershocks of the bubble burst ceased. In the meantime, the ASP of PCs continued to decrease. The CPU ASP decline in 2001 and 2002 indicates the impact of the platform developed by Intel, which proved to be effective in preventing the CPU ASP from falling. The platform established by Intel contained a closed interface, which helped the price of its internal parts (more specifically, the CPU) to remain stable when the platform became diffused.

Intel's platform strategy opted for an open interface for the portion outside the platform. The main components in this outside portion, such as the DRAM and HDD, were connected via standardized open interfaces, guaranteeing compatibility among products. Thus, it was hard to have a variety of products for the DRAM and the HDD. The standardization of interfaces promoted a shift from competition revolving around differentiation to competition over investments in mass production capacity for identical products.

This shift in the competition pattern had different impacts on the firms in developed countries and those in emerging countries. Figure 5.8 tracks changes in the DRAM

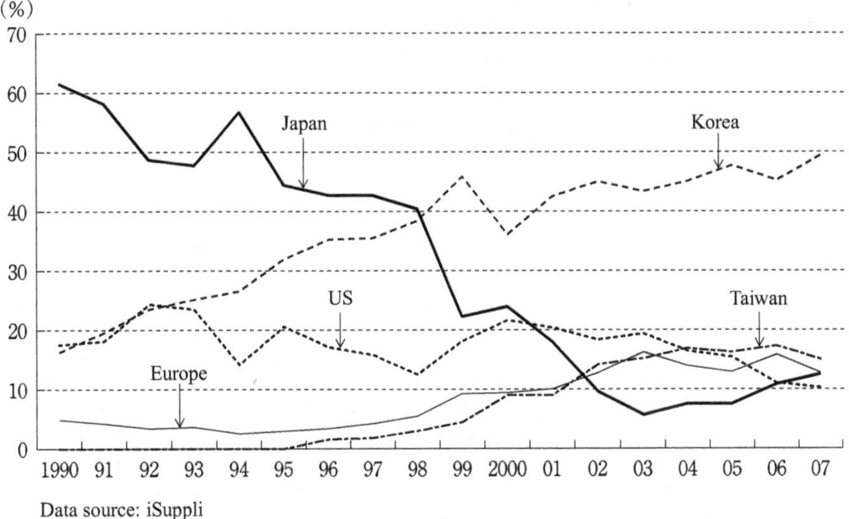

Fig. 5.8 DRAM market share by country

market share by country based on the sales amounts of the top 20 firms.[20]

Some researchers noted that South Korea topped the global DRAM market in 1992 (Itami 1995, p. 256). Yet, this does not necessarily reflect a general tendency. It is true that Samsung Electronics Co., Ltd. gained the largest DRAM market share by corporation that year but, in terms of nationality, Japan retained its superior position well into the 1990s.

It was only after the mid-1990s that Japan's prominence started fading, exactly at the time when Intel's platform strategy transformed the competition focus of the DRAM and HDD segments from product differentiation to scale of investment. Japan's DRAM industry lost much of its market share around 2000, whereas Korean DRAM providers gained ground. The change in the competition style, triggered by the implementation of the platform, helped the Korean DRAM industry to grow, taking a large share away from its Japanese counterpart.

Nonetheless, a comparison between Japan and South Korea is not sufficient; attention needs to be paid to Taiwanese DRAM providers, too. The DRAM industry, which appeared among the top 20 firms in or after 1995, was generally recognized as a highly competitive, low-profit segment, but that was not the case in emerging countries. Its low profit margins, unappealing to firms in developed economies, were still significant for firms in emerging economies. Moreover, any firm could supply DRAMs to the PC market, as long as the connection with the open interface was provided, which was a favorable condition for new entrants.

The growth of the Taiwanese semiconductor industry was also somewhat related to an increased presence of the European DRAM industry. European DRAM providers strategically licensed their DRAM technologies to Taiwanese firms while, at the same time, subcontracting production to them. Around 2000, the Taiwanese DRAM sector comprised three groups: (1) suppliers licensed and subcontracted by Infineon, a European DRAM manufacturer (e.g., Mosel, ProMOS, Nanya and Windbond), (2) suppliers licensed and subcontracted by Elpida, a Japanese manufacturer (e.g., Powerchip Semiconductor) and (3) other (Nakane 2002a). The success of group (1) was largely driven by the performance of the European DRAM industry. Indeed, the alliance between Infineon, the largest European DRAM supplier, and its Taiwanese licensees gained fourth position in the global DRAM market (Nakane 2002b).[21]

---

[20] The sales amounts of major DRAM manufacturers were aggregated by year. In some years, fewer than 20 firms were active in the market.

[21] The development of the Taiwanese DRAM industry took off when Infineon separated its semiconductor business from its main business in 2006 and founded Qimonda. The name of this spin-out contained the element *Qi*, coming from the Chinese language, which shows how seriously the firm took its collaboration with Chinese and Taiwanese semiconductor suppliers (PC Watch 2007). Qimonda ranked third in the market in 2007, but it went bankrupt in 2009 as a result of severe competition. Currently, the business operates as Qimonda Licensing and specializes is the licensing of semiconductor-related patents. Elpida ranked third in the market in 2008, but it had to file a bankruptcy-reorganization plan under the Corporation Reorganization Law in 2012, which was approved. The firm later became a subsidiary of Micron, a US firm. At present, the main players in the DRAM industry are Samsung Electronics and Hynix, based in South Korea, and the US DRAM provider Micron.

The semiconductor industries in emerging nations, such as the Korean and Taiwanese DRAM industries, seized the opportunity to grow as mega suppliers in the expanding PC ecosystem driven by Intel's platform strategy. On the contrary, the DRAM industries of developed countries, particularly Japan, could not technically differentiate themselves from competitors because of the platform and largely lost their market shares as investment competition intensified.

5.6.2 *Impact on the Peripheral Industries: Growth of Taiwan's Motherboard Industry*

The platform strategy that Intel implemented was aimed at the growth of its CPU business, but its benefits were far-reaching. Indeed, it was Taiwanese motherboard firms that expanded their business the most by aligning with Intel's strategy. After the motherboard standardization (ATX 1.0 standard) in 1995, the Taiwanese industry surged forward and soon satisfied 70–80% of the global demand for motherboards. In 2000, its export value was eight times higher than in 1990 and, by then, it had become a major industry supporting the Taiwanese economy. Figure 5.9 evidences such growth by plotting the production of motherboards and notebook PCs in Taiwan.

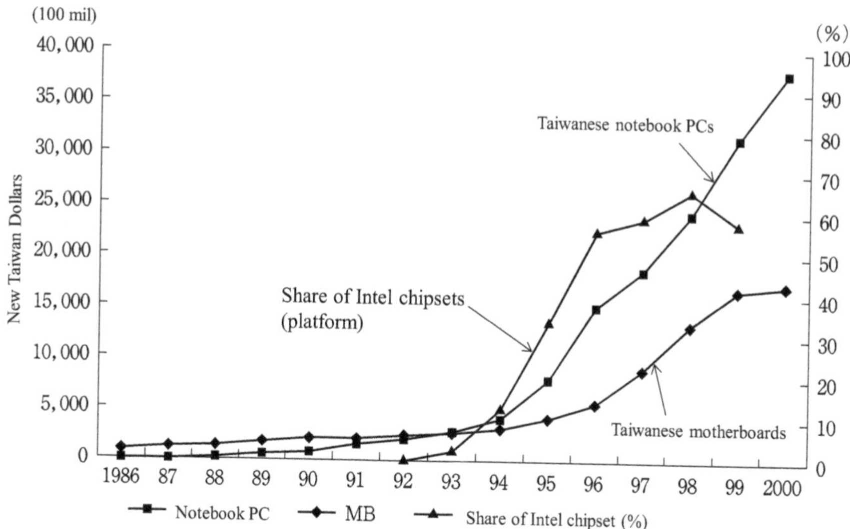

Data sources:
Data on motherboard and PC production come from the Internet Information Search System, Department of Statistics, Ministry of Economic Affairs, R.O.A., while data regarding chipset market share are provided by Dataquest.

Fig. 5.9 Market share of Intel chipsets and Taiwanese production of notebook PCs and motherboards

When Intel launched the Pentium CPU in 1993, it mainly produced its genuine motherboards in its foundry in Puerto Rico. There were mixed views among the analysts on this strategy of a CPU supplier providing not only chipsets but also motherboards. Many argued that Intel should have refrained from threatening suppliers of complementary goods to its CPU, meaning Taiwanese motherboard producers.

Motherboards compatible with the Pentium used a high-speed signal line called the PCI bus. As the timing of signal transition was restricted, their development was more difficult than that of conventional motherboards. Hence, in view of the business risks involved, Taiwanese motherboard suppliers were reluctant to develop Pentium-based motherboards. Additionally, there was the possibility of rampancy of poor quality motherboards, not complying with the signal transition timing. Therefore, Intel's decision to produce motherboards by itself was rational, also because it ensured that suitable motherboards would be put on the market from early on.

When Intel started production of its Pentium-based motherboards in 1993, it had already asked Taiwanese suppliers to manufacture them. This request, however, meant producing motherboards for the most cutting-edge CPU, a new product with a diffusion rate of just a few percentage points. Although the Taiwanese suppliers might well have been able to successfully develop Pentium-based motherboards, they were extremely concerned about sales risks. Therefore, they were unwilling to agree to Intel's request, which left the firm with no alternative but to self-produce. At the beginning, when the risks were still high, the platform firm itself had to engage in the supply of complementary goods.

The demarcation between Intel and Taiwanese motherboard suppliers in 1995 to 1996 is worth noting. Intel earmarked 1995 as an important year for the diffusion of the Pentium and produced Pentium-based motherboards on a very large scale. This mass production plan was communicated to the Taiwanese suppliers in advance in 1994, so that they would also produce large quantities to match Intel's mass supply. In fact, Intel failed to achieve the 10 million target of its 3-2-1 Project but succeeded in extensively diffusing Pentium-based motherboards.

Interestingly, Intel announced the ATX standard (ATX 1.0) in July 1995. This standard defined the layout and other details of the motherboard so thoroughly that it could be used as purchasing specifications. In 1996, the platform firm limited the amount of its own production of motherboards and subcontracted the production of ATX-based motherboards to Taiwanese suppliers. As a result, the Taiwanese motherboard industry grew fourfold over the course of five years, from an annual gross output of 40 bil NTD in 1995 to 170 bil NTD in 2000. The technical prowess and production capacity nurtured during this process also contributed to a quick expansion in the production of notebook PCs. Figure 5.8 clearly shows the rapid growth of both the motherboard and the PC industries of Taiwan. Intel bore the early-stage risk of developing a new motherboard for the Pentium and standardized the product (ATX standard), which made it easier for the Taiwanese firms to supply motherboards to PC manufacturers.

The predecessor of the ATX standard was the AT standard, used in desktop PCs and adopted by IBM as its internal standard specifically developed for the IBM PC/AT machine. Some areas of the AT standard had remained rather unspecified, such as the position of screws and electrical power supply features, which often caused physical inconsistencies. In fact, when a PC manufacturer procured a motherboard based on the AT standard, it had to make special arrangements to fit it inside its PC case. Thus, manufacturers of IBM-compatible PCs had to define the motherboard specifications in full detail, together with the Taiwanese suppliers, for each of their PC models prior to placing an order for the motherboard.

As for chipsets, before the Pentium generation, chipset suppliers sold their own chipsets, whereas PC manufacturers sometimes designed chips by themselves, specifically for their PC models. Therefore, the Taiwanese motherboard suppliers were expected to have the expertise to manage such a variety of chipsets, which caused a risk in product development.

However, from the Pentium generation onward, this scenario changed. Intel supplied an enormous amount of Pentium-specific chipsets, and most Taiwanese motherboard suppliers used them, reducing the risk of incompatibility. Hence, Taiwanese motherboard suppliers competed over how quickly they would equip Intel's latest CPU and its associated chipsets onto their motherboards and start mass production. In other words, technical differentiation was no longer relevant and competition shifted to the areas of quality control, delivery schedule and production cost. The transition to the ATX-based motherboard made it easier for Taiwanese motherboard suppliers to continuously invest in the new technology, by minimizing the risk of customizing for individual customers.

After 1995, once the standard for the motherboard was established and copious amounts of key components were supplied by Intel, the Pentium-based PC experienced a fast rise in sales. Taiwanese motherboard suppliers grew rapidly during the same period, also because they did not ignore the change in competition scope from technical differentiation to mass production of standardized products.

Thanks to the fact that the platform provider was located in a developed country, the global division of labor driven by standardization offered a developing country like Taiwan opportunities for tremendous economic growth.

5.6.3 How Intel Overcame Its Difficulties in Diffusing the Pentium

Let us now look at how Intel overcame the difficulties explained in Sect. 5.6.2 by implementing and diffusing its platform.

5.6.3.1 Threat of the Emerging Compatible CPU Suppliers

Intel integrated the motherboard and chipsets into one design, thereby establishing a platform product. It also provided chipsets to Taiwanese motherboard suppliers. As a consequence, Intel's platform product diffused on a global scale. The platform firm made its external interfaces completely open and kept the inside as a black box, often protected by patents or non-disclosure agreements (NDAs). The external portion was put in the open area, whereas the internal details were kept in the closed area.

Compatible CPU suppliers, such as AMD and Cyrix, supplied their own CPUs as alternatives to Intel's previous-generation CPU, the 486. A typical example were pin-compatible CPUs.[22] Being pin-compatible, these alternative CPUs could replace Intel CPUs while maintaining the bus and chipsets developed by Intel as they were. Intel's containment strategy, however, forced compatible CPU suppliers to develop their own chipsets and promote their products to motherboard suppliers by themselves, incurring the burden of all related costs. Consequently, the market shares of compatible CPU suppliers contracted but Intel's share remained high.

Intel's rival, Cyrix, failed to develop and promote a proprietary chipset and eventually withdrew from the CPU market for general PCs. Cyrix launched an integrated CPU for low-price PCs named MediaGX in 1998. The product, a one-chip microcomputer integrating the CPU with the image processor for the 1,000-dollar PC segment, was adopted by Compaq and enjoyed a certain level of success. In 1998, however, Intel acquired Chips & Technologies, which owned the image processing technologies for the low-price segment, and launched a CPU integrated with the graphics processor, which took the MediaGX's market share. As for Cyrix, in 1997 it had been acquired by National Semiconductor. The Cyrix division was then sold to VIA Technologies, Inc. of Taiwan in 1999 and withdrew from the CPU business for PCs.

The other rival, AMD, decided to obtain a license from Intel in 1995 and agreed to stop developing pin-compatible CPUs after the P6 generation. Since AMD could no longer use the chipsets supplied by Intel, specialized manufacturers developed dedicated chipsets for AMD, but their diffusion was quite minor compared to the entire chipset market size. Until then, AMD had cyclically supplied low-price CPUs every time Intel CPUs had become obsolete. Yet, because only Intel was now able to use Intel's platform, this cycle disappeared. As a consequence, the gap between the market shares of Intel and AMD significantly widened.

5.6.3.2 Reduction in PC Prices Due to Competition Among System Suppliers

Intel's platform strategy provided three benefits during the phase in which PC prices dropped.

Firstly, by also offering the chipsets, Intel could ensure a smooth transition to its next-generation CPU, thus being able to constantly offer high-end CPUs. Prior to the platform strategy, system suppliers had developed the chipsets themselves, which

[22] Pin compatibility meant that the compatible CPU had exactly the same interface as the Intel CPU. If the Intel CPU was replaced with the compatible CPU, the motherboard performed just as originally designed.

sometimes hampered the smooth transition to new-generation CPUs. PC manufacturers first equipped their servers with new, premium CPUs and only later did they launch high-end PCs featuring those CPUs. Because of this generation window strategy of PC makers, it always took a while for PCs equipped with the new CPUs to become widespread. Intel succeeded in substantially shortening this time period by supplying the chipsets itself.

Secondly, Intel standardized various functions of the PC and integrated them into its own chipsets. Subsequently, most of the PC functions became incorporated into the chipsets. Since the integrated functions were standardized, PCs equipped with Intel chipsets, regardless of their manufacturer, had the same standardized functionalities. Owing to this, the PC soon turned into a commodity and the area of differentiation for PC manufacturers shrank considerably. The PC manufacturers that had in-house R&D capabilities, such as Compaq, lost their power, while emerging firms without any R&D capability, such as Dell and Gateway2000, gathered momentum by concentrating their resources on expanding distribution networks and minimizing overheads.[23]

Thirdly, although PC prices declined, the average sales price of CPUs remained high, as illustrated in Fig. 5.7. By contrast, the ASPs of the HDD and the DRAM, which are both located outside the platform, plummeted. The drop in the ASP of the PC promoted the diffusion and supply of the system. Capitalizing on this, Intel achieved an eightfold growth in sales during the 1990s, while maintaining its gross margin at high levels.

These three benefits reversed the position of system suppliers and Intel, a device supplier. Intel moved up the ladder from key device supplier to platform leader and redesigned the PC ecosystem by placing itself at the center of innovation.

5.6.3.3 Rise of RISC CPU Manufacturers

Between the late 1980s and the early 1990s, the ACE Consortium failed to diffuse RISC CPU-based PCs and finally disappeared. The primary cause of this failure was that the Consortium did not manage to reduce the price of RISC CPU-based systems. Because of the slow diffusion and limited production of such systems, the cost of RISC CPUs could not be lowered, so their supply remained low. This persistent vicious cycle put high-performing RISC CPUs, once superior to Intel CPUs, into a difficult situation, as RISC CPU makers had no capital to invest in developing next-generation products.

On the other hand, Intel's CPUs had an increased number of transistors every time a new generation was launched and achieved parallel processing capability, ultimately outperforming RISC CPUs. Likewise, Intel's abundant investments in

[23]The average ratio of general administrative expenses to total sales between 1987 and 1990 was 7% for Compaq and 5% for Dell. In relation to marketing expenditure, the ratio was 12% for Compaq and 14% for Dell. In and after 1991, Compaq reported a combined figure for general administrative expenses and marketing expenditure; a comparison between the two firms has been impractical since.

process technologies and production facilities led its CPUs to surpass the operation frequency of RISC CPUs—originally their key advantage—and finally oust them from the market.[24]

5.6.3.4 Inconvenient Legacy Technology

As the PCI bus was standardized by PCI-SIG, the ISA bus became a legacy technology working at low speed under the PCI bus. The VL bus for high-speed graphics devices was progressively replaced by the PCI bus, which soon became the mainstream. For low-speed devices, however, the ISA bus remained the focus of technology development. Intel set up a bus bridge (the south bridge) between the PCI bus and the ISA bus so as to secure compatibility and remove the legacy issue altogether.

5.7 Summary and Discussion

5.7.1 Findings

The case study in this chapter examined the platform strategy of Intel in the 1990s, which is summarized as follows.

1. Intel standardized the PCI bus and supplied considerable amounts of PCI-based chipsets and motherboards. Taiwanese motherboard suppliers were also stimulated by Intel's strategy and supplied large amounts of motherboards to the global market. These motherboards carried Intel chipsets and were dedicated to Intel CPUs. Consequently, the production amount of Taiwanese motherboard suppliers experienced an eightfold growth during the 1990s and eventually satisfied more than 80% of the global demand for motherboards.
2. Intel reorganized its company structure and integrated the chipset division into the CPU division, so that the same roadmap could be shared between the CPU development team and the chipset development team and the latest CPU would be launched together with its associated chipsets. The CPU and the chipsets became fully integrated and functioned as key components of the platform. The chipsets incorporated new functions, like the USB capability, that converted the high performance of the CPU into value for the users. If a compatible CPU manufacturer used such chipsets without a license from Intel, Intel always filed a patent suit against that manufacturer. Eventually, compatible CPU suppliers were excluded from the system relying on Intel's chipsets.
3. At first, the CPU-based platform introduced by Intel was not accepted by PC manufacturers. Traditionally, the chipsets dedicated to the latest CPU had been

[24]As of 2016, the RISC CPU was available in non-PC markets, especially in areas requiring high energy efficiency. Firms like ARM, SH and MIPS are still active players in this arena.

designed and developed by specialized chipset manufacturers. It was Taiwanese motherboard suppliers that accepted and diffused Intel's platform, which was composed of the CPU and the chipsets. These suppliers achieved an eightfold growth over the 1990s and secured a share higher than 80% in the global market for motherboards.

4. Thanks to Taiwanese motherboard suppliers, the PC, equipped with its standardized functions, was adopted worldwide and became increasingly commoditized after 1995. By 2003, the average sales price (ASP) of a PC had dropped to 60% of its 1995 level and that of the HDD, a key component of the PC, to 40% of its 1995 level. In the same period, instead, the price of Intel CPUs, protected by the platform, only went down to 90% of its original level. This mere 10% drop over eight years demonstrates that the business environment was stable for the platform firm.

5.7.2 Entering Peripheral Markets and Open Standards

5.7.2.1 Entry into Peripheral Markets as a Lock-in Strategy

Intel's entry into the chipset market contributed to its lock-in strategy. By developing the chipsets and the CPU according to a shared roadmap, both were launched simultaneously as a platform product. The latest CPU and associated chipsets constituted an integrated platform sold as a bundle. Intel equipped its chipsets with cutting-edge capabilities that required the very high processing power of the latest CPU. Many of such capabilities were standardized through open specifications, as seen in the case of the USB standard.

The productization of the platform by concurrently developing the chipsets and the CPU functioned as a kind of bundling strategy, made effective by regulating the number of licensees of the patents contained in the interface. Eventually, the platform firm abandoned licensing pin compatibility, and compatible CPU suppliers could no longer use systems carrying Intel's chipsets. If anyone was found using the interface without a license from Intel, the platform firm took legal action against such an intellectual property infringement. On top of this, no technical information concerning the interface was disclosed unless an NDA was signed. By contrast, technological information was openly shared about the interfaces external to the chipsets, which belonged to the open area.

The CPU and the chipsets were made into a platform product by developing both at the same time, following a shared roadmap. The external area around the platform was kept open, whereas the inside of the platform was kept in the closed or licensed area. Intel successfully developed a structure under which the CPU inside the platform could only be supplied by Intel, no matter how widely the platform was actually adopted.

Since the open area was standardized, connecting devices were commoditized and diffused in a short period of time, but they often faced severe price competition. The

HDD and the DRAM, for example, experienced a massive expansion in demand but, at the same time, they were affected by significant price slashing. Intel, on the other hand, achieved a distinctive competitive advantage, since its CPU was positioned inside the platform and no compatible CPU could replace it. Accordingly, the firm dominantly supplied the latest-generation CPUs.

As mentioned, when it developed the platform product combining the CPU and chipsets, Intel reorganized the CPU division and the chipset division to integrate them into a single business unit. There are two important aspects to this change. One is the timing of the reorganization, which almost coincided with the establishment of the PCI standard. To expand the ecosystem by means of open standardization, the platform firm planned to embed the open technology into the chipset and solidify its competitive advantage. Indeed, the expansion of the ecosystem and the solidification of its competitive advantage were closely linked. The other important aspect is that both businesses were equally incentivized. The platform firm redesigned its incentive mechanism by merging the high-profit CPU division and the low-profit chipset division, so as to coordinate the development of both technologies and successfully bundle the two product types. If, in light of low profitability and potentially high risks, the chipset division had decided to postpone the start of the development of the associated chipsets until after the broad adoption of the latest CPU, the bundling strategy would have been jeopardized. Hence, to ensure that the chipset division would follow the moves of the CPU division, an integrated division had to be set up. This restructuring was indispensable for the bundling strategy to work in the platform firm's favor.

5.7.2.2 Entry into Peripheral Markets as a Stimulus

The case study regarding Intel's entry into the motherboard market shed light on how smartly the platform provider acted to expand the ecosystem. In the early stages, the platform firm developed, manufactured and supplied its own motherboards. Later, in 1995, it established a standard for the motherboard and started outsourcing its production to Taiwanese motherboard suppliers, which eventually grew into the main source of motherboards in the global market. What Intel intended to achieve with its entry into the peripheral market was to stimulate an expansion in the production of the latest CPUs by Taiwanese suppliers. The goal was not the lock-in of the motherboard business; rather, it had to do with encouraging Taiwanese motherboard suppliers to adopt the PCI standard and invest in the production of motherboards based on Intel's latest CPU. This stimulus strategy was highly successful and the Taiwanese motherboard industry soon came to satisfy 80% of the global demand.

Open standardization is an important strategy for the expansion of the ecosystem, but it may not be enough on its own. As seen in the motherboard case, a stimulus may be needed to convince symbiont firms to apply the standard. If this is the case, the entry of the platform firm itself into peripheral markets is an effective way to revitalize them.

From the viewpoint of the conventional theory discussed in Chap. 2, the entry into peripheral markets by platform firms may, at first glance, appear to be a bundling strategy for the sake of lock-in. However, an in-depth analysis may show that the strategic purpose of this entry is actually to stimulate the peripheral markets and to encourage the symbiont firms to embrace the standards set by the platform firms. The entry into a peripheral market by the platform firm is effective for the growth of the ecosystem and not for the lock-in of customers. Hence, establishing an open standard in a peripheral market further enhances the effectiveness of the strategy. For instance, Intel established and published the ATX standard for the motherboard, while also producing the motherboard by itself.

When a platform provider enters a peripheral market, careful observation will reveal whether its behavior points to the lock-in strategy or stimulus strategy.

5.7.2.3 Rise of Platform Firms: Established Firms Versus Emerging Firms

In the course of entering the chipset and motherboard markets as part of its platform strategy, Intel could not avoid intensifying friction with traditional PC manufacturers, including IBM and Compaq. These PC manufacturers with consolidated technical capabilities developed motherboards and chipsets by themselves as an important means of product differentiation. If Intel were to provide self-made chipsets and motherboards, they would lose their source of differentiation. Thus, they supported compatible CPU suppliers in an attempt to deprive Intel of its bargaining power.

On the other hand, emerging PC manufacturers, such as Dell and Gateway, welcomed the mass supply of Intel-made chipsets and motherboards associated with the latest CPU. These emerging system makers did not usually develop chipsets in house but procured them from outside. However, the outsourced chipsets became available only some time after the launch of the latest CPU, which put them at a disadvantage in the market for PCs carrying the latest CPU. Indeed, emerging PC manufacturers did not like this delay; therefore, they preferred Intel's chipset, which were simultaneously launched with the latest CPUs.

The emerging PC manufacturers were also pleased to see an increased supply of motherboards and notebook PCs by Taiwanese firms, which resulted from the stimulus strategy implemented by Intel in the Taiwanese motherboard and notebook PC ODM industries. The PC-related industries in Taiwan benefited the most and expanded their production capacity eight times, eventually meeting 80% of the global demand.

An examination of such a conflict of interests points to the fact that the platform strategy has the potential to transform the symbiont firms in the ecosystem. This change is caused by the platform provider absorbing some functions fulfilled by symbiont and user firms into the scope of its platform product. In so doing, the platform firm establishes its competitive advantage. Sometimes the new platform structure is beneficial to the new symbiont and user firms as well, since the functions absorbed into the platform are not their source of competitiveness. Rather, it is convenient for them if such functions are available as a part of the platform product. In consideration of this, when the platform firm implements its platform strategy, the composition of symbiont firms is likely to change.

5.7.3 *Conclusions*

This chapter carried out a detailed case study to understand the actuality of the platform strategy. Intel, a platform firm, conducted strategic standardization and established the open area and the closed area in the PC product architecture. In the process, it created a mechanism through which it could gain added value as the PC ecosystem expanded.

As suggested by our analysis, a platform firm smartly develops its relationship with symbiont firms. In the case of the chipset business, Intel entered the peripheral market to pursue a lock-in strategy, whereas, in the case of the motherboard business, its entry into the peripheral market was intended to invigorate it. Platform providers invest considerable resources in developing strong relationships with symbiont firms, exhibiting many strategic behaviors.

Our investigation also found that a platform firm manages the ecosystem by entering peripheral markets. This behavior has two different purposes: (1) to enhance its bargaining power through lock-in and (2) to expand the ecosystem by stimulating peripheral business domains. An important takeaway here is that a platform firms enter peripheral markets for one or the other strategic purpose, as a means to wisely manage its ecosystem.

This chapter examined the ecosystem management by platform firms from the macroscopic perspective (viewpoint of industrial structure). The next chapter explores the ecosystem management by platform firms more closely from the microscopic perspective (viewpoint of inter-firm relations). Indeed, the case study introduced in Chap. 6 looks at the collaborative problem-solving process between Intel and Taiwanese motherboard suppliers in the development of motherboards associated with the latest CPUs, in order to understand how a platform firm manages its relationship with symbiont firms.

References

Burgelman RA (2002) Strategy is destiny: How strategy-making shapes a company's future. Free Press, New York

Gawer A, Cusumano MA (2002) Platform leadership: How Intel, Microsoft, and Cisco drive industry innovation. Harvard Business School Press, Boston MA

Gawer A, Henderson R (2007) Platform owner entry and innovation in complementary markets: Evidence from Intel. J Econ Manag Strategy 16(1):1–34

Itami H (1995) Naze Mittsu no Gyakuten ha Okottanoka–Nihon no Handoutai Sangyou (Why the three reversals happened: Japan's Semiconductor Industry). NTT Press, Tokyo (in Japanese)

Mizuhashi Y (2001) Denshi Rikkoku Taiwan no Jitsuzou (The reality of Taiwan as Electronic Nation). JETRO, Tokyo (in Japanese)
Nakane Y (2002a) Hanyou Buhin Shijou ni Henka DRAM deha Gappei Kyoutei ga Kaishou TFT ni EMS Oote Sannyuu (Changes in the electronic components market: Merger agreement dissolved at DRAM, Major EMS supplier entry into TFT). Nikkei Microdevices 58 (in Japanese)
Nakane Y (2002b) Taiwan Nanya to Doitsu Infinion Teikei no Igi to Taiwan DRAM Gyoukai Saihen (Meanings of partnership of Nanya and Infineon and Taiwanese DRAM industry restructuring). Tech-on, 08 May 2002, Nikkei BP. http://techon.nikkeibp.co.jp/members/01db/200205/1000296/. Accessed 26 Aug 2006 (in Japanese)
Nihon Kougyou Shinbun (1997) Chiku Sei Tai Hatsu Taiwan Jouhou Kiki Sangyou Hatten no Shinario 7 (Future growth scenario of Taiwanese information appliance industry 7). Nihon Kougyou Shinbun, Tokyo (in Japanese)
PC Watch (2007) Qumonda no CEO ga Rainichi. Nihon ha Hijouni Juuyouna Shijou (Qimonda's CEO comes to Japan, saying Japan is a very important market). PC Watch, 22 Feb 2007. http://pc.watch.impress.co.jp/docs/2007/0222/qimonda.htm. Accessed 08 Dec 2016 (in Japanese)
Uchida T (1994) Intel wo Houi shite Totsunyuu shita Micro Processor Shin Sengoku Jidai–Beikoku Computer Shijou Repoto (Microprocessor Warfare Era and Intel–US computer market report). Interface 1994 Apr 232–234 (in Japanese)
Yu A (1998) Creating the digital future: the secrets of consistent innovation at Intel. Free Press, New York

Table 6.1 Comparison between the two types of inter-firm networks

Product architecture dealt with by the network	Integral architecture	Modular architecture
Typical example	Automobiles	PCs
Characteristics	Functions and components are connected on a many-to-many basis in a complicated manner. Interfaces between parts are not clearly defined	Functions and components are connected on a one-to-one basis. Interfaces between parts are clearly defined
Coordination mechanism for problem-solving	Strong coordination capability needs to be put in place for sharing knowledge with other entities. Business partners are classified according to length of transaction history and level of competence and evaluated based on trust	The interfaces between components defined by open standards enable the development of final products without knowledge sharing or any other coordination among relevant entities
	Relation-specific expertise and assets are accumulated, requiring a mutual coordination mechanism for problem-solving	Open standard-based interfaces create an autonomous coordination mechanism for problem-solving
Underlying inter-firm network	A core network is formed, comprising a limited number of component providers, with high levels of relation-specific expertise, and having the final product manufacturer at its center	An open network is formed with platform firms at the center, without the need for relation-specific assets, thus allowing new entrants to easily join
Barrier to new entry	High	Low
Example of the network	Supplier networks for automobiles (*keiretsu*)	Networks observed in the PC industry
Characteristics of final products	– High integrity – Difficult to quickly expand production as it requires skillfulness	A wide variety of final products resulting from various combinations of diverse components
Innovation	Systemic innovation through coordination and integration of multiple modules	Modular cluster-type innovation through combinations of diverse modules

components are connected on a one-to-one basis and the interfaces between the components are clearly defined. The automobile is a typical example of integral architecture and the PC of modular architecture (Fujimoto 2007).

A large number of studies have looked into cross-boundary problem-solving mechanisms by focusing on integral architecture products, such as automobiles, and important insights have been gained (Fujimoto et al. 1998). These works point out the

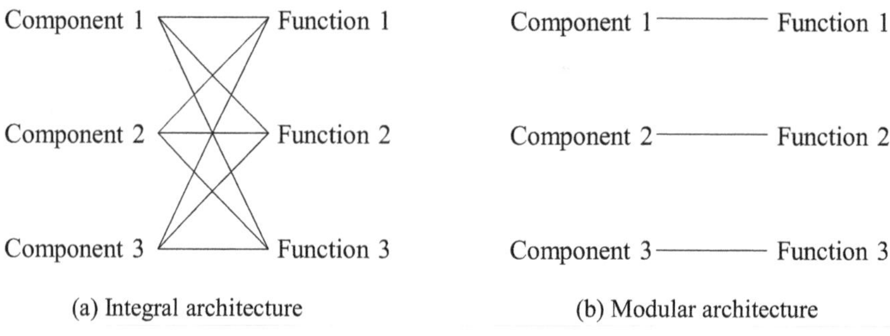

Fig. 6.1 Two types of architecture

importance of knowledge sharing among firms for the efficient solving of common issues (Dyer and Nobeoka 2000). Additionally, in order to ensure effective coordination with suppliers, firms need to build sophisticated coordinating capabilities in house, relying on knowledge sharing (Takeishi 2001). As a result of jointly pursuing efficient problem-solving, final product makers and component providers accumulate relation-specific expertise and assets in house by engaging in long-term business relations, categorizing business partners according to their competence and assessing their capabilities based on trust. This leads to efficient problem-solving practices under a mutual coordination mechanism (Williamson 1979; Asanuma 1989; Sako 1991).

On the other hand, cross-boundary problem-solving for modular architecture products requires a different coordination mechanism. In the modular architecture, the interfaces between the components are clearly defined, based on open standards, and final products are easily manufactured by assembling the necessary components following prescribed rules. Thanks to these unambiguous interfaces, manufacturers providing components for modular architecture products do not need inter-firm knowledge sharing and coordination. They can concentrate their knowledge and efforts on their own business domain (Baldwin and Clark 2000). Accordingly, contrary to integral architecture, modular architecture does not require accumulating relation-specific expertise and assets.

6.2.2 Knowledge Scope and Business Task Scope

To illustrate the difference between the two types of architecture, Fig. 6.2 displays the problem-solving mechanism in each architecture type in terms of the boundaries of the knowledge scope and the business task scope. Companies A and B share the same tasks in both cases. The task scope represents the purview of the business tasks that a company performs. The task scopes of the two companies look the same, meaning that the division of labor between them is the same in both situations. Conversely,

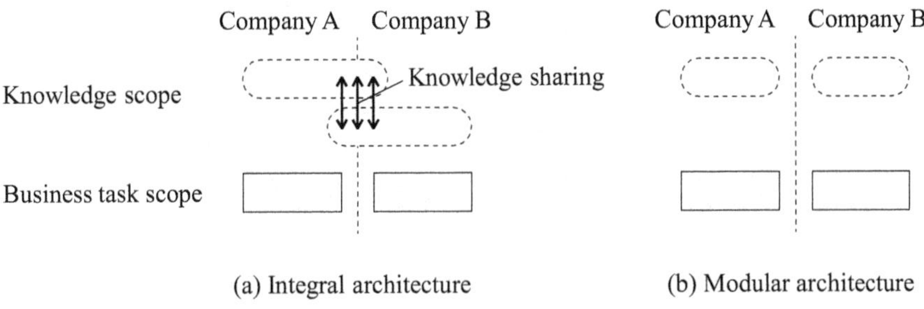

Fig. 6.2 Knowledge scope and business task scope

the knowledge scope, which represents the extent of knowledge that a company has behind the business tasks that it performs, greatly differs between the two cases.

In the integral architecture case, i.e., case (a), Companies A and B have and share knowledge beyond the boundaries of their business scopes. Due to the intricate correlation between functions and components of an integral architecture product, the firms involved need to possess knowledge beyond the boundaries of their business task scopes (cross-boundary knowledge ownership) and share knowledge with other entities (knowledge sharing). This pattern of joint problem-solving requires high levels of organizational capability. In addition, problem-solving by multiple firms in conjunction with integral architecture products means investing vast amounts of money. The resulting knowledge is prone to becoming *sticky information* (von Hippel 1994), which ends up needing a division of labor with the participation of a selected group of partners. An increase in cross-boundary knowledge ownership and sharing makes it difficult to maintain the alignment (consistent arrangement) of the knowledge scope and the business task scope; in such a case, the inter-firm network can easily lose modularity.

On the other hand, in the modular architecture case, i.e., case (b), the knowledge scopes of the firms correspond perfectly with their business task scopes. There is no need for cross-boundary knowledge ownership or knowledge sharing (Baldwin and Clark 2000). In the division of labor between the two firms, the scopes of knowledge and business tasks are consistently aligned. This pattern of joint problem-solving does not require high levels of organizational capability, and thus solves problems fairly quickly. When the alignment of the knowledge and business task scopes is secured, the inter-firm network can maintain modularity without difficulty; thus, it does not have to limit membership to a few selected firms and can welcome a wider range of players.

Actual products on the market often feature a mixture of integral architecture and modular architecture. This requires firms to strategically align their knowledge and business task scopes (Sosa et al. 2003). In the case of inter-firm networks, where task sharing spans across multiple companies, aligning the knowledge and business task scopes is even harder to achieve.

6.2.3 Inter-firm Networks

Because the two architecture types have different cross-boundary problem-solving mechanisms, the characteristics of their inter-firm networks are also different. In the inter-firm network for the integral architecture, the more participating firms pursue efficient cross-boundary problem-solving, the more they accumulate relation-specific expertise and assets. This eventually leads to the formation of an inter-firm network comprised of component providers skilled in relation-specific capabilities and having the final product manufacturer at its center.

Such a network demonstrates superior problem-solving abilities via knowledge sharing and mutual coordination and lends high integrity to the final product (Dyer and Nobeoka 2000). However, the relation-specific assets become a hurdle for new players wanting to join the network, as building such assets requires sharing sticky tacit knowledge that can only be acquired over a long period of time (von Hippel 1994). Hence, an inter-firm network of this kind tends to form a core network with a limited number of participants (Langlois and Robertson 1992). Supplier networks in the Japanese automobile industry (often called *keiretu* networks) are a good example of this situation.

The inter-firm network supporting the modular architecture, on the other hand, does not require relation-specific expertise and assets, which allows new players, with little or no accumulation of assets, to join. We call this type of network an open network (Kokuryo 1999). The network for the modular architecture does not require the participating firms to have strong mutual coordination abilities. Instead, the coordination mechanism works in an autonomous way through interfaces. As a result, a flexible combination of diverse components is achieved, producing a wide variety of final products (Sanchez and Mahoney 1996). Furthermore, the absence of relation-specific assets allows for a sudden production increase by accepting an active inflow of new companies into the network. Starting with the PC industry in the 1990s, emerging industries have been supported by open networks, where modular cluster-type innovations take place very actively (Baldwin and Clark 2000).

The platform firm that provides the technological platform plays an important role in modular cluster-type innovation (Gawer and Cusumano 2002). In an open network, with the platform firm at its center, cross-boundary problem-solving takes place based not on a mutual coordination mechanism but on an autonomous coordination mechanism via interfaces. Since the network can accommodate many new entrants, it develops into a gigantic ecosystem that fosters modular cluster-type innovations (Iansiti and Levien 2004).

6.2.4 Dilemma of Core Networking

The platform leader is important to the open network, and so is the open network to the platform leader. This is because what determines the added value of the platform is the modular cluster-type innovation arising from the ecosystem using the platform. As modular cluster-type innovations occur through different combinations of diverse modules, they cannot be easily achieved by a core network, which limits its members to a handful of skilled firms. The platform firm, therefore, has to prevent the open network from becoming a core network (core networking).

However, a serious dilemma is posed in terms of the platform firm's business strategy if it is positioned at the center of technological innovation. Indeed, the platform firm accelerates product innovation by intermittently incorporating technological innovations, but this activity entails the risk of depriving the inter-firm network of modularity.

The modular architecture makes product development easy and flexible thanks to its clearly-defined interfaces but, at the same time, it requires an enormous workload and a certain level of capability for system integration and testing (Baldwin and Clark 2000). If the platform firm engages in incessant technological innovation, the financial burden of system integration and testing becomes unsustainable, so that, even for modular architecture products, the autonomous coordination mechanism becomes insufficient and what is actually required is a mutual coordination function (Brusoni and Prencipe 2001). Yet, an expansion of the mutual coordination function is bound to destroy the open network supported by the autonomous coordination mechanism of the modular architecture, potentially causing the collapse of the very ecosystem that determines the value of the platform.

This is the dilemma faced by platform leaders: the more they innovate, the more they destroy the modularity of the open networks on which their business relies.

Core networks are essentially ideal for collaborative problem-solving. Giving strong priority to collaborative problem-solving turns open networks into core networks. If core networking progresses, it becomes ever more difficult for newcomers to participate in the open network, and this eventually hampers the expansion of the ecosystem.

Platform firms need to develop their platforms while dealing with the *dilemma of core networking*, which is practically unavoidable if the ecosystem is to expand. They have to establish a collaborative work process that assures the diffusibility of the platform without reliance on a particular group of firms.

The matters discussed above, which have hardly been touched upon in existing research, led us to conduct an exploratory study on the process of cross-boundary problem-solving in open networks. This chapter discusses the case of Taiwanese motherboard suppliers and Intel, the developer and provider of a technological platform for the PC, which is a perfect example of a modular architecture product.

6.3 Case Study

6.3.1 Research Subject and Method

6.3.1.1 Method and Case Selection Criteria

In this study, we performed thorough analyses of multiple cases concerning a single phenomenon, i.e., inter-firm transactions at the dyad level rather than at the network level. Our research explored the collaborative work process between Intel, the PC processor market leader providing a technological platform, and Taiwanese motherboard suppliers, which adopted Intel's platform and eventually came to satisfy more than 90% of global demand.

6.3.1.2 Data

We obtained the data to be analyzed through a two-year field study on the PC industry. The data mostly consisted of primary sources from the interviews that we conducted between November 2006 and March 2008 and secondary sources from related papers. The secondary sources included industrial journals, academic journals, reports by industry specialists and technical handbooks by specialized publishers. Prior to carrying out the interviews, we tried to gain a better understanding of the technological milestones in the industry by going through these secondary sources (Tatsumoto 2007).

The interviews were conducted to understand how Intel and Taiwanese motherboard suppliers collaborated between the 1990s and the 2000s. In 1993, Intel started providing not only CPUs but also chipsets for the peripheral circuit; by 1995, it had completed the establishment of its platform. The platform firm has since been integrating various innovations, contributing greatly to the evolution of the PC.

We also performed interviews with three groups of firms, in addition to Intel and the Taiwanese motherboard suppliers, in order to ascertain the validity of our primary sources. The first group consisted of Japanese and American PC manufacturers that were customers of the Taiwanese firms. The second group comprised electronic design automation (EDA) vendors, which communicated with both Intel and the Taiwanese motherboard sector. The third group featured component suppliers, which had opportunities to communicate with various motherboard manufacturers. These interviews made sure that the data used in our study were more objective.

We held a total of 31 interviews with Intel, the main subject of this study, motherboard manufacturers using Intel's technological platforms and PC manufacturers with internal procurement departments, as well as with four tool and component suppliers that were assumed to have objective views on the relations between Intel and the motherboard suppliers. This corresponded to 18 firms altogether, as detailed in the Interview List attached at the end of this book. Most of the interviews were conducted in a semi-structured fashion, and each of them took about two hours.

Our work chiefly concerns the relationships between Intel, the platform firm, and Taiwanese motherboard suppliers, but we also interviewed a wider variety of firms. This is because multiple angles were needed to remove biases and more accurately assess the relationships under investigation. In order to rule out possible biases due to the location of the interviewees, the interviews were conducted in their offices in Japan and the US, as well as in Taiwan. For example, the seven interviews with Intel took place in its offices in Taiwan, Japan and the US.

6.3.1.3 Industrial Structure

Figure 6.3 shows the relationship between Intel, the platform firm, and the Taiwanese motherboard suppliers, i.e., its symbiont firms. The platform firm sells CPUs to PC manufacturers, which, in turn, need motherboards to house the chips. It is those Taiwanese vendors that develop and manufacture the motherboards. Intel also provides chipsets to these motherboard vendors.

Intel sells CPUs to PC makers at premium prices, while providing chipsets to the motherboard suppliers at discount prices. As discussed in Sect. 5.6.1 (Chap. 5), the price of CPUs is maintained at higher levels than that of other electronic components. The motherboard suppliers sell motherboards carrying Intel's chipsets to PC makers.

As can be seen in Fig. 6.3, Intel's CPU sales strategy is a typical two-sided market strategy. Technologically speaking, the CPU is close to the chipsets and, considering only this technological aspect, it would seem natural for the platform firm to provide CPUs to Taiwanese motherboard suppliers. Yet, Intel sells CPUs to PC manufacturers and chipsets to motherboard suppliers as a means to implement the two-sided market strategy, which gives it its source of bargaining power to control CPU prices. Sustaining this market structure requires the timely mass supply of motherboards supporting the latest CPUs by Taiwanese suppliers, which, in turn, relies on joint problem-solving practices between Intel and the Taiwanese firms, a matter that is discussed in detail in the following subsections.

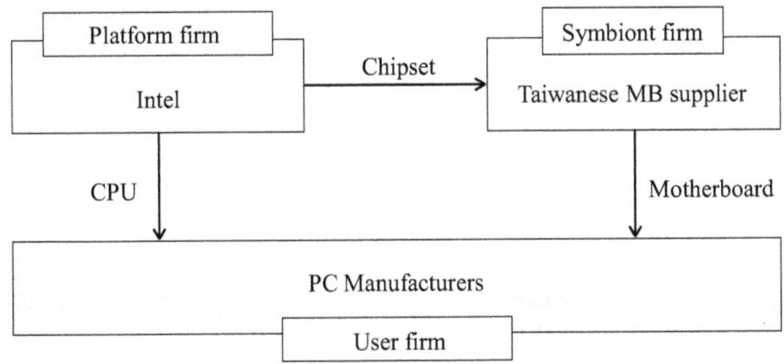

Fig. 6.3 Relationship between Intel and Taiwanese MB suppliers

6.3.1.4 Technology: Motherboard, Chipset and CPU

The motherboard, one of the primary components of the PC, is a printed circuit board with chipsets, DRAM and other parts mounted onto it. The CPU, on board the motherboard, accesses the DRAM and HDD via chipsets, which work as controllers of other devices.[1]

Intel develops both the CPU and associated chipsets and provides them jointly as a technological platform to motherboard manufacturers. The motherboard carries approximately a hundred electronic devices and dozens of connectors, all connected via circuitry. Although the CPU and the chipsets are core components, they are only a portion of what constitutes the motherboard. In this sense, the motherboard may be regarded as a system product.

The motherboard is clearly separated from the CPU and the chipsets via interfaces. Nonetheless, the motherboard and the core electronics are very closely linked from the perspectives of software and hardware. In terms of software, the Basic Input/Output System (BIOS), which resides on the motherboard, is the underlying software that controls the CPU, chipsets and various I/O ports. Intel provides the CPU and chipsets to motherboard suppliers, but they have to obtain the BIOS on their own, either by developing it themselves or by purchasing it from third parties. With the chipsets and the BIOS working together, USB devices (e.g., a USB mouse or USB memory stick) can easily be connected to the PC. New functions, in addition to the USB capability, are constantly incorporated into Intel's chipsets, many of which are made possible thanks to the interaction between the chipsets and the BIOS.

What is most important to Intel is relatedness on the hardware side. Intel has been steadily improving the performance of its CPUs, which means that it has also improved the speed of electronic signals running on the motherboard. Increases in the speed of electronic signals on the motherboard give rise to various problems. For example, faster signals make it difficult to synchronize signal timings, which results in possible failures in acquiring signals by the circuit wirings on the motherboard. This is called the problem of signal integrity, and extensive testing has to be carried out upon launching a new chipset to ensure that it is not present.

---

[1]Since CPUs are expensive, motherboard suppliers do not make purchases directly from Intel. Instead, PC manufacturers buy CPUs from Intel and install them onto the motherboards when they assemble their PCs. The chipsets reach the motherboard vendors following two different paths: either the motherboard suppliers purchase them directly or the PC manufacturers make purchases and lend them to the motherboard suppliers. In both cases, the chipsets are designed by the motherboard suppliers, installed along the motherboard production line and delivered to PC manufacturers already on the motherboards.

Table 6.2 Segments of the motherboard market

MB Segment	Market size	Market Characteristics
Own brand	– High margin – Small market	– Own channel for DIY market – High reliability – Differentiation needed, such as latest functions
OEM/ODM	– Low margin – Large market	– For PC manufacturers – High reliability
No brand	– Low margin – Large market	– For developing countries – Low reliability – Low price

6.3.2 Findings from the Field Study

6.3.2.1 Profiles of Motherboard Manufacturers and Their Motivations

(1) Segments of the Motherboard Market

Three segments exist in the Taiwanese motherboard industry: own-brand, OEM/ODM[2] and no-brand products. Table 6.2 explains the characteristics of these three segments.

Own-brand motherboards are sold to the DIY market[3] via the manufacturers' own distribution channels. They yield high margins, but the market size is small. The market for OEM/ODM motherboards is characterized by low profitability but it is large, as it satisfies the vast demand coming from PC manufacturers. The Taiwanese industry supplies 90% of the total demand for motherboards and the ratio between own-brand and OEM/ODM products is 25:75. No-brand motherboards are also sold to the DIY market, but not via the manufacturers' distribution channels, which is why it is difficult to gather statistical data about them. However, this market is thought to be quite large, especially in developing economies. No-brand products are regarded as relatively low in quality; hence, their prices tend to be lower than in the other segments.

(2) Profiles of Motherboard Firms

Our field study revealed that Taiwanese motherboard suppliers can be grouped into four categories. In this analysis, we pick and describe a representative company for each category (Companies A to D).[4] Table 6.3 shows the profiles of these firms.

---

[2]Original Equipment Manufacturing (OEM) subcontractors make products under the brand names of their customers. Original Design Manufacturing (ODM) subcontractors design and make products under the brand names of their customers. The difference lies in whether, on top of manufacturing, the subcontractors also design the products (Kawakami 2012).

[3]DIY stands for Do-It-Yourself. It is a market for end users who build personal computers by assembling purchased components.

[4]After 2000, small capitalized enterprises, like Company D, have decreased in number due to competition, so that now the Taiwanese motherboard industry mostly features firms like Companies

Table 6.3 Segment-based profiles of MB suppliers

Company	Segment represented	Characteristics	MB product portfolio			Share
			Own brand	OEM/ODM	No brand	
A	Technological leader	– Mainly own-brand MBs – Known for its technical prowess. Latest tech on MBs – Collaboration with Intel (early involvement) – Segment leader	70%	30%	–	31.5%
B	Follower	– Mainly own-brand MBs – Follower – Technology accumulations by working with Intel	60%	40%	–	11%
C	Mass production (for OEM/ODM)	– Economy of scale in production – Strong electronics supply chain – Major player in the OEM/ODM segment	–	80–90%		12.3% (44.8% as whole segment)
D	Small-lot production (for consumers)	– Little technological accumulation – Dependent on Intel's platform product – Small-scale, flexible and swift business development – Many companies in the same segment	–	–	100%	Small (12.7% as whole segment)

Company A started its motherboard business with own-brand products. In 2000, however, it entered the OEM/ODM business too, in an effort to compete in a decreasing price environment. The current ratio of the two segments is 70% for own-brand items and 30% for OEM/ODM products. The firm has been successful in building its own brand, thanks to its extensive technological strengths. It is also one of the first vendors in the Taiwanese motherboard industry to collaborate with Intel. In order to maintain its brand equity, the firm gives utmost priority to reliability compared with other motherboard manufacturers. Hence, it develops the BIOS on its own and does not outsource. It is particularly eager to adopt cutting-edge technologies in its motherboards and it has sufficient capabilities to detect and solve problems that may occur when new technologies are implemented.

Company B's motherboard business is composed of own-brand products, accounting for 60% of the total, and OEM/ODM products, accounting for 40%. Similarly to Company A, Company B also places its own-brand business at the center of its operations. Since it has not been as successful as Company A in establishing its brand and securing a large market share, it is positioned as a follower. Therefore, it is highly motivated to accumulate technological knowledge by collaborating with Intel, so as to acquire the latest information as early as possible.

Around 80–90% of Company C's motherboard business is OEM/ODM. Its strengths lie in scale economy in manufacturing and a strong supply chain featuring electronics suppliers. Despite low margins, the OEM/ODM business enjoys enormous demand. To meet such mass production demand, having the capacity for large-scale manufacturing is essential, and there are only a few firms, including Company C, that can guarantee this level of capacity. Mass production relies on purchasing large quantities of electronics, which drastically reduces costs.

Company D produces mainly no-brand products. Its technological knowledge is limited but, since it is small, it can be very agile and flexible in expanding its operations. The firm's basic business strategy is to release motherboards compatible with the latest CPU and associated chipsets as fast as possible, in order to derive maximum benefit. Suppliers grouped in the same category as Company D are mostly those that entered the market in the 1990s, when Intel started providing its platform for the PC. The number of players in this segment is quite large.

The market share of each firm in 2004 was 31.5% (A), 11% (B), 12.3% (C) and a few percentage points (D). Note that the category represented by Company C comprises many players operating in similar ways and accounts for 44.8% of the total market. Likewise, many suppliers operate in the category represented by Company D, and their combined market share is estimated to be 12.7%. As discussed earlier, however, this no-brand category is hard to quantify in statistical terms and features a large number of companies; hence, it is reasonable to assume its actual share to be larger (data source: Citigroup Investment Research).

A–C. From the mid-1990s to around 2000, however, there were many firms like Company D in the industry.

6.3.2.2 Process of Platform Development

As clearly indicated by the interviews conducted for our case study, Intel established a process involving knowledge sharing with specific Taiwanese motherboard suppliers, such as Companies A and B, while not having to do so with the majority of market participants, such as Companies C and D (Fig. 6.4).

Intel designs chipsets on its own until engineering samples (ESs) come out of its foundries. Once ESs are ready, the platform firm enters into an NDA with Company A and shares with it technological knowledge about the CPU and the chipsets.

Company A, equipped with the new technological knowledge, along with the new CPU and ESs of the chipsets, tests the system performance and stability of its motherboard carrying the new CPU and chipsets. In addition to Intel's products, the motherboard features third-party devices and the BIOS that Company A developed. So, its reliability is tested when all of these elements are combined and connected. When a hardware or software problem is detected in the CPU or a chipset, Company A performs any necessary tuning on its own, while also giving feedback to Intel. Intel relies on this information mainly to test its semiconductors but does not use it for its reference designs, as discussed later.

Company A has the privilege to obtain additional details about the CPU and chipsets from Intel. This allows it to adjust its motherboard based on Intel's internal

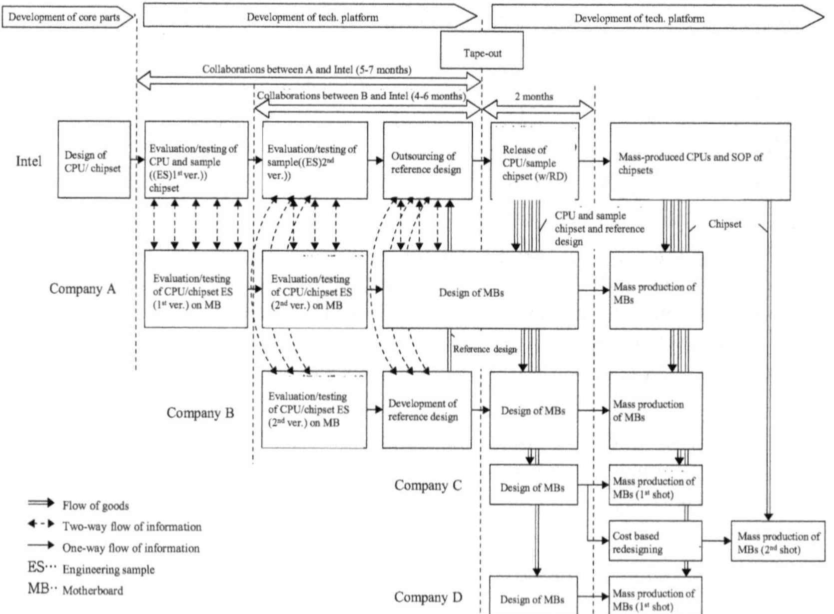

Fig. 6.4 Collaboration process between Intel and Taiwanese motherboard suppliers

information, so that it can achieve higher performance and reliability than its competitors. Such a system that boosts the reliability of its products is what supports Company A's own-brand motherboard business.

Intel carries out integration tests on its CPU and chipsets together with Company A five to seven months before tapeout (the release of a final semiconductor design). At the same time, Intel asks Company B to make a reference design after completing the verification of the first-version ESs. Four to six months during the reference design development phase are used by Intel to solve problems with Company B through mutual coordination. A reference design is a prototype design of a motherboard with the new CPU and chipsets installed and it is provided to motherboard suppliers along with Intel's CPU and chipsets.

Until the mid-1990s, Intel developed the reference design on its own and then provided it to Taiwanese motherboard suppliers. The firm realized, however, that this approach could not solve the systematic problems that the Taiwanese vendors faced in developing their motherboards. It was difficult for Intel, a semiconductor manufacturer, to fully understand the issues with which its customer manufacturers, i.e., that Taiwanese motherboard suppliers, struggled. For example, the reference designs drawn by Intel contained general electronic components that were not available in Taiwan; as a consequence, the Taiwanese firms had to use equivalent components that were slightly different from those chosen by Intel.

When a motherboard is designed using equivalent components, signal integrity problems may occur. As Intel's CPU performance went up, it became more difficult to determine the criteria for components to be regarded as *equivalent* components.[5] On the other hand, if Intel, with its huge technological capabilities, had developed the reference design by itself, it would have swiftly identified suitable equivalent electronics. This explains why the platform firm could not easily see that finding equivalent components could even be an issue.

That being the case, Intel started to ask Taiwanese motherboard manufacturers to develop reference designs in the late 1990s. Over time, the quality of these reference designs has increased to such an extent that they can be employed for mass production as they are. The BOM,[6] which can readily be used for production, and the mount pattern data, which can be entered directly into the mounter, are attached to the reference designs. A motherboard supplier can thus ramp up mass production without much system testing because it can simply draw the circuit patterns as per the reference designs, which dramatically shortens development and production lead times.

Intel obtains ownership rights to each reference design in exchange for outsourcing it to Company B and bearing the development costs. This reference design developed

[5]This problem applied not only to hardware but also to the BIOS software that Intel recommended in its reference design. The vendor of the recommended BIOS was American, but Taiwanese motherboard suppliers often used BIOS products developed by other third parties for cost-cutting purposes.

[6]Bill of Materials.

by Company B reflects the design preference of Company B, a Taiwanese motherboard manufacturer, which entails high feasibility for other Taiwanese vendors, too.

Working as a subcontractor of reference designs is not necessarily favorable for any motherboard supplier, since a reference design with the firm's own technology embedded is distributed to competing vendors along with the CPU and the chipsets. The firm's expertise—or a portion of it, at least—is leaked to the outside. Therefore, Company C does not assume the role of reference design subcontractor to Intel.

One of the reasons why Company B develops reference designs despite this risk has to do with its market position. Company B engages mainly in the own-brand business, so it is rarely in competition with Company C and other OEM/ODM providers. Therefore, even if its reference designs are distributed to other motherboard makers, the potential business loss is minimal. In actual fact, Company B is much more focused on its role as follower of Company A in its core business area, where it has a smaller market share. It attaches more importance to achieving a sufficient level of quality to increase its brand value by accumulating technologies and acquiring motherboard development capabilities recognized by Intel. Developing reference designs ordered by Intel also gives Company B the advantage of acquainting itself with Intel's latest CPU and chipsets ahead of its competitors.

Company C has a large share primarily in the OEM/ODM market and, differently from Company B, it does not need to risk its know-how being leaked by developing Intel's reference designs. Once the latest CPU is released, the supplier purchases the associated chipsets, to which the reference design is attached. The so-called first-shot motherboard is the product version created by applying the reference design with barely any modification in the mounting line. The first-shot motherboard can be released to the market almost at the same time as the latest CPU becomes available. Subsequently, the vendor redesigns the motherboard by focusing on cost-cutting and adding features that appeal to users and releases it as the second shot, soon followed by a third-shot version.

Of the four companies, Company D has the least technological accumulation; yet, it can still release motherboards for the latest CPU in a short period of time by using the reference design. The firm's basic strategy is to release the motherboard supporting the latest CPU at the earliest and enjoy the ensuing time-to-market premium. It competes against large enterprises, such as Company C, in the first-shot motherboard market. With its inferior development capability resulting from small-scale capital, Company D loses out to Company C in a product design race under usual circumstances, but it can compete on equal terms by using the reference design. In the first-shot motherboard market, Company D has a chance to beat Company C by establishing competitive advantage in agile decision-making or any aspect other than the amount of capital.

To summarize Intel's platform development process, the firm implemented collaboration processes with Companies A and B but did not do so with Companies C and D, which had the largest market share. The purpose of collaboration was not the same for Companies A and B. In the case of Company A, the platform firm placed emphasis on verifying semiconductor development from the system perspective. In the case

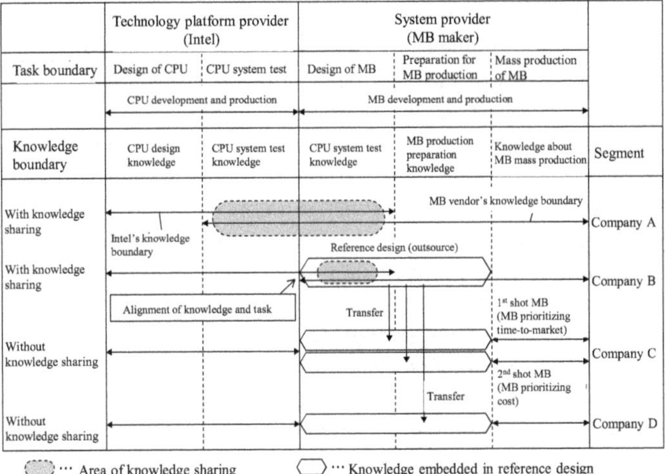

Fig. 6.5 Differences in the boundaries of the knowledge and business task scopes between the technological platform provider and the system makers

of Company B, Intel gave priority to transferring system development knowledge to reference designs, enabling suppliers, like Companies C and D, to smoothly design motherboards and start mass production in a short period of time.

6.3.2.3 Management of the Boundaries of Knowledge and Business Tasks

Figure 6.5 outlines the processes revealed by the field study from the perspective of managing the knowledge scope and the business task scope.

Intel classifies motherboard manufacturers based on their technological level and market position and, by managing relationships and knowledge sharing in different manners, it facilitates the joint problem-solving process with each of them. Intel has been successful in turning problems that tend to be integral into modular solutions by adjusting the boundaries of the knowledge and business task scopes.

In the first type of relationship (Company A example), Intel solves problems by going beyond the boundaries of business tasks, collaborating and sharing knowledge with a limited number of very capable vendors. In this case, the problems to be solved are chiefly those identified through testing of the CPU and chipsets from the system perspective. In other words, the platform firm's own semiconductors are verified with the help of system knowledge. At this point, the platform developed largely takes Company A's capability as a given fact; thus, its diffusibility is not secured.

In the second type of relationship (Company B example), the platform firm prepares solutions in such a way that those receiving that information can easily understand it. In the first relationship type, problems are still integral, as they lie across the two firms, i.e., Intel and Company A. On the other hand, in this second relationship type, as seen in the Company B example, by formulating problems not exceeding the boundaries of business tasks, integral problems are restructured as modular problems. At this stage, the platform gains diffusibility.

In the third type of relationship (examples of Companies C and D), no knowledge sharing process is implemented. Instead, the reference design is distributed as a solution ensuring alignment of the knowledge and business task realms. In this way, the reference design is accepted by motherboard manufacturers through competition. As a result of transferring the scope of knowledge to the reference design, even small businesses with limited technological accumulation can receive knowledge transfer and share tasks while maintaining modularity, just as large firms can.

Simply put, platform providers successfully align the knowledge and business task scopes by managing a combination of different types of relationships with symbiont firms, so as to encourage many other companies to undertake the development and manufacture of products utilizing their platform.

6.4 Discussion

6.4.1 Dilemma of Core Networking and Construction of Inter-firm Networks

The aim of this study was to shed light on how platform firms manage the dilemma of core networking. Platform firms construct open inter-firm networks that ensure the modularity of their products by strategically managing the collaboration processes with other players. In this way, they prevent open networks from becoming core networks.

Platform firms share knowledge with a minimum number of relevant players by managing their relationships with multiple manufacturers of final products and they can quickly reconcile the boundaries of the knowledge and business task scopes. At the same time, they develop reference designs, thus creating platforms that do not require knowledge sharing. By encouraging many firms to develop and manufacture products using these platforms, platform firms maintain the open network-based ecosystems in which they thrive.

The processes identified in this study offer new insights into the architecture of products and the structure of inter-firm networks. More specifically, the product architecture determines the structure of the inter-firm network, whereas the strategy regarding how to construct the inter-firm network also contributes to determining the product architecture. Firms have to develop strategies to strengthen the influence of the product architecture on the inter-firm network, and vice versa.

Previous studies have focused solely on product architecture strategies, but our investigation pays due attention to inter-firm network strategies, too. These two strategies are two sides of the same coin; they are complementary to each other, as well as reciprocal. Employing the two strategies together exerts unexpectedly profound effects. For example, Intel started the platform strategy of providing chipsets along with the CPU. Concurrently, it implemented the division-of-labor strategy of providing the chipsets to Taiwanese motherboard suppliers, which caused a seismic shift in the PC industry from the vertical to the horizontal form.

Needless to say, constructing such an inter-firm network requires strong management. This kind of network structure cannot be shaped as a matter of course. Inter-firm networks that actualize modular architecture need to be constructed strategically through effective management, with final blueprints in mind. Platform firms have to find potential collaborators on their own initiative and think for themselves about what they should collaborate on and with whom they need to establish collaboration processes. This study illuminated the process in which a platform firm achieved diffusibility of its platform by choosing various collaborators with different levels of technology accumulation and market positions, changing the scope of knowledge sharing depending on the collaborator, and sometimes deciding not to collaborate at all.

Next, let us explore the generality of overcoming the dilemma of core networking. Platform firms overcome the dilemma of core networking by leading technological innovation, while they also maintain inter-firm networks as open networks to ensure the sustainable growth of the ecosystem by managing their relationships with collaborators.

Examples of this can be observed in the digital product markets that grew rapidly during the 1990s. In the Chinese GSM mobile phone market, for instance, the baseband semiconductor provided by MediaTek, a Taiwanese firm, formed a platform. The platform firm succeeded in securing diffusibility of its platform by collaborating with mobile phone unit design firms (design houses) and developing reference designs together. Knowledge was not shared between the semiconductor provider and final product manufacturers; hence, the inter-firm network did not become a core network. Thanks to this mechanism, the Chinese GSM mobile phone market welcomed many small-sized entrants with little technological accumulation, so that an ecosystem based on the platform provided by MediaTek was formed (Imai and Kawakami 2007; Marukawa 2007; Yasumoto and Shiu 2007). This diffusion strategy employing reference designs is very effective, and this is why Qualcomm took the same approach when it launched its latest baseband chips for the Chinese smartphone market in the 2010s, consequently securing a majority market share.

The semiconductor industry has experienced the same evolution observed in cross-boundary problem-solving for CPUs and motherboards. Since the 1990s, it has seen continuous technological evolution and progress in design rules (i.e., a reduction in minimal linewidth). When this started to happen, the Japanese semiconductor industry argued that rapid technological evolution would make it difficult to ramp up mass production of the state-of-the-art generation with simple acquisitions of manufacturing equipment, urging the foundries and equipment providers to collaborate closely. Japanese semiconductor companies expected the industry to move toward greater vertical integration and hoped to gain an advantage thanks to their proximity to Japan's huge equipment industry.

What happened in reality was different, however. Leading equipment providers, whose equipment was closely related in terms of manufacturing process, created an alliance and jointly developed manufacturing recipes, a kind of reference design, for the latest technologies. They offered these recipes when they provided their equipment to foundries. Following this new approach, the foundries were able to ramp up production of latest-generation semiconductors without needing knowledge sharing with equipment providers.

Some of the more capable equipment providers became recognized as platform firms. They ensured that the ecosystem would remain open and welcomed new businesses into it. The fabless-foundry model was one of the main examples of this new business, vis-à-vis traditional IDM (integrated device manufacturer) models. The fact that they acted as the platform in terms of the semiconductor manufacturing process was the basis for the growth of Korean and Taiwanese semiconductor firms, such as Samsung Electronics and TSMC. On the other hand, Japanese semiconductor companies misjudged the dominant trend and waned (Shintaku et al. 2008).

The background commonly observed in several cases is that the participating firms calling for the platform to be open are new entrants from developing countries. They have very limited technological accumulation and would thus require a vast amount of time if knowledge sharing were essential. To achieve fast growth, they need platforms that can be used immediately, without any knowledge sharing. Platform leaders maintain the network open by continuously forming relationships with such new entrants from emerging countries, so that the ecosystem can continue to grow. Intel is a good example; the platform firm built relationships with Taiwanese, not American, motherboard manufacturers. Taiwanese manufactures were willing to join the open ecosystem stemming from Intel's platform products. Conversely, American manufactures were not willing to do the same because they had enough technological accumulation and wanted to avoid the risk of leakage of their technological know-how. This observation offers important clues as to the establishment of an ecosystem and its growth.

6.4.2 Point of Transition to an Ecosystem-Type Industry

This study has made it clear that changes in product architecture depend on the structure of the inter-firm network; hence, the strategy for a new inter-firm network structure affects the product architecture. Figure 6.6 contrasts the findings from our research and existing theories.

The traditional theories contend that, when continuous innovations occur, inter-firm collaboration based on knowledge sharing is needed to solve problems and the inter-firm network becomes a core network. As shown by (1) in Fig. 6.6, the core network behind the integral architecture is strengthened, as it requires deeper knowledge sharing (Dyer and Nobeoka 2000). Likewise, with innovations constantly appearing, also the open network behind the modular architecture, which did not use to require knowledge sharing, starts to need it, inevitably becoming a core network,

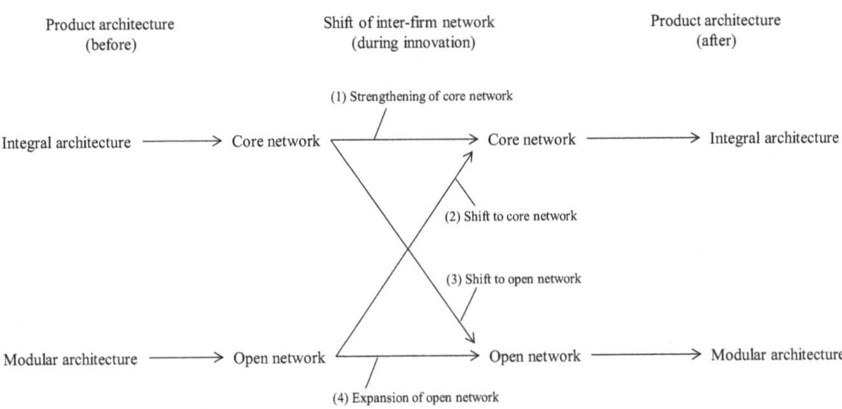

Fig. 6.6 Changes in product architecture and inter-firm network

as shown by (2) in Fig. 6.6 (Takeishi 2001). Accordingly, the product architecture becomes somewhat closer to the integral architecture. For example, the Japanese automobile industry, which is rapidly being computerized, is going through core networking, driven by the development of the in-vehicle electronics network pursued jointly by auto manufacturers and component suppliers.

This study, however, points to the possibility that, even when continuous technological innovations occur, the inter-firm network does not become a core network. This implies that modular architecture products do not transform into integral architecture products thanks to the effect of the inter-firm network structure. Overcoming the dilemma of core networking based on the inter-firm network strategy shown in the present book prevents the open network from becoming a core network (Fig. 6.6(2)) and expands it through continuous innovations (Fig. 6.6(4)). This mechanism of keeping the network open may have more significant effects than any practitioner or researcher has presumed thus far.

With respect to global ecosystems, the fact that advanced and emerging economies have strong complementarity underlies the above mechanism, and the presence of the platform firm, which makes use of the relationships among them for its business, enhances such complementarity. In digital product markets, an international network of firms is in place, in which firms from advanced countries provide the platforms and new market players from developing countries develop and manufacture the final products. There exists a strong mutually complementary relationship between platform providers from advanced countries, accumulating technological knowledge, and newly entered symbiont firms from developing countries, seeking opportunities for growth. This relationship functions as the engine that keeps the inter-firm network open and sustains the growth of the ecosystem.

The semiconductor industry is a perfect example of this mechanism. Since 2000, the design rule for logic semiconductors has been going through miniaturization, making the product architecture more and more integral. The more semiconductors become miniaturized, the more complicated the correlation between functions and physical composition becomes, making it harder to maintain clear interfaces between the functions. Therefore, the inter-firm network between designing and manufacturing was expected to become a core network for the sake of very close coordination. Practitioners and researchers presumed that vertically-integrated semiconductor manufacturers would gain an advantage as a result of core networking.

What actually happened was exactly the opposite: the horizontal division of labor between design (fabless) firms and manufacturing firms (foundries) stayed the same, driving the evolution of technological generations. Fabless firms, such as the American Qualcomm, designed new semiconductors for smartphones and achieved remarkable success. In the meantime, TSMC, a Taiwanese foundry, implemented an open innovation platform (OIP) strategy to maintain the network open and firmly protected the horizontal separation of designing and manufacturing, which is what provides the basis for the inter-firm network (Semiconportal 2011). With the OIP strategy, TSMC offered design kits to fabless firms, thereby creating an environment where a wide range of fabless firms can now use its contract manufacturing services.

When the product architecture becomes integral, the inter-firm network usually becomes a core network ((2) in Fig. 6.6). Yet, platform firms constantly strive to invite new entrants from developing countries as symbiont firms into their inter-firm network, so as to prevent core networking. They regard the diffusibility of their platforms as a fundamental condition and keep working toward it, no matter how much effort they have to expend. As a result, it may be difficult for an inter-firm network, once it is established as an open network, to revert to being a core network.

Finally, let us explore under what conditions a core network becomes an open network, based on the findings of this and the previous chapters (Fig. 6.6(3)). As explained in the macroscopic analysis in Chap. 5, Intel repeatedly carried out strategic standardization as a trigger for constructing an open network of firms. The firm set an open standard for motherboards, for example, to provide clear interfaces and convert the product architecture into a modular one. At the same time, Intel entered the motherboard market to stimulate it and enticed Taiwanese motherboard suppliers into its inter-firm network to make them develop motherboards compatible with its latest CPU. In so doing, as seen in the current chapter, Intel maintained the process of enabling the development of motherboards, while ensuring modularity by distributing reference designs.

If a strategy for ensuring modularity is pursued in relation to both product architecture and inter-firm network, integral architecture products are converted into modular architecture products, due to strong influence. The product architecture trails an inter-firm network behind it and, because of the inertia of the network, it does not lead to an architectural shift simply by virtue of technological change. We need to understand architectural change from the perspectives of both product architecture transformation and changes in the inter-firm network.

6.5 Conclusions

This chapter discussed the management of the relationships between platform firms and their symbiont firms. Platform firms prevent core networking by providing reference designs to align the knowledge scope and the business task scope and manage their relationships with symbiont firms to encourage the growth of the ecosystem.

The next chapter deals with how platform firms manage their relationships with user firms, which are as important to them as symbiont firms. From the perspective of user firms, platform firms are core component providers. Hence, Chap. 7 presents a comparative case study to identify how core component providers adopting the platform strategy manage their relationships with user firms and how those adopting the product strategy manage those same relationships.

References

Asanuma B (1989) Manufacturer-supplier relationships in Japan and the concept of relation-specific skill. J Jpn Int Econ 3(1):1–30

Baldwin CY, Clark KB (2000) Design rules: the power of modularity. MIT Press, Cambridge MA

Brusoni S, Prencipe A (2001) Unpacking the black box of modularity: technologies, products and organizations. Ind Corp Change 10(1):179–205

Chesbrough HW (2003) Open innovation. Harvard Business School Press, Boston MA

Chesbrough HW, Teece DJ (1996) Organizing for innovation: When is virtual virtuous? Harvard Business Review January–February, p 65–73

Dyer JH, Nobeoka K (2000) Creating and managing a high-performance knowledge-sharing network: the Toyota case. Strateg Manag J 211:345–367

Dyer JH, Singh H (1998) The relational view: Cooperative strategy and sources of interorganizational competitive advantage. Acad Manag Rev 23(4):660–679

Fujimoto T (2007) Architecture-based comparative advantage: a design information view of manufacturing. Evol Inst Econ Rev 4(1):55–112

Fujimoto T, Nishiguchi T, Itou H (eds) (1998) Readings Sapuraiya Sisutem: Atarashii Kigyoukan Kankei wo Tsukuru (Readings supplier system: creating new inter-firm relationship). Yuhikaku, Tokyo (in Japanese)

Garud R, Kumaraswamy A (1995) Technological and organizational designs for realizing economies of substitution. Strateg Manag J 16(S1):93–109

Gawer A, Cusumano MA (2002) Platform leadership: How Intel, Microsoft, and Cisco drive industry innovation. Harvard Business School Press, Boston MA

Iansiti M, Levien R (2004) The keystone advantage: what the new business ecosystems mean for strategy, innovation, and sustainability. Harvard Business School Press, Boston

Imai K, Kawakami M (2007) Higashiajia no IT kikisangyou: Bungyou Kyousou Sumiwake no Dainamizumu (The IT equipment industry in East Asia: Dynamics of division of labor, competition and segregation). Institute of Developing Economies, Japan External Trade Organization, Chiba (in Japanese)

Kawakami M (2012) Ashuku sareta Sangyo Hatten: Taiwan Note Pasokon Kigyou no Seichou Mekanizumu (Accelerating the growth mechanism of the Taiwanese notebook computer industry). The University of Nagoya Press, Nagoya (in Japanese)

Kokuryo J (1999) Open architecture Senryaku: network Jidai no Kyoudou Moderu (Open architecture strategy: collaboration models for network era). Nikkei Inc., Tokyo (in Japanese)

Langlois RN, Robertson PL (1992) Networks and innovation in a modular system: lessons from the microcomputer and stereo component industries. Res Policy 21:297–313

March JG, Simon HA (1958) Organizations. Wiley, New York

Marukawa T (2007) Gendai Chugoku no Sangyou: Bokkou suru Chuugoku Kigyou no Tsuyosa to Morosa (Modern industries in China: the strength and fragility of rising Chinese companies). Chuoukoron-Shinsha Inc., Tokyo (in Japanese)

Powell WW, Koput KW, Smith-Doerr L (1996) Interorganizational collaboration and the locus of innovation: networks of learning in biotechnology. Adm Sci Q 41:116–145

Sako M (1991) The role of 'Trust' in Japanese buyer-supplier relationships. Ricerche Economiche 45(2–3):449–474

Sanchez R, Mahoney J (1996) Modularity, flexibility, and knowledge management in product and organization design. Strateg Manag J 17:63–76

Semiconportal (2011) Taiwan TSMC ga 28 nm no Dezainkitto wo Soroeru 14 Seihin no Tapeout Kanryou (TSMC to launch 28 nm design kit, completing 14 products tapeout). https://www.semiconportal.com/archive/editorial/technology/design/110628-tsmc.html. Accessed 28 Jun 2011 (in Japanese)

Shintaku J, Tatsumoto H, Yoshimoto T, Tomita J, Park E (2008) Seihin akitekutya kara miru Gijutu Denpa to Kokusai Bungyou (Technology diffusion and international division of labor from the viewpoint of product architecture). Hitotsubashi Bus Rev 56(2):42–61 (in Japanese)

Sosa ME, Eppinger SD, Rowles CM (2003) Identifying modular and integrative systems and their impact on design team interactions. J Mech Des 125(2):240–252

Takeishi A (2001) Bridging inter- and intra-firm boundaries: management of supplier involvement in automotive product development. Strateg Manag J 22:403–433

Tatsumoto H (2007) PC no Bus Architecture no Hensen to Kyousou Yuui-Naze Intel ha Platform Leadership wo kakutoku Dekitaka (Historical trends in PC bus architecture: Why did Intel get platform leadership in the PC industry) MMRC Discussion Paper 171:1–62

Tatsumoto H (2013) Architecture Saikou (Reconsideration of architectural view in innovation). In: Fujimoto T (ed) Jinkoubutsu Fukuzatuka Jidai: Sekkei Rikkoku Nihon no Sangyou Kyousouryoku (The design era of complex products: The competitiveness of Japanese industries with Product Design Power). Yuhikaku, Tokyo (in Japanese)

Ulrich KT (1995) Product architecture in the manufacturing firm. Res Policy 24:419–440

von Hippel E (1994) "Sticky Information" and the locus of problem solving: implications for innovation. Manag Sci 40(4):429–439

West J, Salter A, Vanhaverbeke W, Chesbrough H (2014) Open innovation: next decade. Res Policy 43(5):805–811

Williamson EO (1979) Transaction-cost economics: the governance of contractual relations. J Law Econ 22(2):233–261

Yasumoto M, Shiu JM (2007) An investigation into collaborative novel technology adoption in vertical disintegration: Interfirm development process for system integration in the Japanese, Taiwanese, and Chinese mobile phone handset industries. Ann Bus Adm Sci 6:35–68

Chapter 7
Management of the Relationship with User Firms: A Comparative Case Study of Bosch and Denso

In Chap. 6, we discussed the relationship between platform firms and symbiont firms from the microscopic point of view (inter-firm relations). This chapter continues our microscopic analysis by exploring the relationship between platform firms and user firms.

From the perspective of user firms, platform firms are a special kind of core component supplier. The key difference between core component suppliers and platform firms is in the management of inter-firm relationships. Core component suppliers adopt a close-relational approach, offering their products as customized ones to user firms, whereas platform firms use an open-industrywide approach, publishing open standards and providing their products based on them.

This chapter compares Bosch and Denso, which manufacture and provide the Chinese market with a core automotive component for the car engine, i.e., the Electronic Control Unit (ECU). Bosch pursues a platform strategy,[1] which was described in Chap. 6. On the other hand, Denso's strategy is typical of traditional core component suppliers. Their ways of managing their relationships with user firms, i.e., carmakers, are markedly different. Our comparative case study offers insights into the performance of these two distinct strategic patterns and their impact on the Chinese auto industry.

[1] The expression *platform firm* refers to "a firm with monopolistic market share and strong bargaining power". In the auto industry, it is automobile manufacturers that have strong bargaining power, so it is hard to apply the definition to component suppliers. However, if we carefully observe corporate behaviors, some component suppliers do appear to act like platform firms.

H. Tatsumoto, *Platform Strategy for Global Markets*,
https://doi.org/10.1007/978-981-33-6789-0_7

7.1 Management of Relations with User Firms: Two Communication Patterns

Platform firms are a special kind of core component supplier from the perspective of user firms, but they differ greatly from the other, general core component suppliers in how they manage their relations with user firms. Some recent studies have pointed out that the unique communication pattern followed by platform firms accelerates the rapid international transfer of industries (Imai and Kawakami 2007; Marukawa 2007; Marukawa and Yasumoto 2010; Kawakami 2012). Table 7.1 categorizes how core component suppliers from developed nations manage their relations with user firms, especially in global business.

The first method may be described as an *open-industrywide approach.* Core component providers adopting this approach aim to bolster their competitiveness by defining clear standard interfaces for components through open standards, which helps reduce excessive time and resources needed for communication and avoid redundancy in investment costs. Since the 1990s, global standards (globally compatible and unified industrial standards) have been frequently created as the industrial environment has changed. This is partly because, with the easing of anti-trust laws, the activities of consortia and international standardization organizations, such as the International Standardization Organization (ISO) and the International Electrotechnical Commission (IEC), have become more intense. Additionally, firms are ever more aware of the merits of using industrial standardization as a strategic tool (Tatsumoto 2012). In this type of corporate strategy, companies set clear standards

Table 7.1 Global business strategy of core component companies

Company relationship	Open-industrywide approach	Close-relational approach
Changes in the industrial environment	Frequent establishment of international open standards	Liberalization of FDI into former communist and developing countries
Strategy	– Provide standard-based core components by setting clear standards for component interfaces – Development completed in a short period of time since it is done according to standard templates – Customization expenses are unnecessary because own product is prepared as standard commercial product	– Foster engineers in local development centers – Complex problems can be solved by technical support through close communication – Costs tend to be high since customization is usually performed for every customer
Tendency of corporate nationality	Mainly Western companies	Mainly Japanese companies
Strategy type	Similar to platform companies	Similar to product companies
Key firm in the case study	Bosch	Denso

for the interfaces between components by establishing industrial standards, reduce the time and costs associated with communication and avert the risk of redundant investments. They spare no effort to increase their competitive advantage. This firm behavior, exhibited by core component suppliers, is part of the platform strategy discussed in Chaps. 3–6.

The second corporate strategy may be called *close-relational approach.* Firms following this approach aim to bolster their competitiveness by using human communication to efficiently transfer technical know-how in the development and production of a technology whose knowledge is inherently difficult to transfer. They excel in product development, through a joint problem-solving process based on close information sharing with customer makers (Dyer and Singh 1998; Dyer and Nobeoka 2000). In the 1990s, former socialist countries and emerging countries started opening up their markets to direct investment (establishment of factories and development bases) by developed countries. Along with foreign direct investment, technological knowledge was transferred across borders. By using efficient human communication to transfer inherently complex development and manufacturing knowledge, firms enhanced their competitive edge. The strength of this strategy lies in the product development process through joint problem-solving based on sharing information with user firms. Core component suppliers implementing this strategy are very similar to traditional manufacturing companies.

The two types of core component suppliers in Table 7.1 both accelerate technological transfers from developed countries to developing countries, but the technological information transfer path is entirely different. Within the open-industrywide approach, the technology transfer from core component suppliers takes place through open standards, while, within the close-relational approach, technology is transferred through technological spillovers triggered by foreign direct investment (FDI).

Interestingly, core component suppliers in the US and Europe tend to take the open-industrywide approach and Japanese firms tend to adopt the close-relational approach. One reason that might explain this difference is their strategic tendency. US and EU firms employ the open-industrywide approach as part of their platform strategy, whereas Japanese firms opt for the close-relational approach as part of their product strategy. From the strategic viewpoint, the two types of core component suppliers compete in the global market.

In cases when the international technological transfer of complex products is involved, core component suppliers often play an essential role; yet, firms oriented toward the platform strategy and those oriented toward the product strategy exhibit contrasting features. What happens if these strategically different firms compete in the same emerging market? What kind of changes are required of core component suppliers as the industry in the emerging country grows?

To answer these questions, the present chapter takes the automobile as an example of a complex product and focuses on the ECU for the engine as a core component. We examine how core component suppliers based in developed countries conduct their business in the Chinese market.[2]

7.2 Data

The comparative case study on the two core component suppliers in the Chinese in-vehicle electronics market was performed as part of a larger exploration of the industry. The data used in this chapter, including its Appendix, consist of technological literature and interviews with various relevant firms. We conducted 46 interviews from 2009 to 2016 with 29 firms, including five automobile makers, three suppliers, nine development tool software providers and semiconductor manufacturers (see the Interview List attached at the end of the book for details). All the firms interviewed operate globally and develop their products catering to the needs of local markets, while communicating well with offices in other areas. To ensure a global point of view, we held these interviews in Japan, Europe (Germany, Belgium and France), India, China and a few ASEAN countries. The interviews followed a semi-structured format and each lasted approximately two hours.

The case study concerned two firms (Bosch and Denso) in the Chinese engine ECU market, but we deemed it insufficient to only interview their Chinese representatives. So, for both companies, interviews in their home countries—Germany for Bosch and Japan for Denso—were also organized, since core component companies develop products according to their global development roadmaps.

Additionally, the in-vehicle electronics industry has been very active in consortia and standardization activities since 2000. Thus, we needed to listen to what the players in each segment of the ecosystem had to say, including carmakers, parts suppliers, development tool software providers and semiconductor manufacturers. At that time, global open standards were not yet very impactful on market performance, since the standardization activities began in the 2000s, but their impact was already felt on ongoing product development processes. The Appendix to this chapter provides a detailed description of the AUTOSAR consortium as an example of global open standardization activity.

[2]The content of this chapter is mostly based on interviews conducted between 2009 and 2016. Note that the Chinese automobile and ECU markets were going through a transition period at that time, as touched upon in Sect. 7.4, and they might experience further drastic changes in industrial structures.

7.3 Automobile Architecture and the Role of the ECU

7.3.1 Engine ECU: The Control Device for the Engine

Let us start by explaining in-vehicle electronics, which are complex core components, in an easily understood manner.

With advancements in computer technology, software components that specifically control hardware have emerged. These components are called embedded systems and have been implemented in various products to achieve complex control. The specific electronic component for automobiles is referred to as the Electronic Control Unit, or ECU. The ECU that controls the engine is called the engine ECU.[3] The ECU was first introduced in automobiles in the 1970s to control the engine by means of a computer, so as to satisfy stringent gas emissions standards.

The engine ECU is an essential core component in modern automobile development and its designing and manufacturing requires technological knowledge of the automobile as a whole. Accordingly, it is one of the areas in which component suppliers from developing countries cannot easily catch up with the developed world; so, the majority of engine ECUs for automobiles in developing markets are provided by suppliers from developed nations.

Simply put, the automobile is a “vehicle which moves its body by producing moving power (horsepower) through controlling an internal combustion device called the engine”. When higher speed is needed, the engine produces more power to increase the flow of gasoline pumped into the engine. On the other hand, when the flow of gasoline decreases, so does the speed of the car. This is the basic control mechanism of the engine and, in this sense, the engine is the heart of the car.

The ECU was originally developed as a supplemental device to control the engine. *Supplemental device* here literally means a device that works supplementally, but now the ECU has become indispensable for any automobile.

Roughly speaking, today’s engine consists of a large casting called an engine block and the ECU, a computer that controls the engine block. The engine block is a mass of large mechanical parts, and die machining know-how is extremely important in order to manufacture one. On the other hand, the ECU is a small computer, comprised of microprocessors and memories that store programs, that controls the engine block based on various external conditions. To draw an analogy, it may be said that the engine block is akin to the muscles and the ECU to the brain.

Gasoline-fueled engines draw air from the outside environment, add gasoline to it, ignite the fuel-air mixture in the cylinder and rotate the engine. This entire sequence is completed almost instantly, depending on the external conditions. It is not hard to imagine that engine control is a very complicated process. Nevertheless, motorists can enjoy driving without being aware of such a complex procedure at all, thanks to the ECU (Fig. 7.1).

---

[3]On 18 Sep 2015, the US Environmental Protection Agency (EPA) announced that Volkswagen, a major German auto manufacturer, was suspected of not complying with gas emissions standards (Wall Street Journal 2015). The engine ECU is the component that controls the exhaust gas purifier.

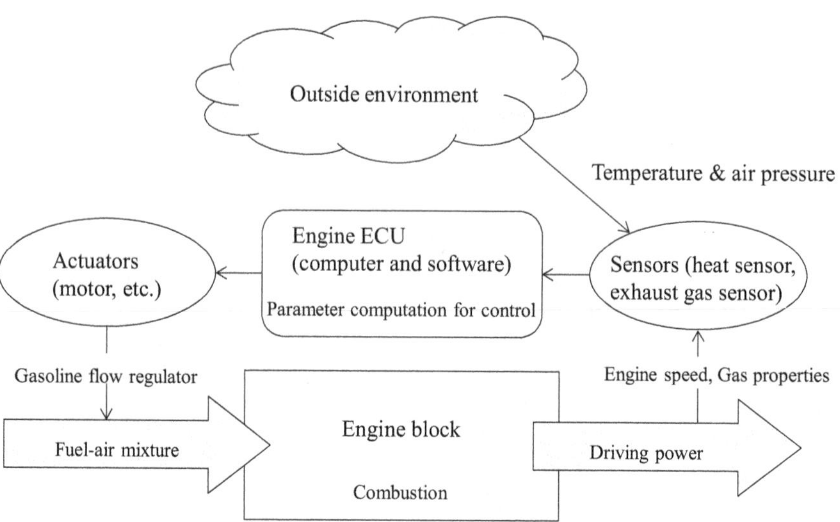

Fig. 7.1 Engine management system

Three types of devices are used to control the engine, namely, sensors, actuators and computers. The sensors check the external environmental conditions and the status of the output. The actuators change the input, while the computer calculates the input level according to the external environment and the output level. The sensors range from the intake air temperature sensor to the O_2 sensor. The actuators include the fuel injection device (motor), which controls the amount of fuel to be injected. The computer is the ECU. Its role is to receive inputs from the sensors, perform calculations and send signals to the actuators.

The ECU controls the engine not only to extract driving force (horsepower) in a steady way but also to combust the fuel within the limits of gas emissions regulations and improve fuel efficiency. Furthermore, it has to extend the life of the engine block as much as possible. Developing ECUs requires deep knowledge of internal combustion engines. In other words, ECUs are packed with know-how to use the engine at best.

As seen above, today's engine development does not involve just making engine blocks, but it inevitably requires the development of ECUs. ECUs are now an integral part of automobiles. Interestingly, while the manufacture of engine blocks is a specialty of auto manufacturers, ECUs are, in most cases, not made by them. Some carmakers do have the capability to develop ECUs, but this activity is mostly left to specialized providers, which are typically leading in-vehicle electrical parts suppliers, such as Denso, Bosch, Continental and Delphi.

In brief, the engine ECU is a procured component, rarely produced by auto manufacturers themselves. As explained before, the ECU features microprocessors and memories; it is a large set of electrical parts, also covering peripheral sensors and actuators. Hence, it is often more logical for automobile makers to procure it from electrical parts suppliers than to develop and produce it in house.

7.3.2 Development and Calibration of Engine ECUs

This section digs deeper into the manufacturing process of engine ECUs. There are two important steps in the making of ECUs: the development and production of the ECU itself (ECU development and production) and the setting of optimal numerical values for the ECU (ECU and engine calibration).

In the 1970s, when computer-based engine control was introduced, auto manufacturers began developing ECUs. In the US, ECU development was first made necessary by the enactment of the Muskie Act of 1970, which strictly regulated gas emissions. Today, the basics of ECU-based engine control have been mastered by the industry, and roles are shared between electrical parts suppliers, which develop and produce ECUs, and automobile manufacturers, which procure ECUs from them and customize the purchased products to fit their own vehicles.

As for the calibration of ECUs, major automobile manufacturers do it themselves, while small to mid-sized manufacturers usually outsource it to specialized companies. Even major manufacturers do the same for derivative models. The reason why the calibration work can be outsourced to specialized companies is that the technology for controlling engines is generic. The providers of calibration services handle the whole spectrum of vehicles that use engines, from automobiles to motorcycles, motorboats and jet skis. Regarding four-wheeled vehicles, for example, their calibration activities cover agricultural vehicles (tractors), as well as motor sports cars that compete in F-1 races. Besides electrical parts makers that develop and manufacture ECUs, there are some engineering service companies, such as Ricardo, providing ECU design and calibration services.

A delicate relationship exists between auto manufacturers and component manufacturers when it comes to ECU development and calibration, because these tasks require architectural knowledge (overall knowledge) of automobiles. Many of the electrical components other than the ECU are much less interdependent and can thus be treated individually. As these components use component knowledge only, auto manufacturers have little trouble determining whether to make them in house or outsource them. The ECU, however, requires a great deal of architectural knowledge, i.e., overall knowledge of the automobile, which, for auto manufacturers, is a source not only of bargaining power over component providers but also of differentiation of their automobile products. For example, the calibration of the engine ECU may range from a basic level, like tabulating optimal values to comply with gas emissions regulations, to a much more sophisticated level, such as identifying appropriate combinations of values to make driving more comfortable.

In sum, ECU-based engine control allows auto manufacturers to abide by gas emissions regulations and provide an enjoyable driving experience. The ECU has become indispensable in today's automobiles. ECU development and ECU calibration are two processes that auto manufacturers have to approach with great care.

7.3.3 Engine ECU and Integrated Control

At first, the engine ECU was the only electrical computerized component installed on board cars; later, various components came to be controlled by ECUs in automobiles for the developed world. Today, even low-priced models are equipped with about ten ECUs, while high-end models carry dozens or even up to a hundred ECUs. Since the year 2000, these ECUs have been connected with one another via an in-vehicle network, so that they collaborate to function through an integrated control system. The driving control is a good example of integrated control. The integrated control of multiple ECUs is an enabler of today's autonomous driving.

For example, the antilock braking system (ABS) and electronic stability control (ESC), preventing the tires from being locked and facilitating stable driving during a sudden braking event, are made possible through the integrated control of multiple ECUs. As one can easily imagine, it is far more difficult to develop an integrated control ECU concerning multiple systems than to develop an ECU controlling a single system.

Figure 7.2 summarizes what has been discussed above. The ECUs for the engine and the brakes form a layered structure with the driving control ECU, which provides integrated control. The ECU markets in developing countries are better understood if this structure is taken into account.

In each single control layer, an ECU is designed to control a single function module, such as the engine ECU, transmission ECU or brake ECU. As mentioned

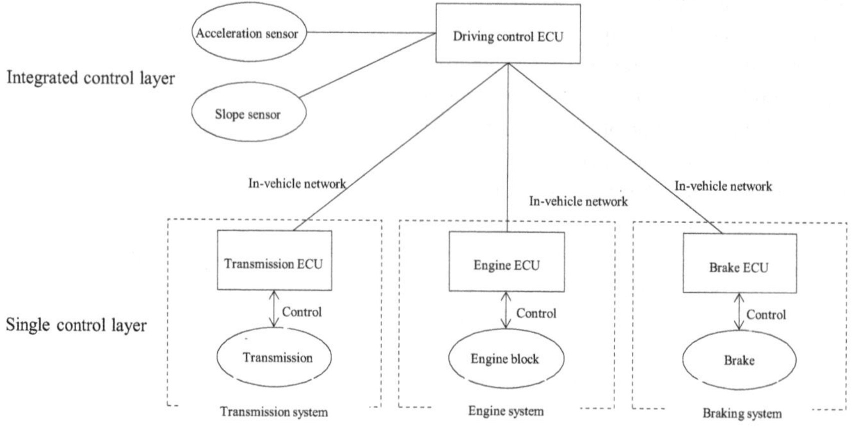

Fig. 7.2 Control layers

before, these ECUs are developed as auxiliary devices to control individual functional components. They are all important from the standpoint of automobile control, but the engine ECU, in particular, is critical for achieving efficient driving, while also complying with gas emissions regulations around the world. Most of the ECUs currently on board vehicles in developing countries are of this single control type.

On the other hand, the integrated control layer is a new feature that emerged as the independent ECUs became increasingly connected via the in-vehicle network. Traditionally, drivers were responsible for controlling the individual functions, but the networking of the engine ECU and the brake ECU has enabled computers to control driving. ECUs in this integrated control layer are a recent introduction, and this market is expected to boom and determine the competitiveness of the future automobile industry. Today, the ECUs used in passenger cars for emerging nations are still of the single-control type, but they will need to become integrated-control ECUs before long.

Whether of the single-control or integrated-control type, the engine ECU is one of the most important ECUs, since it provides core functions of the automobile. Additionally, it has a strong relationship with open standards in terms of both single-control and integrated-control layers. As detailed in Sect. 7.3.4, the open standards relevant to the engine ECU concern gas emissions control for single-control ECUs and electronics platforms for integrated-control ECUs.

7.3.4 Engine ECU and Open Standards

There are two main open standards related to the engine ECU. One regards gas emissions control and the other electronics platforms.

(1) **Emissions Control**

Let us start with gas emissions control. As explained in Sect. 7.3.2, the engine ECU was first developed as a complemental device for controlling gas emissions. Emissions control is enforced at the national level, but its regulation (i.e., open standard) goes beyond country borders and has become a kind of international standard (Fig. 7.3). Automobiles can be imported and exported freely among countries adopting the same regulations. If the regulations differ in the importing and exporting

region	04	05	06	07	08	09	10	11	12	13	14	15
US(Federal)	tentative							Tier 2				
US(California)	LEV I							LEV II				
EU	EURO3	EURO4					EURO5				EURO6	
Japan	new short term		new long term regulation				post new long term regulation					
China	EURO 1		EURO 2				EURO 3					
India	EURO 1		EURO 2									

source: Ministry of the Environment (2009) pp.180-192

Fig. 7.3 Gas emissions regulations

countries, the models to be exported must be certified through additional checks and approved by the importing country. This becomes an issue when importing and exporting used cars. As for new cars, they have to be developed according to the regulations of the destination countries.

As seen in Fig. 7.3, Europe's gas emissions regulations, the EURO regulations, are adopted in China, India and other developing countries. Generally speaking, it is easier to develop models for overseas markets that follow the same regulations as the home country. Since Europe's gas regulations are prevalent in developing countries, European car electronics suppliers have an advantage. The Chinese market, the focus of this study, adopts the EURO 3 standard for its emissions control, just like the EU.[4] This means that auto manufacturers with expertise in developing vehicles for European markets are in a particularly favorable position.

Information related to emissions control is open to anyone, so that any firm can comply with the relevant regulations. Since it is shared by all firms, it is obviously an open standard; yet, it is slightly different from the de facto standard or the consensus standard discussed in Chaps. 3–6. Gas emissions regulation is a typical de jure standard, which is involuntarily under the supervision of each government. Any car model existing in a country must be certified as compliant with the current regulation by the local government. Any engine ECU (and vehicle) that does not abide by the regulation cannot be sold in that country.

Gas emissions regulations also affect other functions of the automobile, for instance, fuel efficiency. It requires strong technological competency to achieve maximum fuel efficiency while complying with gas emissions regulations. Hence, it is said that de jure standards, such as the gas emissions standard, represent a main deterrent to new market entries.

(2) **Electronics Platforms**

Let us now look at electronics platforms. The second open standard regarding the engine ECU originated from the complexity of electronics themselves. The engine ECU is, in principle, the same as a PC but features a wide range of elements, including software, semiconductors and networks, that complicate its development. The level of complication has rapidly gone up, as ECUs are increasingly becoming connected via the in-vehicle network and operated under integrated control.[5]

To reduce complexity, open standards are used in various domains. This trend has intensified dramatically since 2000 and several consortia have been set up to create open standards. The famous AUTOSAR consortium, established in 2003, is designed to promote the standardization of auto electronics platforms. It was formed in Europe, but it also features a number of American and Japanese auto manufacturers and component suppliers. In addition, membership has been extended to auto manufacturers, component suppliers and software developers from China

[4]As of 2016, China followed a EURO 4-equivalent regulation (EURO 5 in some areas).

[5]A recall incident resulting from the increased complexity of electronic control systems involved Toyota Motor Corporation. Managing this complexity has been recognized as an industrywide issue in the automobile industry (MacDuffie and Fujimoto 2010).

and India. Its standardization activities include software programs, semiconductor interfaces and development processes, especially in the areas of basic driving control functions, like the powertrain and the braking system. European ECU suppliers, such as Bosch and Continental, actively engage in the standardization activities of AUTOSAR.

In the last few years, new consortia have been formed to develop open standards other than AUTOSAR. In 2014, Google LLC and four auto manufacturers established the Open Automotive Alliance (OAA), with the aim to encourage the adoption of the Android platform[6] in vehicles. Until recently, the automobile industry had rarely seen this kind of consortia but, as the introduction of electronics has increased technological complexity even further, their initiatives have intensified (see the Appendix "About the AUTOSAR standard" for more details). The consensus standards developed by these consortia are expected to boost efficiency and expand the market because they make it easier to ensure compatibility and reliability of electronics and software.

7.4 Engine ECU Market in China

7.4.1 Background to the Introduction of Engine ECUs in China

The engine ECU is an essential electronic component that controls the engine and, as discussed above, its calibration is a critical process, able to determine the value of automobiles. The calibration work requires deep knowledge of physics and internal combustion, as well as sensitivity to the user's point of view. These various aspects of know-how become a source of competitive advantage for automobile manufacturers and companies providing calibration services.

To develop and calibrate engine ECUs, it is essential to have architectural knowledge of the automobile as a whole. Carmakers in developed nations possess this knowledge, whereas it takes parts suppliers a long time to acquire the capability to develop and/or calibrate ECUs. Even when developed-country automakers procure ECUs from electronic component makers or outsource ECU calibration to service providers, they can still differentiate their cars from others using the knowledge that they have. In addition, various influential electrical component suppliers and calibration service providers exist in the developed world. This is not the case in developing countries, where technological accumulation for automobile manufacturing is still insufficient. Let us explain this by taking China as an example.

In the Chinese automobile industry, the engine ECU was first introduced during the 1990s. However, at the time, there was no Chinese firm developing and producing ECUs, so the industry needed assistance from foreign suppliers to facilitate the

[6] Android is an OS for smartphones.

adoption of the technology. Meanwhile, electrical component makers from developed countries were seeking an opportunity to enter China, which was expected to become a gigantic market. Direct investment in the Chinese market by electrical component makers boomed twice, in 1992–1994 and around 1997. The first boom was fueled by their motivation to provide electrical components to the foreign-funded auto manufacturers that had already set up joint ventures in China.

From the perspective of the engine ECU business, the second boom is more important. It was triggered by the Chinese government announcing the introduction of new gas emissions regulations (EURO 2) in 1998.[7] As explained earlier, engine ECUs and high-precision fuel injectors are needed to comply with gas emissions regulations. Electrical component suppliers engaging in the engine ECU business perceived this as a business opportunity and made direct investments in China.

Because of the Chinese government's regulations on the production of finished products (automobiles), no foreign capital was allowed to set up a wholly-owned subsidiary in the country; joint ventures with local businesses were needed instead. On the contrary, no such regulations existed with respect to components, allowing 100% foreign capital entities to be established.[8] Since it was easy to start a corporation in the country, Bosch, Denso, Delphi and other global enterprises providing engine ECUs now have a presence in China through direct investment. This has intensified competition in the Chinese engine ECU market.

7.4.2 *Engine ECU Business in China*

The Chinese automobile industry was mostly dominated by joint-venture carmakers in its early days. Later, a rush of new entries into the industry, combined with the motorization wave observed in and after 2000, brought about the rapid growth of pure Chinese automakers. Figure 7.4 presents the numbers of passenger cars sold in China by year and the shares of automakers by country. In the figure, *Chinese* refers to those manufacturers purely funded by Chinese capital, whereas *German*, *Japanese*, and other nationalities represent joint ventures between firms from developed countries and Chinese capital; more specifically, *German* indicates joint-venture carmakers created by German auto manufacturers and Chinese capital.

Although the statistics on market shares contain inconsistencies regarding, for instance, the coverage of models, it can be seen that the share of Chinese carmakers is roughly 30–40%. Owing to a sudden increase in the number of new entrants and the rapid growth of Chinese carmakers, quite a few firms were weeded out in a short period of time. The China-funded survivors, however, have been growing much faster than joint-venture manufacturers.

---

[7]In reality, the EURO 2 regulation was first implemented in urban areas only and it was extended to all parts of China after 2004.

[8]As of 2016, in case of a component supplier for environmentally friendly (new energy) automobiles, the establishment of a joint venture is required.

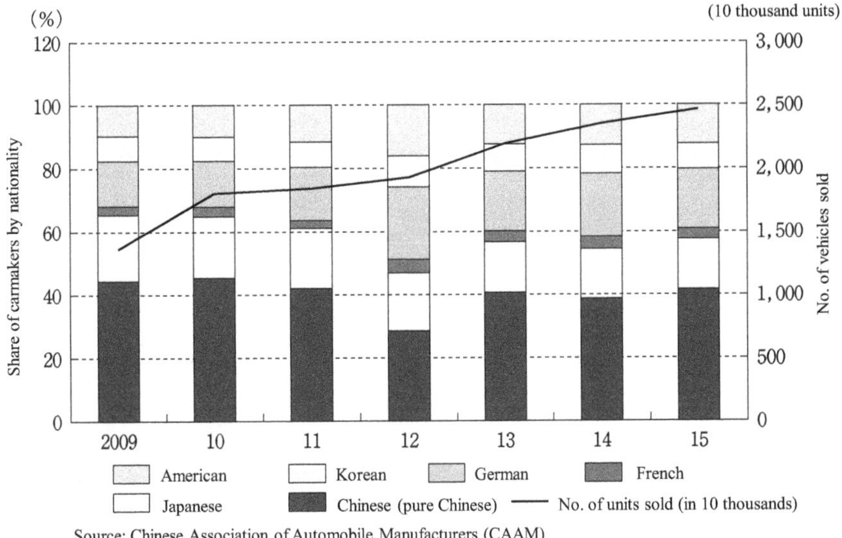

Fig. 7.4 Passenger cars sold in China by year and shares of automakers by country

From the standpoint of the engine ECU business, the Chinese automobile industry can be divided into three segments, summarized in Table 7.2. The first comprises models manufactured by joint ventures between companies from developed countries and Chinese local capital. The main products of joint ventures are those licensed specifically for the Chinese market, based on models originally created by foreign carmakers for their domestic markets in developed countries. The engine ECUs for these licensed models are typically provided by the suppliers to the original models. Therefore, it is usually European electrical component suppliers that provide engine ECUs to joint ventures between Europe and China and Japanese suppliers to joint ventures between Japan and China.

The second segment regards original models developed by joint ventures. These are new models designed and manufactured in China,[9] so engine ECU suppliers need to possess the necessary product development capability in China. Unlike licensed models, the sales areas of which are sometimes restricted, original models can be freely exported. This encourages the joint ventures to actively produce original models, and the Chinese government backs this movement.

The third segment includes automobiles developed and manufactured by Chinese local automakers. Like in the second segment, ECU suppliers are expected to be capable of developing products in China. The Chinese government supports the development of original models by local auto manufacturers, too. This segment is extremely promising for the future of the ECU business.

[9]These models are largely dependent on technology transfer from the joint ventures' parent companies in developed countries.

Table 7.2 Market segments in the Chinese engine ECU Market

Business segment	Target vehicle model	Design location	Characteristics
Supply of engine ECUs to joint ventures	Vehicle models licensed to joint ventures by automobile manufacturers from developed countries	Home country (developed country)	– Vehicle models are designed in the home country, so engine ECU companies need a development base in the home country – Export may be restricted
Supply of engine ECUs to joint ventures for own models	Vehicle models developed by joint ventures	China	– Vehicle models are designed in China, so engine ECU companies need a development base in China – Export is not restricted
Supply of engine ECUs to local companies	Vehicle models developed by local companies	China	– Vehicle models are designed in China, so engine ECU companies need a development base in China – Export is not restricted

7.5 Background and Current Situation of Entry into the Chinese Market by Bosch and Denso

7.5.1 ECU Business of the World's Two Largest Suppliers in China

Bosch and Denso are the two largest suppliers of engine ECUs in the world. Bosch's total sales in 2015 corresponded to 70.6 billion euro (78.3 billion dollars), of which 41.6 billion euro (46.2 billion dollars) came from the automobile business. Denso, on the other hand, reported 4,524.5 billion yen (37.3 billion dollars), almost all of which was automobile related.[10] Figure 7.4 plots the sales of auto parts of the two suppliers.[11] This section focuses on explaining the difference between the operations of Bosch and Denso in China.

[10]The sales figures and other data were derived and summarized based on the financial database SPEEDA.

[11]The sales figure for Bosch was derived by converting euro into yen using an annual average of exchange rates.

7.5.2 *Bosch's ECU Business in China*

7.5.2.1 Background to Bosch's Entry into the ECU Market in China

Robert Bosch GmbH (from now on, Bosch), founded by Robert Bosch in 1886, is a company based in Stuttgart, Germany, and its main business is in precision machines and electronics. It began early on to expand its operations overseas and it has now become a multinational firm with offices all over the world.

Bosch has four main business units (as of 2015). Its automobile business is responsible for the largest sales, 59% of the total, and deals with car electronics and other auto parts. The second largest unit is consumer products, accounting for 24.3%, and the third is industrial technology, accounting for 9.4%. The remaining portion of the total sales is provided by the energy construction division.

Bosch has an investment management company in Shanghai (Bosch China), which invests in 32 subsidiaries (100% owned) and 11 joint ventures with local Chinese firms. It employs a total of about 26,000 workers in China (as of 2010, when we conducted our interviews) and expects this number to grow. Approximately half of Bosch's business in China is attributed to the engine ECU (for both gasoline and diesel cars), followed by ABS and the body ECU. The Chinese market is already large for Bosch, but further rapid growth is forecast in the coming years. In 1995, in order to expand its ECU business in China, the firm established United Automotive Electronic Systems Co. Ltd. (UAES), a joint venture with a local Chinese firm in Shanghai. UAES is the development center of engine ECUs in China.

Today's automobiles are equipped with many electrical components; of these, the engine ECU, ABS and airbag system, in particular, are indispensable. The engine ECU plays an even more vital role, as it is needed to comply with gas emissions regulations; thus, the relevant technologies were actively introduced into China with a strong political intent. A competition was held to decide by whom the engine ECU technologies would be introduced, inviting Bosch, Denso and other companies. Bosch won the competition. Consequently, UAES was established by Bosch together with a joint venture of Chinese automobile companies.

UAES is a joint venture between Bosch and a local automaker but, in actuality, Bosch contributed 41% of the capital, Zhonglian Automotive Electronics—which is itself a joint venture of eight local automobile companies, including Shanghai Automotive Industry—49% and Bosch China 10%. Overall, Bosch's total share accounted for 51%. In terms of its ECU business in China, the establishment of UAES was a significant step for Bosch.

7.5.2.2 Business Policy and Main Customers

UAES had three business objectives: (1) contribute to the development of the Chinese automotive industry by providing powertrains,[12] (2) be a partner liked by customers and (3) make sufficient profit and achieve above-average growth. Each is meaningful, but the third objective is especially interesting in terms of competitive strategy, since it indicates that UAES refuses to pursue an extreme price strategy to gain ground, but it rather aims to expand its market share by providing customer-friendly systems.

All the major suppliers of engine ECUs already have a presence in China and, among them, Bosch has seized a particularly favorable business opportunity. The other suppliers essentially operate in accordance with the entries by the auto manufacturers of their home countries into the Chinese market. Therefore, their major customers in China are often joint ventures funded by those same home-country automobile manufacturers. For example, Delphi, a US supplier of electrical components, is present in China to support GM (Shanghai GM). This scenario limits the business opportunities for engine ECU suppliers to their existing customer base.

Bosch, on the other hand, does business not only with joint ventures but also with Chinese automobile manufacturers. In fact, most Chinese-capital carmakers and major engine makers are supplied by Bosch. One reason why Bosch has earned such a large share in the Chinese market is that it has succeeded in dealing with both joint ventures and Chinese-capital firms. This extraordinary success has made its products a de facto standard in the Chinese engine ECU market.

7.5.2.3 Localization of Management

Bosch's Chinese engine business has been localized, with 80% of the engineers engaged in Research and Development being Chinese and a fairly low turnover compared with the national average. Bosch believes that the source of its competitive advantage is its people, and it has been a long-standing policy to actively hire local talents. The accumulation of ECU-related technology by Chinese local automakers is not high. Then again, there are still many other automobile-related technologies in which they lag behind the developed world, so they do not regard the engine ECU as a vital area for improvement. As a consequence, a wide technological gap remains between Bosch and local Chinese auto manufacturers.

7.5.2.4 Division of Labor with Home Country

Since the growth of the Chinese market has been remarkably fast compared with other parts of the world, Bosch has developed product models dedicated to the Chinese

---

[12] *Powertrain* refers to the whole set of devices that deliver the driving force produced by the engine to the wheels. The engine EUC is a core component of the powertrain.

market, aside from its global platform roadmap,[13] and UAES has played a central role in this. The joint venture has about 3,800 employees (as of 2010) and started providing engine ECUs in 1996.

UAES's technology originates from Bosch in Germany. The Chinese gas emissions regulations are based on those of Europe and UAES has earned a dominant position by transferring the technologies developed by Bosch in Germany. The technologies transferred, however, are rather basic and the individual product models (i.e., ECUs), especially those dedicated to the Chinese market, are developed in China. The direct investment that Bosch made ahead of the other engine ECU suppliers underpins its success in the country.

Despite initially relying on technology transfer from Bosch, since 2000 UAES has worked to develop new products for the local market and improve its development capability in China, so that its products can be regarded as originally made in China. In addition, platforms developed in China are starting to appear on the global market. In 2008, for example, the TCU (Transmission Controller Unit) developed by UAES was incorporated into Bosch's global product portfolio.

The engine ECU that UAES supplies in the Chinese market is fundamentally a single-model standard product, rather than a customized one. Since customized products tend to be costly and require longer development times, Chinese auto manufacturers usually refrain from choosing them. They prefer standard products because of their lower cost and shorter delivery times. These standard products, however, are not exactly identical. They come with different combinations of sensors and actuators and are delivered as suitable EMSs (Engine Management Systems) to individual customers. Since the engine ECU is a control unit, it is highly versatile. UAES customizes it by changing parameter settings in the specification document working with the customers but, in essence, its business relies on having standard products as baseline. There is a 5% difference in the price applied to joint ventures and Chinese auto manufacturers.

The engine ECU business of UAES usually starts with a proposal. The specification document describing the EMS functions proposed by UAES extends well beyond 100 pages, with more than 1,000 parameters to be set. Using this template, UAES finds out what the customer requires and determines each parameter to complete the final version of the specifications.

This is the basic flow of determining the function specifications, but the actual process is slightly different depending on whether the customer is a joint venture or a Chinese firm. Joint ventures tend to require a larger amount of documentation, since they need to cater to the customization needs of the auto manufacturers back in their home countries, from which they receive technology transfer. On the contrary, Chinese automakers make small changes, merely adding some extra unique specifications. In the case of newcomers to the market, the standard products often suffice.

[13]Bosch planned to integrate its platform roadmap at the global level with its new engine ECU platform (MDG1) to be launched in 2015.

7.5.3 *Denso's Business in China*

7.5.3.1 Background to Denso's Entry into the ECU Market in China

Denso Corporation is an electrical component supplier for automobiles headquartered in the city of Kariya, Aichi Prefecture, Japan. It was established in 1949 as a spin-off of Toyota Motor's electric components and radiators division, which was losing money at the time. *Nihon Denso* (meaning *Japan Electrical Components*) was the initial name, with the mission of "serving all carmakers in Japan", which was changed to simply *Denso* in 1996. In 1953, the supplier made a technology alliance with Bosch and, by actively accumulating technologies, Denso gained competitiveness in its technological level and product quality. Backed by the motorization trend in Japan in the 1950s, it grew rapidly to become one of the largest engine ECU suppliers in the world.

Denso strictly focuses on automotive components, with consolidated sales of 4,524.5 billion yen (fiscal year ending March 2016). The company's customer base consists of the Toyota group (45.3%) and non-Toyota customers (44.2%), while general commercial products (10.5%) make up the remaining sales (source: Denso's presentation on financial results for fiscal year 2016).

Denso entered the Chinese market ahead of any other auto parts suppliers from Japan. In 1987, after identifying the country as a promising market, it set up a representative office in China and, starting from the mid-1990s, it built manufacturing plants of car air conditioners and starters/alternators. In 1997, it established Tianjin Denso Electronics Company in Tianjin City as an engine ECU production base. The decision stemmed from hopes of further growth of the Chinese market and the prediction that China would introduce gas emissions regulations (EURO 2 regulations) in 1998 (though this actually happened in 1999). China's accession to the WTO in 2000 led auto manufacturers from developed countries to expand their business in China, which, in turn, led Denso to increase its production there.

Tianjin Denso plays a central role in Denso's production of car electronics in China. Its majority share (93%) is owned by Denso Corporation and the remaining 7% by Toyota Tsusho. Its main products include engine ECUs, meters, car navigation systems and fuel pumps.

7.5.4 *Business Policies and Main Customers*

Denso's business policy in China is to be a component provider to the Chinese subsidiaries of auto manufacturers from developed countries (joint ventures). Hence, the key to its success lies in the improvement of design skills in the home countries (Japan, US and Europe). It has strong ties with joint ventures operating in China, especially those between Japanese carmakers and Chinese firms. Indeed, Tianjin Denso's main customers include FAW Toyota, Guangzhou Toyota, Guangzhou Honda and

Jilin Suzuki. However, its closest connections are with Toyota-funded joint ventures; in some product categories, Toyota-affiliated customers account for as much as 90% of Tianjin Denso's business.

Joint-venture automakers produce models licensed by auto manufacturers based in developed countries. Therefore, an important factor that determines a supplier's competitiveness is participating as early as possible in the designing process of these developed-country auto manufactures, so as to earn *design wins*, i.e., have its products integrated into the automobile design. This means that Denso China needs to work closely with the development bases of auto manufacturers from developed countries.

Since its business in China centers mainly around joint-venture carmakers, Denso strategically strengthens its development resources and sales force in the home countries and increases its production capacity in China. With this policy, Denso's production in China has come a long way for what concerns quality and technology accumulation.

In the late 2000s, however, local vehicle development in China started to expand, as joint-venture carmakers began designing their own models and Chinese automakers were steadily growing. This created a pressing need for Denso to intensify its relationships with on-site Chinese auto manufacturers and expand its development center in the country. The firm was keenly aware of the importance of collaborating with fast-growing Chinese carmakers. Consequently, as well as bolstering development and sales resources in China, it implemented a development, production, and sales framework tailored to the local market in terms of balance between quality and price.

7.5.5 Localization of Management

Tianjin Denso is wholly owned by Denso. Compared with join ventures, this makes it more difficult to recruit and train local managers, i.e., to localize corporate management. When adding a production item, Denso's head office in Japan dispatches Japanese personnel from the divisions concerned, such as production engineering, quality assurance and manufacturing. As a result, the number of Japanese managers increases, hindering the growth of local managers. However, hiring talented resources in the Chinese labor market is a challenge, while promoting insufficiently qualified local employees to managerial positions makes things more complicated. One possible idea would be to hire many local employees as managers and later demote those who do not demonstrate sufficient abilities. Yet, the Japanese tend to be averse to demotion, so this is not a practical idea. Thus far, Denso has not been successful in developing local managers, which naturally takes time, and this is one of the priority issues that need addressing.

7.5.6 Division of Labor with Home Country

The division of labor between Denso China and Denso Japan is that the engine ECUs are designed in Japan and manufactured by Tianjin Denso in China. Currently, China depends on Japan (or on the home countries of other Western auto manufacturers) for engine ECU designs. Denso China's main customers have traditionally been joint-venture carmakers, which rely on the decisions made by their design groups back home, i.e., the auto manufacturers in developed countries. This is why Denso has worked toward strengthening its design resources in the developed countries and increasing its manufacturing capability in China.

Denso's efforts to improve its production capacity in China have been successful. In practical terms, the firm takes the following steps when a new product is developed, and then manufactured in China. First, in the home country, i.e., usually in Japan, the manufacturing process is designed based on the product design. This process design includes the process control specification sheets. When the new product is a derivative model of an existing product, it is Tianjin Denso that creates the process control specification sheets. The sheets define the specifications for jigs and automated machines. Tianjin Denso also prepares operation manuals, detailing installation procedures, quality check points and safety precautions that are needed for the actual manufacturing floor. In sum, the process control specification sheets and operation manuals for new products are made in China, in collaboration with the production management team in Japan, whereas those for derivative products are made solely in China. As far as derivative products are concerned, Denso has accumulated sufficient technologies to allow the designing processes to be completed by Chinese personnel only.

Facing fierce market competition, joint-venture automakers are keen on the product designs to be made in China. Besides the simple production of licensed models, automobile development itself, including platforms, has been shifting to China, which implies that substantial development capabilities are required on site. Chinese auto manufacturers also want to see Denso China enhance its developing capabilities, because they cannot succeed in creating platforms on their own, without the cooperation of Denso China's development center. These movements keep providing Denso with new business opportunities.

To meet the growing demand coming from both joint-venture and Chinese carmakers, Denso has rapidly been expanding its development center in China. Although the basic design of engine ECUs is the same for all customers, the firm anticipates that diversification will increase to meet the customers' individual needs (custom designs). Unless additional engineers are hired to dramatically expand the ECU calibration potential, Denso believes that it will not be able to meet the needs of auto manufacturers in the future.

7.5.7 *Market Performance of the ECU Business in China*

The market size of passenger cars in China was about 13 million vehicles in 2009 and approximately 25 million in 2015 (Fig. 7.3). Clearly, all these vehicles carry engine ECUs. The main suppliers of engine ECUs in China are foreign-funded firms from Japan, the US and Europe, such as Bosch (Germany), Denso (Japan), Delphi (US), Visteon (US) and Continental (Germany). There are no precise statistical data on their respective market shares because the engine ECU is merely a component and, unlike the automobile itself, it is not statistically tracked. Nonetheless, inferring from various sources, the engine ECU market shares for 2009 can roughly be estimated as Bosch (UAES) having 40–60%, Delphi 10%–20% and Denso around 10%. Undeniably, Bosch holds the top share of the Chinese engine ECU market.

The Chinese market has been more lucrative than the European market for Bosch. This results from its impressive business model, which deserves admiration. Indeed, the firm provides engine ECUs as turnkey solutions, i.e., standard products. Because it sells off-the-shelf products, it does not need to tailor them to different customers, avoiding the high costs associated with customization. By distributing a single model to a wide range of customers, Bosch has achieved high profitability in the Chinese market.

Such a standard product requires less technological accumulation; thus, it greatly benefits Chinese automobile manufacturers, eager to catch up with the developed world. Firstly, no need for customization minimizes the price of engine ECUs. Secondly, standard products can be delivered with shorter lead times, which contributes to reducing the time for automobile development. Thirdly, since standard products do not require detailed specifications to be defined by the automobile manufacturers, their lack of technological accumulation does not matter, while, as described above, a shorter time to market is still ensured. Finally, since engine ECUs are ubiquitous, engineers can efficiently learn and accumulate expertise in developing them as general skills, and carmakers can more easily hire mid-career engineers. These advantages have caused more Chinese automobile manufacturers to choose Bosch as their engine ECU supplier and have led the company to earn such a large market share that its product have become the de facto standard.

Bosch entered the Chinese market earliest among global ECU providers—and it has thus accumulated the longest experience—but this is not the only reason why it is successful there. The excellent model that it established for the engine ECU business is what has truly strengthened its competitive advantage in the Chinese market.

7.6 Future Trend of the Chinese Automobile Industry

7.6.1 Technological Accumulation of the Chinese Automobile Industry: Two Future Visions

The Chinese automobile industry has been growing very rapidly. The industry develops products catering to the practical needs of the Chinese market, based on the technologies created by automobile industries from developed countries as available resources.

The automobiles manufactured in China in the 1990s (licensed models produced by joint-venture makers) were modifications of those made in developed countries, tailored to the Chinese market. On the contrary, the models and brands developed by pure Chinese carmakers since the late 2000s have gone one step further from relying solely on base models and have come to mean original models locally developed in China. It is believed that Chinese automobile makers usually go through the four stages described in Table 7.3 until they launch completely original models and brands.

The first stage is to make partial modifications for the Chinese market to models already sold in developed countries. The product development is easy, since it only involves modifying some parts of an existing model. In the second stage, the modules related to driving (mainly the lower body) are used as they are in the existing model, but the exterior design of the body and the interior are created anew. In other words, the development of the upper-half modules (upper body) is the focus.

The third stage implies a major leap from the second stage, as the makers design the basic functions of the vehicle from scratch, including driving, braking and turning. For this purpose, single-function ECUs have to be maximally utilized. To control vehicle movement, the developers need to use ECUs in the integrated control layer. The modules involved in vehicle driving (lower body) are called a platform, and individual automobile manufacturers are expected to have the development capabilities for platforms. In the fourth stage, the automobile makers develop the vehicle in its entirety.

The interviews carried out in 2010–2011 indicated that most Chinese automobile manufacturers, whether joint ventures or pure Chinese makers, were transitioning from the first stage to the second stage and, as of 2015, more and more of them managed to reach the third stage. In the very near future, they are highly likely to tackle the fourth stage, i.e., development of the entire vehicle including integrated control systems. As a matter of fact, the Chinese government's industrial policy endorses the transition to the fourth stage.

Table 7.3 Technological stages of automobile development by Chinese manufacturers

First stage	Mainly partial modifications of base models
Second stage	Development of the upper body only
Third stage	Development of the platform as a whole (running gear and chassis)
Fourth stage	Development of the whole vehicle including control components (ECU, etc.)

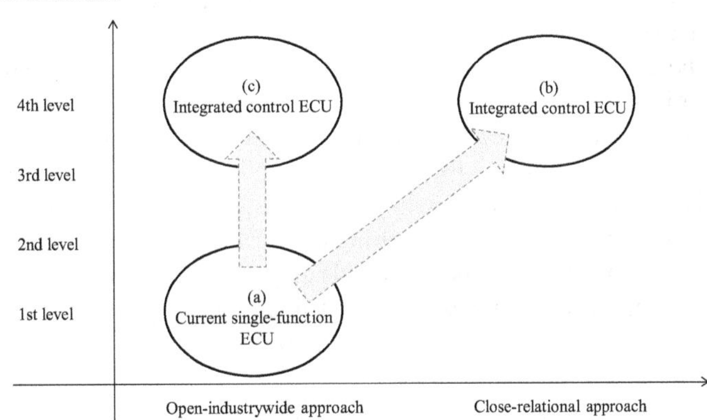

Fig. 7.5 Future image of the Chinese ECU market

In today's Chinese engine ECU market, the communication pattern most frequently observed between auto manufacturers and component suppliers is similar to the provision of turnkey solutions, represented by (a) in Fig. 7.5.

When the technology level of Chinese auto manufacturers shifts from the first and second stages to the third and fourth, the trade patterns between auto manufacturers and ECU makers will probably change. As for the direction of the change, however, there are two distinct views.

The first group of experts believes that there will be closer communication between the two sides and they will start exchanging technological information more regularly. The inter-firm communication pattern will thus resemble the close-relational approach. In this case, it will be preferable to exchange technological information face to face and ECU suppliers will be most importantly expected to have local development capabilities. This theory predicts that integrated control will become more and more necessary and the communication pattern will shift to (b) in the upper right corner of Fig. 7.5. If that is the case, demand for customization will increase, and engineers from local Chinese suppliers will need to be deeply involved in the car development projects of Chinse manufacturers. In the first stage, they will simply have to develop products based on the models already present in the home countries; yet, in the second and third stages, they will have to develop platforms by themselves. This situation provides greater opportunities for ECU suppliers from developed nations to transfer necessary technology and knowledge. Denso, in particular, pursues this approach with determination.

The second group argues that, while demand for customized ECUs will increase for sure, demand for standard products will still be greater. The inter-firm communication pattern will thus be closer to the open-industrywide approach. It is believed that, even if integrated control is needed, the communication pattern between automobile manufacturers and component suppliers will remain unchanged and simply move up to (c) in Fig. 7.5. Assuming this view to be true, component suppliers will likely be expected to provide more comprehensive solutions, i.e., turnkey-like solutions. The Chinese market is extremely competitive and pressure to reduce costs is high. In order to satisfy this need, ECU manufacturers too will need to pursue scale economy. In doing so, they will have to be careful not to depend too much on face-to-face communication by, for example, simplifying the technical specifications; otherwise, they will end up needing an enormous amount of work for technological and knowledge transfer and bearing considerable costs. Higher costs will mean lower profits and greater difficulties in dealing extensively with local Chinese automobile makers. Bosch intends to address this issue by promoting the provision of comprehensive solutions.

7.6.2 Pros and Cons of the Two Approaches

So far, the Chinese market has undoubtedly grown following the open-industrywide approach. But, if it is to grow further at the same pace, which approach, close-relational or open-industrywide, will be more effective? They both have advantages and disadvantages and it is hard to tell which will prevail.

The former approach, with emphasis on communication, is advantageous in that it comes with adequate support services, which may be welcomed by local auto manufacturers trying to accumulate technologies. The engine ECU supplier customizes the interface of its product and provides each customer with a tailored ECU. The close-relational approach will encourage customized interfaces.

The most important point in this case is whether the engine ECU will become the focus of technological accumulation (catch-up) for Chinese auto manufacturers. As discussed earlier, their level of technological accumulation needs improving in many areas if they are to catch up with the developed world. Under these circumstances, it is unclear whether the engine ECU will be the main area for catch-up or whether Chinese automakers will concentrate on bettering the overall package of the automobile to increase integration and make the product more attractive.

Nonetheless, it should not be forgotten that this approach has a disadvantage too: since it involves building up strong business relationships, its associated costs tend to escalate. For example, ECU makers have to expand their design centers and technical sales force in a short period of time. The question is whether they can develop products that meet cost requirements, while keeping the burden of investment increases as low as possible.

The latter approach, on the other hand, has the advantage of reduced costs associated with business trading, since it emphasizes standard interfaces. The engine ECU being provided as a standard product is attractive to automobile makers in terms of shorter delivery times and lower costs. Engine ECU suppliers also benefit because they can sell a single product model to a wide range of customers, which brings in more profits that can be reinvested in R&D.

One problem with this approach is that it fosters differentiation competition among auto manufacturers, and this makes it difficult to sell engine ECUs as standard products. The engine ECU is a component that directly relates to primary performance indicators of the automobile, such as engine efficiency and gas emissions control. Therefore, automobile manufacturers are always motivated to differentiate their products from others in this field.

In an environment where new players incessantly join the market, there are many auto manufacturers with low levels of technological accumulation, which keeps the demand for standard engine ECUs high. On the other hand, in an environment where new entries have come to a halt, auto manufacturers start to differentiate based on their accumulated technologies, also in the field of engine ECUs; as a result, competition relying on differentiation may pose a threat to any business that revolves around standard ECUs. Yet, even in such a situation, if Chinese auto manufacturers remain in the third stage and compete mainly by differentiating their upper bodies, the standard engine ECU business may still survive. The possibilities of industrial evolution are complex and it is too early to clearly predict its future.

An external factor that deserves consideration has to do with the standardization activities carried out in the car electronics field since 2000 (Tokuda et al. 2011). The increasing complexity of car electronics has been a serious problem also in developed countries and, in order to reduce it, auto manufacturers and component suppliers, accompanied by tool makers, semiconductor manufacturers and software companies, have gathered together to actively carry out standardization activities. A good example is the AUTOSAR consortium, which is an open standardization organization established in Europe (see the Appendix at the end of this chapter). The standard specifications, roadmaps and tools compatible with those introduced by such consortia affect not only developed countries but also developing countries. If a global standard is created and a business ecosystem arising out of it expands, the industry as a whole tends to move toward the open-industrywide approach. This is a key change that needs to be watched with great attention.

7.7 Conclusions

As pointed out at the beginning of this chapter, international technological transfer is difficult for developed-country industries dealing with complex products. In reality, however, these industries are spreading to developing countries at an astonishing rate. In this pattern of industrial transfer, core component providers from developed countries play a particularly important role. In this chapter, we divided the policies of core component providers concerning inter-firm relationships into two types, the open-industrywide approach and the close-relational approach, and then compared them. The former approach was typically observed in platform-oriented firms, i.e., those that pursue a platform strategy by enhancing the ecosystem, and the latter in product-oriented firms, i.e., those that pursue a product strategy by developing differentiated products.

A major difference emerged from our case studies on two suppliers to the Chinese automotive industry. Bosch, which follows the open-industrywide approach, helps its user companies develop new products in a short period of time and is widely accepted by Chinese-capital automakers with low levels of technological accumulation. In previous studies, firms of this type have been called technology enablers or technological platform owners (Gawer and Cusumano 2002). More recently, much academic attention has been devoted to how platform firms create an ecosystem that encompasses both developed- and developing-country firms while fostering technological transfer (Ogawa 2008; Shintaku et al. 2008; Tatsumoto et al. 2009). This industrial structure is ideal for developing countries because it greatly contributes to their domestic economic growth (Ogawa 2011; Tatsumoto 2012).

In the Chinese automotive industry, pure Chinese carmakers that still have limited technological accumulation work well with global-scale ECU suppliers. The former are willing to adopt the platform components offered by the latter while they complete their technological catch-up, so they welcome platform firms. Conversely, joint-venture carmakers may see the rise of platform firms as a problem, since platform ECUs are available to all the players in the ecosystem and are likely to deprive them of their sources of differentiation. In the auto ecosystem, a further growth of Chinese-origin automakers will likely expand the business opportunities offered to platform firms in China.

On the other hand, when auto joint ventures want to develop their own models for export, ECU suppliers from developed countries, which provide different carmakers with customized interfaces based on the close-relational approach, are preferable, so that technological information can be actively absorbed. In this case, ECU suppliers have to deal with the increasing costs of inter-firm communication. One viable solution may be to concentrate the firm's resources on co-development with auto manufacturers and outsource the peripherals to capable local developers. In this scenario, however, a cluster of local development firms needs to be in place as a prerequisite.

For firms in both developed and developing countries, platform-based industrial transfer has its economic rationality. Generally speaking, cost pressure is high in developing countries and firms from developed countries have a hard time earning profits there. Nonetheless, if an industrial structure based on open standards is created, developed-nation firms can still make sufficient profits in developing economies, which accelerates industrial transfer. By having the platform as their bedrock, firms from both developed and developing countries can share work in an industrial ecosystem. At the same time, platform firms can achieve both the commoditization of their products and high profitability (Ogawa 2008). This is the key to understanding the strategy of platform firms in developing countries.

Such a strategy for business expansion into developing countries exists as a background to fast industrial transfer across national borders and largely affects industrial evolution in emerging economies. Platform-based industrial transfer, called platform-separated model (Tatsumoto et al. 2010), is characterized by universality and rationality as a competitive strategy for developing markets and its importance for firms from developed countries is likely to grow in the coming years.

Appendix: About the AUTOSAR Standard

In the mid-1990s, in-vehicle electronics (from now on, referred to as car electronics) started to become outstandingly complex and the industry realized that this would lead to an increase in development man-hours and cause problems with quality assurance. The importance of electronic technologies, especially software, rippled across enterprises as a key element for delivering the functionality of automobiles.

(1) Car Electronic Components

In terms of cost, the ratio between mechanical parts and electronic parts is seven to three in general car models (Fig. 7.A.1); hence, car electronics by no means account for most of the cost of producing a vehicle. A closer look at the breakdown of costs reveals a fundamental difference between the two kinds of automotive parts. When dividing the car components into in-house parts and purchased parts, the ratio for mechanical parts is three to four, whereas that for electronic parts is roughly three to twenty-seven, which translates into ninety percent of parts being outsourced. This extreme proportion plagues automobile manufacturers in terms of not only procurement capability but also accumulation of expertise.

Car electronics are essentially classified into four categories, depending on where in the vehicle they are used. They include powertrain parts, which generate the driving force, chassis parts, which control driving, body parts, which provide a comfortable interior environment, and information parts, which handle multimedia, such as the car navigation system (Fig. 7.A.2). More recently, a fifth category, safety parts, has become a regular feature. The four categories are sometimes grouped into lower

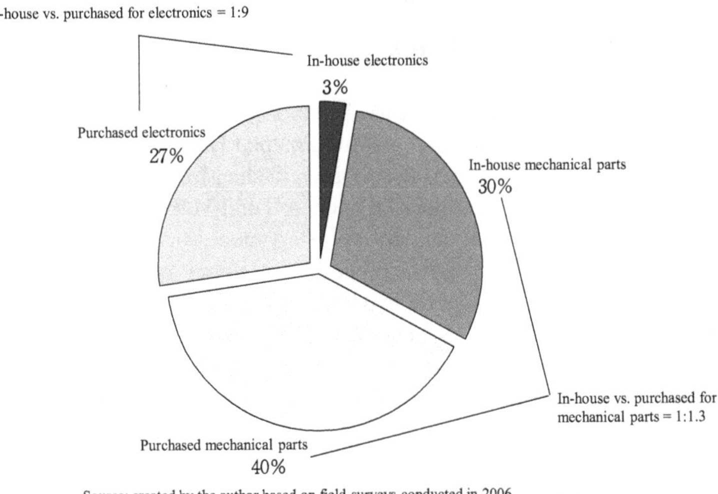

Fig. 7.A.1 Comparison between the costs of mechanical parts and of car electronics

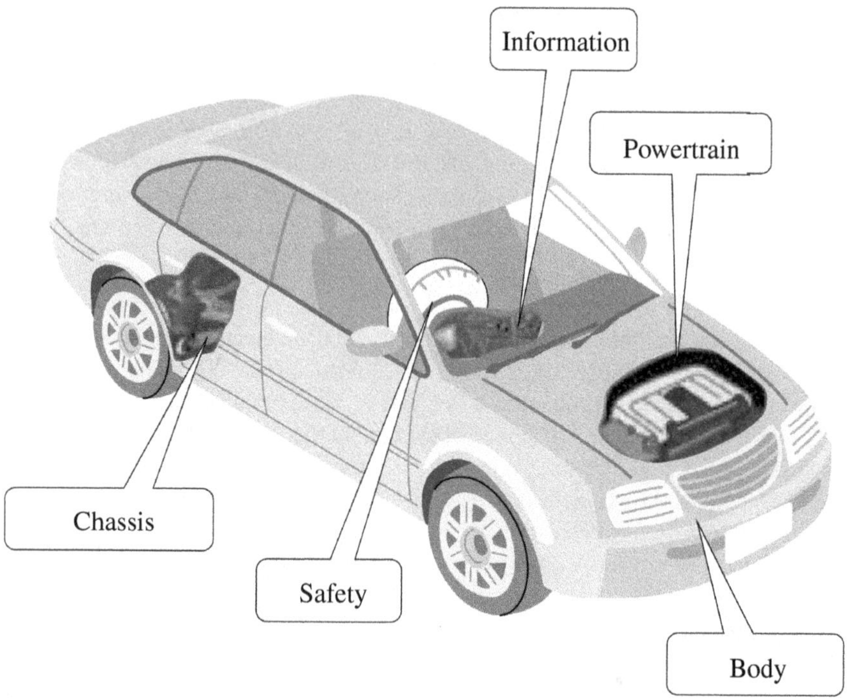

Fig. 7.A.2 Four plus one categories of car electronics

body (powertrain and chassis parts) and upper body (body and information parts). The scope of the AUTOSAR standard is the lower body of the car.

(2) Standardization of Car Electronics

Efforts to standardize car electronic parts began in Europe, with five German automotive manufacturers setting up a consortium named Hersteller Initiative Software (HIS) in 2001. Its members were Audi AG, Bayerische Motoren Werke (BMW) AG, Porsche AG, Daimler (then Daimler-Chrysler) AG and Volkswagen (VW) AG. The consortium intended to define standard software modules, software testing, flash programming of ECUs, development process assessment and standard simulation processes and tools. Hence, its participants aimed to standardize common requirements for car electronic parts, associated software and development environment from the standpoint of automakers. This initiative, however, fell through without the participation of suppliers. Nevertheless, the formation of HIS was significant in letting the whole industry know that there was a major movement in the car electronics domain.

After this experience, European mega suppliers quickly took action. In the following year, 2002, Daimler-Chrysler, Robert Bosch GmbH (Bosch) and Continental AG jointly announced that they were preparing to set up a partnership dedicated to car electronics, which would later become the AUTOSAR consortium. It is worth noting that this time the members comprised an automaker, Daimler-Chrysler, and two suppliers, Bosch and Continental.

In July 2003, with the joining of BMW, Siemens AG and VW, the partnership transformed into the AUTOSAR (AUTomotive Open System ARchitecture) consortium, featuring three automobile manufacturers and three suppliers. All its participants remained European, until Ford of the US signed up as a core member in November 2003. Membership in AUTOSAR became increasingly global with the participation of PSA of France and Toyota of Japan in December 2003 and General Motors of the US in the following year. As a result, the consortium developed into a forum aimed at defining global standards.

AUTOSAR planned its activities in three-year periods: Phase 1 would cover the period from 2004 to 2006, Phase 2 from 2007 to 2009 and Phase 3 from 2010 to 2012. A set of standard specifications would be released in each phase. The consortium's scope of standardization was broad, with ECUs at its center, which inevitably required a large numbers of participating firms, categorized into core partners, premium members and associate members, depending on their role and authority within the consortium. As of 2005, AUTOSAR comprised 10 core partners, 46 premium members and 24 associate members from the automobile and semiconductor industries, as well as parts suppliers, software vendors and tool providers.

AUTOSAR targeted four main aspects as objectives of its standardization activities: (i) the interface of the microcontroller (semiconductors), (ii) the internal components of basic software (BSW), (iii) data formats for applications and (iv) the process and methodology of development. The microcontroller in objective (i) refers to the semiconductor chip in the ECU that executes processing, analogous to the CPU in personal computers. Objective (ii) means standardizing the set of software components that make up the BSW; it is equivalent to standardizing the internal components of the Windows OS. Objective (iii) concerns the data formats to be used by applications; an analogy would be standardizing and sharing the format of Word files across the industry. Objective (iv) was pursued in order to improve developing tools. The above objectives and their scopes are summarized in Fig. 7.A.3.

As the figure illustrates, the AUTOSAR standard defined standard specifications for the internals of the ECU and associated elements, such as the data formats for applications. The consortium split the entire scope of standardization into smaller sections, called work packages, dedicated to the areas covered by the four objectives. One of the work packages, for example, was called MCAL; member and partner companies concerned gathered to discuss and develop a standard for the interface of the microcontroller, which would later be reviewed for approval.

The level of accomplishment of the four objectives, that is, how detailed the specifications in their scopes were standardized, differed significantly. Table 7.A.1 lists the results of the efforts made on the work packages and how much detail was standardized: ◎ means that the target area was fully standardized, ○ represents a reasonable level of detail, while △ indicates insufficient standardization. The insufficient result

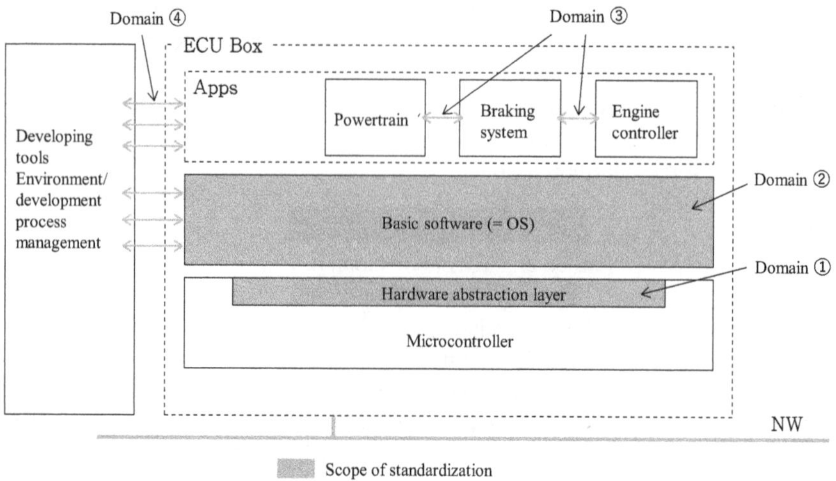

Fig. 7.A.3 Scope of AUTOSAR standardization

Table 7.A.1 Level of standardization in the four AUTOSAR domains

Domain	Scope of standardization	Outcome
①	Interface of microcontroller	◎
②	Basic software	◎
③	Data formats for applications	△
④	Tools and methodologies (development process)	○

was mainly caused by the failure to consolidate different approaches into one and the reluctance of participating firms to provide technical information.

The table shows that the standardization activities were successful in objectives (i) and (ii), while they were not in objective (iii). Referring to the architectural separation framework presented in the discussion on strategic standardization (Chap. 3), this outcome can be interpreted as follows: the interface of the microcontroller and the BSW made it into the open area, whereas the data formats for applications were kept in the closed area. This architectural division is, in fact, aligned with the intent of the founding members of AUTOSAR, which were automakers and mega suppliers. Applications and the various elements associated with them are an area for differentiation for both automakers and suppliers; or rather, applications are actually the suppliers' core competence. It was no surprise that the standardization efforts concerning data formats for applications did not see major progress. On the other hand, the interface of the microcontroller and the BSW were actively standardized, since these components were typically purchased by both automakers and suppliers and their domains did not overlap with the companies' business segments.

(3) Global Expansion of the AUTOSAR Standard

These standardization activities led to the wide adoption of car electronic systems compatible with the AUTOSAR standard among European automakers. Figure 7.A.4 tracks how the AUTOSAR standard was adopted by European carmakers over time.

As AUTOSAR ended up being a global organization, it was not only European firms but also firms from other parts of the world, such as Asia, that engaged in its standardization activities. Figure 7.A.5 shows the geographical distribution of AUTOSAR members around 2011. The numbers next to the area names indicate the number of participating firms, with increases from the previous year reported in parentheses.

European firms participating in the AUTOSAR consortium were the most numerous, i.e., 72 firms in total. This is no surprise considering that the original forum was established in Europe. The second largest group was from Asia, with a total of 64 firms, including 41 from Japan, 9 from China and 8 from India. So many Japanese firms joined AUTOSAR, despite geographical distance from its origins, because Japanese parts suppliers had long been trading with European carmakers and had a strong interest in the standard.

Figure 7.A.6 shows the size of automobile markets in major regions of the world as of 2012. China was the largest market that year, with 19 million new vehicles sold. As the Chinese auto industry had been seeking an opportunity to introduce technology from Europe, it closely followed technical trends developing there. This does not necessarily mean that Chinese automakers wished to implement the AUTOSAR standard in their own market; it simply explains why many Chinese firms were motivated to join the consortium.

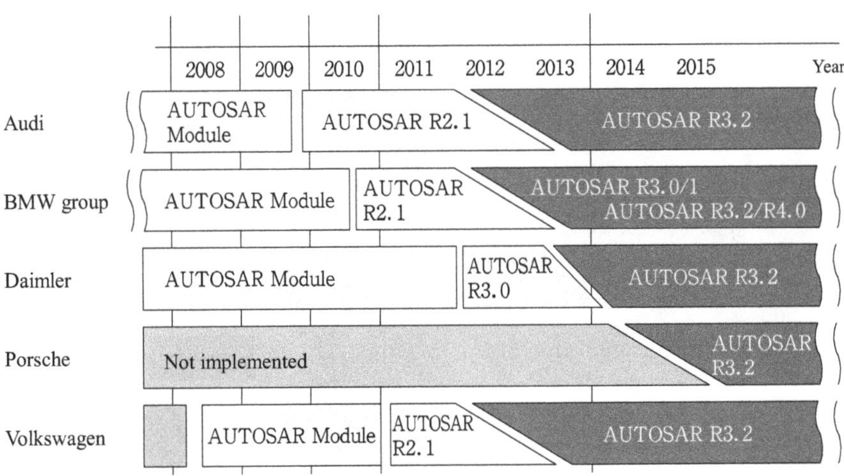

Source: Tokuda, Tatsumoto, Ogawa (2011)

Fig. 7.A.4 Status and prospects for the implementation of AUTOSAR specifications

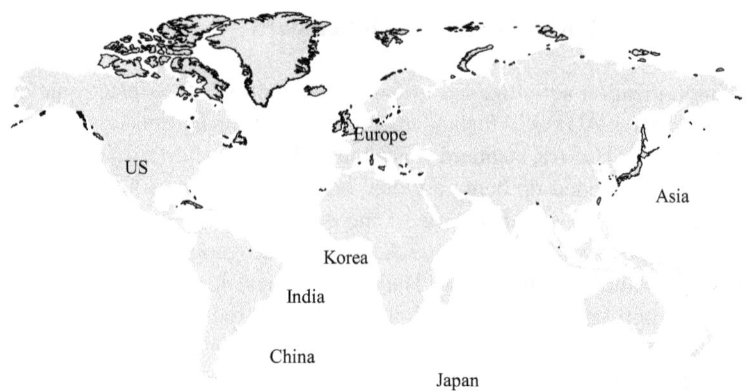

Note: Numbers in parentheses represent increments from the previous year
Source: AUTOSAR presentation material

Fig. 7.A.5 Geographical distribution of AUTOSAR member firms (around 2011)

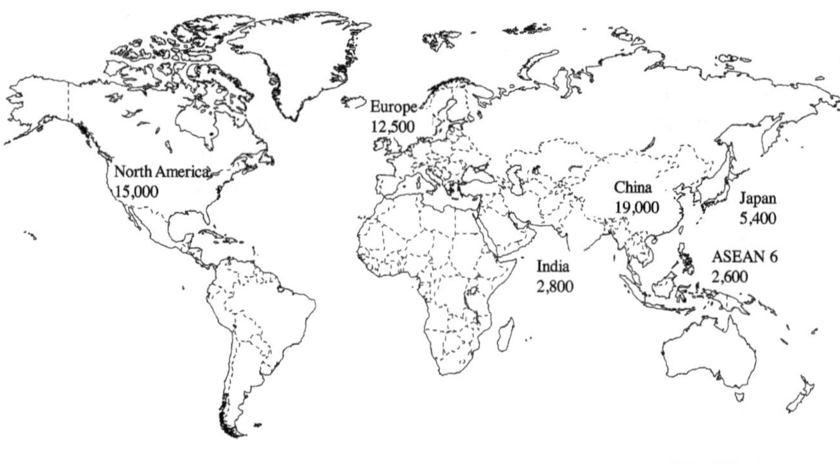

1) ASEAN 6 refers to Thailand, Malaysia, Indonesia, the Philippines, Singapore and Vietnam

2) The numbers of vehicles are rounded numbers of new vehicles sold based on the 2012 data from JETRO, except the number for Japan based on JAMA data and that for ASEAN 6 based on JETRO data for 2011

Fig. 7.A.6 Automotive market sizes in the world (2012)

What is noteworthy is the significant number of Indian firms among the consortium participants from Asia. At that time, the Indian auto market was still small and featured mostly compact cars; thus, it was not suitable for the wide implementation of the AUTOSAR standard. Clearly, the consortium's Indian members had other goals in mind when they joined.

Indeed, AUTOSAR's Indian participants were mostly leading offshore firms working as software development subcontractors for foreign firms. Bangalore in southern India is well known for its large cluster of such offshore developers. They undertake costly processes, most typically detailed designing, coding and unit testing, on behalf of advanced-nation firms, using India's engineering power. Although it was a minor automobile market, the country was growing as a hub of software development for vehicles, and an open standard would facilitate the outsourcing of automotive software by advanced-nation carmakers. The spreading of the AUTOSAR standard seemed to offshore developers to be a good opportunity for business expansion. Accordingly, they invested in strengthening their development bases with a view to working with AUTOSAR.

There are two types of offshore developers in India. The first type comprises firms established as subsidiaries of European suppliers, which made direct investment in offshore developers that exclusively undertake their projects. Europe's leading suppliers, such as Bosch and Continental, have large-scale development bases in Bangalore. The other type comprises locally-funded developers, subdivided into those engaged mainly in IT software as a whole, including automotive software, such as Wipro and TATA Consultancy Services, and those specialized in the automotive segment, such as KPIT. In either case, Indian software developers perceived AUTOSAR as a chance for business expansion and augmented their development capacity.

(4) **Bosch's Actions Leveraging the Open Standard**

Bosch took additional strategic actions within the AUTOSAR process. Firstly, at the World Automotive Congress in 2012, the firm announced that it would develop and launch a new microcontroller compatible with the AUTOSAR standard in 2015 (Rueger et al. 2012). This microcontroller, called MDG1, would be the first 32-bit chip built from scratch in compliance with the AUTOSAR standard. Bosch also revealed that it would release the software environment at the end of 2012, prior to the launch of the chip itself. Bosch designed the chip but subcontracted its manufacturing to three semiconductor firms (Freescale Semiconductor, Inc., Infineon Technologies and STMicroelectronics), adopting the so-called fabless model. MDG1 was designed to be a scalable microcontroller,[14] with three grades, i.e., 1 core, 2 cores and 4 cores, with more cores providing more capabilities. The three grades had the same API,[15] so that any of them could run the same application software.

---

[14] Scalable microcontrollers are a family of microcontroller products that can be switched to higher performance when the processing capability needed goes up. The development efficiency is higher, as no change needs to be made to the software.

[15] API stands for application programming interface and it is the interface between hardware and software.

Secondly, Bosch pushed forward with regard to making basic software (BSW) open. The supplier worked with ETAS[16] and they jointly released their BSW as open-source software (OSS) (Rüping and Trechow 2014). This BSW was then provided to a development consortium called COMASSO Association as a development resource. Developers gained access to the Bosch-developed BSW by becoming members of the association.

Thirdly, the firm released its application library interface, existing on top of the BSW, on the web[17] as a de facto standard. It named it VeMotionSAR and made it available for open access to the library. The use of the library, however, is not free because it is Bosch's proprietary asset.

These additional standardization efforts paid for by the mega supplier were overlaid onto the AUTOSAR standard. While AUTOSAR offered a standard set of specifications for the BSW, the OSS released by COMASSO was the actual source code. Since it is available for free, it is expected to have a strong impact as a de facto standard. In the meantime, Bosch also provided MDG1 as a product for the bottom layer of the BSW and released VeMotionSAR for the top layer of the BSW. The firm means to grow these businesses into new important sources of revenue.

The standardization of AUTOSAR is still in progress and it is too early to assess its impact or predict whether it will spread across the global ecosystem. Yet, the above description of the AUTOSAR initiative highlights the corporate behaviors of the European auto parts suppliers, which strategically engage in standardization activities, and those of the Indian offshore firms, which perceive this kind of open standardization as a business opportunity.

In recent years, the automotive industry, like many others, has experienced the tremendous impact of electronics, due to be further amplified by the arrival of self-driving cars and connected cars. Today no one can develop a vehicle without software, and the scale of software programs to be developed is ever growing. New services are also expected to emerge, as cars become connected to external networks, such as the Internet. In this scenario, the industry has been exposed to more and more opportunities for various firms to collaborate on open standardization. Traditionally, standardization experiences have been fewer in the auto industry than in the IT electronics industry, but recent innovations, including autonomous driving, have triggered a vigorous movement in support of open standardization.

AUTOSAR and the Open Automotive Alliance (OAA), an organization promoting the Android platform for automobiles established at the end of 2014, are good examples. Putting self-driving into practice will require further standardization efforts involving the legal field and many other aspects. Another example of open standardization is the Vehicle-to-everything (V2X) communication system, including cellular technologies. A global partnership for the mobile broadband standard, 3GPP, published V2X specifications based on LTE technology in 2016. They are referred

[16]ETAS is a wholly-owned subsidiary of the Bosch Group, established in 1994 as a solution provider for the development of embedded systems.

[17]http://www.bosch-vemotionsar.com/. Accessed 04 Jan 2017.

to as C-V2X and are expanding to cover 5G technology, too. C-V2X connects the two industries, auto and telecom, to form one ecosystem. Players in the ecosystem are expected to have a broad perspective and to think from a strategic point of view.

References

Dyer JH, Nobeoka K (2000) Creating and managing a high-performance knowledge-sharing network: The Toyota case. Strateg Manag J 211:345–367

Dyer JH, Singh H (1998) The relational view: Cooperative strategy and sources of interorganizational competitive advantage. Acad Manag Rev 23(4):660–679

Gawer A, Cusumano MA (2002) Platform leadership: How Intel, Microsoft, and Cisco drive industry innovation. Harvard Business School Press, Boston MA

Imai K, Kawakami M (2007) Higashiajia no IT kikisangyou: Bungyou Kyousou Sumiwake no Dainamizumu (The IT equipment industry in East Asia: Dynamics of division of labor, competition and segregation). Institute of Developing Economies, Japan External Trade Organization, Chiba (in Japanese)

Kawakami M (2012) Ashuku sareta Sangyo Hatten: Taiwan Note Pasokon Kigyou no Seichou Mekanizumu (Accelerating the growth mechanism of the Taiwanese notebook computer industry). Nagoya University Press, Nagoya (in Japanese)

Marukawa T (2007) Gendai Chugoku no Sangyou: Bokkou suru Chuugoku Kigyou no Tsuyosa to Morosa (Modern industries in China: The strength and fragility of rising Chinese companies). Chuoukoron-Shinsha Inc., Tokyo (in Japanese)

Marukawa T, Yasumoto M (2010) Keitai Denwa Sangyou no Shinka Purosesu: Nihon wa naze Koritsu shitanoka (Evolution in the mobile phone industry: Why does the Japanese mobile phone industry isolate in the global market). Yuhikaku, Tokyo (in Japanese)

MacDuffie J, Fujimoto T (2010) Why dinosaurs will keep ruling the auto industry. Harvard Bus Rev 88(6):23–25

Ministry of the Environment of Japan (2009) Jisedai Jidousya Fukyuu Senryaku (Next generation vehicle deployment strategy). http://www.env.go.jp/air/report/h21-01/. Accessed 28 Sep 2015

Ogawa K (2008) Waga Kuni Erekutoronikusu Sangyou ni miru Platform no Keisei Mechanism (Mechanism of building platform business in Japanese electronics Industry). Akamon Management Review 7(6):339–407 (in Japanese)

Ogawa K (2011) Kokusai Hyoujunka to Hikaku Yuui no Kokusaibungyou Keizaiseityou (International standardization, international division of labor and economic growth). In: Watanabe T (ed) Global Biziness Senryaku (Business strategy for global market). Hakutou Shobou, Tokyo (in Japanese)

Rueger J, Wernet A, Kececi H, Thel T (2012) MDG1: The new, scalable, and powerful ECU platform from Bosch. In: Proceedings of the FISITA 2012 World Automotive Congress 194, Lecture Notes in Electrical Engineering:417–425

Rüping T, Trechow P (2014) Association goes beyond AUTOSAR. RealTimes Jan 2014:18–19 ETAS

Shintaku J, Tatsumoto H, Yoshimoto T, Tomita J, Park E (2008) Seihin akitekutya kara miru Gijutu Denpa to Kokusai Bungyou (Technology diffusion and international division of labor from the viewpoint of product architecture). Hitotsubashi Business Review 56(2):42–61 (in Japanese)

Tatsumoto H (2012) Platform Kigyou no Kyousou Senryaku (Competitive strategy of platform firms) MMRC Discussion Paper 396:1–33 (in Japanese)

Tatsumoto H, Ogawa K, Fujimoto T (2009) The effect of technological platforms on the international division of labor: A case study on Intel's platform business in the PC industry. In: Gawer A (ed) Platforms, markets and innovation. Edward Elgar, Cheltenham UK and Northampton MA

Tatsumoto H, Ogawa K, Shintaku J (2010) Opun Inobesyon to Purattofomu Bijinesu (Open innovation and platform business). Kenkyu Gijutsu Keikaku 25(1):78–91 (in Japanese)

Tokuda A, Tatsumoto H, Ogawa K (2011) Opuen Inobesyon Sisutemu – Oushuu ni Okeru Jidousya Kumikomi Sisutemu to Hyoujunka (Open innovation system: Development and standardization of in-car electronics systems in Europe). Kouyou Shobou, Kyoto (in Japanese)

Wall Street Journal (2015) EPA accuses Volkswagen of dodging emissions rules. http://jp.wsj.com/articles/SB10063581187792594737804581241441337997546. Published 19 Sep 2015, accessed 21 Sep 2015

Chapter 8
Establishment of a Global Ecosystem and Its Expansion: Does the Platform Strategy Trigger a Transformation in the Structure of the International Division of Labor?

This chapter attempts to provide a comprehensive picture of the strategies of platform firms, relying on inputs from the case studies and empirical studies presented in Chaps. 3–7. The picture is then examined in order to verify the propositions introduced in Chap. 2.

Our discussion leads to the conclusion that the emergence of platform firms in global ecosystems triggers a transformation in the structure of the international division of labor, since it accelerates the shift from existing firms to new firms. Within the context of a global ecosystem, existing firms are likely to be from developed countries, whereas new firms are likely to be from developing countries.

This evolution is commonly observed among the ecosystems investigated in this book in Chaps. 3–7, and is characterized by three major factors: the presence of platform firms, open area and closed area in product architecture and international division of labor between developed and developing countries. Besides, our analysis offers some insights into the effects of this transformation on symbiont and user industries.

8.1 Fundamental Proposition and Subordinate Propositions

8.1.1 Ecosystems Discussed in This Book

Table 8.1 outlines the business ecosystems discussed in Chaps. 3–7. All the industries covered in those chapters display the ecosystem-like industrial structure defined in Sect. 2.4.2 of Chap. 2: platform, symbiont and user firms are involved in an ecosystem, where network effects resulting from an open standard bind the platform firm and symbiont firms together.

H. Tatsumoto, *Platform Strategy for Global Markets*,
https://doi.org/10.1007/978-981-33-6789-0_8

Table 8.1 Platform firms and symbiont/user firms discussed in this book

Chapters	Business ecosystem	Open standard	Platform firm	Symbiont firms	User firms
3	Mobile communications	GSM	Communications equipment provider (Ericsson)	Communications device suppliers	Communications operators
4	Semiconductor manufacturing equipment	SEMI	Semiconductor manufacturing equipment supplier (Applied Materials)	Materials, semiconductor manufacturing equipment, production control system providers	Semiconductor manufacturers
5	Personal computers (electronic parts)	PCI, ATX, etc.	Semiconductor provider (Intel)	Memory semiconductors, HDD providers	Personal computer makers
6	Personal computers (motherboards)	PCI, ATX, etc.	Semiconductor provider (Intel)	Taiwan motherboard suppliers	Personal computer makers
7	Car electronics	Gas emissions control, AUTOSAR	ECU provider (Bosch)	Software, semiconductors, development tool providers	Automobile manufacturers

It can be inferred from Table 8.1 that a platform firm, symbiont firms and user firms exist in each of the business ecosystems referred to in the various chapters. The platform firm shown in brackets is the most representative in that ecosystem; yet, there may be more than one platform firm in some cases. In addition, an open standard plays a key role in each ecosystem, generating strong network effects within it. In the example of mobile communications examined in Chap. 3, the GSM system was the critical open standard. As for semiconductor manufacturing equipment (Chap. 4), the SEMI standard, which defined the 300 mm specifications, played the vital role. So did PCI and ATX for personal computers in Chaps. 5 and 6 and emissions control regulations and the AUTOSAR standard for automotive electronics in Chap. 7. Taking these ecosystems as subjects, the present chapter tries to determine whether the propositions put forward in Chap. 2 hold true. Let us first look at the framework used for this examination.

8.1.2 Framework for Examination

Chapter 2 articulated our fundamental proposition and four subordinate propositions. The fundamental proposition is as follows:

Fundamental Proposition: "When an open standard prevails in a global ecosystem, the platform firm gains a dominant competitive position. The success of the platform firm triggers a sudden transformation in the structure of the international division of labor".

Subordinate propositions (1)–(4) are categorized into those concerning the main effects of the platform strategy, i.e., (1)–(3), and one regarding its side effects, i.e., (4). The first three are related to the platform firm's corporate behavior to attain competitive advantage; thus, they are about the main effects of the platform strategy. The fourth one is about its side effects, as it deals with the outcomes generated by the strategic behavior of the platform firm.

Subordinate propositions:

Main effects

(1) Platform firms make strategic use of open standards to gain competitive advantage.
(2) (2) Platform firms gain competitive advantage by positioning themselves at the hub of transaction networks and by passing on information among multiple markets.
(3) (3) Platform firms gain competitive advantage by implementing two-sided market and bundling strategies, managing relations with suppliers of complementary goods and adopting other strategies based on the market structure.

Side effects

(4) The rise of a platform firm during the formation of a global ecosystem triggers a sudden transformation in the structure of the international division of labor.

The findings from the studies in Chaps. 3–7 are aligned with the above propositions according to the framework detailed in Fig. 8.1. In this diagram, the process of a business ecosystem's growth is divided into an establishment phase and an expansion phase. The strategic behaviors of the platform firm(s) and the responsive behaviors of the symbiont and user firms are also reported for each phase. Since subordinate propositions (1)–(3) are related to the platform firm's strategy, its behaviors are placed in cells A and C. It must be noted that the platform firm takes strategic action in consideration of the responsive behaviors of symbiont and user firms, which means that the strategy of the former relies largely on the behaviors of the latter. Cells A to D, therefore, also describe the behaviors of symbiont and user firms. Subordinate proposition (4) concerns the outcome generated, as a byproduct, by the strategic behaviors of the platform firm. This is why subordinate proposition (4) is placed outside cells A to D.

The two axes in Fig. 8.1 and the content of each of the cells, A to D, are as detailed below.

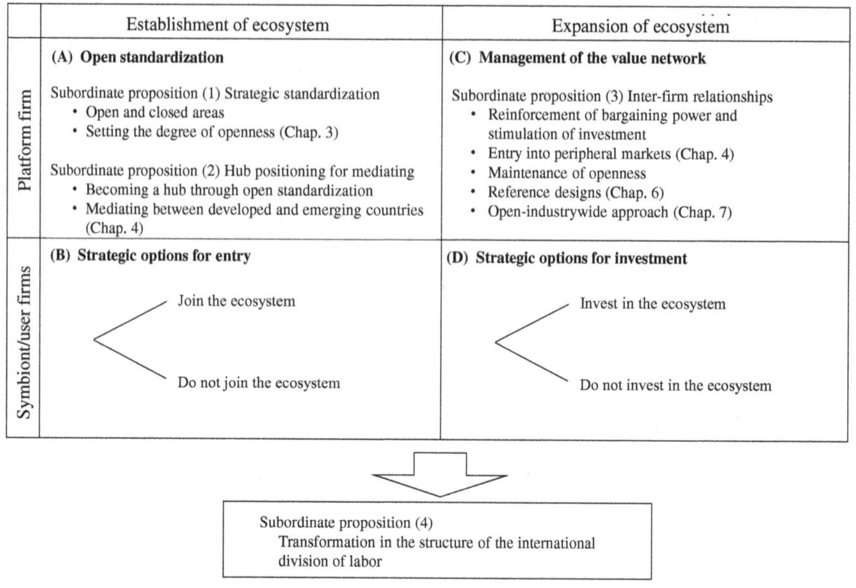

Fig. 8.1 Correlation among the four subordinate propositions

Vertical axis: The vertical axis divides the firms operating within the ecosystem according to their roles. As made clear in Chap. 2, a business ecosystem contains firms with three different roles, i.e., platform, symbiont and user firms.

Unlike product manufacturers, the platform firm cannot complete a system product or service on its own. Its system product or service is completed and made available to user firms when complementary goods and direct goods missing in the system are supplied by symbiont firms. This whole chain forms a business ecosystem, which is why looking solely at the platform firm is not sufficient to analyze a business ecosystem and attention must be paid to the symbiont and user firms as well.

Horizontal axis: The horizontal axis represents the two phases of an ecosystem-type industrial structure, i.e., establishment and expansion. A business ecosystem goes through the two phases as it comes into being and grows to affect the global economy. The establishment phase ends when symbiont firms and user firms join the ecosystem. With the participation of symbiont and user firms, a two-sided market is created. The expansion phase takes off when those symbiont and user firms, in addition to the platform firm(s), make investments and the ecosystem expands accordingly, thereby starting to exert global influence. The development process of business ecosystems is divided into these two phases because the platform firm needs to have a different strategic viewpoint in each phase. Similarly, symbiont and user firms need to make different strategic decision in the two phases.

Cells: The cells list the basic strategies of the firms in both phases. The basic strategy of the platform firm in the establishment phase is to promote the participation of symbiont and user firms in the ecosystem by means of open standardization, thus creating a two-sided market. In so doing, the firm establishes open and closed areas based on strategic standardization and positions itself at the hub among multiple markets. The symbiont and user firms respond to the platform firm's strategic behavior by choosing whether or not to join the ecosystem.

The basic strategy of the platform firm in the expansion phase is to expand the ecosystem globally, while reinforcing its bargaining power through the management of the value network. The platform firm invests to expand the ecosystem. What is crucial, however, is whether or not the other players in the ecosystem, that is, symbiont and user firms, make investments too. Investments by these firms are indispensable for the growth of the ecosystem. Therefore, the platform firm manages the value network in order to stimulate the symbiont and user firms and make it easier for them to invest. More specifically, it manages the network by, for example, entering peripheral markets for investment stimulus, developing reference designs to maintain the openness of the network and constructing inter-firm relations based on the open-industrywide approach.

8.1.3 Options for the Platform Firm's Strategy

Cells A to D help us understand how platform firms strategically act and how symbiont and user firms respond in the ecosystem establishment and expansion phases. These corporate behaviors are displayed in an extensive form in Fig. 8.2.[1]

This graphical representation makes it easier to appreciate the difference and relationship between the establishment and expansion phases. The establishment phase deals with the platform firm's strategic behaviors until symbiont and user firms join the ecosystem. The platform firm cannot complete a system product or service on its own, so the existence of symbiont firms is indispensable. For the ecosystem to become established, which is the goal of the platform firm, the entry of symbiont firms is a must. Thus, the platform firm implements open standardization as a means to encourage such entries.

Even when the ecosystem is established, it may exist as a tiny cluster with little influence unless it grows. For the ecosystem to expand, investments must be made by symbiont and user firms. In this phase, the platform firm supports the symbiont and user firms and stimulates them to increase their investments through the management of the value network.

[1] Figure 8.2 ② refers to a state in which the openness of the ecosystem is not maintained, although symbiont and user firms invest. In this case, because very few symbiont and user firms commit financial resources, the investment is unlikely to lead to expansion into a global ecosystem. Maintaining the openness of the ecosystem is the main topic in Chaps. 6 and 7.

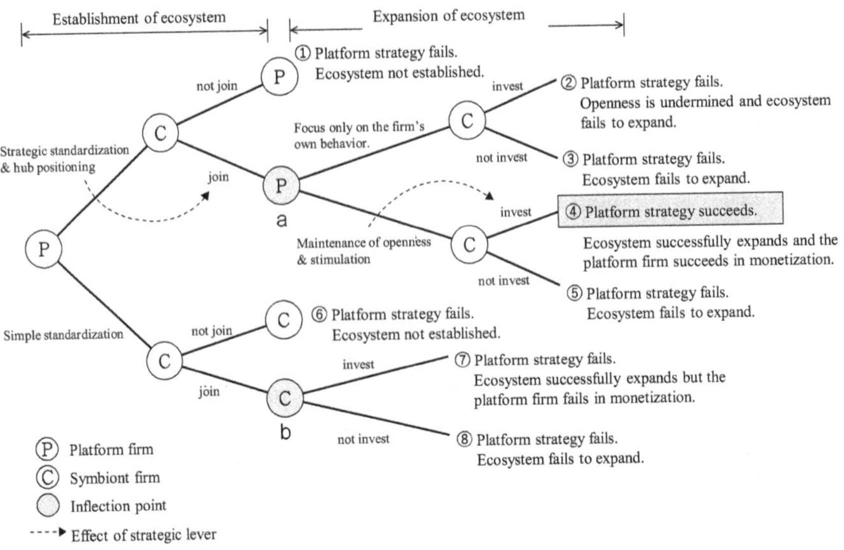

Fig. 8.2 Tree of the platform strategy

Strategic levers: The strategic levers appearing in Fig. 8.2 are noteworthy. The dashed arrows correlate the platform firm's strategic levers with the corporate behaviors of the other firms. The corporate behaviors of the platform firm at the beginning of the dashed arrow have been called strategic levers in earlier studies (Gawer and Cusumano 2002). According to them, a strategic lever is a strategic behavior of the platform firm that influences the responsive behaviors of symbiont and user firms, i.e., their next move. For instance, if the platform firm chooses strategic standardization combined with hub positioning, this will influence the next decision to be made by symbiont and user firms about whether or not they should enter the ecosystem. The elements of the strategic levers that influence the probability of entry by symbiont and user firms are explained later, in Sect. 8.2.

8.1.4 Move at the Inflection Point: Difference Between Simple Standardization and Strategic Standardization

A closer look at Fig. 8.2 reveals that the platform strategy consists of a first half of the game up to the end of the establishment phase and a second half covering the expansion phase. In this book, the move that transitions from the first to the second half is called the inflection point. Figure 8.3 is a simplified version of Fig. 8.2 for explanatory purposes and it features two inflection points, a and b. The difference between the two is who makes a move, which really matters to the success of the platform strategy.

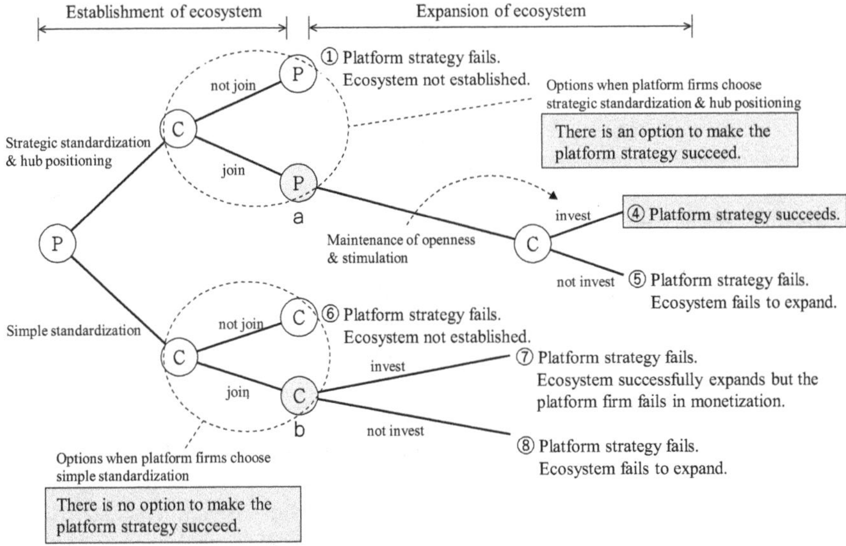

Fig. 8.3 Difference between simple standardization and strategic standardization

The move at point a is made by the platform firm, the one at point b by the symbiont and user firms.[2] Whether the platform firm chooses the strategic standardization plus hub positioning strategy or the simple standardization strategy determines what move to make (or who makes a move) at the inflection point. This is because the former strategy secures the source of bargaining power for the platform firm, whereas the latter does not. With its bargaining power secured, the platform firm gets to make a move at inflection point a, but it loses that chance at inflection point b.

In case of the former strategy (inflection point a), the platform firm protects the closed area, while standardizing the open area based on a strategic approach. The closed area contains classified information and/or patented interfaces, serving as the source of the platform firm's bargaining power. In addition, the platform firm positions itself at the hub between the two areas, so as to further reinforce its already strong bargaining power. Greater bargaining power enables the platform firm to take strategic action and shift the phase from ecosystem establishment to expansion ahead of symbiont and user firms.

In the other case, i.e., the simple standardization strategy (inflection point b), the platform firm just establishes an open area through standardization and does not

[2]This is easier to understand when we consider that the moves at inflection points a and b are made by chance, i.e., they are chance moves. The platform firm wins the move with a probability of p and the symbiont and user firms win the move with a probability of (1-p). The platform firm can increase probability p by implementing strategic levers (strategic standardization plus hub positioning). Rigorously speaking, both the platform firm and the symbiont and user firms have the chance to make a move at both inflection points a and b; for the sake of simplicity, the diagram depicts the player with the higher chance.

create a closed area that can provide a source of bargaining power. It is also not positioned at the hub connecting the two areas, meaning that it may not secure any bargaining power.

To sum up, the initial choice as to whether to pursue the strategic standardization and hub positioning approach or the simple standardization approach determines whether the platform firm gets to make a move at the inflection point (a or b); in other words, it determines whether or not the platform strategy will be successful.

The inflection point gives the platform firm the option to make a move; using the strategic levers of *maintenance of openness and stimulation*, it may influence the next move of symbiont and user firms about investing or not. As discussed in Chap. 5, for example, the Taiwanese motherboard firms, or symbiont firms, initially hesitated to invest in the development and production of motherboards supporting the Pentium CPU (Central Processing Unit) in personal computers. Intel Corporation, the platform firm, responded by entering the motherboard market in order to stimulate investment by these firms. Thanks to this move, personal computers carrying Pentium CPUs forged a global ecosystem and the Taiwanese motherboard firms derived enormous profits. If the Taiwanese firms had decided to refrain from investing, as had seemed the case at the outset, this global ecosystem would not have taken shape.

On the contrary, the move at inflection point b is made by the symbiont and user firms. In this case, the firms can choose whether or not to commit financial resources, independently of the strategy of the platform firm. This allows the symbiont and user firms to decide to invest (⑦) if they believe that they can make money or not to invest (⑧) if they do not believe that they can. ⑧ indicates that the ecosystem fails to expand, which is equivalent to the failure of the platform strategy.

What about situation ⑦? Here the ecosystem expands thanks to the entry of symbiont and user firms. Importantly, however, the investment by symbiont and user firms as such does not translate into profit for the platform firm itself, since the investment decision by the former is made regardless of the strategy adopted by the latter.

The symbiont and user firms invest at inflection point b for the purpose of making their own business profitable. If their profits come from the expansion of the ecosystem, the platform firm should not worry. Nevertheless, in some cases, the profits that the platform firm is supposed to earn go to the symbiont and user firms. If the move at the inflection point is made by the platform firm (case a), it can act to prevent such a situation. Conversely, if the move at the inflection point is made by the other firms (case b), the platform firm has no means to escape this predicament. In situation ⑦, therefore, the platform firm often fails to profit.

Let us take a look at the DVD market, examined in earlier research, to exemplify the situation described above. Ogawa (2009) presented in-depth case studies on the DVD system, which was standardized on the initiative of Japanese firms. It showed that the Japanese electronics firms leading the standardization of the DVD format held patents that were essential for the standard, so they had an undisputable advantage in terms of both technology and patent portfolio. Nevertheless, they did not adopt the strategic standardization approach that any platform firm should pursue. The DVD specifications were developed as the result of endless compromises, without any well-defined business model.

In this scenario, the Japanese electronics makers assumed the role of platform firms, with the platform being the system to deliver content compatible with the DVD format. Yet, their basic strategy focused on selling large quantities of DVD players and DVD drives, which is typical of product manufacturers. They did not pay attention to the overall picture of the business ecosystem or to their relations with symbiont firms, i.e., their standardization was not strategic. As a consequence, these electronics firms, which were supposed to be platform firms, failed to benefit from the DVD ecosystem. On the other hand, the film software industry, as symbiont sector, made vast profits, and so did other symbiont firms, such as media producers (manufacturers of disks onto which to record DVD data), makers of core parts for DVD drives and semiconductor fabs.

Shintaku et al. (2006) reported on changes in the added value of the DVD ecosystem (Fig. 8.4), which grew from one billion dollars in 1998 to 700 billion dollars in 2004. The Japanese and European platform firms that led the standardization activities earned an added value of 9.18 billion dollars in 2004 (only 13% of the total). The rest, or the vast majority, went to the film industry. According to estimates by Shintaku et al., of the 700 billion dollars of added value generated by the DVD ecosystem, 50 billion dollars were earned by film software providers. In other words, it was the symbiont firms, rather than the platform owners, that secured most of the added value.

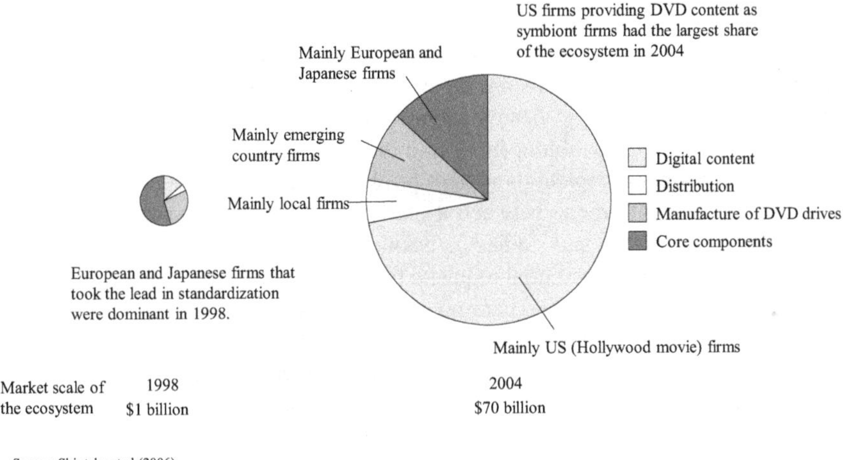

Fig. 8.4 Distribution of added value in the DVD ecosystem

In the DVD case, the platform firms failed to make money, although the ecosystem itself was successfully formed. This provides a typical example to show the difference between simple standardization and strategic standardization. The DVD platform firms missed their move at the inflection point, because they did not implement strategic standardization and hub positioning, ultimately failing to bring in the expected profit.

As Fig. 8.2 illustrates, the choice between simple standardization and strategic standardization combined with hub positioning comes at the very beginning for the platform firm. The difference between the two approaches may seem quite subtle, but it is actually substantial when looking at the overall picture. Up until the point when the ecosystem is established, the only option that allows the platform strategy to succeed is the path leading to situation ④. Without opting for strategic standardization and hub positioning, the firm cannot reach ④, i.e., ensure the success of the platform strategy, via inflection point a. If it opts for simple standardization, there is no path at all that leads to the success of the strategy. This implies that the platform firm must adopt the strategic standardization and hub positioning option at the very beginning.

8.2 Strategic Levers of Platform Firms: Subordinate Propositions (1)–(3)

8.2.1 Strategic Levers

The strategic behaviors of platform firms designed to influence the responsive behaviors of symbiont and user firms are called strategic levers (Gawer and Cusumano 2002). As its basic strategic behavior during the ecosystem establishment phase, the platform firm calls symbiont firms into the ecosystem and makes it work. The platform firm cannot complete its system product or service on its own. This is the most fundamental difference between a platform firm and any product or service firm considered in traditional studies on business strategy.

Symbiont firms are an essential requisite for the platform firm. In other words, the participation of symbiont firms is paramount for the establishment of an ecosystem by the platform firm. An ecosystem also needs user firms that adopt the system provided jointly by the platform firm and symbiont firms. Furthermore, the expansion of the ecosystem depends largely on the behaviors of symbiont and user firms. To expand the ecosystem, it is not only the platform firm but many other symbiont and user firms that need to make investments. A critical strategic behavior to achieve this end is to stimulate investments by symbiont and user firms by entering peripheral markets, while maintaining openness in the value network.

The following subsections look at the strategic levers, the combination of strategic standardization and hub positioning and the combination of openness maintenance and stimulation, in light of subordinate propositions (1)–(3) by reflecting on the case studies in Chaps. 3–7.

8.2.2 *Subordinate Proposition (1): Strategic Standardization*

Chapter 3 analyzed the case of the GSM ecosystem for mobile phones. It identified the establishment of the open and closed areas and the maintenance of openness as the key elements of strategic standardization. In the GSM example, communications equipment manufacturers played a central role in the standardization process and set the phone device area as open and the communications infrastructure area as closed. The establishment of these open and closed areas was consistent with their business model. In addition, communications equipment manufacturers defined the standard specifications for the device in order to achieve a high level of openness, so as to entice device manufacturers and device component manufacturers into the ecosystem. This example is perfectly coherent with subordinate proposition (1) "Platform firms make strategic use of open standards to gain competitive advantage".

The platform firm engages in standardization activities to develop an open standard, with the aim to create an ecosystem (strategic standardization). The open standard is intended to entice symbiont firms and foster the growth of the ecosystem. At that moment, the platform firm attracts symbiont firms not at random but in accordance with its business model. This point distinctly differentiates strategic standardization from simple standardization. Here follows an explanation of the two elements of strategic standardization: open and closed areas and degree of openness.

8.2.2.1 Open Area and Closed Area

(1) Business model and strategic standardization

Open area here refers to the portion of the product architecture that falls within the scope of standardization. As seen in Chap. 3, a system product that may create a business ecosystem is gigantic. When standardizing strategically, the standard setters do not deal with the entire system in depth but draft detailed specifications for a certain subsystem. The subsystem for which detailed specifications are provided is called the open area. In the open-standardized subsystem sector, technical information is widely shared, which encourages new entrants to join the ecosystem. In the closed area, on the other hand, classified information and patents build a barrier to entry, making it difficult for newcomers to access the market. It must be noted that a closed area is not simply equivalent to an unstandardized area.

In the case of Chap. 3, out of the three relevant domains, i.e., switches, base stations and devices, the most meticulously defined area was the device domain. That is to say, the device domain was rendered open. Conversely, the other two domains, switches and base stations, were not thoroughly standardized and were left as closed areas. A large number of Chinese local firms entered the device market but not the base station market. So, the GSM standard came to be composed of the open device sphere and the closed base station and switch spheres.

This way of demarcating the open and closed areas strongly reflects the business models of the European communications equipment manufacturers that took the initiative in establishing the GSM standard, or platform firms. At that time, they provided all kinds of communications equipment across the device, base station and exchanger markets. The communications infrastructure products, including base stations and switches, were the main contributors to their profits, which explains why they were reluctant to make their technical knowledge about communications infrastructure equipment open.

Table 8.2 summarizes the areas made open and closed in the strategic standardization process for the cases presented in each chapter. There are some commonalities in the demarcation of the open and closed areas deriving from how platform firms carry out strategic standardization: they typically keep the areas where they provide their own products and/or services closed and make the areas of the symbiont and user firms' products and services open. In sum, to platform firms strategic standardization means establishing the open area and the closed area according to their business model. In order to do this, they need to identify what their core business is and what it is not before undertaking standardization, so as to ensure that such core business is not standardized and remains a closed area.

If a platform firm has components as its core business, its products and services are part of a larger system and the firm will try to make the whole system open, except the components that it provides. The earlier examples of personal computers and in-vehicle electronics fall into this category. In the case of personal computers, CPUs and chipsets were rendered closed and the other areas, including interfaces and buses, were set as open. As for car electronics, the methods for providing fuel efficiency and the applications inside the ECU were kept closed, whereas the fuel mileage measuring methods and interfaces for development tools were made open.

If a platform firm has end products as its core business, it provides a large-scale system composed of several subsystems. Looking at these subsystems, the platform firm will pinpoint the areas where it brings in the largest profits and set them as closed, while leaving the other areas open. The earlier examples regarding the GSM mobile phone and semiconductor manufacturing equipment correspond to this pattern. In the case of the GSM mobile phone, the infrastructure segment, including network base stations, was kept closed, whereas the device segment was made open. For what concerns semiconductor manufacturing equipment, the internal mechanisms of the machines remained classified, i.e., closed, whereas the interfaces between the machines and standard layouts of fabrication plants became open.

In both situations, the platform firm needs to retain technical knowledge of the entire system. By virtue of its comprehensive understanding of the technology, it shares its technical knowledge of the subsystem(s) assigned to the open area in the form of open standards across the entire ecosystem, in accordance with its business model. In this way, the firm may entice symbiont and user firms to join the ecosystem.

There are two patterns for the sharing of technical knowledge about the open area. One is followed when the firm operates in the open area and already possesses technical knowledge about it. The other is for when the firm does not do business in the open area, so it has no technical information about it.

In the former case, the possession of technical knowledge is, of course, a strength, but some organizational coordination is required to share it with others and make it

Table 8.2 Open and closed areas

Chapters	Business ecosystem	Open standard (strategic standardization)	Platform firm	Open area	Closed area
3	Mobile communications	GSM	Communications equipment provider (Ericsson)	Phone devices	Communications infrastructure (base stations, exchangers)
4	Semiconductor manufacturing equipment	SEMI	Semiconductors manufacturing equipment supplier (Applied Materials)	Shape of silicon wafers, standard layout of foundries, communication protocols between machines, interfaces between machines, automated transfer equipment	Internal mechanism of manufacturing equipment
5	Personal computers (electronic parts)	PCI, ATX, etc.	Semiconductor provider (Intel)	Specifications of buses inside personal computers, external interfaces, system designs	CPU and chipsets
6	Personal computers (motherboards)	PCI, ATX, etc.	Semiconductor provider (Intel)	Shape of motherboards, layout of electronic parts	CPU and chipsets
7	Car electronics	Gas emissions control, AUTOSAR	ECU provider (Bosch)	Fuel mileage measuring method (for gas emissions control), OS, semiconductor API, interfaces of development tools (esp. in the AUTOSAR standard)	How to achieve fuel economy (for gas emissions control), applications inside the ECU (esp. in the AUTOSAR standard)

open. When openly standardized, a business domain will come to feature new players, resulting in intensified competition. Fearing such fierce competition, the business division in charge of that domain would most likely oppose the idea of making the technology an open standard. This is why any firm employing the divisional system faces difficulties in operating a platform business. A solution might be to integrate the divisions in charge of the open and closed areas, as well as their incentives, so as not to lose sight of the goal of standardization, i.e., promoting the establishment of an ecosystem by making the technical knowledge open and encouraging symbiont and user firms to join it. Profits from the open area business should not be the only criterion for evaluation. The business in both the open area and the closed area needs to be integrated and managed as one, so that a shared roadmap can be followed. In the example of the GSM mobile system referred to in Chap. 3, the strategy of making the technical information about the device openly available may work at the organizational level only when the device business and station business are regarded as one.

In the latter case, when the platform firm does not operate in the open area, the lack of technical knowledge poses an obstacle. Technical knowledge, however, is obtainable in many ways other than by doing business in a certain sector. These include hiring knowledgeable personnel from other firms, acquiring firms in that sector and gathering information from partner firms through the smart utilization of trade relations. In the example of motherboards for personal computers cited in Chap. 6, Intel strategically managed its trading relations with symbiont firms, collected the technical information on motherboards that they had accumulated and ultimately made that information open as reference designs. The case of ECUs for automobiles in Chap. 7 demonstrates that the establishment of inter-firm relations using a light approach allows the platform firm to trade with a wide range of user firms, giving it the opportunity to ascertain their levels of technical knowledge.

Furthermore, the consortium, the venue for standardization activities, provides firms that lack technical knowledge with the perfect chance to obtain it. The personal computer example in Chap. 5 shows that Intel became involved in consensus standardization activities on several occasions. In these consensus standardization projects, leading symbiont and user firms, other than Intel itself, circulated technical information and helped establish the ecosystem. In the example of car electronics in Chap. 7, the automotive makers and ECU manufacturers created a consortium called AUTOSAR, which was also joined by semiconductor manufacturers and development tool developers that contributed wide-ranging information, resulting in the successful development of open standards.

(2) Barriers to entry into the closed area

In the context of strategic standardization, *closed area* does not mean the area outside the scope of standardization, but the area protected from entry by other firms owing to the barrier built around it. The closed area corresponds to the core business of the platform firm, and how the firm builds a barrier around it rarely becomes evident, since this is exactly the source of its competitive advantage. Nonetheless, an overarching look at the studies described in the previous chapters reveals the existence of certain entrance deterrence methods.

Table 8.3 summarizes the entrance deterrence methods emerged from the case studies in Chaps. 3–7. A common approach across all the cases is not to include the area in the scope of standardization. Hence, the table lists the methods other than

Table 8.3 Entrance deterrence for the closed area

Chapters	Business ecosystem	Entrance deterrence method
3	Mobile communications	– Envelopment of the extension market
4	Semiconductor manufacturing equipment	– Prevention of standardization
5	Personal computers (electronic parts)	– Confidentiality of technical information (need for NDAs)
		– Protection of interfaces through patents
		– Non-disclosure of interfaces by integrating multiple components
6	Personal computers (motherboards)	– Collaboration only with a handful of firms for joint problem-solving
7	Car electronics	– Prevention of standardization

"not standardizing", which can be categorized into two types, i.e., those implemented during the standardization process and those adopted outside the process.

The former were observed in Chaps. 3, 4 and 7. The communications infrastructure firms in Chap. 3 installed control equipment at base stations that could initially be accessed only by their personnel, thereby putting up barriers against new entrants wishing to come into the extension market (i.e., building of additional base stations). This was made possible by defining the base station control equipment as a subsystem having both an open interface and a closed interface. The platform firms in Chap. 4 excluded the business areas of their core competence (internal mechanisms of manufacturing machines) from the scope of the 300 mm standardization. A similar case is the example of AUTOSAR in Chap. 7. The platform firms proactively led the standardization to ensure that the business areas of their core competence would remain outside its scope.

The latter were seen in Chaps. 5 and 6, which presented examples of entry deterrence created outside of the standardization process. Chapter 5 examined multiple methods: keeping technical information confidential and allowing other firms to obtain it only by entering non-disclosure agreements (NDAs) with the platform firm, patenting internal interfaces and licensing to a handful of firms only, and so forth. Because the internal interfaces were patented, any firm that entered the market without a license would have to face fierce disputes over intellectual property. Besides, platform firms integrated several components and hid their interfaces, thereby putting barriers in place to protect the closed area. In Chap. 6, the platform firm involved only a very limited number of partners in the cross-boundary problem-solving process, so as to prevent technical spillovers, and protected the closed area by installing barriers through the smart management of inter-firm relations.

In sum, establishing a closed area during the process of strategic standardization does not simply mean excluding it from the scope of standardization, but it goes well beyond that. As a consequence, it requires organization-level integration of the divisions responsible for the standardization activities. This underscores that strategic standardization is a strategic action occurring at the level of the whole organization.

8.2.2.2 Setting the Degree of Openness

Once the open area is specified in strategic standardization, the next step is to define the degree of openness. It is determined by two factors: (i) how detailed the standard specifications should be and with what other firms they should be shared and (ii) how to assign intellectual property rights to the standard, i.e., what intellectual property rights policy to follow.

The degree of openness has a considerable impact on the diffusion of a standard. The higher it is, the faster the standard will spread, because there will be more and more new players adopting the system or supplying components that support it.

(1) Extensiveness and detailedness of the standard

When a standard is designed to have a larger scope and specifies the technical information in detail, the degree of openness is high.

As seen in Chap. 3, the standard written as a result of the GSM standardization activity had a high degree of detailedness in the area of phone devices. This allowed a large number of device manufacturers and device component providers to join the ecosystem. In the example of the Chinese GSM market discussed in the chapter, the Chinese phone manufacturers that made an entry were able to develop and produce GSM-compatible devices within a short period of time, thanks to the components supplied by component providers.

Intel, examined in Chap. 5, is a CPU provider, yet it carried out standardization in various areas of personal computers from the 1990s onward, leading to their diffusion on a massive scale. One such example is the standardization of motherboards, in terms of their standard shape, power source, interfaces, etc. Personal computer makers with strong technical expertise had previously developed and produced motherboards for the most advanced CPUs in house, in order to use them in premium products as part of their lock-in strategy. Once standardization made it possible to manufacture standard motherboards compatible with the most advanced CPUs, Taiwanese firms drastically increased their production volumes. Without having to produce them internally, PC manufacturers were able to procure vast amounts of motherboards compatible with the latest CPUs from them, and a variety of personal computers supporting state-of-the-art CPUs became available. The most modern CPU now spreads fairly quickly after its launch on the market.

Openness may sometimes be increased not just by setting standard specifications but by distributing reference designs to be followed as part of the standard. The management of inter-firm relations between Intel and Taiwanese motherboard providers, explored in Chap. 6, depended largely on reference design development. Intel produced a reference design for motherboards based on components available in the local market by managing its relationships with a limited number of Taiwanese firms. The reference design was then distributed to a larger group of Taiwanese motherboard manufacturers along with chipsets. Some Taiwanese MB makers had previously pursued the strategy of providing low-cost motherboards through mass production, which meant that they could begin mass production immediately with the help of a reference design. The distribution of the reference design further increased the degree of openness and accelerated the spread of technology for the open area, compared with the development of the standard alone.

(2) Standard Essential Patents (SEPs)

The degree of openness is greatly affected by how the patents involved in the open standard are dealt with. Patents residing in open standards have drawn the attention of researchers, especially in recent years, since the matter of patents is crucial for standards. Standard Essential Patents (SEPs) are patents deemed indispensable for creating a system specified by a standard. It is typically a firm's intellectual property right (IPR) policy that determines how to deal with SEPs. The IPR policy can be of (i) the Gentlemen's Agreement type, (ii) the FRAND (Fair, Reasonable and Non-Discriminatory) type or (iii) the Royalty Free (RF) type. Which type the firm chooses as its IPR policy affects the degree of openness.

With the first option, a Gentlemen's Agreement, the rule is to decide nothing pertaining to patents during the standardization process. Any conflicts arising later are to be resolved through coordination among the parties concerned. When (ii) FRAND is selected, the rule is to set license fees for SEPs at non-discriminatory and reasonable levels. Licensing may be either free or paid for. Lastly, in (iii), or the RF type, SEP licensing and license fees are free.

As mentioned, the degree of openness varies according to which type of IPR policy pertaining to SEPs is chosen. The Gentlemen's Agreement policy tends to reduce the degree of openness, because patent holders usually set expensive license fees in pursuit of profits. Conversely, the RF policy, which does not require license fee payment, results in high levels of openness. Among the three options, the FRAND type may be regarded as middle ground in terms of degree of openness provided. It ensures openness due to non-discriminatory licensing and reasonable license fees; however, the *reasonable* license fees may sometimes be set at unexpectedly high levels, as described below.

The type of IPR policy to be adopted depends on the standardization approach. The platform firm must decide which standardization process to follow in light of whether it is a patent holder in the area in question. Table 8.4 outlines the

Table 8.4 Standardization and IPR policies

Standardization process	IPR policy preferences
De facto	Advantageous to the firm
De jure	FRAND, in general
Consensus	Varies (depending on the strategy) (i) Gentlemen's agreement: deciding not to decide anything, solving issues among the parties as they arise (ii) FRAND: non-discriminatory licensing is the ground rule, license fee may be free or paid for (iii) Royalty free: licensing SEPs is a must but is free of charge

relationship between the standardization process and the IPR policy.

In the de facto standardization process, only one firm sets the standard; hence, it can choose the IPR policy that is most advantageous to itself. If the priority is the prevalence of the standard, the firm may adopt the RF type policy and, if the priority is making money, it may opt for the Gentlemen's Agreement type.

The de jure process encompasses legal legitimacy, so the type of IPR policy to be adopted is constrained. In many cases, the FRAND type is chosen. For example, at ISO and IEC, the application of the FRAND policy is a requirement. As SEPs included in de jure standards are to be non-discriminatorily licensed for reasonable fees, according to the FRAND conditions, their level of openness tends to be high. In reality, however, some say that the fees are indeed *reasonable,* while others claim otherwise. There have been instances of lawsuits initiated because unexpectedly expensive license fees were set, despite the FRAND approach. Nonetheless, recent verdicts have tended to deny expensive license fees when an IPR policy of the FRAND type is adopted (Ueki 2013).

The consensus standardization process has a much shorter history and the IPR policy chosen varies depending on the actual conditions of the consortium or forum.

Nowadays, firms typically opt for a combination of the consensus approach and the RF type of policy. The fact that the consortium, the basis for consensus standard development, consists of many different firms allows a wide range of patents to be released royalty free at once. Platform firms often strategically choose this combination to secure greater openness and attract symbiont and user firms. This approach is called *patent release.*[3]

Of the case studies analyzed in this book, the example of personal computers in Chap. 5 tells a most remarkable tale about the disclosure of essential patents. The USB standard, an interface standard for personal computers, made the patents falling within its scope open and free of charge. Because the consortium disclosed the patents, openness went up, which propelled the development of USB-compatible peripheral devices. This is a typical example of the disclosure of essential patents lowering the entry barrier and rendering the market more dynamic. The cases reviewed in the other chapters do not explicitly address IPR policies.

SEPs and IPR issues have garnered much attention of late, but in the 1980s and 1990s there were not clear rules. A firm's IPR policy, therefore, tended to be devised in a relatively ambiguous and confused way.[4] More recently, an increase

[3]In actuality, there are various types of patent release: unlimited approval of patent use, approval of patent use for a set period of time and others. Sometimes, the firm wanting to use the released patent is restricted in exercising its own patent rights in the relevant field. In other cases, licensing is conditional on the firm benefitting from the use of a patent not initiating patent disputes with the firm releasing the patent.

[4]In the GSM standardization process, discussions around patent rights were held based on the Gentlemen's Agreement approach. According to Bekkers et al. (2002), five communications equipment providers (Ericsson, Nokia, Motorola, Alcatel and Siemens) cross-held SEPs. In such a scenario, SEPs function as a kind of cartel and, to enter the device market, a newcomer must

in disputes over SEPs has accelerated the clarification of the legal interpretation of IPR policies (Ueki 2013), providing legal decisions on reasonable license fees for SEPs and on whether SEPs have the right to suspension under the FRAND conditions referred to earlier.

The Gentlemen's Agreement approach leads to lower openness, while the RF type makes it higher and the FRAND type stands in the middle. Generally speaking, firms have come to select their IPR policy from among these options in line with their strategy. In recent years, for instance, Toyota Motors has disclosed its patents pertaining to hydrogen fuel automobiles (Yamada 2015; Mochizuki 2015), confirming that platform firms release patents in order to strategically encourage the entry of symbiont and user firms into their ecosystem.

8.2.3 Subordinate Proposition (2): Positioning at the Hub

The empirical analysis in Chap. 4 demonstrated the effectiveness of platform firms positioning themselves at the hub of transaction networks in the process of implementing their platform strategy. This corresponds to subordinate proposition (2): "Platform firms gain competitive advantage by positioning themselves at the hub of transaction networks and by passing on information among multiple markets".

This proposition about hub positioning by platform firms has been reported in many previous studies and somehow regarded as an obvious fact; nevertheless, no demonstrative evidence for it has been provided. Considering that hub positioning is part of a platform firm's basic strategy, it is critical to gather evidence to support this proposition, and Chap. 4 dealt with this issue head-on.

Associating a mere increase in the number of transactions with hub positioning is simply wrong. A hub becomes vital only when both the rate of information transfer is high and the contribution of the node to information transfer is large. The contribution of the node to information transfer means that information does not flow without the presence of the node. If the node mediates among multiple communities, for example, its betweenness inevitably grows. The network index describing this feature is called betweenness centrality.

Chapter 4 attempted to prove subordinate proposition (2) by using both statistical analysis and network analysis. The statistical analysis shed light on the strong interactions among betweenness centrality, sales rates of open standard-compatible products and sales ratios in emerging countries. It identified the positive effects on

pay royalties. If the newcomer itself holds SEPs, it can make trade-offs concerning royalties but, if it holds none, the total amount of royalty fees can be rather substantial. This issue is referred to as *royalty stack*. In the GSM environment, component providers and software vendors were not asked for patent licenses, and these industries went through accelerated growth thanks to the open standards. Additionally, it is difficult to ensure that SEP licenses are safeguarded in emerging economies, where the protection of intellectual property is not so strict, while it is easy in developed countries. Hence, addressing openness through SEPs is not necessarily a perfect strategy. Lastly, the handling of intellectual property (SEPs) based on Gentlemen's Agreements is no longer recommended from the standpoint of competition laws.

sales values, or market performance, of the positioning of semiconductor manufacturing equipment firms at the hub, on condition that they had high sales ratios in emerging economies. We also learned that firms placed at the hub reinforce their market performance by increasing their sales rates of open standard-compatible products. The combination of hub positioning and strategic use of open standards is a typical strategy pursued by platform firms. The demonstration of the effectiveness of the hub positioning strategy is an important contribution of this book. As described earlier, for these strategies of platform firms to work, the condition of high sales ratios in emerging markets is paramount. This point is relevant to subordinate proposition (4) and is further examined later, in Chap. 9.

The subsequent network analysis in Chap. 4 revealed a more interesting fact through the identification of hub nodes using the node function method. Figure 8.5 presents the ratios of node functions on an interannual basis, showing that hub nodes appeared in transaction networks in 1996, 2001 and from 2003 to 2006. In the node function method, nodes linking communities are categorized as connector nodes or hub nodes. The difference between connectors and hubs lies in the absolute size of betweenness centrality. The nodes that simply mediate within communities are categorized as connector nodes, while those that mediate among different communities and have extremely high betweenness centrality are classified as hubs.

Figure 8.5 shows that connector nodes played a central role in terms of inter-community linkage between 1994 and around 2002. After 2003, however, as hub nodes appeared one after another, connector nodes rapidly decreased in number and turned into peripheral nodes. So, the nodes for inter-community linkage gradually became hub nodes only. The constant presence of hub nodes and drop in the number of connector nodes indicate that the function of mediating among communities was

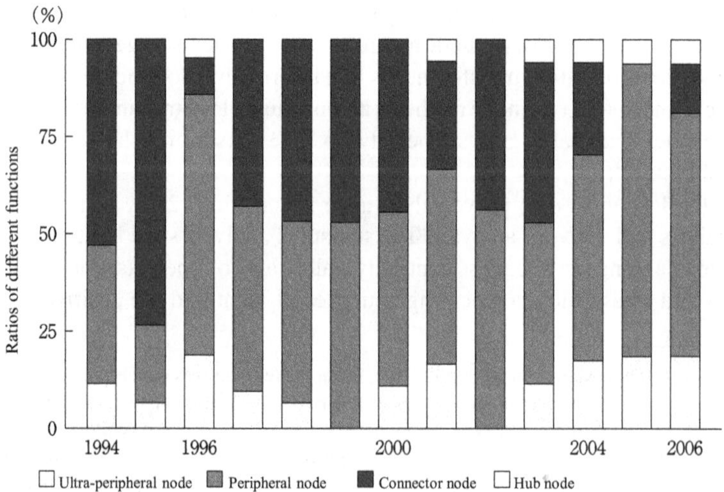

Fig. 8.5 Interannual changes in the ratios of nodes functionality

concentrated into hubs. This transition period corresponded to the phase when products compatible with the 300 mm standard were launched and became prevalent on the market. The prevalence of the open standard is thought to have caused the function of inter-community betweenness to converge into hubs, in turn reducing the number of connectors.

Figure 8.5 also answers a long-standing question in platform strategy studies, i.e., whether accidental positioning at the hub makes a firm a platform firm or whether positioning at the hub is an intentional strategic behavior adopted by a platform firm. The findings from Chap. 4 support the latter.

The firms were able to position themselves at the hub due to their circumstances, not just because they were platform firms. Then, they proactively promoted open standardization, thereby heightening the betweenness centrality of platform firms. The connector nodes that used to serve the role of inter-community betweenness, on the other hand, quickly disappeared, as open standards became widespread. This is because much of the information that relied on connector nodes to flow among communities was made open, which eliminated the need for connector nodes to pass on information in the first place. In brief, the function of mediating among communities converged into a small number of connector nodes. These nodes, in turn, grew in their betweenness centrality, or in the function of passing on information, and transformed into hub nodes. Later, the hub nodes became a permanent feature and the ones that survived long enough turned into platform firms.

This mechanism may be summarized as follows: (i) the prevalence of open standards heightens the betweenness centrality of platform firms; (ii) the prevalence of open standards decreases the inter-community betweenness of connector nodes and concentrates this function into platform firms; (iii) the betweenness centrality of platform firms becomes extremely high and the nodes of platform firms change from connector nodes into hub nodes.

From this perspective, strategic standardization and hub positioning are two strategies that are closely interconnected with each other. Strategic standardization enables the development of open standards, and the ensuing prevalence of open standards converts the nodes of platform firms from connector nodes into hub nodes. Reflection on this sequence of events suggests that platform firms strategically position themselves at hubs.

Unfortunately, other than in Chap. 4, it was not possible to conduct direct verification on transaction networks, since accessing transaction network data is extremely difficult and, as a consequence, hardly any research of this kind exists. Nevertheless, various studies have determined that platform firms position themselves at hubs. The communications equipment providers in the US and Europe that were analyzed in Chap. 3 positioned themselves in places with high betweenness centrality by building a wide range of transaction networks relying on their role as existing firms. Chapters 5 and 6 explained how Intel, as a platform firm, indisputably positioned itself at the hub by building far-reaching transaction networks with personal computer providers (user firms) and Taiwanese ODMs (symbiont firms). Bosch, one of the subjects of Chap. 7, is considered to have positioned itself near the hub because it had been trading with most joint-venture firms and local OEM firms in China.

In these examples, platform firms do not only carry out strategic standardization in the ecosystem establishment phase but also continue their standardization efforts later on. Continuous standardization is effective, in that the prevalence of open standards makes the inter-community betweenness converge into hubs. The case study in Chap. 4 illuminated the situation in which the prevalence of an open standard shifted the inter-community betweenness function from connector nodes to hub nodes. In addition, the studies in Chaps. 3, 5, 6 and 7 revealed that continuous standardization enabled platform firms to gradually position themselves at hubs and expand their competitive advantage.

8.2.4 Subordinate Proposition (3): Management of the Value Network

In the ecosystem expansion phase, platform firms pursue the strategy of stimulating the expansion of their ecosystem to establish their competitive advantage. Chapters 5–7 showed that platform firms largely adopt two types of strategic behavior. The first is entry into peripheral markets (Chap. 5), the other is maintenance of the open network in the ecosystem by effectively managing relations with symbiont firms (Chaps. 6 and 7). Platform firms expand their ecosystems and develop them into gigantic global ecosystems through these two types of strategic behavior. The combination of entry into peripheral markets and maintenance of the open network based on the management of relations with symbiont firms echoes subordinate proposition (3): "Platform firms gain competitive advantage by implementing two-sided market and bundling strategies, managing relations with suppliers of complementary goods and adopting other strategies based on the market structure".

8.2.4.1 Entry into Peripheral Markets

(1) Reinforcement of bargaining power

One of the typical methods used by platform firms to reinforce their bargaining power and exert influence on the open area is the bundling strategy, introduced in Chap. 2. Specifically, the platform firms' bundling strategy for complementary goods is also called platform envelopment (Eisenmann et al. 2011). By bundling complementary goods with the platform product, platform firms can achieve higher levels of competitiveness than symbiont firms selling the complementary goods unbundled. One example of this strategy is Intel's entry into the chipset market, explored in Chap. 5.

Intel came to exert its influence, earned through its substantial market share in the CPU market, on the chipset market, which was a peripheral market. The purpose of this move was not simply to boost profits but to implement an interface standard on chipsets for personal computers that would be advantageous to Intel itself and spread it worldwide. In the 1990s, the firm released interface standards in quick succession, while rapidly growing its share in the chipset market. The ecosystem of personal computers soon expanded, as Taiwanese ODM firms engaged in the mass production of personal computers with Intel chipsets installed.

(2) Revitalization of peripheral markets

There is another type of entry into peripheral markets, the purpose of which is quite the opposite of the lock-in strategy, meant to exercise influential power on the open area. It is the platform firm's entry into peripheral markets for the purpose of revitalizing complementary goods markets. Though the move itself is the same, the strategic purpose behind it is radically different. Of the two cases of Intel's entry into peripheral markets discussed in Chap. 5, the entry into the chipset market was a lock-in strategy, while the entry into the motherboard market was intended to revitalize it.

Indeed, Intel made a sensational entry into the motherboard market in 1995, but it soon started outsourcing production to Taiwanese ODM firms. It developed a set of standards regarding the shape of the motherboard and other aspects (such as the ATX standard) and signed technical transfer agreements with Taiwanese ODM firms, before pulling away from the market itself. An objective observation of Intel's behavior in these circumstances suggests that it entered the motherboard market in order to boost its activity and widely spread motherboards able to support its latest CPU. This was a strategic move that the platform firm made to stimulate the symbiont firms and revitalize that peripheral market.

In the studies about entry into peripheral markets featured in the other chapters, we frequently observed cases of the entry for the purpose of increasing one's bargaining power.[5] Chapter 3 looked at communications equipment manufacturers, serving as platform firms, which carried out some of the tasks of communications operators as a service or solution business. Ericsson, for example, provided equipment installation design services for communications operators with limited accumulation of technical expertise—something that requires either great skill in optimal communications network design or the system operation service and the communications equipment combined as a package. In the scenario presented in Chap. 4, the semiconductor manufacturing equipment firms, i.e., the platform firms, made their way into peripheral markets by acquiring the business of peripheral machines in addition to their core business. In the example of automotive electronics in Chap. 7, car electronics firms that were platform firms entered peripheral markets very frequently in parallel with the AUTOSAR standardization activities (Juliussen and Robinson 2010). Continental, for example, bought the automotive electronics division of Siemens (Siemens VDO) in 2007 and was acquired by the Schaeffler Group in the same year, which resulted in the establishment of a gigantic car electronics firm. Continental also entered peripheral markets in 2015 by purchasing the car electronics division of Elektrobit Automotive GmbH, which dealt with the basic software (BSW) and the development tools for AUTOSAR. In 2016, Denso announced its plan to establish AUBASS CO., LTD., jointly with eSOL Co., Ltd. and NEC Communication Systems,

[5]As this was not a theme in these studies, it was not exhaustively described in the chapters.

Ltd., which would develop and license BSW and other tools related to AUTOSAR and provide related engineering services.

The series of studies conducted shed light on cases in which platform firms make entries into peripheral markets to trigger their revitalization. In the AUTOSAR car electronics example in Chap. 7, Bosch released the BSW as open-source software together with ETAS (Rüping and Trechow 2014), primarily to stimulate the firms providing development tools or software and to revitalize their markets. Activities concerning open-source software carried out by platform firms are, as seen in this case, instances of entry into peripheral markets for the purpose of revitalizing them.

In sum, our case studies point to the fact that entry into peripheral markets serves as an important strategic lever that platform firms can use to enhance their bargaining and stimulate peripheral markets.

8.2.4.2 Management of Inter-firm Relations in the Value Network

(1) Reference designs

The expansion of an ecosystem requires the maintenance of openness by preventing a network comprising certain firms from becoming a core network. The subject of analysis in Chap. 6 was the relationship between Intel and Taiwanese motherboard manufacturers in the process of developing motherboards supporting Intel's latest CPU. Intel created a detailed reference design and distributed it to several motherboard manufacturers in Taiwan endowed with different levels of technological accumulation. The design even allowed firms with almost no technological accumulation to develop and produce motherboards compatible with latest-generation CPUs.

In order to develop and manufacture such motherboards, a firm needs to possess technical knowledge about the latest CPU, besides technical knowledge about the latest motherboard itself. In other words, no firm can develop and produce the most modern motherboard unless it absorbs technological knowledge covering two domains (system knowledge). With a reference design, however, it can develop and manufacture the new motherboard despite a low level of technical knowledge about the cutting-edge CPU. This approach does not result in the construction of entry barriers due to lack of system knowledge, which, in turn, prevents a value network from becoming a core network. Core networking means that a value network is created with only a handful of leading firms. For an ecosystem to successfully expand, core networking must be precluded.

(2) Open-industrywide approach

It was observed that platform firms implement the management of openness also vis-à-vis user firms. In Chap. 7, a comparison analysis was conducted on the Chinese engine ECU market, featuring Bosch and Denso as core ECU suppliers. In the situation analyzed, Bosch displayed a platform firm-like strategic behavior, taking the open-industrywide approach in its relations with user firms. In contrast, Denso's strategic behavior was typical of product manufacturers, centered on relationships with its user firms of the close-relational type. Chinese automotive makers currently seem to prefer inter-firm relations of the open-industrywide type, as pursued by Bosch, because they enable faster catch-up with the developed world.

Differently from the close-relational approach, the open-industrywide approach does not require the formation of assets specific to the relationship. Hence, it can easily attract new firms into the value network. This has proven to be an effective method for expanding an ecosystem fairly quickly.

Chapters 6 and 7 investigated the platform firms' strategic behaviors of using reference designs in the PC industry and of opting for the open-industrywide approach in relations with user firms in the automotive electronics industry, respectively. These behaviors prevent value networks from becoming core networks and secure openness. Adopting this perspective, we can find many similar behaviors in other platforms as well. The platform firms that created the GSM standard, examined in Chap. 3 about mobile communications, continued their standardization activities even after the standard began commercial service in Europe in 1992. This continuity in open standardization secured the openness of the value network, thus allowing a large number of component manufacturers and software providers to join the ecosystem of mobile communications as symbiont firms and begin investing in development and production. Similarly, user firms joined the ecosystem one after the other to supply GSM-compatible phones all over the world. In the semiconductor manufacturing equipment industry introduced in Chap. 4, the platform firms, or equipment providers, encouraged new semiconductor manufacturers to join the ecosystem by selling their manufacturing equipment compatible with an open standard to semiconductor foundries in emerging markets. These observations also back the argument that platform firms strive to maintain the openness of the value network as a stepping stone toward the expansion of their ecosystems.

8.2.5 Mechanism of Action: Discussion of Subordinate Propositions (1)–(3)

Subordinate propositions (1)–(3) make the case for the effectiveness of the strategic levers that platform firms employ, such as strategic standardization, positioning at the hub and management of inter-firm relations. The series of studies in this book examined these subordinate propositions using case studies and empirical analyses, and the evidence emerging from them supports the effectiveness of these strategic levers.

The significance of strategic standardization and hub positioning, the two strategic levers in the ecosystem establishment phase, is twofold. First of all, they encourage symbiont and user firms to step into the ecosystem. Secondly, they create the source of bargaining power that the platform firm needs to make a move at the inflection point.

Standardization alone functions as a way to accelerate the participation of other firms in the ecosystem. It does not, however, provide the platform firm with an opportunity to make a move at the inflection point. If the move is not made, symbiont and user firms do not make investments in the ecosystem expansion phase; consequently, the ecosystem may not expand. Even when the platform firms themselves invest to expand the ecosystem, profitability is not guaranteed. This means that the use of standardization alone is a failure in terms of platform strategy. If the latter is to be successful, a combination of standardization and hub positioning is needed. These strategic levers go beyond the remit of simple standardization because they are based on the precondition of the business model adopted by the platform firm (scoping of core and non-core businesses). Moreover, the integration of multiple business divisions is a must to make the demarcation of the open and closed areas work, which means that it is highly strategic.

The management of inter-firm relations is a strategic lever in the ecosystem expansion phase, but it carries strategic meaning in another sense as well. An ecosystem cannot be expanded by platform firms alone; it requires investment by symbiont and user firms to grow. Platform firms, therefore, need to take strategic action with consideration given to the reactions of symbiont and user firms.

It was mentioned earlier that platform firms propel the expansion of their ecosystems by adopting certain strategic behaviors, such as entry into peripheral markets to stimulate the value network and draw investments to expand the ecosystem, maintenance of openness of the value network through the use of reference designs, as well as use of the open-industrywide approach to prevent the construction of entry barriers. These strategic levers require a good understanding of the situation in which the symbiont and user firms find themselves. More concretely, when managing the value network, platform firms need to gather and understand information about all the players in the entire ecosystem. While typical product manufacturers tend to concentrate on their own business, platform firms have to collect as much information as possible about their symbiont and user firms, analyze it and comprehend it, since they rely heavily on these firms.

The series of case studies and empirical analyses in this book indicated that the strategy of platform firms depends largely on the circumstances of their symbiont and user firms. They also revealed that the symbiont and user firms that the platform firms select have a commonality: they are newcomers to the ecosystem, or firms that want to catch up with traditional firms.

Preexisting symbiont firms have sufficient levels of technical knowledge and fully understand the context of their industry. In many cases, they already have the information that the platform firms can provide. The strategic levers that platform firms use act to increase the number of new entrants because they make technical information open. Weighing up the advantage of gaining technological information and the disadvantage of intensified competition due to new entries from a holistic point of view, the strategic levers of platform firms are deemed to be disadvantageous to preexisting symbiont firms.

Newcomer symbiont firms, on the other hand, regard a possible entry into the ecosystem as an immense opportunity for gaining additional profits, because they are invited to operate in a new industry. This is why the strategic levers of platform firms work more effectively on newcomers than on traditional symbiont firms. The same is true for user firms. The strategic levers have a stronger impact on new user firms than on existing ones.

It is now essential to understand what consequences this asymmetry brings about, which is the point addressed by subordinate proposition (4), explained in Sect. 8.3 below.

8.3 Secondary Effects of the Platform Strategy: Subordinate Proposition (4)

8.3.1 Prevalence of Open Standards and Formation of Global Ecosystems

Because open standards are patternized technological information, they can easily go beyond national borders. Hence, it is no surprise that they become international or global standards. When an ecosystem continues to grow, while relevant open standards prevail internationally, a global ecosystem is established.

A global ecosystem will eventually involve firms from both developed and developing countries. If so, in order to establish a global ecosystem, should platform firms promote the open standard among firms in developed countries? Or would it be better to promote the standard among firms in emerging countries? As observed in the review of past studies in this field (Chap. 2), none of the preceding research has offered an explicit answer.[6]

This question actually corresponds to subordinate proposition (4): "The rise of a platform firm during the formation of a global ecosystem triggers a sudden transformation in the structure of the international division of labor". The logic behind the proposition is that platform firms choose to collaborate with newcomer firms that have scarce technological accumulation and limited understanding of the industrial context, rather than with traditional symbiont and user firms. Newcomers strive to catch up with the traditional firms in developed countries and, in many cases,

[6]It is not self-evident that firms in emerging countries grow as symbiont firms while the ecosystem expands globally. In the automotive industry, for example, when the industries in developed countries advanced into the global market, major component suppliers from those countries advanced along with the automotive manufacturers by making foreign direct investment. Such FDI included not only their own capital but joint ventures as well. The trend of open standardization in the automotive industry, explained in Chap. 7, began in the 2000s, when automotive electronics became prevalent.

newcomer firms in the global economy happen to be from emerging nations. This is because the success of platform firms is always accompanied by the growth of emerging-country firms.

Chapters 3 and 4 clarified some of the issues raised by subordinate proposition (4). The GSM mobile communications case in Chap. 3 showed that Chinese local firms emerged and grew in the mobile phone segment, which was specified as the open area in the GSM standard. As a consequence, the mobile phone market in China expanded thanks to the entry of these domestic firms. The platform firms were communications equipment providers from the US and Europe and, to them, *existing symbiont firms* meant mobile phone manufacturers in the US and Europe, while *newcomer firms* meant local mobile phone manufacturers in China. The communications equipment providers from the US and Europe were also mobile phone providers; thus, Chinese mobile phone providers would present themselves as competitors.

In the example of the Chinese mobile phone industry in Chap. 3, it may be rather exaggerated to say that the platform firms proactively selected Chinese local companies as symbiont firms from the outset. They did not, however, attempt to implement the bundling strategy to lock in the mobile phone market. If they had truly wanted to implement the bundling strategy, they could have taken an even more aggressive approach. For example, they could have prohibited the most prevalent mobile phones in China at that time from connecting to the network, as many of these devices were not compliant with the standard.

Moreover, the communications equipment providers from the US and Europe had a considerable number of standard essential patents (SEPs), because they led the standardization process. Therefore, they were in a position to demand expensive royalty fees when licensing to local Chinese providers, which would in effect create an entry barrier. Alternatively, the platform firms could have exploited their influence by exercising their patent rights vis-à-vis semiconductor firms.

The US and European communications equipment providers, however, did not show any signs of wanting to introduce similar kinds of deterrence on a large scale. If the mobile phone market expanded thanks to the efforts of local firms in China, the communications equipment market, their core business, would expand as well. In brief, the platform firms in question prioritized their core business over their mobile phone business.

Remarkably, Nokia took a different stance. It pursued an expansion of its share in the mobile phone market as well, while providing communications equipment to the Chinese market. Nokia was trying to counter local firms in China's mobile phone segment by constructing a surprisingly efficient supply chain for a firm in a developed country. Yet, this attempt did not bear fruit. The firm had to continuously cut profits and gradually became burned out; following another failure in the shift to smartphones, it ended up selling its mobile phone business to Microsoft.

To sum up, in the above example about the mobile communications industry, the US and European communications equipment providers drew a line between the open and closed areas; they gave priority to their core business (communications equipment) and left the mobile phone business (open area) to new entrants from emerging economies. As platform firms, they acknowledged that their communications equipment core business was what they had to focus on and let their symbiont firms deal with the mobile phone business. They chose emerging-country firms as their symbiont firms.

The empirical analysis performed on the semiconductor manufacturing equipment industry in Chap. 4 confirmed that platform firms select emerging-country firms as their user firms. The platform firms examined are leading semiconductor manufacturing equipment providers, while the symbiont and user firms are complementary manufacturing equipment providers and semiconductor foundries, respectively. The mass production of semiconductors needs a wide variety of manufacturing equipment, such as exposure devices (steppers), development devices, etching machines and heat treatment equipment, in one production line. These machines are developed and supplied to foundries by different manufacturers, but they must all belong to the same generation in order to work together. Hence, standardization is highly beneficial for them.

Chapter 4 examined the activities to establish the standard for the 300 mm wafer generation. Among the manufacturing equipment firms, Applied Materials (AMAT) and Tokyo Electron (TEL) regarded this open standardization as a good opportunity and started to pursue a platform strategy. Interestingly enough, the providers of steppers, which were considered the most critical devices for the whole process at that time, did not adopt a platform strategy. Since AMAT and TEL provided foundries with multiple processes, they were able to ascertain the links among all the processes and they opted for the platform strategy.

The empirical analysis identified a set of conditions for the platform strategy to be effective. As previously defined, the basic strategy of platform firms consists in positioning themselves at the hub of transaction networks and making strategic use of network effects produced among multiple markets. In other words, their basic strategy is to escalate their betweenness centrality to boost their sales values. Against this basic strategy, we examined the impact of sales rates of open standard-compatible products (Ro300) and of sales ratios in emerging countries (EMSR). Our evidence indicated that the effectiveness of the basic strategy improves when the sales rates of open standard-compatible products grow, which is probably because higher sales rates enhance the inter-market network effects. This finding is consistent with the theoretical models about the competitive strategy of platform firms, discussed in Chap. 2.

Digging deeper, this outcome emerging from the empirical analysis suggests that the impact of an open standard on the basic strategy does not become positive until sales ratios in emerging markets grow large enough, as illustrated in Fig. 8.6. The marginal effect (ME) of positioning at a node with high betweenness centrality (bts) on market performance (sales of equipment) is displayed on the Y axis, while the sales rate of open standard-compatible products (Ro300) appears on the X axis. If the regression line in the figure shows a downward slope, the more open standard-compatible products are sold, the less impact betweenness centrality has on the sales

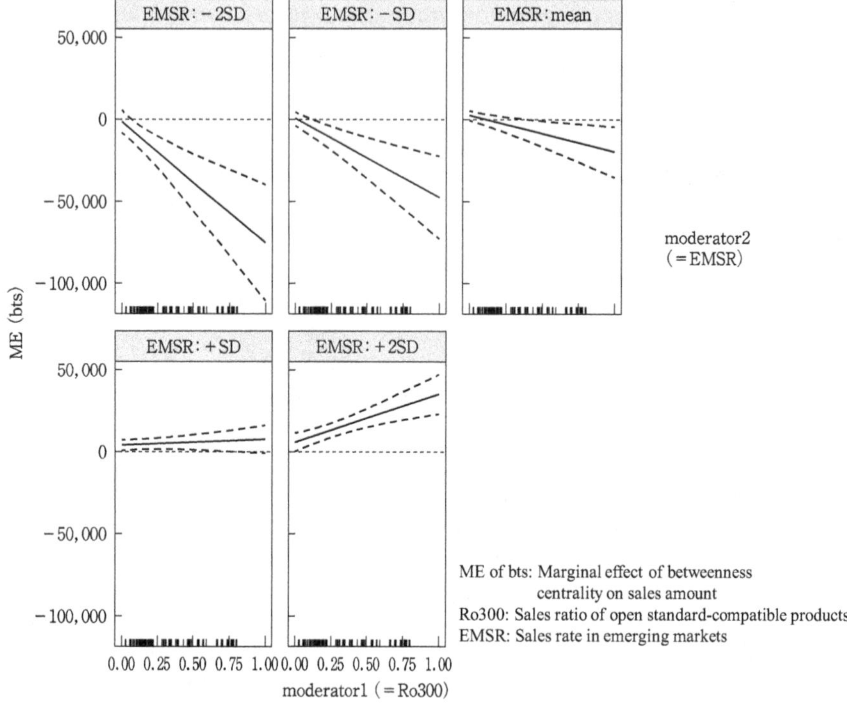

Fig. 8.6 Marginal effects of betweenness centrality, Ro300 and EMSR

value of equipment (or the smaller the marginal effect of betweenness centrality is). If the regression line shows an upward slope, the more the products are sold, the greater the marginal effect.

Figure 8.6 depicts five panels according to EMSR, i.e., the sales ratio in emerging markets. The *mean* plot represents a situation with average sales ratio in emerging markets, whereas -SD are -2SD are cases with a smaller standard deviation by one and two, respectively, and +SD and +2SD are the opposite.

With the mean EMSR, no matter how high Ro300 (sales rate of open standard-compatible products) becomes, the marginal effect of betweenness centrality (ME of bts) is relatively decreasing. As the sales rates of open standard-compatible products increase, the effect of the platform strategy of positioning at the hub with high betweenness centrality becomes relatively diluted.

When the standard deviation of EMSR is lower by one or two, higher sales rates of open standard-compatible products mean a distinctly negative marginal effect of betweenness centrality. This shows that, if platform firms deal solely with developed markets, the effect of the strategic use of open standards is not maintained or may even become negative.

Conversely, when the standard deviation of EMSR is higher by one or two, higher rates of open standard-compatible products mean a distinctly positive marginal effect of betweenness centrality. Hence, if platform firms achieve higher sales rates of open standard-compatible products, the effect of the strategic use of open standards becomes positive.

The above can be translated into the assumptive result that the platform strategy of using open standards works most effectively in a global ecosystem in which the sales ratio in emerging countries is high. Such a situation indicates that more semiconductor firms in emerging countries than in developed countries buy manufacturing equipment compliant with the open standard from the platform firms. The background to this is that, when manufacturing equipment firms adopted the platform strategy based on open standards, semiconductor firms in emerging countries saw this as an opportunity for technological catch-up with developed countries and actively invested in manufacturing equipment compliant with the open standard.

8.3.2 *Subordinate Proposition (4): Transformation of the Structure of the International Division of Labor*

The logic behind subordinate proposition (4) "The rise of a platform firm during the formation of a global ecosystem triggers a sudden transformation in the structure of the international division of labor" is that platform firms choose to collaborate with newcomer firms that have scarce technological accumulation and limited understanding of the industrial context, rather than with traditional symbiont and user firms. Newcomers strive to catch up with the preexisting firms in developed countries and, in many cases, *newcomer* firms in the global economy happen to be from emerging nations. This is because the success of platform firms is always accompanied by the growth of emerging-country firms.

The above reasoning actually consists of two parts. The first half is about how platform firms choose new firms as symbiont and user firms, while the second half is about emerging-country firms being the *new firms* in the global economy and growing following the success of platform firms. Let us take a look at these two aspects one by one.

First, let us verify if the rise of platform firms motivates new firms to catch up with preexisting firms and triggers a transformation in the industrial structure. Table 8.5 shows whether such catch-up was observed in the symbiont and user segments explored in this book, by presenting a list of new firms and existing firms in both segments. In the mobile communications industry studied in Chap. 3, no new firm joined the user community due to the presence of regulations to control new entries.

The far-right column about the transformation of the industrial network deals with a possible shift in the balance between traditional firms and new firms in the industry. It actually suggests that the catch-up with traditional firms by new firms was frequently observed in both the symbiont and user segments.

Table 8.5 Transition of the industrial structure from existing to new firms

Chapters	Business ecosystem	Symbiont firms		User firms		Transformation of the industrial network	
		New	Existing	New	Existing	Symbiont	User
3	Mobile communications	Communications device suppliers (Chinese firms)	Communications device suppliers (Western firms)	None	Communications operators (China Mobile, etc.)	Yes	No
4	Semiconductor manufacturing equipment	Semiconductor manufacturing equipment suppliers (automated transfer equipment, CIM software)	Semiconductor manufacturing equipment suppliers (steppers, etc.)	Semiconductor manufacturers (Taiwanese foundries, Korean memory makers)	Semiconductor manufacturers (US and Japanese semiconductor manufacturers)	No	Yes
5	Personal computers (electronic parts)	Korean memory makers (Samsung Electronics, etc.) Taiwanese ODM firms	US and Japan memory semiconductor providers	Emerging PC firms (Dell, Gateway 2000, etc.)	Existing PC firms (IBM, Compaq)	Yes	Yes
6	Personal computers (motherboards)	Taiwanese motherboard firms	In-house manufacturing division of existing PC firms	Emerging PC firms (Dell, Gateway 2000, etc.)	Existing PC firms (IBM, Compaq)	Yes	Yes
7	Automotive electronics	Emerging developers (Indian and other offshore firms)	Electronics devices, software, semiconductors, tools	Chinese automotive firms	Foreign-funded/state-run joint ventures	–	–

Secondly, let us check if this kind of industrial structure transition from preexisting to new firms also transformed the international division of labor. In Table 8.6 below, the firms shown in bold are developed-country firms, whereas the underlined areas refer to emerging-country firms. The far-right column about the transformation of the international division of labor indicates whether or not a phenomenon in agreement with subordinate proposition (4) was observed, i.e., whether firms from emerging countries caught up with or even overtook those from developed countries.

A comparison between Table 8.5 (Transition of the industrial structure from existing to new firms) and Table 8.6 (Transformation of the international division of labor between developed and developing countries) reveals that the transition from the old to the new is often accompanied by the international transformation. However, this may not always be the case. The personal computers industry, analyzed in Chaps. 5 and 6, featured a reversal between the old and the new in the user segment; yet, the firms involved were American and, in terms of nationality, no international shift took place.

Although the emerging PC firms were based in the US, they had strong relations with Taiwanese Original Design Manufacturing (ODM) firms. Indeed, the former were the outsourcers of PC and laptop production to the latter and, through this mechanism, the US firms backed the growth of the Taiwanese ODM firms. What can be seen here is strong complementarity between new user firms in developed countries and symbiont firms in emerging countries.

A closer look at the column "Transformation of the international division of labor" in Table 8.6 suggests that, in our examples, such a transformation occurred on the symbiont side much more than on the user side. This is because regulations were in place concerning new entries (communications operators in Chap. 3) or, in the cases in which we analyzed the user segment, because some new and existing firms were actually based in developed nations (PC firms in Chaps. 5 and 6). The presence of entry regulations may appear to be quite special, yet they are commonly implemented in infrastructure industries. Similar examples of regulations may include store opening regulations. On the contrary, if no such regulations exist and the distribution channels or other factors do not constitute an entry deterrence, new firms in developed countries immediately emerge also in the user segment, as observed in the PC case.

In the mobile phone sector discussed in Chap. 3 and the PC industry cases of Chaps. 5 and 6, no transformation of the international division of labor took place on the user side. In contrast, the symbiont firms that supported those user firms went through a large-scale transformation. The international transformation on the symbiont side becomes massive when the user industry grows larger and larger, since the industrial transformation in the symbiont industries strongly encourages the growth of the user industry. These findings may be condensed into the following three points:

(i) The rise of platform firms in a global ecosystem produces strong pressure for international industrial transformation;

Table 8.6 Transformation of the international division of labor between developed and developing countries

Chapters	Business ecosystem	Symbiont firms		User firms		Transformation of the international division of labor	
		New	Existing	New	Existing	Symbiont	User
3	Mobile communications	Communications device suppliers (Chinese firms)	**Communications device suppliers (Western firms)**	None	Communications operators (China Mobile, etc.)	Yes	No
4	Semiconductor manufacturing equipment	**Semiconductor manufacturing equipment suppliers (automated transfer equipment, CIM software)**	**Semiconductor manufacturing equipment suppliers (steppers, etc.)**	Semiconductor manufacturers (Taiwanese foundries, Korean memory makers)	**Semiconductor manufacturers (US and Japanese semiconductor manufacturers)**	No	Yes
5	Personal computers (electronic parts)	Korean memory makers (Samsung Electronics, etc.) Taiwanese ODM firms	**US and Japanese memory semiconductor providers**	**Emerging PC firms (Dell, Gateway 2000, etc.)**	**Existing PC firms (IBM, Compaq)**	Yes	No
6	Personal computers (motherboards)	Taiwanese motherboard firms	**In-house manufacturing division of existing PC firms**	**Emerging PC firms (Dell, Gateway 2000, etc.)**	**Existing PC firms (IBM, Compaq)**	Yes	No
7	Automotive electronics	Emerging developers (Indian and other offshore firms)	**Electronics devices, software, semiconductors, tools**	Chinese automotive firms	**Foreign-funded/state-run joint ventures**	–	–

Bold font: developed-country firms
Underlined font: Developing-country firms

(ii) Between the symbiont industry and the user industry, the former is more prone to a transformation of the international division of labor;
(iii) When entry regulations are in place or a shift between existing firms and new firms occurs early on in the user industry, a transformation of the international division of labor does not take place there. Instead, the pressure for such a transformation concentrates on the symbiont firms, bringing about profound changes in the symbiont industry.

In sum, subordinate proposition (4) holds true only under a rather complicated set of conditions.

8.4 Surprising Similarity in the Evolution of Ecosystems: Platform Firms, Open and Closed Areas and the International Division of Labor Between Developed and Developing Countries

As pointed out in the previous sections, the platform strategy has a powerful impact on the industries concerned, which is why we set out to explore it thoroughly. In that process, the similarities detected between the platform strategy described in the studies of this book and the resulting evolutions of business ecosystems provided useful insights.

Chapters 3–7 examined diversified ecosystems, namely, mobile communications, semiconductor manufacturing equipment, personal computers and automotive electronics. Even when the uniqueness of each of these ecosystems is taken into account, there are rather striking similarities in their industrial evolution, as revealed by the case studies and empirical analyses. The three elements of similarity that are present in all the situations are platform firms, open and closed areas and the international division of labor between developed-country firms and emerging-country firms. Figure 8.7 illustrates the relationships among these three elements.

Firms that implement a platform strategy only serve as the engine for the industrial evolution of the ecosystem. The competitive strategy of these platform firms brings about an architecture that has both open and closed areas and a structure of division of labor between developed countries and emerging countries.

The competitive strategy of platform firms is very different from that of product manufacturers. The platform strategy starts by artificially altering the architecture of a certain product, which is divided into an open subsystem and a closed subsystem. This division is achieved by means of strategic standardization. With strategic standardization, platform firms draw up an open standard defining the architecture of a product as two subsystems, open and closed. This is the separation of architecture. The open subsystem is called the open area and the closed subsystem the closed area. The scopes of the open and closed areas are determined depending on the business models of the platform firms.

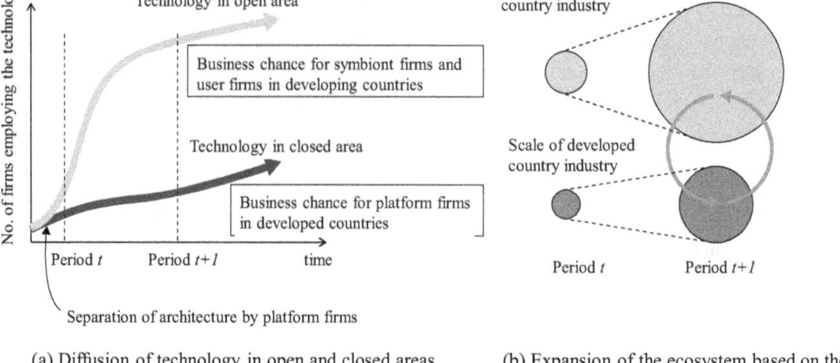

Fig. 8.7 Similarity in the industrial evolution of ecosystems

When an architecture is divided, the markets of the two areas undergo changes in terms of intensity of new entries. The open area, where new entries happen at a fast pace, is the source of growth for the expansion of the ecosystem. If the open area market grows, the closed area market will follow suit. The two areas used to be a single system; therefore, a network effect is at play between them. Simply put, if either of them grows, so does the other. Platform firms position themselves at the hub and mediate between the two areas, while operating their business in the closed area.

Both industries in the open and closed areas develop, but their profitability is different. The growth of the open area industry is driven by new entries, while that of the closed area industry by network effects. This difference is what determines the profitability of the two areas. Since it features fewer companies, the closed area industry promises to be lucrative. Platform firms keep their own business in the highly profitable closed area and earn profits from the growth of the ecosystem.

If no further action is taken, however, this profitability will soon be lost. Competitors will not just sit back and watch their rivals bring in huge earnings in the fast-growing industry. In addition, there will be continuous new entries in the closed area too. Platform firms can prevent this situation from happening by entering into peripheral markets to reinforce their bargaining power and by managing their relations with symbiont firms and user firms, as seen in Chaps. 5, 6 and 7, respectively. Platform firms also work to strengthen the competitiveness of their core business in the closed area.

Intellectual property (IP) management is another critical component of the platform strategy. In Chap. 5, when other firms tried to step into the closed area, Intel, the platform firm, aggressively staged patent disputes. IP management directly linked with their business strategy is extremely effective for platform firms, because they need to implement a powerful lock-in strategy in a certain area of the ecosystem.

Hence, the platform strategy clearly involves more than simply offering quality products. These efforts might not be as conspicuous as strategic standardization but they are just as important for the success of the platform strategy.

Furthermore, platform firms need to take various measures to expand the open area, as well as to reinforce their bargaining power in the closed area. Even when strategic standardization does lead to the creation of an ecosystem, the ecosystem will not grow spontaneously, it will require various interventions and stimuli. As seen in Chaps. 5–7, stimulation through entry into peripheral markets, distribution of reference designs, adoption of the open-industrywide approach and other forms of stimulus are necessary to ensure that the openness of the value network is maintained and the expansion of the ecosystem takes place smoothly. Platform firms manage their ecosystem by defining the open area as the area of ecosystem growth and by consistently managing its expansion.

This book has repeatedly pointed out that the platform strategy cannot be brought to fruition by platform firms alone. A platform firm is unable to complete its system on its own and always needs to involve symbiont firms. Symbiont firms are absolutely essential for platform firms.

The industries of emerging countries that enter the global economy constitute a vast pool of symbiont firms. In the open area, created through strategic standardization, new entrants come in one after the other, which drives down expected profitability. Yet, low profitability does not necessarily mean that the business in the open area is not attractive. On the contrary, it represents an ideal chance for the new entrants to distribute their products to a sizable global market, as long as they comply with the open standard. The advantage of being able to enter the world market with little or no technical accumulation and a poor understanding of the industrial context significantly overweighs any possible disadvantages. Besides, the open area market expands as the ecosystem expands. A growing industry means a chance of growth for the firms of emerging economies. The analysis in Chap. 5 demonstrated that the Taiwanese ODM industry and the South Korean memory semiconductor industry fully exploited this opportunity and caught up with developed countries.

The rise of platform firms appears to offer an opportunity for catching up with the industries of developed countries not just as symbiont firms but also as user firms. As described in Chap. 4, the semiconductor industries in emerging nations, such as the South Korean memory industry and the Taiwanese foundry industry, successfully caught up with developed countries during the process of diffusion of the 300 mm standard for semiconductors manufacturing equipment. In the case of the engine ECU market in China reported in Chap. 7, the engine ECU provided by the platform firms in developed countries presented local automotive manufacturers with a perfect opportunity for technological catch-up.

Strategic standardization by platform firms defines an open area and a closed area. While the open area provides firms in emerging countries with a perfect business opportunity, the growth of the open area also drives up the growth of the closed area; the closed area presents the platform firms in developed countries with a business opportunity as well. Following the strategic standardization by platform firms, a global ecosystem is established where firms from both developed and developing countries operate. The global system rapidly expands, thanks to the international division of labor created by the industries from developed and emerging countries. These movements stem from the opening of emerging-country markets in the 1990s and the subsequent participation of the emerging economies in the world economy, and they are further supported by the growth of the industries in emerging countries.

This thought process leads us to conclude that the global strategy of platform firms does not simply mean that platform firms have expanded globally, but that they have taken advantage of the changes in the world's industrial environment since the 1990s in order to grow. In the 1990s, the liberalization of markets in emerging countries occurred, leading their industries to join the world economy. The global strategy of platform firms provides an excellent opportunity for emerging-country industries with low levels of technological accumulation and a poor understanding of the industrial context to catch up with developed countries.

Furthermore, strategic standardization, which serves as the first step in the global strategy of platform firms, is a consequence of the relaxation of antitrust laws in the US and Europe in the mid-1980s. As explained in Chap. 1, the formation of an international open standard relies on the activities of consortia, or similar organizations. The relaxation of antitrust laws in the 1980s enabled consortium-based standardization and underpins the frequent formation of international open standards.

Against the backdrop of these industrial movements, the effectiveness of the platform strategy will not be a unique occurrence in the electronics industries, but it will extend to other industries too. As a matter of fact, the car electronics industry, examined in Chap. 7, is not a pure electronics industry but more of a combination of mechanics and computer software. Cyber Physical Systems (CPS) and the Internet of Things (IoT) are similar systems; hence, the effectiveness of the platform strategy may be substantial in this area. Needless to say, the discipline of network services is a key target for the application of the platform strategy. Other industries further away from the electronics industry, including the medical, energy and agricultural sectors, may also be potential targets for successfully implementing the platform strategy. All of this will be backed by the division of labor between the industries of developed and emerging countries, given the ecosystem-type industrial structure that has developed there. The platform strategy does not just bring profits to platform firms but expands ecosystems; thus, it is expected to trigger a new wave of international economic growth.

It cannot be emphasized enough that giving consideration to the platform strategy, the open and closed areas and the international division of labor between developed and emerging countries, as introduced in this book, is crucial. This will allow us to thoroughly understand which direction the evolution of ecosystems and the competitiveness of different firms are going to take, while, at the same time, enabling us to plan competitive strategies suited to the current age.

8.5 Conclusions

This chapter summarized the case and empirical studies conducted in Chaps. 3–7 using our analytical framework, thereby determining whether the four subordinate propositions presented in Chap. 2 are corroborated. The first three subordinate propositions, i.e., (1)–(3), concern the main effects of the platform strategy and they were examined as strategic levers of platform firms.

Strategic standardization by platform firms, the subject of subordinate proposition (1), was verified in all the case and empirical studies. We also learned that defining the open and closed areas and determining the degree of openness are critical.

Subordinate proposition (2), "Platform firms gain competitive advantage by positioning themselves at the hub of transaction networks and by passing on information among multiple markets", was investigated in the empirical analysis of Chap. 4 and statistically endorsed. The network analysis also identified that strategic standardization and hub positioning are closely related. Although this proposition is not directly touched upon in the other chapters, we can conclude that it is adequate, based on the evidence regarding the situation of platform firms.

The management of the value network, addressed by subordinate proposition (3), was described by looking at how platform firms manage their ecosystems in the personal computer industry (Chaps. 5 and 6) and the car electronics industry (Chap. 7). We saw that the entry into peripheral markets, investigated in Chap. 5, has two purposes for a platform firm: revitalization of such markets and strengthening of its bargaining power. Chapters 6 and 7 revealed that platform firms support the openness of the value network and prevent core networking by managing inter-firm relationships, in order to accelerate the expansion of the ecosystem.

Subordinate proposition (4) concerns the side effects of the platform strategy. We discussed the impact that it has on global ecosystems when platform firms successfully make use of the strategic levers in subordinate propositions (1) to (3). The findings from Chaps. 3–7 suggested that the rise of platform firms is very likely to induce a transformation in the international division of labor, which tends to affect symbiont firms more often than user firms. By examining the situations in which such an international transformation did not take place in the user segment, we found that at times entry regulations were in place (Chap. 3) and, in those cases, some firms from developed countries were included as symbiont and user firms (Chap. 5 and 6). The presence of entry regulations may appear to be a rare occurrence but, as a matter of fact, it is common practice in the infrastructure industry. In the PC industry, where developed-nation firms are both of the new and the old type, no international transformation took place in the user industry because a shift in industrial structure came about between old and new firms in the developed nation.

If, like in the case of PC production, an international industrial transformation does not happen in the user industry, the symbiont industry goes through a more serious transformation of the international division of labor. This is because new firms in the user industry select as their symbiont partners new entrants that are trying to catch up with traditional firms from developed countries. For example, as seen in Chap. 6, the computer industry of the US witnessed an increase in newcomers in the user segment. The new user firms chose the Taiwanese ODM industry—symbiont firms in developing countries—as partners. This resulted in a proxy war between developed- and emerging-nation firms in the symbiont segment linked to the industrial structure shift from existing to new firms in the user segment.

In conclusion, all of the subordinate propositions are deemed legitimate. Among these, however, only subordinate proposition (4) "The rise of a platform firm during the formation of a global ecosystem triggers a sudden transformation in the structure of the international division of labor" entails a complicated set of preconditions, as follows:

(i) The transformation of the international division of labor takes place more easily among symbiont firms than user firms;
(ii) When entry regulations are in place or a shift between existing firms and new firms occurs early on in the user industry, a transformation of the international division of labor does not take place there. Instead, the pressure for such a transformation concentrates on the symbiont firms, bringing about profound changes in the symbiont industry.

In all the cases explored in Chaps. 3–7, the rise of platform firms caused an industrial structure transformation. This derived from the competitive strategy of platform firms, promoting open standards in order to fill gaps in terms of technical accumulation and information on the industrial context between old and new firms and trigger an industrial transition.

This power of industrial structure transformation is augmented in a global ecosystem. Since changes in the industrial structure influence all the participants in the ecosystem, each of its players, not just platform firms, needs to decide how to respond to the strategy of platform firms. Given its centrality, further discussion and examination of the platform strategy is of paramount importance going forward.

References

Bekkers R, Verspagen B, Smits J (2002) Intellectual property rights and standardization: the case of GSM. Telecommun Policy 26:171–188

Eisenmann T, Parker G, Van Alstyne M (2011) Platform envelopment. Strateg Manag J 32:1270–1285

Gawer A, Cusumano MA (2002) Platform leadership: How Intel, Microsoft, and Cisco drive industry innovation. Harvard Business School Press, Boston MA

Juliussen E, Robinson R (2010) Is Europe in the driver's seat? The competitiveness of the European automotive embedded systems industry. Institute for Prospective Technological Studies, Joint Research Center, European Commission. https://ec.europa.eu/jrc/sites/jrcsh/files/JRC61541.pdf. Accessed 26 Jan 2017

Mochizuki S (2015) Toyota ga FCV Tokkyo wo Mushou Kaihou shita Shin no Nerai ha? (What was Toyota's aim in licensing the FCV patent for free?) IP Manag Rev 19:38–47. http://www.ip-edu.org/library/pdf/ipmr/IPMR19_38_47.pdf. Accessed 26 Dec 2016 (in Japanese)

Ogawa K (2009) Kokusai hyoujunka to Jigyou Senryaku (International standards and business strategy). Hakuto Shobou, Tokyo (in Japanese)

Rüping T, Trechow P (2014) Association goes beyond AUTOSAR. RealTimes Jan 2014:18–19 ETAS

Shintaku J, Ogawa K, Yoshimoto T (2006) Architecture-based approaches to international standardization and evolution of business models. In: International standardization as a strategic tool: commended papers from the IEC centenary challenge 2006. International Electrotechnical Commission, Geneva

Ueki M (2013) Hyoujunka Hissu Tokkyo no Roiyariti Kijun wo Bei Chisai ga Shimesu. Sumaho Google Jineini Dageki (US District Court shows the valuation criteria for Standard Essential Patents, dealing a blow to smartphone, google camp). Nikkei Technology Online. http://techon.nikkeibp.co.jp/article/COLUMN/20130530/284689. Accessed 26 Dec 2016 (in Japanese)

Yamada Y (2015) Toyota ga Ireino Senryaku FCV Tokyokaihou no Hitsuzen (Toyota's unexpected move to open license of its FCV patents, but it's inevitable) Toyo Keizai Online, Jan 9 2015. https://toyokeizai.net/articles/-/5573. Accessed 26 Dec 2016 (in Japanese)

Chapter 9
Conclusions

This final chapter verifies that the studies conducted in Chaps. 3–8 corroborate the fundamental proposition and the four subordinate propositions introduced in Chap. 2. It then considers the academic and business implications of this book and prospects for further investigation.

The appendix that follows summarizes the history of architecture research, since the evidence and discussions presented here are largely influenced by past investigations. Finally, we suggest possible future directions for architectural studies.

9.1 Summary

Against the backdrop of the frequent formation of international open standards since the 1990s, we carried out a series of case studies and empirical analyses on the basis of our fundamental proposition: "When an open standard prevails in a global ecosystem, the platform firm gains a dominant competitive position. The success of the platform firm triggers a sudden transformation in the structure of the international division of labor".

Our case studies and empirical analyses provided the following three insights into the process through which platform firms gain competitive advantage in global ecosystems:

(1) Platform firms make strategic use of open standards to gain competitive advantage (subordinate proposition 1);
(2) Platform firms gain competitive advantage by positioning themselves at the hub of transaction networks and by passing on information among multiple markets (subordinate proposition 2);
(3) Platform firms gain competitive advantage by implementing two-sided market and bundling strategies, managing relations with suppliers of complementary goods and adopting other strategies based on market structure (subordinate proposition 3).

H. Tatsumoto, *Platform Strategy for Global Markets*,
https://doi.org/10.1007/978-981-33-6789-0_9

These three statements actually correspond to the strategic levers that platform firms implement to gain greater competitiveness in their respective global ecosystems. When using these levers, in order to maximize their strategic effect, platform firms select firms from emerging countries with low levels of technological accumulation and a limited understanding of the industrial context as their symbiont and user firms. Participating in a global ecosystem presents these emerging-country firms with a crucial opportunity for catching up with the developed world. The series of studies featured in this volume revealed that the success of the platform strategy brings about the following side effect (subordinate proposition 4):

(4) The rise of a platform firm during the formation of a global ecosystem triggers a sudden transformation in the structure of the international division of labor.

A closer look at this evidence directs our attention to the following two conditions:

(i) The transformation of the international industrial structure, or of the international division of labor, occurs more easily in the symbiont segment than in the user segment.
(ii) When entry regulations are in place or a shift between existing firms and new firms occurs early on in the user industry, a transformation of the international division of labor does not take place there. Instead, the pressure for such a transformation concentrates on the symbiont firms, bringing about profound changes in the symbiont industry.

The findings from (1) to (4) underpin the corresponding subordinate propositions (1)–(4). In conclusion, the case studies and empirical analyses performed in this book collectively support the fundamental proposition.

9.2 Academic Contributions

This book aimed to shed light on the competitive strategies of platform firms in global ecosystems, a topic not exhaustively researched so far, and to explain, through case studies and empirical analyses, how the rise of platform firms affects the international division of labor.

Much of the past research on platform firms tacitly assumed domestic firms to be the platform firms and took little notice of international conditions. This disregard for internationality is strikingly odd, when considering the impact that platform firms have on the global economy. The case studies in the present volume addressed the competitive strategies of platform firms in global ecosystems, in response to the academic requirements of the times.

In this analysis, prior studies were summarized at the outset, pointing out that the strategic behaviors of platform firms originate from the ecosystem-type industrial structure that bears network effects (Chap. 2). The following chapters introduced a series of case studies and empirical analyses to examine several ecosystem-type industries, including those for the production of mobile phones, semiconductor manufacturing equipment, personal computers, and car electronics. These examples were used to investigate the corporate behaviors of platform firms in detail and identify the competitive strategies that are specific to them.

Platform firms frequently engage in strategic standardization with the aim of establishing an ecosystem. The case study on the mobile communications industry, discussed in Chap. 3, found that strategic standardization demarcates the open and closed areas in the architecture of a system product for the purpose of maximizing network effects. This separation of architecture allows firms in emerging countries to enter the open area, thereby forging a global ecosystem. In the meantime, the platform firms may expand their business in the closed area.

Moreover, the study on the semiconductor manufacturing equipment industry in Chap. 4 revealed that platform firms augment their competitiveness by positioning themselves at the hub of global ecosystems and by passing on information among multiple communities. It described how the platform firms rolled out their technology among firms in emerging countries using open standards.

During the ecosystem expansion phase, platform firms adopt various tools to manage the value network. This was seen in Chap. 5, which analyzed the personal computer industry and observed how platform firms make strategic entries into peripheral markets. They enter peripheral markets for two distinctive purposes, i.e., to stimulate and revitalize those peripheral market and to lock them in, thus strengthening the competitiveness of their own business.

Platform firms also provide the technological knowledge gathered from certain symbiont firms to other symbiont firms, in the form of reference designs. This is done to prevent the value network from becoming a core network, i.e., a network depending solely on a small group of select symbiont firms (study on the motherboard industry in Chap. 6), and to manage inter-firm relations with a broad spectrum of user firms based on the open-industrywide approach (study on the car electronics industry in Chap. 7).

Except Chaps. 3–7 all featured case studies that comprised extensive analyses relying on numerous interviews and a wide range of secondary information. Hence, they were able to illuminate the details of the strategic behaviors of platform firms not understood by earlier research. Chapter 4, meanwhile, presented an empirical study using transaction network data on semiconductor manufacturing equipment. Very few previous works on platform firms performed empirical analyses. However, the relationship among different strategic behaviors or the conditions under which these behaviors exert effects can be understood only through empirical analysis based on statistical data.

As a result of our investigations about the preconditions needed for the platform strategy to exert effects, we learned that the platform strategy has positive outcomes only when three strategic behaviors are implemented as a package. These behaviors are positioning at the hub (high betweenness centrality), high sales rates of open standard-compatible products and high sales ratios in emerging markets. The simultaneous pursuit of the three strategic behaviors produces interaction effects on a considerable scale. A platform firm achieves a statistically significant effect by increasing its sales rate of open standard-compatible products when it positions itself at the hub and its sales ratios in emerging markets are high enough.

Chapter 8 wrapped up the analysis of the multiple ecosystems reviewed in this book. It examined the side effects of the success of the platform strategy in global ecosystems, showing that the rise of platform firms triggers a transformation in the international division of labor. When platform firms make use of their strategic levers, they choose emerging-country firms, i.e., newcomers to the global economy, as symbiont firms and user firms to maximize the impact of such levers.

The rise of platform firms in the world economy has become indisputably conspicuous in recent years, but the international phenomena that it may bring about have not been well understood, also due to the limited amount of existing research. The series of studies in this book intends to fill that gap and provide answers about such a complex subject.

9.3 Business Implications

This book has three business implications, explained below.

The first has to do with understanding the strategic standardization that platform firms implement. Platform firms use strategic standardization as a strategic trigger that can potentially have an impact on other firms. Previous studies, however, have not clearly explained how platform firms push forward with standardization activities and what strategic objectives they aim to reach. This book reveals that the purpose of strategic standardization is to divide the architecture into an open area and a closed area, so as to establish an ecosystem.

This architectural separation is not necessarily undesirable to symbiont and user firms either. Rather, they may benefit from the establishment and expansion of the ecosystem. If their business domain is specified as part of the open area, a deep transformation of the industrial structure may occur, in which case, they need to plan a strategic response in advance. To examine such a scenario, the mechanism of strategic standardization explained in the present volume may be effective.

Secondly, our analysis thoroughly describes the strategic levers, such as strategic standardization, positioning at the hub and management of the value network, to business practitioners trying to plan a platform strategy as their competitive strategy. The details of the levers were presented in Chaps. 3–7. In addition, Chap. 8 provided an overview of the relationships among these strategic levers from a broad perspective, emphasizing that strategic standardization, the initial strategic lever, is not pure standardization. Since it is carried out according to the platform firms' business models, it goes beyond simple standardization activities. Hub positioning is inseparable from the prevalence of open standards, and their promotion among firms in emerging countries allows platform firms to position themselves at the hub in global ecosystems.

Our evidence highlights that, if strategic standardization and hub positioning tactics are implemented at an early stage, platform firms can take strategic action at the inflection point between the ecosystem establishment phase and the expansion phase, ahead of symbiont and user firms. Furthermore, regarding the strategic lever of managing the inter-firm network, it is critical to obtain bargaining power and stimulate peripheral markets by entering them and to prevent the network from becoming a core network by maintaining it open, to encourage new entrants to join the ecosystem. The use of strategic levers in the ecosystem expansion phase requires broad knowledge and comprehension of the entire ecosystem, rather than a limited focus on the platform firm's own business.

Thirdly, this book identifies the relationship between the platform strategy and transformations in the industrial structure, which may be of interest to business practitioners and policy makers. For example, firms that follow a platform strategy are entering the automotive industry today thanks to the opportunities offered by the development of autonomous driving. The present volume also introduces a framework to evaluate what kinds of effects an industry experiences when going through such changes. The platform strategy is not all bad news to traditional firms because it entails an expansion of the ecosystem. On top of this, the promotion of new entries may bring about innovations.

At the same time, however, the platform strategy is likely to trigger transformations both in the industrial structure between old and new firms and in the international division of labor. Indeed, the platform strategy has a truly immeasurable impact. This is why, as touched upon at the start of Chap. 1, the EU is headed toward imposing regulations on platform firms. This book provides the foundations for examining both the advantages and disadvantages of the platform strategy.

9.4 Contemporary Significance of This Book: Expansion of Ecosystem-Type Industries

9.4.1 Significance for Traditional Product Manufacturers

This book analyzes the strategic behaviors of platform firms from the viewpoint of an industrial structure of the ecosystem type. Yet, also for industries not necessarily of the ecosystem type, understanding the strategic behaviors of platform firms acquires considerable practical significance from two perspectives.

The first is associated with the hierarchical nature of product architecture. In terms of hierarchy of product architecture, whether or not an industry is of the ecosystem type is a relative issue. A complex product system usually takes on a layered structure; some of the layers may come from an ecosystem-like industrial structure and others from a very traditional structure, not of the ecosystem type.

For example, the automotive industry has long been well known for its non-ecosystem-like industrial structure. More recently, however, with the introduction of self-driving technology and the arrival of car dispatch service providers, a new layer has become part of the existing product architecture.[1] As a result, the value network behind it might transform radically, creating a situation of the ecosystem type. In such a case, it will be necessary to understand what strategic behaviors platform firms will adopt vis-à-vis traditional automotive makers and component suppliers. Indeed, platform firms may appear to them to be core parts providers but, in actual fact, they are completely different. The key to success is to fully understand the strategies of platform firms and collaborate with them.

The other perspective has to do with comparing platform-oriented and product-oriented strategies. The platform strategy differs substantially from the strategy of conventional product manufacturers, centered on developing and marketing quality products. If we look at firms in the real world, discriminating between platform- and product-oriented strategies may well be difficult, and only relative differences may emerge. In some cases, the two may even reside in one firm. Apple Inc., for example, acts like a platform firm in the smartphone market, but it is also well known for its strong design management to improve its product brands. Improving product brands is a typical case of the product-oriented strategy.

In sum, firms in the real world operate the platform- and product-oriented strategies in parallel. Firms in an ecosystem-like industry cannot maintain their competitive advantage unless they make wise use of these two strategies. In this sense, again, it is important for traditional product firms to understand the platform strategy explained in this book.

9.4.2 New Sources of Network Effects: Emergence of IoT/Big Data/AI and Data-Driven Industrial Structures

The ecosystem-type industrial structure is characterized by network effects. The business ecosystems examined in the present volume have the formation of international open standards as their source of network effects. Yet, a new source of network effects has become visible in recent years, i.e., data. This trend is sometimes called the fourth industrial revolution.

A data-driven industrial revolution has been predicted for quite some time, but how such a revolution may change industries has not been clarified. If big data are randomly accumulated with no specific goal, they are of no use to firms and end up being discarded.

---

[1] In 2016 Alphabet Inc., the parent company of Google Inc., established a subsidiary dedicated to self-driving cars, called Waymo LLC. The firm announced a plan to conduct a joint research project with Honda R&D Co., Ltd., a research and development subsidiary of Honda Motor Co., Ltd., on autonomous driving technology in the US (ITmedia 2016). Also, Uber and other car dispatch services have been spreading globally, intensifying market competition. The relationship between these firms and traditional automotive firms is attracting the attention of researchers (Wall Street Journal 2016).

More recently, phenomena like the penetration of Internet of Things (IoT) devices, the establishment of Big Data technology and the productization of artificial intelligence (AI)—machine learning, in particular—have provided a generic framework for the use of data in business. In detail, the key steps consist in collecting data using IoT devices with various sensors, accumulating the collected data, extracting information from the archive on demand thanks to the power of Big Data technology and, lastly, creating prediction models from such data using AI (machine learning algorithms). AI-based prediction models offer high-accuracy predictions for smart matching, i.e., the efficient matching of demand and supply. The co-use of IoT, Big Data, and AI increasingly enables the diffusion of data-driven businesses. Data-driven companies generate strong network effects, since they usually offer their business solutions as APIs (application protocol interfaces) in the cloud. Consequently, they serve as a powerful engine to transform an industrial structure into an ecosystem-type one.

More concretely, driving data from automobiles are perfect for building prediction models for autonomous driving and car dispatch services. There are also big business opportunities in matching with peripheral services (e.g., accommodation and sightseeing). Once this smart matching becomes popular, the automotive industry, self-driving technology firms, dispatch service firms and accommodation providers will enjoy the network effects of using the same APIs. In this way, IoT, Big Data and AI will transform traditional industries into ecosystem-type industrial structures. Data-driven industrial revolutions are anticipated not only in the automotive industry but also in many other areas, among which precision agriculture and data health care.

It goes without saying that platform firms exert a strong influence on ecosystem-type industries. In new ecosystems based on IoT, Big Data and AI, the discussions on the platform strategy presented in this book will most likely be of relevance. Firms will also need to constantly consider whether they should pursue the platform strategy, or platform-oriented strategy. If they choose not to do so, they will have to address the big issue of how to deal with platform firms. From this standpoint, the logic behind the platform strategy examined in this book will prove useful to many firms.

9.5 Challenges and Visions

This book elucidates the global strategy employed by platform firms. Of course, our analysis also has limitations, in that many specific aspects remain uncertain and need to be better understood.

First of all, much is left to be addressed for what concerns the organization-level decision-making process inside platform firms. The present volume focuses on corporate behaviors relevant to market competitiveness and does not cover what platform firms do in terms of internal decision-making. It is well known that very few Japanese firms follow the platform strategy and most platform firms today are concentrated in the US. Whether a correlation exists between this fact and internal decision-making processes is a matter that draws both practical and academic attention and may represent a key area for future investigations.

The second area of uncertainty regards the strategic nature of platform firms. The strategy of platform firms depends heavily on the response of symbiont and user firms, so not everything can be planned ahead. If symbiont and user firms behave in an unfavorable way, platform firms may have to apply their strategy by using stimulus measures. As the platform strategy depends on the other firms' behaviors, accidentality comes into play. Although platform firms behave based on their strategic intentions, they also have to act to make maximum use of unexpected, accidental elements.

Today's studies on platform firms mainly concentrate on analyzing the former, i.e., the strategic intention-based behaviors of platform firms. In reality, while some of their actions are founded on plans, platform firms most often react to other firms' behaviors. If this is the case, scholars must look at their strategies with the notion of uncertainty in mind, rather than in a deterministic manner. We need to apply more probabilistic models theoretically, while also conducting empirical studies aimed at assessing multiple strategic options that platform firms can select in response to the behaviors of symbiont and user firms.

Thirdly, it is difficult to say what kind of strategies symbiont and user firms may implement in response to the rise of platform firms. Most of the firms participating in an ecosystem are not platform firms; indeed, they are either symbiont firms or user firms. Under these circumstances, the responsive strategy to the platform strategy carries greater value than the platform strategy itself. Nevertheless, the number of studies dealing with this issue is extremely small. In sum, the responsive strategy seems to be a stimulating topic for further research.

The fourth area concerns studies to better understand international business or international competitiveness and platform firms as a subject of regulatory control when it comes to cross-border activities. This book adds a new variable to the research on platform firms, i.e., the international division of labor, and uncovers a portion of the mechanism of how platform firms establish global ecosystems. Yet, this exploration barely scratches the surface.

One of the numerous unanswered questions is why so many platform firms are Western, particularly American. Another is why so few Japanese firms implement the platform strategy. Are there any industrial environmental factors in Japan that hamper the growth of platform firms? What industrial conditions are needed for a platform firm to emerge in a global ecosystem from the viewpoint of international competitiveness? From the perspective of the international division of labor, are these influential platform firms truly advantageous? Or should they be regulated for the sake of healthy competition and economic growth? The analyses in this book are devoted to the *firms* side, the players in ecosystems, and lack the perspective of consumers. If consumers are taken into consideration, are regulations controlling platform firms necessary after all? These questions require further examination.

As pointed out above, the strategic behaviors of platform firms need to be studied in greater depth. The global strategy of platform firms, described in this work, also deserves more extensive discussion. I would be truly delighted if this book contributed to future research on platform business.

Appendix 1: Architecture Research

The platform strategy is also analyzed in studies on innovation strategies for complex artifacts, or system products. In these studies, architecture is an essential concept. Likewise, this book is strongly affected by the concept of architecture and, to gain a better understanding of it, let us first explore the history of architectural studies in this Appendix.

What is Architecture Research

Architecture research refers to investigations that clarify the relationship between the structure of an artifact and the structure of the division of labor. Architecture is one of the core topics in studies on the management of technology. Furthermore, architecture research has an impact on many disciplines concerning artifacts, ranging from product development to production management, inter-organizational relationships, industrial organization and corporate strategy. In recent years, the concept of architecture has yielded useful insights and achieved high levels of refinement, while discussions around it have grown more complex and intense. However, architectural studies started out with an extremely simple idea and clever observation.

The term *architecture*, first used by Simon (1962) to speak about the design of artifacts, refers to the state of the bonds between design elements. That means, architectural studies developed from the straightforward notion of looking at dependencies among elements as a feature of artifacts.

Dependency among elements is one of the features that any artifact has. In other words, everything has an architecture. In fact, Simon (1962) mentioned precision machines (e.g., watches), corporate organizations (i.e., organizational structure), human body and other bodily systems (e.g., the brain and other organs), and symbol systems (e.g., musical notes and mathematical formulas) as examples of artifacts that have an architecture. Economic systems and digital control systems have an architecture too. The classic study on architecture by Alexander (1964) argued that architecture exists in city planning and culture. We are surrounded by a wide variety of architectures in our daily life, which is why architecture is worth studying and architectural research has a broad spectrum of applicability.

Now, while we have learned how important architecture research is, why does architecture attract the interest of researchers to such an extent? Because architectural studies hypothesize that complex systems have a common architecture. More specifically, although we are surrounded by many different architectures, complex systems have certain architectural features in common.

Simon (1962) asserted that any complex system, whether a precision machine or corporate organization or bodily system, has a common architecture, that is to say, a common dependency pattern among design elements. This surprising insight has been a strong motivation in architectural studies. Similar concepts can be seen in contributions on general systems and cybernetics (Wiener 1948). Some research on cybernetics, for example, argued that sustainable complex systems have in common the characteristics of feedback and homeostasis, although they slightly differ from one another depending on whether emphasis is placed on the state of dependency of artifacts or on the patterns of information flows among them. Fujimoto (2009) extended this notion by describing how economic systems, precision machine control and axiomatic design methods are all based on this assumption. Many researchers have been fascinated by academic inquiry around the common characteristics of complex systems.

Architecture of Complex Artifacts

This section is devoted to exploring the following two questions, based on the concept of architectural studies of the early days (Simon 1962):

(i) Why do complex artifacts have a common architecture?
(ii) What does this common architecture shared by complex artifacts look like?

Earlier Studies on Architecture

Reasons Why Complex Artifacts Have a Common Architecture

There are two reasons why complex systems have a common architecture. One has to do with the fact that the cognitive capacity of human beings is limited, the other with the process through which a complex system is created.[2]

Let us start by explaining the first factor, i.e., why limitations of the human cognitive capacity produce a common architecture. As discussed by Okuno et al. (2006), humans have a limited level of cognitive abilities. This makes people perceive some related elements as one chunk, or a complex system as an aggregate of a certain number of chunks.

More concretely, we understand the human body as an assembly of the head, the torso and the limbs. We cognitively group smaller elements into chunks at a certain level. Thus, the head consists of the eyes, ears, mouth, brain, skull and so on. Okuno et al. (2006) used the term *coordination system* to denote the fact that we consider a complex system as a set of chunks of smaller design elements related to each other. In other words, we do not regard the human body as consisting directly of nerve cells,

---

[21] Simon (1962) provided a detailed description of the design evolution process but not as much information on the limitations of the human cognitive capacity.

muscle cells and epithelial cells. Rather, we first of all consider it as an aggregate of the head, torso and limbs.

We do not recognize the human body as a hierarchical aggregation of countless tiny cells, though that is the truth, due to the limitations of our cognitive abilities. If we are to cognize nerve cells, we take consecutive steps and cognize the limbs first, then the hands and fingers and only later the cells. Each step, or layer, is also made up of chunks, such as the head, consisting of the eyes, ears, mouth, etc., the body comprising the thorax, abdomen, etc., and the limbs including the arms, hands, fingers etc., as if they were pulling design elements together.

A complex system, therefore, is perceived as an aggregation of layers, each of which consists of chunks comprised of design elements. This is the common architecture of complex systems or, more precisely, this is how humans recognize the architecture of complex systems. Nowadays, these *chunks* are known as *modules*. Because human cognitive abilities are limited, a complex system is understood as having an architecture made up of layers, each consisting of modules.

So far, we have discussed how our limited cognitive capacity creates a common architecture. Let us now introduce a different point of view, i.e., how the process through which a complex system is produced creates a common architecture.

A complex system involves numerous design elements. That is to say, it takes a long time to assemble a complex system from so many individual design elements. The process is fraught with obstacles, or noise, which hamper its completion. If and when a complex system is finally put together, it has gone through several intermediate states during its creation process. This is because, if an obstacle gets in the way and hinders the completion of the system, the in-process system—that is, its intermediate state—can be reused and a complex system can be built from it. Restarting the building process from such an intermediate state makes it more probable for a complex system to be completed than going back to square one and redesigning everything from scratch.

Simon (1962) made similar observations by explaining the process to manufacture watches. A watch is a precision device made up of various components. The watchmaker first assembles small parts, such as the hands, spring and gear, into several subassemblies, or intermediate states.

What if the maker tries to assemble a watch directly from the small parts without going through the various subassembly states? If something goes wrong during assembly, the process has to be restarted from the beginning. On the other hand, the maker has a much better chance of completing the assembly of a watch if he/she builds several subassemblies first and then assembles the subassemblies into the final form of a watch.

Intermediate states are effective for completing a complex system. In the intermediate state, several design elements that are related to each other are built into a module. In the example of watchmaking, the subassemblies correspond to modules. In other words, when intermediate states are included in the process of creating a complex system, the architecture of an artifact may be divided into the level of assembling multiple design elements into modules and the level of assembling modules into the end state of the complex system. Ultimately, the architecture of complex systems is characterized by modularity and a layered structure.

No matter which explanation is chosen, either the limited capacity of humans for recognizing complex systems or the process of creating complex artifacts, the architecture of complex systems is understood as having the common features of modularity and layered structure. Systems displaying these common features are called *nearly decomposable systems* (Simon 1962).

Nearly Decomposable Systems

Nearly decomposable systems have the following three crucial characteristics:

(i) The mutual dependency among the elements of a module is very strong, whereas the mutual dependency among the elements of different modules is extremely weak or non-existent.
(ii) The movement of each module is independent of the other modules over a short period of time (i.e., approximately).
(iii) In the long term (i.e., collectively), the movement of each module affects the other modules.

The first feature essentially refers to the fact that a complex system has a layered structure. Though a complex system is *complicated*, not all its design elements are necessarily closely interwoven. There are some places where no dependency is observed, while in other places very strong dependency exists among elements. This clearly indicates that a system can be understood as a hierarchical structure.

The second statement means that the movement of a complex system is an approximation of the movements of its constituent modules over a short period of time. A complex system may be treated as an aggregation of modules for a short period of time, when a certain set of design elements is treated as a module.

The third characteristic, on the other hand, points to the fact that a complex system does not exhibit simple behaviors that can be easily assessed as the sum of the behaviors of its constituent modules. That is to say, when different modules are aggregated as a system, the interactions among the modules unexpectedly exert a strong impact and affect the entire system in the long run.

Application of the Concept of Architecture to the Industries of Complex Artifacts (Studies in the Early 1990s)

Hierarchy of Architecture

Around the early 1990s, architectural studies focused specifically on the first characteristic of nearly decomposable systems (Clark 1985; Henderson and Clark 1990; Christensen 1992a, b; Henderson and Cockburn 1994). These analyses divided a complex system into an *upper layer*, being the end state of the complete product, and a *lower layer*, or its components. The upper layer is an architectural level that requires overall knowledge, or knowledge of the dependencies among the modules, whereas

Table 9.1 Architectural layers and impact of innovation

Architectural layer	Impact on competition
Upper (architecture-level)	– Any architecture-level innovation, no matter how small, has a major impact on competition – As their organizational structure is excessively compatible with the preexisting architecture, traditional firms overlook the shift to the new architecture and fail to respond
Lower (component-level)	– Any component-level innovation, no matter how large, has no major impact on competition – Traditional firms may respond to component-level innovation by extending the life of the current technology or by employing the new technology

the lower layer concerns the component level, which requires core knowledge, or knowledge of the dependencies among the elements inside a module.

Henderson and Clark (1990) were the first scholars to point out that architecture-level innovation and component-level innovation are different in nature. They conducted case studies on the semiconductor manufacturing equipment industry and discovered that, when architectural innovation occurs, no matter how small its scale, incumbent firms cannot react and are defeated by entrant firms (Table 9.1). The reason for this, they explained, is that incumbent firms already have an information processing structure suitable for the preexisting architecture and cannot embrace (or are inclined to ignore) the changes featured in the new architecture. In other words, according to Henderson and Clark, innovations are disregarded by traditional firms due to limited cognitive abilities of organizations.

To make the same case, Henderson and Cockburn (1994) carried out empirical analyses using data on research and development productivity in the pharmaceutical industry. They demonstrated that firms purposefully taking enterprise-wide initiatives in architecture-level innovations are the most productive in research and development. This evidence is in line with Christensen's studies on the hard disk industry in the 1970–1990s (Christensen 1992a, b). Christensen showed that the introduction of a new component-level technology ended up having a limited impact on the structure of competition, because the incumbent firms were able to respond to the emergence of the new technology by extending the life of the prevalent enabling technology back then or by implementing the new technology. Component-level technologies, in other words, do not pose a threat to preexisting firms.

Architecture-level innovation is a different story. Christensen reported that the hard disk industry went through five waves of innovations at the architectural level in the period from the 1970 to the 1990s. Each time, the incumbent firms were defeated by the entrant firms. The reason behind the defeat of the preexisting players was attributed by Christensen to the organization-level cognition capability.

An architectural innovation means the creation of a new product segment. In the case of hard disks, the disks for mainframes and those for desktop computers belong to two different segments. In addition, each segment is characterized by different customer preferences. In many cases, an architectural innovation brings about lower prices and lower performance. It is not existing customers but new customers that prefer the new product. Because incumbent firms are too loyal to the needs and preferences of existing customers, they neglect to listen to new customers. Furthermore, the products arising from architectural innovations tend to be less profitable and less reliable than existing products. Therefore, preexisting firms, or incumbents, fail to rationally consider—or cannot organizationally respond to—architectural innovations. Christensen concluded that this is why incumbent firms are defeated by new firms and called such a situation *the innovator's dilemma.* In a broad sense, this issue is equivalent to the limitations of the cognitive capacity of organizations noted by Henderson and Clark (1990).

Relationship Between Architectural Innovation and Organizational Capacity

Architectural innovations matter greatly for complex systems, and how an organization responds to such innovations has an impact on its performance. This thought is commonly observed in studies on product development dating back to the first half of the 1990s. Clark and Fujimoto (1991) made a comparative study on the development projects of 20 automotive firms in the US, Europe and Japan, showing that efficient projects in terms of product development and production entailed responses to architecture-level innovations at the organization level. Here, organizational capability means knowledge integration by heavyweight product managers and promotion of knowledge exchanges between processes by having them partly overlap with each other.

Some scholars also reported that a similar mechanism is observed not only inside one firm but between firms, or organizations, too. Clark (1989) paid attention to the trade patterns between automobile makers and auto parts suppliers and concluded that these patterns vary from country to country and differences in patterns make a difference in the productivity of automobile development. The Japanese automobile industry, in particular, has a unique propensity for close communication between different organizations. This capacity is called a relationship-specific asset (Williamson 1979) or relationship-specific capability (Asanuma 1989). It is regarded as highly effective for solving problems at the architectural level. Later studies demonstrated that the relationship-specific capability exists in inter-organizational relations in the automotive industry and greatly contributes to development efficiency across the production network (Dyer and Nobeoka 2000). Furthermore, the relationship-specific capability is positively proportional to the integration capability of individual organizations (Takeishi 2001).

These investigations around product development strongly endorsed the idea that architectural innovations are essential for complex systems and organization-wide responses to innovation influence a firm's performance. In sum, the studies in the early 1990s emphasized that (i) architecture-level innovations have a larger impact on the industrial structure than component-level innovations and (ii) solving architecture-level problems requires organizational capabilities, or the organization's capability to integrate a wide range of knowledge through overlapping between processes, cross-cutting organizations, centralized leadership (heavyweight product managers), inter-organization relationship-specific abilities and so on.

Yet, the above inquiries only dealt with the first of the three characteristics of nearly decomposable systems identified by Simon (1962), without bringing the other two characteristics into focus. This means that they did not address the questions: "Are there more important success factors than inter-organizational integration when it comes to other module dependency patterns?" and "How do innovations at the module level collectively affect the architecture level?" The first question evolved into research about the differences among architecture types from the mid-1990s onward and the second question led to examinations of dynamic processes in architecture after 2000.

Differences in Inter-organizational Relationships According to the Types of Architecture (Studies in the Mid-1990s)

Integral Architecture and Modular Architecture

The mid-1990s saw a significant rise in the number of studies focused on the second and the third characteristic of nearly decomposable systems. Scholars believed different states of dependency among modules to require different organizational capabilities.

This change in the direction of research in the mid-1990s reflected the changes in the innovation pattern observed in the US industry. At the time, the US industry was characterized by three aspects: (i) innovations were concentrated in certain industries, particularly modular architecture-based industries, such as that of information technology; (ii) entrant firms, not incumbent firms, led innovations; and (iii) innovations were accelerated using resources existing outside—not inside—the innovator firms, among which industrywide standards, industry-academia collaborations and outsourcing (Miyata 2001). These characteristics differed greatly from the traditional style of US innovations promoted by vertically-integrated firms and the firms' central research centers. The shift from linear innovation to open innovation that occurred in the 1990s seemingly had a significant impact on scholarly reflection.

Ulrich (1995) was the first among architecture researchers to highlight this point. He distinguished between modular architecture, which has simple and clear states of dependency among modules, and integral architecture, which has complicated states of dependency among modules. In an architecture of the modular type, a combination of multiple modules does not have a major collective impact, which, in turn, means that organizational integration is not that important. In an integral architecture, however, this collective impact may be unexpectedly vast. Ulrich argued that integral architecture requires a cross-cutting, horizontal team or heavyweight product manager, so that it can be managed across all its functional units. The bottom line is that different types of architecture require different organizational structures.

A similar insight was also derived in the field of inter-organizational (inter-firm) relations (Langlois and Robertson 1992; Robertson and Langlois 1995). Langlois and Robertson (1992) examined how organizations achieved coordination in the stereo system and microcomputer (personal computer) industries. Inter-organizational coordination in these industries is quite simple, thanks to the presence of compatible standards. It does not involve dense communication, specialized trade patterns, or any other kinds of abilities unique to the inter-organizational relationship.

In the stereo system example, for instance, a consumer can choose a speaker from one manufacturer, an amplifier from another, and a player from yet another, at his or her discretion, and combine the three components into a stereo system. This is because compatible standards are pervasive across the industry. In other words, the system product is completed through an autonomous supply chain, not a centralized supply chain. Langlois and Robertson also predicted that autonomous innovations and decentralized innovations occurring in autonomous supply chains would gain increasing importance going forward.

Baldwin and Clark (2000) ascertained that the modular architecture had become the mainstream in the digital industry and underlined that the product development patterns of the modular architecture were inducing a new type of industry-level innovation, i.e., modular cluster innovation. A typical example of this is the computer industry in Silicon Valley.

In modular architecture, firms can mix and match different components with little or no inter-organizational coordination, since they share design rules (Baldwin and Clark 2000). In this context, *design rules* are virtually analogous to open standards in inter-firm relations. More combination options mean that the potential added value of the product increases exponentially. Besides, openly available design rules allow different firms in an industry to develop different components concurrently—part providers can develop their specialty parts on their own, without any coordination with other firms—and this brings about overwhelmingly rapid innovations.

Studies based on trade costs also tackled the question of what kind of inter-organizational coordination, organizational integration or division of labor, is most desirable for an industry that deals with complex systems. In the mid-1990s, academics working in this field held the view that different types of architecture correspond to different patterns of inter-firm relations (Chesbrough and Teece 1996).

Trade cost-based studies prior to the 1990s had regarded organizational integration as the most critical aspect for industries dealing with complex systems. According to Teece (1986), a complex system comprises a complicated dependency relationship among design elements, hence requiring a strong dependency relationship in innovation activities (research and development, manufacturing, etc.) Even when a firm achieves a remarkable innovation in research and development, it is not guaranteed to occupy an advantageous position in terms of competition. A firm excelling in manufacturing may actually earn more money utilizing other firms' innovations. This argument apparently came from the tacit presumption, widespread in trade cost-based studies of the early days, that all complex systems are of the integral architecture type.

This point of view needed correction, as a new innovation pattern, i.e., modular architecture-based innovation, emerged in the 1990s and quickly gained ground. Ten years after his initial study (Teece 1986), Teece extended his discussion by suggesting that the pattern of inter-organizational integration depends on the innovation pattern

(Chesbrough and Teece 1996). Inter-organizational integration remains vital when an innovation requires a complementary innovation and has a strong relationship of dependency with this complementary innovation. Teece called this kind of innovation *systemic innovation.*

Nonetheless, when the relationship with the complementary innovation can be clearly identified based on open standards, inter-organizational integration is no longer important. Each organization independently produces innovations, or autonomous innovations. In this case, inter-organizational integration loses its central role and what truly matters is how well each organization handles its own area of specialty (Chesbrough and Teece 1996).

The point made by Chesbrough and Teece was that inter-organizational integration is crucial for products of the integral architecture type, whose components are intricately and mutually interdependent, whereas it is not important when components are clearly modularized based on open standards, i.e., in the case of modular architecture.

Similarities and Differences Between the Studies in the Early 1990s and in the Mid-1990s

Table 9.2 summarizes the similarities and differences between the studies carried out in the early 1990s and those of the mid-1990s and later years.

In both periods, it was pointed out that complex artifacts have a layered structure, which corresponds to the first characteristic of nearly decomposable systems. The design elements are not equally dependent on each other across the architecture; some have strong dependency (within a module) and some have weak dependency (between modules). The layered structure is made up of these modules.

Differently put, a complex system has two separate layers: the upper-level (architecture-level) layer of inter-module dependency and the lower-level (component-level) layer of intra-module dependency.

Table 9.2 Similarities and differences between studies in the early 1990s and in the mid-1990s

		Early 1990s	Mid-1990s
Similarities	Target artifacts	Complex artifacts	Complex artifacts
	Layered structure (modularization)	Focused	Focused
Differences	Target architecture	Integral	Modular
	Bonding state between modules	Complicated	Simple
	Success factor	Inter-organizational integration	Control of industrywide standards
	Reason for traditional firms being defeated by entrant firms	Traditional firms fail due to the limitations of their own cognitive capacity	Entrant firms built their competitive edge based on network effects

The difference between the studies in the two aforementioned periods has to do with the matter of where, in a layered architecture, an innovation should occur to bring about a critical situation that completely changes the traditional structure of competition.

The studies in the early 1990s stressed that architecture-level innovation is what truly matters. Even if an innovation is implemented in one of the components, the innovator cannot realize a product without the other components. Hence, component-level innovation does not matter to incumbent firms. That is to say, innovations at the architecture level are more important than those at the component level. This thought originated from the implicit assumption that all complex systems have an integral architecture.

Architectural research in the early 1990s explored the semiconductor manufacturing equipment industry (Henderson and Clark 1990), the hard disk industry (Christensen 1992a, b) and the pharmaceutical industry (Henderson and Cockburn 1994). Additionally, a study on the automotive industry (Clark and Fujimoto 1991) presented a view consistent with the outcomes of the above analyses. According to the classification system proposed by Ulrich (1995), these industries are categorized as integral architecture with complicated relationships among design elements.

In this first period, little attention was paid to innovations at the component level, since the importance of innovations at the architecture level was seen as paramount and repeatedly highlighted. Researchers also noted that, when an innovation occurs at the architecture level, entrant firms have a better chance of beating preexisting firms and the management of architectural innovations needs to go beyond the boundaries of organizations.

The studies in the mid-1990s and onward, on the other hand, took the second and the third characteristic of nearly decomposable systems into consideration and argued that different states of architecture-level dependency—meaning how interdependent modules are—require that priority be given to different items on the management agenda. They pointed out that architectural innovations, or inter-organizational integration, are not necessarily always crucial.

Inter-organizational integration is, without a doubt, important in integral architecture, characterized by strong dependency among modules. Conversely, in modular architecture, inter-organizational integration is not a main concern. Modular architecture does not require extensive efforts to achieve coordination among modules, because the modules share an open standard, or a set of design rules, so that anyone can create the product by combining its compatible parts according to the standard. This feature is commonly observed in nearly all the segments of the digital industry.

What is more important is that the two types of architecture result in two different scenarios accounting for the phenomenon of entrant firms defeating incumbent firms. This phenomenon is a feature repeatedly detected in the innovation pattern of the US industry during the 1990s, as described earlier (Miyata 2001).

With integral architectures, entrant firms defeat existing firms when the latter fail to respond to architectural innovations. Incumbent firms are beaten due to the limitations of their organizational cognitive capacity, or their inability to act despite recognizing that a reaction is necessary. Nevertheless, inter-organizational integration remains crucial.

With modular architectures, on the contrary, entrant firms, which provide components, may defeat existing firms by attaining strong competitiveness, not on account of the mistakes made by incumbent firms. Open standards play a vital role here. Intel, Microsoft, Cisco and other emerging enterprises of this kind used to be mere providers of subsystems belonging to a gigantic system. These firms beat IBM and other incumbent firms by having open standards on their side. Once an open standard prevails, network effects start being produced and the firm that has control over the standard grows stronger and stronger (Shapiro and Varian 1999; Economides 1996). In a modular architecture-based industry, an emerging firm may become the central player, regardless of whether preexisting firms make mistakes.

The importance of open standards has become ever more evident and they have been described using various names, including *compatible standards* (Langlois and Robertson 1992), *standards* (Chesbrough and Teece 1996), *design rules* (Baldwin and Clark 2000) and other expressions. As far as modular architecture is concerned, open standards, or standardization, take center stage in place of inter-organizational integration. This is why research started to move its focus to standardization processes after 2000 (Gawer and Cusumano 2002; Iansiti and Levien 2004; Winn 2005; Chesbrough et al. 2006; Greenstein and Stango 2007; Shintaku and Eto 2008; Ogawa 2009; Tatsumoto and Takanashi 2010).

From Static Studies to Dynamic Studies (Studies After 2000)

The studies on architecture shifted from static ones to dynamic ones around the year 2000. Static studies revealed that the type of architecture determines the innovation pattern and particularly affects inter-organizational integration. Because the two architecture types require different approaches to inter-organizational integration, the management of innovation also differs between them. Inter-organizational integration is indispensable for the success of the integral architecture. For the modular architecture, on the other hand, the smart exploitation of open standards is a more crucial strategy. If so, the essential question in terms of technology management regards the circumstances under which an architecture becomes integral or modular, which is a matter of dynamic processes of architectural change.

Trajectories of the Design Evolution Process

Simon (1962) was the first academic to put forward the notion of the design evolution process. This concept, however, was long ignored and received hardly enough attention also in the studies on dynamic processes in and after 2000. In examining how to measure architecture, it is essential to establish and model how the design evolution process dynamically changes, as described in Sect. 3???.

The design evolution process of complex artifacts tends to move toward a reduction in complexity. The routes that it takes are not a single path; rather, they entail various options. The general perception that any complex artifact will evolve into modular architecture in any case is an over-simplified argument and may risk overlooking the essence of the matter.

The key is to be aware that different artifacts may potentially take several different evolution paths into modular architecture. Once again, design evolution does not follow a single path. We can tell what kind of modular architecture a complex artifact may come to take on by examining its design evolution path in detail. As the design evolution path is not a single trajectory, modular architectures developing from it are not of a single type.

Several different types of modular architectures are viable as a result of modularity-building. This means that some modular architectures serve a certain firm and some do not. Consequently, firms have to contribute, either directly or indirectly, to the evolution path, in order to bring about a modular architecture that is advantageous to themselves from the point of view of management.

Baldwin and Clark (2000, pp. 123–146) proposed the notion of *modular operators*, which are design activities that determine the evolution path to modular architecture. This concept brings together two elements, i.e., what kind of simplifying method a designer chooses in order to reduce complexity and what kind of modularization that decision leads to. In the example of watchmaking cited by Simon (1962), the creation of the intermediate state called *subassembly* is one of the modular operators. Baldwin and Clark (2000) introduced six design operators and argued that each of them results in a different modular architecture. However, they provided detailed descriptions of only a few of the six operators and did not examine the conditions under which a certain operator is chosen. Therefore, when reading their work, one might have the impression that modularity-building is always repetitive and consistent. Besides, the six modular operators were proposed simply based on design activities at the individual level, rather than at the organizational or business strategic level.

There is one more aspect that needs attention with regards to modularization. Modularization is actually a two-step process, consisting of module-building and modularity-building. Module-building is the process of splitting a complex artifact into several modules. It separates design elements and dependencies into those inside the modules and those between the modules. By contrast, modularity-building refers to the process of changing the inter-module dependencies, after the module-building phase is completed. It makes the dependencies among the modules well-defined, clear and simple. This allows design rules (e.g., protocols and interfaces) to be set according to the inter-module dependencies and helps provide compatibility among modules.

Modularization is the overall process of module-building followed by modularity-building. Module-building can take place on its own and is not necessarily always accompanied by modularity-building. In some cases, integrity-building—not modularity-building—takes place after the module-building phase.

Integrity-building strengthens the dependency between two modules and puts them in a dependency state, in which they are coupled. This refers to design activities that improve the performance of an artifact at the cost of modularity.

From the standpoint of design science, complex artifacts should ideally acquire a modular architecture through the process of modularity-building; in reality, however, integrity-building often takes place. In the domain of software design, for example, Gabriel (1989) pointed out that worse is better, meaning that a design that seems wrong in terms of design science might prove to be a better design for most users. There are two major reasons for this. Firstly, the right design tends to become too complicated. Complete modularity requires a lot of buffers, also called *fat*, which make the design highly complex. Secondly, it is very often the case that the right design causes functionality to be poor because of too much fat.

The architecture of an artifact will be modular when it is split into modules and more modularity than integrity is created. This whole process is called modularization. If integrity is created more than modularity after the module-building process, the architecture of the artifact will be integral. It is the division criterion of the artifact, as explained later, that determines whether more modularity-building takes place than integrity-building, or vice versa.

Sections 2.4.2??? and 2.4.3??? explain module-building operators and granularity of modules, two critical factors when discussing the design evolution process.

Module-Building Operators: Encapsulation and Commonization

Architecture is a subject investigated not only in management studies but also by design science. The object-oriented design method,[3] which is used in software designing, provides a number of clues to the discussion on modular operators. A closer look at this approach reveals that there are two essential modular operators: one is an encapsulation operator and the other is a commonization operator (Fig. 9.1).

The former is focused on the *has-a* relationship in the modularization process. If a design element envelops another design element, these two elements are dependent in terms of the *has-a* relationship. Bringing together design elements by means of this relationship will yield sub-assy type modularization, as exemplified by the watch-making case presented by Simon (1962). Since the encapsulation operator encloses design elements and dependencies within sub-assies and hides their complexities from the outside, it functions as an information concealment tool.

The commonization operator, on the other hand, is focused on the *is-a* relationship between elements in the modularization process. The *is-a* relationship has to do with whether a module and another module are essentially the same or different. If they are the same, they can come together and form a module based on the example (basis) of a similar module, with only slight modifications and without the need to create a wholly new module. This process is called *inheritance* in the object-oriented design method and can be regarded as analogous to commonization of modules. Bringing together design elements linked by the *is-a* relationship will result in a modularization process of the commonization (standardization) type, meaning, for example, that any screw of the same (common) type can be used inside a watch.

The encapsulation operator is often utilized in studies on modularization (Aoki 1995) and some go as far as to say that encapsulation is always the operator for modularization, but this is not correct. In actuality, there are multiple modular operators

[3]The object-oriented design method is an approach to modularization design that gives consideration to the relationship between design elements.

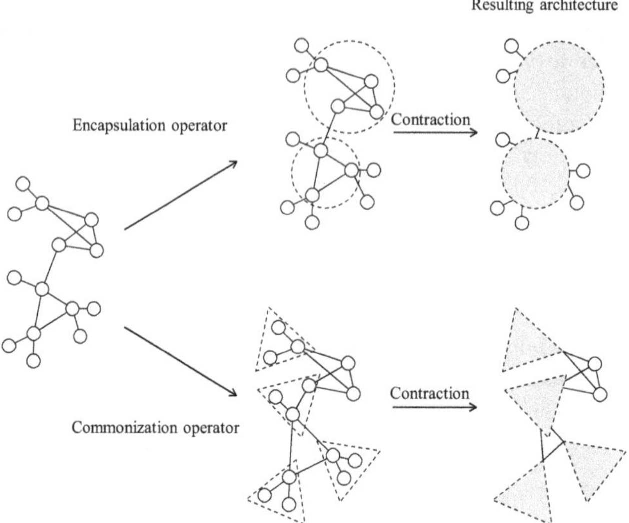

Fig. 9.1 Encapsulation and commonization operators

besides the encapsulation operator and the commonization operator. Any of these operators can facilitate modularity-building. It should be noted, however, that the different operators bring about different forms of modular architectures. Ultimately, an artifact's modular architecture will come in many different variations.

Granularity of Modules: Agglomerativeness and Divisiveness

This subsection explores the issue of granularity of modules. Granularity can be explained using the example of an automobile, which can be regarded as being made up of several hundreds of components or several tens of thousands of smaller parts. The question here is whether we should look at fewer relatively large groups of design elements or at a higher number of smaller groups.

The issue of module granularity can be translated into the question of at what level design elements should be discussed as modules. To address this issue, one has to first be aware that there are two aspects: agglomerativeness and divisiveness.

Agglomerativeness is the quality that defines how to assemble design elements in order to strengthen the dependency inside a module. This process groups design elements into a certain chunk. The module-building operator explained earlier is an example of agglomerativeness.

Divisiveness is the quality that defines how to divide the whole system into modules in order to reduce the dependency between modules. Divisiveness largely affects the design of inter-module dependency; in other words, it affects whether modularity-building occurs more often than integrity-building, or vice versa, in the design process.

Agglomerativeness influences the module-building process by suggesting a wide range of modules as ideas for architecture designing. This also means that several options exist as to how a complex system can be divided over the course of its design evolution. A division criterion sets forth which path to take and, depending on the purpose of division, more than one criterion may be proposed.

Murota (2004) introduced the Dulmage–Mendelsohn (DM) decomposition as a division criterion from the standpoint of graph theories. He described the approach to provide a layered structure composed of modules with maximized intra-module dependency and minimized inter-module dependency. Newman (2006) developed the Modularity Q criterion, which maximizes intra-module dependency and minimizes inter-module dependency in light of community extraction inside the organization. Gabriel (1989), cited above, remarked that the actual realistic scenarios of product use are limited and advocated integral architecture over modular architecture, since the former improves product performance (though with less design flexibility), while the latter attaches more importance to the flexibility of design. Baldwin and Clark (2000) looked at the matter from the economic point of view and suggested the Design Options criterion, which maximizes the ratio between the profits from an aggregate of modules (or the system as a whole) and the financial resources invested in those modules. When the division process needs to take place across the industry, and not in a single organization, these various criteria need to be further analyzed in conjunction with studies on standardization processes.

As numerous division criteria can be adopted, the final choice depends largely on the purpose of division. It is worth noting that the division criteria do not necessarily always favor higher modularity. For instance, when the presence of compatible modules enhances the value of the system from the standpoint of overall optimization, modularity should be built by setting design rules on inter-module dependency. In other instances, integrity should be built by coupling two modules in order to achieve an optimal level of system performance. Thus, architecture does not automatically evolve so as to heighten modularity in the design evolution process. Designers choose between modularity-building and integrity-building depending on the division criterion. In sum, architecture follows a complicated evolution path, in which it sometimes becomes more modular and sometimes more integral.

Example of Design Evolution

This subsection further explains the design evolution process discussed above by means of a diagram.

Figure 9.2 illustrates the design evolution process of artifacts. First, let us look at the artifact being in complex state (a). At this stage, module-building has not yet taken place. In (a), fourteen inter-element dependencies exist. The dependencies among design elements represent the degree of complexity.

Second, let us look at the artifact in (b), i.e., after module-building. Once the modules are built, the inter-element dependencies are separated into intra-module dependencies and inter-module dependencies. At stage (b), four modules have been created, with ten intra-module dependencies and four inter-module dependencies. At this point, designers are also grouped into those who design the inside of the modules

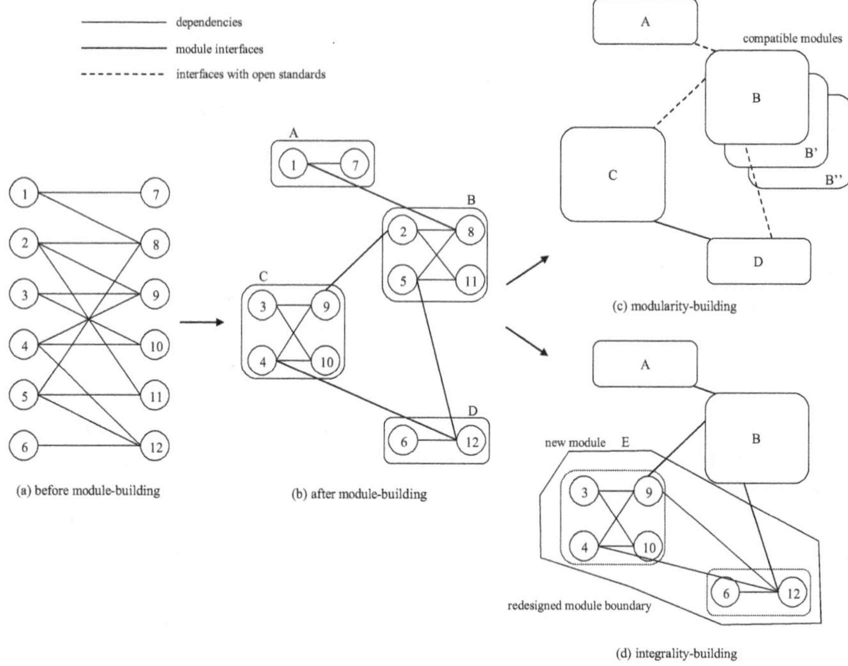

Fig. 9.2 Example of design evolution

(component designers) and those who design the links between the modules (product designers). Product designers have to work only on dependencies between modules. In situation (a), product designers had to deal with fourteen dependencies, but now, in situation (b), they only need to worry about four of them. To the eyes of product designers, the level of complexity of the artifact has decreased. This is the effect of module-building.

Now, if we consider the post-module-building state, the artifact has four inter-module links. Its design evolution can now follow one of two trajectories, (c) or (d).

When (c) is chosen, Modules B′ and B″, which are compatible with Module B, emerge as a result of applying design rules to the inter-module dependencies. If the design rules are set as open standards, Modules B′ & B″ may be provided by firms other than the developer of Module B. These compatible modules sometimes offer different functionalities compared with the original functionality of Module B. The presence of compatible modules increases the level of design flexibility, so that various combinations of modules can be tested. As a consequence, users will have access to diverse products, serving a wide variety of purposes. This is the value of modularity-building.

When (d) is chosen, the inter-module dependencies are revised and Modules C and D are reshaped as one module, Module E. This process of combining two modules into one is precisely the activity of integrity-building. Integrity-building enables design optimization, which could not be attained by using two separate modules. In case (d), a new dependency is added between Design Element 9 and Design Element 12, so as to provide higher product performance. The integrity-building process causes Modules C and D to be in a coupled state, reducing designing flexibility but optimizing performance. This is the effect of integrity-building.

Product designers may opt for design option (c), in pursuit of the effect of modularity-building, or design option (d), in pursuit of the effect of integrity-building. The choice is made based on the division criterion.

Direction of Future Architecture Studies

Framework for the Dynamic Process of Design Evolution

The above discussions can be summarized using three key concepts found in studies on the dynamic processes of architecture.

Let us first discuss the module-building operators. Different module-building operators result in different kinds of modules, therefore leading to different possible architectures. This is why it is critical to verify what impact each module-building operator brings about. Several module-building operators exist, such as the encapsulation operator and the commonization operator, providing multiple architecture options.

Secondly, let us look at modularization. The term *modularization* refers to modularity-building after module-building. Module-building and modularity-building are two different process, and modularization means the same as modularity-building, not module-building. Module-building is a prerequisite process for modularity-building. However, many studies on architecture misuse the term module-building as a synonym for modularization. This confusion causes critical misunderstandings when researchers ascertain whether an architecture is modular or integral. The state of modularity-building is determined by inter-module dependency. Rather than the dependency inside a module, researchers should measure the dependency between modules when they wish to ascertain the type of architecture of an artifact.

Thirdly, the issue of the division criteria is worth pointing out. There are many different division criteria, from among which one is selected according to the purpose of division. Based on the chosen criterion, the designers decide on modularity-building or integrity-building in the design process. If modularity-building is preferred more often than integrity-building, the architecture of the artifact will be modular. If integrity-building is chosen more often than modularity-building, the architecture of the artifact will be integral. In conclusion, the division criterion adopted is critical in determining the type of architecture.

Based on the above three concepts, a framework for dynamic studies on the design evolution of architecture is presented in Fig. 9.3. The studies can be roughly classified into two domains. One domain looks at narrowly-defined design evolutions,

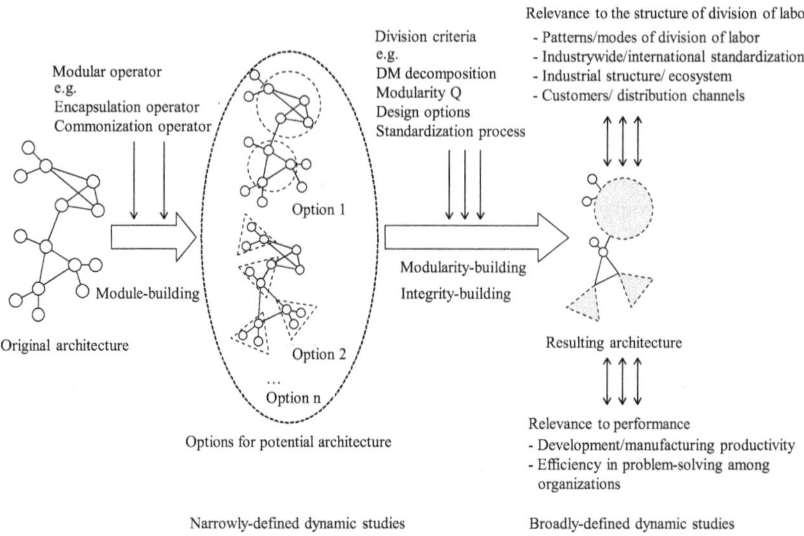

Fig. 9.3 Framework for dynamic studies on architectures

focusing mainly on how an architecture takes shape out of the set of available options. This can be described as the *selection process of architecture.* In this area, investigations on complex networks and social networks are advanced (Watts 2003; Newman 2003). Studies on narrowly-defined design evolutions ultimately concentrate on the properties that complex artifacts have.

The other domain deals with broadly-defined design evolutions. Research in this area looks into how the selection process of architecture is linked to external indicators (e.g., industrial structure or business performance), in order to shed light on the relationship between the design evolution and the industrial evolution of complex artifacts. The external indicators considered may be divided into those relevant to the structure of the division of labor and those relevant to performance. Studies on broadly-defined design evolutions are essential in terms of management of technology.

It was already evident in the days of static research that certain architectures fit well with certain labor division structures. Those static analyses, however, simply compared the architectures and the structures of division of labor existing at that time. They did not examine the strategic options available during the process of architecture selection and what kind of impact this selection might have on structure and performance.

Hardly any of the explorations conducted thus far has assumed that the process of realizing an architecture entails countless options. Also, questions around the primary factors that have direct and indirect impacts on the design evolution or how to make strategic use of design evolution have remained largely unanswered. To discuss complex artifacts from the viewpoint of corporate strategy, we need to examine which kind of architecture should be selected from among multiple options (i.e., potential architecture types).

Dynamic Process Studies Since 2000: Design Evolution and Standardization Process

Since 2000, architecture researchers have been focusing on dynamic processes. They are particularly interested in the fact that large-scale transformations of the industrial structure and/or changes in innovation patterns occur when an integral architecture transitions to a modular one.

The computer industry, for example, used to be characterized by integral architecture in the mainframe period of the 1960s. Later, however, it went through the design evolution stage of modularity-building, so that the personal computer became one of the most representative modular architectures in the 1990s. In turn, the structure of the PC industry rapidly transformed from the vertical integration type to the vertical disintegration (horizontal division of labor) type. Most symbolically, IBM, a comprehensive system firm, declined, while Intel and Microsoft, initially mere component providers, emerged and soon boomed. This trend is commonly observed across digital industries and has been rippling through other industries as well. Even the automotive industry, which used to be regarded as unrelated to digitization, has massively incorporated embedded systems and come to be affected by digitization (Tokuda 2008; Tokuda et al. 2011).

The transition from the integral architecture to the modular architecture goes through two dynamic processes. The first is design evolution, intended to reduce the level of complexity from the standpoint of artifact design. This is why research topics in this domain include module-building operators and division criteria for modularity-building and integrity-building, as seen in the framework of design evolution studies in Fig. 9.3.

Static studies understood modular architecture as being only of one kind, but dynamic studies have placed more emphasis on the variety of modular architectures. Also, dynamic studies have given much consideration to the hierarchical nature of complex systems. Dynamic processes may exhibit different architectural changes in different layers. In some cases, one layer may grow more modular, while another may become more integral. The relationship between dynamic processes in different layers may be another key future topic for dynamic studies.

The second dynamic process is that of standardization, aimed at sharing an interface among organizations. Platform business studies (Gawer and Cusumano 2002) and industrial ecosystem studies (Iansiti and Levien 2004) examined business strategies that make use of standardization. Generally speaking, the standardization process is part of the design evolution process for modularity-building. It is subject to the impact of institutional systems (e.g., antitrust laws and standardization policies); however, it is studied independently of the design evolution process (Ogawa 2009; Tatsumoto et al. 2010; Tatsumoto and Takanashi 2010). The shift in standardization policies by governments across the world in the 1980s (relaxation of antitrust laws, prioritization of regional standards, WTO/TBT treaty) had a strong impact on the standardization process in the 1990s and escalated the importance of standardization-based business strategies. The discussion about strategic standardization presented in this volume is deeply influenced by these investigations.

Research on these two dynamic processes has taken center stage in dynamic architectural studies after 2000. Design evolution and standardization are mutually interactive. Therefore, a comprehensive understanding and strategic use of these processes is key to succeeding in the world of modular architecture. Architectural studies are expected to develop further in terms of exploring dynamic processes.

Appendix 2: Interview List

Chapter	No.	Company name	Category	Date	Place
3	1	Longcheer Technology Co., Ltd.	Handset maker/Design house	2007 January	Shanghai, China
	2	Huaqin Telecom Technology Co., Ltd.	Handset maker/Design house	2007 January	Shanghai, China
	3	AMPLET Communication Laboratory	Handset maker/Design house	2007 May	Tokyo, Japan
	4	Lenovo Mobile Inc.	Handset maker/Design house	2007 August	Amoi, China
	5	Datang Telecom Technology & Industry Group	Equipment supplier	2007 August	Shanghai, China
	6	Commit	Component supplier	2007 August	Shanghai, China
	7	Epson Electronics Device	Component supplier	2007 August	Shanghai, China
	8	NXP Semiconductors	Component supplier	2007 August	Shanghai, China
	9	Motorola, Inc.	Handset maker/Design house	2007 September	Tokyo, Japan
	10	DoCoMo i-mode Europe B.V.	Telecom	2007 September	Amsterdam, Netherlands
	11	European Telecommunications Standards Institute (ETSI)	Standard development organization	2007 September	Nice, France
	12	DoCoMo Communications Laboratories Europe GmbH	Telecom	2007 September	Munich, Germany

(continued)

(continued)

Chapter	No.	Company name	Category	Date	Place
	13	Ericsson Research	Equipment supplier	2007 September	Stockholm, Sweden
	14	Nokia Siemens Networks	Equipment supplier	2007 September	Espoo, Finland
	15	NTT DoCoMo, Inc.	Telecom	2007 November	Tokyo, Japan
	16	Matsushita Communication Industrial Co., Ltd.	Handset maker/Design house	2007 November	Tokyo, Japan
	17	Adcore-Tech Co., Ltd.	Component supplier	2007 November	Yokosuga, Japan
	18	Fiberhome Telecommunication Technologies Co., Ltd.	Equipment supplier	2008 August	Wuhan, China
	19	China Unicom	Telecom	2008 August	Hangzhou, China
	20	Eastern Communication Co., Ltd.	Handset maker/Design house	2008 August	Hangzhou, China
	21	Huawei Technologies Co., Ltd.	Telecom	2008 August	Hangzhou, China
4	1	Japan Electronics and Information Technology Industries Association (JEITA)	Industry association	2005 August	Tokyo, Japan
	2	Semi Japan	Industry association	2005 August	Tokyo, Japan
	3	JFMAT	Material supplier	2005 August	Tokyo, Japan
	4	Shin-Etsu Handotai Co., Ltd.	Material supplier	2005 August	Tokyo, Japan
	5	NEC Electronics Corporation	Device supplier	2005 November	Tokyo, Japan
	6	Murata Machinery, Ltd.	Material handling equipment supplier	2005 December	Tokyo, Japan
	7	TDK Corporation	Material handling equipment supplier	2005 December	Tokyo, Japan
	8	IBM Japan, Ltd.	Software developer	2005 December	Tokyo, Japan
	9	Hewlett-Packard Japan, Ltd.	Material handling equipment supplier	2005 December	Tokyo, Japan
	10	Tokyo Electron Limited	Equipment supplier	2005 December	Tokyo, Japan

(continued)

(continued)

Chapter	No.	Company name	Category	Date	Place
	11	Intel K.K.	Device supplier	2006 January	Tokyo, Japan
	12	Entegris	Material handling equipment supplier	2006 January	Tokyo, Japan
	13	Dainichi Shoji K.K.	Material handling equipment supplier	2006 January	Tokyo, Japan
	14	Texas Instruments Japan Limited.	Device supplier	2006 January	Tokyo, Japan
	15	Arm K. K.	Device supplier	2006 February	Tokyo, Japan
	16	Renesas Electronics Corporation	Device supplier	2006 November	Kochi, Japan
	17	Applied Materials Japan, Inc.	Equipment supplier	2006 December	Tokyo, Japan
	18	ULVAC, Inc.	Equipment supplier	2007 January	Jogasaki, Japan
	19	Fujitsu Limited	Device supplier	2007 March	Mie, Japan
	20	Daifuku Co., Ltd.	Material handling equipment supplier	2008 August	Shiga, Japan
5 and 6	1	Logicool Co., Ltd.	Component supplier	2006 July	Tokyo, Japan
	2	Fujitsu Limited	Personal computer maker/Motherboard supplier	2006 July	Tokyo, Japan
	3	Buffalo Inc.	Component supplier	2006 October	Nagoya, Japan
	4	Renesas Electronics Corporation	Semiconductor supplier	2006 October	Tokyo, Japan
	5	Dell, Inc.	Personal computer maker/Motherboard supplier	2006 October	Amoi, China
	6	Toshiba Corporation	Personal computer maker/Motherboard supplier	2007 April	Tokyo, Japan
	7	Toshiba Corporation	Personal computer maker/Motherboard supplier	2007 June	Tokyo, Japan
	8	Quanta Computer Inc.	Personal computer maker/Motherboard supplier	2007 July	Taipei, Taiwan
	9	Zuken Taiwan Inc.	Development tool supplier	2007 July	Taipei, Taiwan
	10	MediaTek Japan Inc.	Semiconductor supplier	2007 July	Hsinchu, Taiwan

(continued)

(continued)

Chapter	No.	Company name	Category	Date	Place
	11	Gigabyte Technology Inc.	Personal computer maker/Motherboard supplier	2007 July	Taipei, Taiwan
	12	Intel Corporation	Semiconductor supplier	2007 August	Taipei, Taiwan
	13	ASUSTeK Computer Inc.	Personal computer maker/Motherboard supplier	2007 August	Taipei, Taiwan
	14	Intel Corporation	Semiconductor supplier	2007 August	Taipei, Taiwan
	15	Fujitsu Taiwan Ltd.	Personal computer maker/Motherboard supplier	2007 September	Taipei, Taiwan
	16	Compal Electronics, Inc.	Personal computer maker/Motherboard supplier	2007 October	Taipei, Taiwan
	17	Intel Corporation	Semiconductor supplier	2007 October	Taipei, Taiwan
	18	Hitachi East Asia, Ltd.	Personal computer maker/Motherboard supplier	2007 October	Taipei, Taiwan
	19	Renesas Electronics Corporation	Semiconductor supplier	2007 November	Tokyo, Japan
	20	Renesas Electronics Corporation	Semiconductor supplier	2007 November	Tokyo, Japan
	21	Intel K.K.	Semiconductor supplier	2007 December	Tokyo, Japan
	22	Fujitsu Limited	Personal computer maker/Motherboard supplier	2007 December	Numazu, Japan
	23	Renesas Electronics Corporation	Semiconductor supplier	2008 January	Tokyo, Japan
	24	Intel K.K.	Semiconductor supplier	2008 January	Santa Clara, US
	25	Intel Corporation	Semiconductor supplier	2008 February	Taipei, Taiwan
	26	Quanta Computer Inc.	Personal computer maker/Motherboard supplier	2008 February	Taipei, Taiwan
	27	Sony Taiwan Limited	Personal computer maker/Motherboard supplier	2008 February	Taipei, Taiwan

(continued)

(continued)

Chapter	No.	Company name	Category	Date	Place
	28	Hitachi East Asia, Ltd	Personal computer maker/Motherboard supplier	2008 February	Taipei, Taiwan
	29	Intel Corporation	Semiconductor supplier	2008 September	Taipei, Taiwan
	30	Sunonwealth Electric Machine Industry Co., Ltd.	Component supplier	2008 September	Kaohsiung, Taiwan
	31	Taiwan Sanyo Electric	Component supplier	2008 October	Taipei, Taiwan
7	1	Toyota Motor Corporation	Automaker	2009 February	Cologne, Germany
	2	Toyota Motor Corporation	Automaker	2009 February	Brussels, Belgium
	3	Renesas Electronics Corporation	Device supplier	2009 February	Munich, Germany
	4	DENSO AUTOMOTIVE Deutschland	Component supplier	2009 February	Eching, Germany
	5	Honda Motor Co., Ltd.	Automaker	2010 January	Tokyo, Japan
	6	DENSO Corporation	Component supplier	2010 February	Nagoya, Japan
	7	Robert Bosch Engineering India	Component supplier	2010 February	Bangalore, India
	8	Robert Bosch Engineering India	Component supplier	2010 February	Bangalore, India
	9	Robert Bosch Engineering India	Component supplier	2010 February	Bangalore, India
	10	Denso Haryana Pvt.	Component supplier	2010 February	New Delhi, India
	11	Denso Sales India	Component supplier	2010 February	New Delhi, India
	12	Tianjin Denso Electronics Co., Ltd.	Component supplier	2010 April	Tianjin, China
	13	Nissan (China) Investment Co., Ltd.	Component supplier	2010 April	Beijing, China
	14	Bosch (China) Investment Co., Ltd.	Component supplier	2010 April	Shanghai, China
	15	Nissan (China) Investment Co., Ltd.	Automaker	2010 April	Beijing, China
	16	Denso (China) Investment Co., Ltd.	Component supplier	2010 May	Beijing, China

(continued)

(continued)

Chapter	No.	Company name	Category	Date	Place
	17	United Automotive Electronic Systems Co., Ltd.	Component supplier	2010 August	Shanghai, China
	18	DENSO Corporation	Component supplier	2011 March	Kariya, Japan
	19	Robert Bosch GmbH	Component supplier	2011 March	Stuttgart, Germany
	20	Robert Bosch GmbH	Component supplier	2011 March	Stuttgart, Germany
	21	Robert Bosch GmbH	Component supplier	2011 March	Stuttgart, Germany
	22	DENSO AUTOMOTIVE Deutschland	Component supplier	2011 March	Eching, Germany
	23	Renault S.A.	Automaker	2011 March	Paris, France
	24	dSPACE Japan K.K.	Development tool supplier	2011 November	Tokyo, Japan
	25	Vector Japan Co., Ltd.	Development tool supplier	2011 November	Tokyo, Japan
	26	Elektrobit Nippon K.K.	Development tool supplier	2011 November	Tokyo, Japan
	27	dSPACE GmbH	Development tool supplier	2011 November	Paderborn, Germany
	28	Continental Systems	Component supplier	2011 November	Frankfurt, Germany
	29	Vector Informatik GmbH	Development tool supplier	2011 November	Stuttgart, Germany
	30	Toyota Motor Corporation	Automaker	2011 November	Berlin, Germany
	31	Nissan (China) Investment Co., Ltd.	Automaker	2011 December	Beijing, China
	32	Denso (China) Investment Co., Ltd.	Component supplier	2011 December	Beijing, China
	33	Volkswagen Group Japan K. K.	Automaker	2011 December	Tokyo, Japan
	34	DENSO Corporation	Component supplier	2012 August	Tokyo, Japan
	35	KPIT Technologies Limited	Development tool supplier	2013 January	Bangalore, India
	36	KPIT Technologies Limited	Development tool supplier	2013 January	Pune, India
	37	iSOFT International Software Ltd.	Development tool supplier	2013 February	Shanghai, China

(continued)

(continued)

Chapter	No.	Company name	Category	Date	Place
	38	Denso (China) Investment Co., Ltd.	Component supplier	2013 February	Shanghai, China
	39	DENSO Corporation	Component supplier	2013 February	Tokyo, Japan
	40	Honda Motor Co., Ltd.	Automaker	2015 June	Tokyo, Japan
	41	Honda Motor Co., Ltd.	Automaker	2015 June	Tokyo, Japan
	42	Denso International Asia Co., Ltd.	Component supplier	2015 June	Bangkok, Thailand
	43	Nissan Motor Asia Pacific Co., Ltd.	Automaker	2015 June	Bangkok, Thailand
	44	Toyota Kirloskar Motor Private Limited	Automaker	2015 June	Bangalore, India
	45	Honda Cars India Ltd.	Automaker	2015 June	Greater Noida, India
	46	Denso International India Pvt. Ltd.	Component supplier	2015 June	New Delhi, India

References

Alexander C (1964) Notes on the synthesis of form. Harvard University Press, Boston, MA

Aoki M (1995) Keizai Sisutemu no Shinka to Tagensei—Hikaku Seido Bunseki Josetsu (Introduction to the evolution of economic systems and diversity—Comparative analysis of institutions). Toyo Keizai Shinpou Sha, Tokyo (in Japanese)

Asanuma B (1989) Manufacturer-supplier relationships in Japan and the concept of relation-specific skill. J Japanese Int Econ 3(1):1–30

Baldwin CY, Clark KB (2000) Design rules: the power of modularity. MIT Press, Cambridge, MA

Chesbrough H, Teece DJ (1996) Organizing for innovation: When is virtual virtuous? Harvard Bus Rev 74(1):65–73

Chesbrough HW, Vanhaverbeke W, West J (2006) Open innovation: researching a new paradigm. Oxford University Press, Oxford

Christensen CM (1992a) Exploring the limits of the technology S-curve Part I: component technologies. Prod Oper Manage 1:334–357

Christensen CM (1992b) Exploring the limits of the technology S-curve Part 2: architectural technologies. Prod Oper Manage 1:358–366

Clark KB (1985) The interaction of design hierarchies and market concepts in the technological evolution. Res Policy 14:235–251

Clark KB (1989) Project scope and project performance: the effect of parts strategy and supplier involvement on product development. Manage Sci 35(10):1247–1263

Clark KB, Fujimoto T (1991) Product development performance: strategy, organization, and management in the world auto industry. Harvard Business Press, Boston, MA

Dyer JH, Nobeoka K (2000) Creating and managing a high-performance knowledge-sharing network: the Toyota case. Strat Manag J 211:345–367

Economides N (1996) The economics of networks. Int J Ind Organ 14:673–699

Fujimoto T (2009) Fukuzatsuka suru Jinkoubutsu no Sekkei Riyou ni Kansuru Hokanteki Apurochi (Complementary approaches for designing and using complex artifacts). Oukan 3(1):52–59 (in Japanese). https://www.jstage.jst.go.jp/article/trafst/3/1/3_52/_pdf

Gabriel R (1989) The rise of "Worse is Better". https://www.jwz.org/doc/worse-is-better.html. Accessed 9 Apr 2018

Gawer A, Cusumano MA (2002) Platform leadership: How Intel, Microsoft, and Cisco drive industry innovation. Harvard Business School Press, Boston, MA

Greenstein S, Stango V (2007) Standards and public policy. Cambridge University Press, Cambridge

Henderson RM, Clark KB (1990) Architectural innovation: the reconfiguration of existing product technologies and the failure of established firms. Adm Sci Q 35(1):9–30

Henderson R, Cockburn I (1994) Measuring competence? Exploring firm effects in pharmaceutical research. Strat Manage J 15:63–84

Iansiti M, Levien R (2004) The keystone advantage: What the new business ecosystems mean for strategy, innovation, and sustainability. Harvard Business School Press, Boston, MA

ITmedia (2016) Honda Google keiretsu to Jidou Unten Kyoudou Kenkyu—Waymo to Teikei Beino Koudou de Jissyou Jikken he (Honda starts joint research on autonomous driving with Google startup—alliance with Waymo for the field study of autonomous driving in US). IT Media News (in Japanese). http://www.itmedia.co.jp/news/articles/1612/22/news065.html. Accessed 22 Dec 2016

Langlois RN, Robertson PL (1992) Networks and innovation in a modular system: lessons from the microcomputer and stereo component industries. Res Policy 21:297–313

Miyata Y (2001) Amerika no Sangyou Seisaku—Ronsou to Jissen (Industrial policy in the USA—theory and practice). Yachiyo Syuppan, Tokyo (in Japanese)

Murota K (2004) Kongou Gyouretsu no Seijunkei to Kaisou Kouzou (Canonical form and hierarchical structure of mixed matrices). Mathematical Seminar 513:38–43 (in Japanese)

Newman ME (2003) The structure and function of complex networks. SIAM Rev 45:167–256

Newman ME (2006) Modularity and community structure in networks. Proc Nat Acad Sci USA 103(23):8577–8582

Ogawa K (2009) Kokusai hyoujunka to Jigyou Senryaku (International standards and business strategy). Hakuto Shobou, Tokyo (in Japanese)

Okuno M, Takizawa K, Watanabe Y (2006) Jinkoubutsu to Seihin Akitekucya (Complex artifact and product architecture). MMRC Discussion Paper 81:1–27 (in Japanese)

Robertson PL, Langlois RN (1995) Innovation, network and vertical integration. Res Policy 24:543–562

Shapiro C, Varian HR (1999) Information rules: a strategic guide to network economy. Harvard Business School Press, Boston, MA

Shintaku J, Eto M (2008) Konsensasu Hyojun Senryaku (Strategy for consensus standards). Nikkei Inc., Tokyo (in Japanese)

Simon HA (1962) The architecture of complexity. Proc Am Philos Soc 106(6):467–482

Takeishi A (2001) Bridging inter- and intra-firm boundaries: management of supplier involvement in automotive product development. Strat Manage J 22:403–433

Tatsumoto H, Takanashi C (2010) Competitive strategies on standardization: establishing and exploiting consensus standardization. J Jpn Assoc Manage Syst 26(2):67–81. ISSN: 09188282 (in Japanese)

Tatsumoto H, Ogawa K, Shintaku J (2010) Strategic standardization: platform business and the effect on international division of labor. Ann Bus Adminis Sci 10:13–26. ISSN: 1327-4456

Teece DJ (1986) Profiting from technological innovation: implications for integration, collaboration, licensing and public policy. Res Policy 15:285–305

Tokuda A (2008) Jidousha no Erekutoronikusuka to Hyoujunka—Tenkanki ni Tatsu Denshi Seigyo Shisutemu Shijou (Standardization in car electoronics—transition period of car control system market). Kouyou Shobou, Kyoto (in Japanese)

Tokuda A, Tatsumoto H, Ogawa K (2011) Opuen Inobesyon Sisutemu – Oushuu ni Okeru Jidousya Kumikomi Sisutemu to Hyoujunka (Open innovation system: development and standardization of in-car electronics systems in Europe). Kouyou Shobou, Kyoto (in Japanese)

Ulrich KT (1995) Product architecture in the manufacturing firm. Res Policy 24:419–440

Wall Street Journal (2016) Uber's ride-sharing dominance comes under pressure. https://www.wsj.com/articles/ubers-ride-sharing-dominance-comes-under-pressure-1463168731. Accessed 26 Dec 2016

Watts DJ (2003) Six degrees: the science of a connected age. WW Norton & Company, New York

Wiener N (1948) Cybernetics. MIT Press, Boston, MA

Williamson EO (1979) Transaction-cost economics: the governance of contractual relations. J Law Econ 22(2):233–261

Winn JK (2005) US and EU regulatory competition in ICT standardization law and policy. In: IEEE, SIIT 2005 Proceedings, pp 281–291